FRENCH
BATTLESHIPS
1922-1956

FRENCH
BATTLESHIPS
1922–1956

John Jordan and Robert Dumas

Seaforth PUBLISHING

Copyright © John Jordan & Robert Dumas 2009
Colour profiles and plans © Bertrand Magueur 2009

First published in Great Britain in 2009 by
Seaforth Publishing
An imprint of Pen & Sword Books Ltd
47 Church Street, Barnsley
S Yorkshire S70 2AS

www.seaforthpublishing.com
Email info@seaforthpublishing.com

Reprinted, with corrections 2010

British Library Cataloguing in Publication Data
A CIP data record for this book is available from the British Library

ISBN 978-1-84832-034-5

Typeset and designed by Stephen Dent
Printed and in China through Printworks Int. Ltd.

Frontispiece
A bow view of *Richelieu* at anchor in 1952, with a *Gloire* class cruiser in the background.

Contents

ACRONYMS AND ABBREVIATIONS

Organisations

CSM	*Conseil Supérieur de la Marine*	Navy Board (advisory)
DCCAN	*Direction Centrale des Constructions et Armes Navales*	(united technical department created postwar)
DAN	*Direction des Armes Navales*	Naval Ordnance Department
EMG	*Etat-Major Général*	Naval General Staff (NGS)
SCCAN	*Service Central des Constructions et Armes Navales*	(FFNL technical dept 1940-4)
STCAN	*Service Technique des Constructions et Armes Navales*	(replaced latter during late war period)
STCN	*Service Technique des Constructions Navales*	Constructors Department

Technical

ACAD	*Automatique Contre-Avions Double*	Automatic twin AA mounting
BF	*But Flottant*	Anti-surface
BOF	*Boulet Ogival en Fonte*	Exercise round
CA	*Contre Avions*	Anti-aircraft
CAD	*Contre Avions Double*	Twin AA mounting
CAQ	*Contre Avions Quadruple*	Quad AA mounting
CAS	*Contre Avions Simple*	Single AA mounting
OEA	*Obus Explosif en Acier*	HE shell
OPf(K)	*Obus Perforant (Dispositif K)*	AP shell (with colorant)
PBI	*Pont Blindé Inférieur*	Lower armoured deck
PBS	*Pont Blindé Supérieur*	Upper (main) armoured deck

Ranks

CA	*Contre Amiral*	Rear-Admiral
CC	*Capitaine de Corvette*	Lt-Commander
CF	*Capitaine de Frégate*	Commander
CV	*Capitaine de Vaisseau*	Captain
VA	*Vice Amiral*	Vice-Admiral
VAE	*Vice Amiral d'Escadre*	(Senior) Vice-Admiral

Naval Formations

DC	*Division de croiseurs*	Cruiser Division
DCT	*Division de contre-torpilleurs*	Contre-torpilleur Division
DL	*Division de ligne*	Battle Division
DSM	*Division de sous-marins*	Submarine Division
DT	*Division de torpilleurs*	Torpedo-boat Division
EL	*Escadre légère*	Light Squadron[1]

Note:
[1] generally comprised three/four DCT/DT.

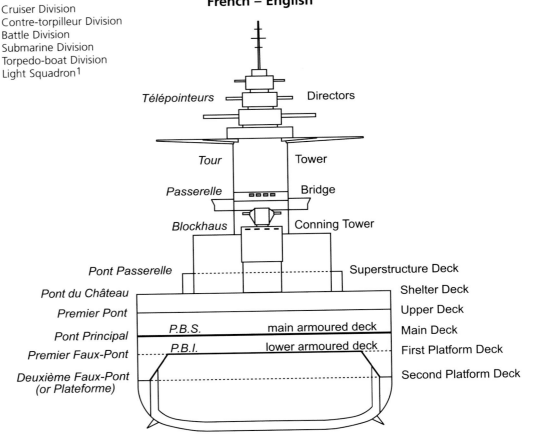

Nomenclature:
French – English

French	English
Télépointeurs	Directors
Tour	Tower
Passerelle	Bridge
Blockhaus	Conning Tower
Pont Passerelle	Superstructure Deck
Pont du Château	Shelter Deck
Premier Pont	Upper Deck
Pont Principal — P.B.S. main armoured deck	Main Deck
Premier Faux-Pont — P.B.I. lower armoured deck	First Platform Deck
Deuxième Faux-Pont (or Plateforme)	Second Platform Deck

PREFACE

The battleships of the *Dunkerque* and *Richelieu* classes were among the most radical and influential designs of the interwar period, and were coveted by the British, the Germans and the Italians following the Armistice of June 1940. *Dunkerque* and her sister *Strasbourg* were scuttled at Toulon in November 1942, but following an extensive refit in the United States, *Richelieu* went on to serve alongside the Royal Navy during 1943-5, and her sister *Jean Bart*, finally completed during the 1950s, was the last battleship in the world to enter service.

This book aims to bring the results of Robert Dumas' original research, first published in a series of French-language monographs during the early 1990s, to English-speaking readers. However, the book is also more ambitious in its scope in that it aims to present these ships in their full historical context, with a greater emphasis on war service and the extent to which that served to highlight the strengths and weaknesses of their design. There is a greater emphasis on the progression of French battleship design from the Washington Treaty onwards, and there is much new material on the technical aspects both of these ships and of their 'paper' predecessors of the 1920s. Finally, the book focuses closely on issues of infrastructure, demographics, strategic thinking, tactical organisation and even national culture which are not always well understood on this side of the English Channel. We hope that this book will give the reader a better understanding not only of the design philosophy and technical characteristics of these ships, but also of the history and traditions of the Marine Nationale during the twentieth century.

THE DRAWINGS

The colour artwork, line drawings and maps were all specially drawn for this book. The colour profiles and plans of Bertrand Magueur are based on original line drawings by Robert Dumas, on official plans currently held by the Service Historique at Vincennes and the Archives de l'Armement at Châtellerault, and on photographs and other documentation.

The line drawings by John Jordan are based on official plans and other documentation located in the French archives. Some of these plans and documents have only recently been made available as part of the *Fonds Potsdam*, an archive of material assembled by the German *Kriegsmarine* during the Occupation and transferred to Berlin, where it was seized by the Russians; the materials were returned to France after the fall of the Berlin Wall and have now been reclassified and distributed among the various French national archives.

ACKNOWLEDGEMENTS
The authors thank the following organisations that have assisted them with their research:

- the Service Historique de la Marine Nationale, Vincennes, Paris
- the Centre d'Archives de l'Armement, Châtellerault
- the ECPA(D), Fort d'Ivry

Sincere thanks are also due: to Richard Worth, whose enthusiasm provided the initial impetus for this book; to Dr Jean Bladé, who provided the watercolour of *Strasbourg* that illustrates the jacket; to Bertrand Magueur, who was responsible for the high-quality colour outboard profiles of the ships; and to Philippe Caresse, Patrick Du Cheyron, Henri Landais, Bertrand Magueur, Max Moulin, Claude Picard, Erminio Bagnasco and Alain Casprak for their assistance with photographic illustration. Bill Jurens, Nathan Okun, John Roberts, Kent Crawford and John Spencer provided support, advice and documentation on the large-calibre guns and shells, and Dag Sundkuist was an invaluable source of information on French coast defence artillery. Bruno Gire provided documentation on the 37,000-ton battlecruiser, the uncompleted battleship *Gascogne* and the NC 420 seaplane, and Harold Winkel kindly permitted us to publish his drawings of the superstructures of *Gascogne*. The authors also wish to extend their thanks to Rob Gardiner (Seaforth Publishing), who has offered support and advice thoughout the project, and to Steve Dent, both for the intelligence and creativity he has displayed in designing the layouts and for the infinite patience with which he has accommodated the inevitable last-minute amendments. Without the collaboration of these people this book would not have been possible.

John Jordan and
Robert Dumas
July 2009

INTRODUCTION

A PRE-HISTORY

IT WAS 1910 BEFORE FRANCE BEGAN THE construction of her first 'dreadnought' battleship. When the British laid down the first of these revolutionary vessels in October 1905 the Marine Nationale was about to embark on a new series of battleships armed with twin 305mm (12in) turrets fore and aft and six twin side-mounted 240mm (9.4in) turrets. Laid down in the same month HMS *Dreadnought* was launched, *Danton* was a classic pre-dreadnought design, with armour plates of graduated thicknesss covering her sides from bow to stern, a protected lower deck of sufficient thickness only to keep out fragments of shell which succeeded in penetrating the armoured belt, and no fewer than four different gun calibres, her armament being completed by sixteen 75mm and ten 47mm anti-torpedo-boat guns. She would be the first French ship to be powered by steam turbines, but maximum speed would be little more than 19 knots as compared with the 21 knots of *Dreadnought.*

Five more ships of the *Danton* class would be laid down, three in 1907 and a further two in 1908, but because of the slow building times endemic in the French shipyards and naval dockyards it would be late 1911 before *Danton* and her sisters entered service. In the interim, the Royal Navy had completed no fewer than ten dreadnought battleships and five dreadnought battlecruisers, and had laid down the first eight of a new type of 'super-dreadnought' battleship armed with 13.5in guns and three similarly armed battlecruisers. The Imperial German Navy had completed the first eight of its own dreadnought battleships together with its first full fledged battlecruiser, *Von der Tann,* and five further battleships and three battlecruisers were on the stocks. Even the United States, not yet regarded as a major naval power, had completed six dreadnought battleships by late 1911 and laid down a further four.[1]

When construction of the dreadnoughts *Courbet* and

Jean Bart began in late 1910 the Marine Nationale was therefore already well off the pace. Two further ships of the class, *Paris* and *France,* would be laid down in November 1911. They would be followed by the three ships of the *Bretagne* class, two of which would be laid down in mid-1912 and the third at the end of the same year. The latter were of similar design, but with ten 340mm guns in five centreline twin turrets replacing the twelve 305mm guns (two superimposed turrets fore and aft plus two on the beam) of the *Courbet* class. The 340mm (13.4in) calibre was adopted in an effort to match the British 13.5in gun. However, displacement, dimensions, protection and propulsion remained essentially unchanged from the *Courbet* class, largely because of the limited dimensions of existing building ways and graving docks.

With the Marine Nationale seriously lagging behind the Royal Navy and the Imperial German Navy in modern battleships, recourse was made to the traditional strategy of putting a large, comprehensive long-term naval programme before the French Parliament. The *Statut Naval* authorised on 30 March 1912 envisaged a powerful battle fleet comprising the following:-

28 sea-going battleships (*cuirassés d'escadre*)
10 scout cruisers (*éclaireurs d'escadre*)
52 fleet torpedo boats (*torpilleurs d'escadre*)

The ships were to be in service by 1920, and the year-on-year construction schedule, as with all such programmes, was fixed in advance. The figure of twenty-eight battleships was to include the eleven modern pre-dreadnoughts of the *République, Vérité* and *Danton* classes (two, three and six respectively – the battleship *Liberté* had been lost to an internal explosion in 1911), and the four dreadnoughts of the *Courbet* class. The remaining thirteen ships were to be laid down over the next five years as follows:

1912: three *Bretagne* class (23,500 tonnes)
1913: two *Normandie* class (25,200 tonnes)
1914: two *Normandie* class (25,200 tonnes)
1915: four *Lyon* class (29,000 tonnes)
1917: two ships of a new type

With the deterioration of the international situation the new programme would be accelerated and compressed during the following two years with a view to having twelve super-dreadnought battleships in service by 1918. The schedule would now be:

1913: four *Normandie* class
1914: one *Normandie* (to make a four-ship division with the *Bretagne* class)
1915: four *Lyon* class

---

[1] The Royal Navy ships were as follows: *Dreadnought,* three *Bellerophon* class, three *St Vincent* class, *Neptune* and two *Colossus* class, with four 'super-dreadnoughts' of the *Orion* class building. Battlecruisers completed were three *Invincible* class and two *Indefatigable* class (a third was building for the Dominion of Australia), with three 13.5in-gun ships of the *Lion* class building. Imperial German Navy: four *Nassau* class and four *Helgoland* class completed with five *Kaiser* class building; the three battlecruisers of the *Moltke* and *Seydlitz* classes were building.
US Navy: two *South Carolina,* two *Delaware* and two *Florida* class battleships had been completed by the end of 1911, with two *Wyoming* and two *New York* class building.

FRENCH BATTLESHIPS 1906-14

	Patrie	*Liberté*	*Danton*	*Courbet*	*Bretagne*
Built	2 ships	4 ships	6 ships	4 ships	3 ships
	1901-06	1903-08	1907-11	1910-14	1912-16
Displacement	14,750t	14,750t	18,500t	23,500t	23,500t
Dimensions	138m x 24.3m	138m x 24.3m	147m x 25.8m	166m x 27m	166m x 27m
Speed	19kts	19kts	19kts	20kts	20kts
Armament	4 x 305mm	4 x 305mm	4 x 305mm	12 x 305mm	10 x 340mm
	16 x 164mm	10 x 194mm	12 x 240mm	22 x 138mm	22 x 138mm
Protection	280mm	280mm	250mm	250mm	250mm

The six battleships of the *Danton* class, laid down between Februrary 1906 and July 1908, were a development of *Liberté*. Although they introduced steam turbines to the Marine Nationale, they were essentially of conservative design, with the classic pre-dreadnought combination of a mixed main battery and graduated armour covering virtually the entire hull. In this class the 305mm twin turrets at the ends of the ship were complemented by six twin 240mm turrets mounted along the sides of the ship. This is *Voltaire* in 1912.

The *Normandie* design was essentially a slightly enlarged *Bretagne* with twelve 340mm guns in four quadruple turrets. Although by this time triple turrets had been adopted by the navies of Italy, Russia and Austria-Hungary, this would have been the first adoption of the quadruple turret by any of the major navies. It was dictated in part by the limited dimensions of the dry docks available to the Marine Nationale, which in turn put a premium on centreline length if large numbers of 340mm guns were to be accommodated.[2] The alternative, the development of a larger-calibre 380mm gun comparable to the latest 15in weapon adopted by the Royal Navy, was not thought to be feasible in the time available for the 1912 programme. The *Lyon* class, which was scheduled to follow the five *Normandie*s, therefore took this process a stage further by mounting no fewer than sixteen 340mm guns in four quadruple turrets. Even so, overall length had now grown from 166 metres in the *Courbet* and *Bretagne* classes to 194.5 metres, and displacement from 23,500 tonnes to 29,000 tonnes. The only existing docks which could accommodate ships of this size were the Missiessy No. 1 and No. 2 docks at Toulon, which had been lengthened to 202 metres between 1909 and 1913. New graving docks 250 metres in length at Cherbourg, Brest and Toulon were therefore an important part of an ambitious infrastructure programme intended to underpin the 1912 *Statut Naval*, and work had begun on these in 1909-11 with a view to completion by 1914-17.

The guns in the quadruple turrets of the *Normandie*

---

[2] Length overall of the *Normandie* class was 176.6 metres; the largest graving docks currently available were the Pontaniou No. 2 and No. 3 docks at Brest, which had been built by combining former building docks during the early 1900s and had a maximum length of 178 metres, and the three docks in the Missiessy Basin at Toulon, one of which was 179 metres long while the other two were currently being enlarged to 202 metres, with work due to complete in 1913.

FRENCH BATTLESHIPS OF THE 1912 NAVAL PROGRAMME

	Normandie	*Lyon*
Built	5 ships	4 ships
	LD 1913-14	(cancelled)
Displacement	25,250t	29,000t
Dimensions	176m x 27m	195m x 29m
Speed	21kts	23kts
Armament	12 x 305mm, 24 x 138mm	16 x 340mm, 24 x 138mm
Protection	280mm	280mm

GRAVING DOCKS AVAILABLE OR UNDER CONSTRUCTION IN METROPOLITAN FRANCE 1914

Cherbourg

Dock	Dimensions	Status
Forme du Homet	249m x 36m	Begun 1909

Brest

Dock	Dimensions	Status
Pontaniou No. 2	178m x 27m	In service
Pontaniou No. 3	178m x 33m	In service
Laninon No. 8	250m x 36m	Begun 1910
Laninon No. 9	250m x 36m	Begun 1910

Note: The two Pontaniou docks were barely large enough to accommodate the *Normandie* class, hence the degree of priority given to the two new Laninon docks, which would be completed in 1916.

Toulon

Dock	Dimensions	Status
Missiessy No. 1	202m x 30.5m	In service
Missiessy No. 2	202m x 30.5m	In service
Missiessy No. 3	179m x 30.5m	In service
Vauban *Grands*	250m x 40.7m	Begun 1911
Bassins	250m x 40.7m	Begun 1911

Note: The larger two of the Missiessy docks, on which work was completed only in 1913, could comfortably accommodate the *Normandie* class, and their dimensions appear to have dictated those of the *Lyon* class. Work on the Vauban *Grands Bassins*, a major engineering project involving reclaimed land, was discontinued during the Great War and resumed only in 1919. The maximum usable length of the two *Grands Bassins* was 408 metres, but in practice each was divided into two docks by watertight caissons.

and *Lyon* classes were paired, the turret being divided by a thick steel partition into two independent gunhouses in order to minimise the chance of a single hit disabling all four guns. The turret itself could still be immobilised on a particular bearing as a result of action damage, resulting in a loss of 33 per cent of main gun power in the *Normandie* class (25 per cent in the *Lyon* class), but the care taken in the two designs to space out the turrets along the ship's axis would ensure that no two turrets could be jammed by a single hit.

Other features of these two designs were less advanced – although the design of the *Lyon* class was never finalised. The *Normandie* class retained the dated protection system of France's earlier dreadnoughts, and concerns about the limited cruise radius associated with direct-drive turbines led to the retrograde step of reverting to triple-expansion engines, which were more economical at lower speeds, for the outer two shafts while retaining turbines for the inner shafts. This mixed propulsion plant attracted considerable criticism within the French Navy: the different properties of the two types of engine when combined at

The first French dreadnoughts, the four units of the *Courbet* class, were laid down during 1910-11 and had an all-big-gun armament of twelve 305mm guns in twin turrets. However, it was still envisaged that battle ranges would be short and shell trajectories correspondingly flat. The protection system therefore continued to based on that of the French pre-dreadnoughts, and the big guns could elevate only to 12 degrees for a maximum range of 13,500 metres, at a time when most foreign battleships had guns which could elevate to 15 degrees and the British Royal Navy was moving to 20 degrees. This is *Jean Bart* in 1916.

Normandie class
25,200 tonnes
176.6m x 27m
12 x 340mm (3 x IV)
24 x 138.6mm
280mm belt
21 knots

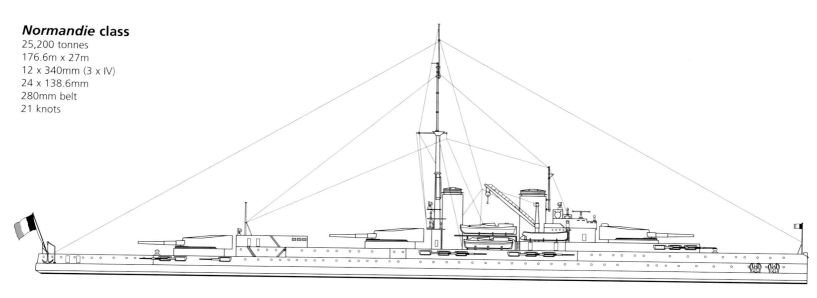

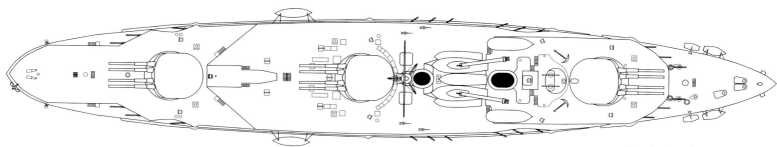

(Drawing by John Jordan © 2009)

higher speeds was an issue, maintenance and the provision of spares would be complicated, and there were also implications for the training of personnel.

These later designs were never put to the test, however, as construction of the *Normandie* class ground to a halt in 1914 and none of the battleships of the *Lyon* class was ever laid down. The outbreak of war in August 1914 resulted in the mobilisation of much of the French industrial workforce, including many of those who worked in the naval dockyards, the *arsenaux*. Priority for both personnel and *matériel* was given to the Army. Only those ships already launched and fitting out would be completed; those laid down would – where possible – be launched to clear the slipways, but construction work would thereafter be suspended. In real terms this meant that the three ships of the *Bretagne* class, all of which had been launched in 1913 and for which the steel, guns, propulsion machinery and other equipment had been ordered and/or delivered, would be completed as quickly as possible with the smaller workforce available; *Bretagne* and *Provence* would complete in 1915 and their sister *Lorraine* the following year. However,

work on the battleships of the *Normandie* class, three of which were launched shortly after the outbreak of war, was quickly abandoned. The fourth ship was finally launched in 1916, but the fifth, *Béarn*, remained on the stocks until the end of the war. Many of the components delivered for these ships were redirected elsewhere: boilers were installed in other ships, and the guns went to the Army; some items were used as replacements for those fitted in the *Bretagne* class after 1918.

THE FRENCH FLEET IN 1918
When the Armistice was signed on 11 November 1918, the most modern battleships in the Marine Nationale were the six *Danton*s, the four *Courbet*s and the three *Bretagne*s. The abandonment of the *Statut Naval* of 1912 in the face of greater priorities on land now meant that the French were even farther behind in numbers and technology. During the war, the British had completed no fewer than ten battleships and two battle-cruisers armed with 15in guns, all of which were significantly larger than the *Bretagne*s; the five ships of the *Queen Elizabeth* class had an oil-fired propulsion plant

A COMPARISON BETWEEN *BRETAGNE* AND THE LATEST FOREIGN CONSTRUCTION (1918)

	Bretagne (Fr)	*Queen Elizabeth* (GB)	*New Mexico* (USA)	*Hyuga* (Jap)	*Hood* (GB)
Built	1912-16	1912-16	1915-19	1915-18	1916-20
Displacement	23,500t	27,500t	32,000t	31,260t	41,200t
Dimensions	166m x 27m	197m x 27.6m	190m x 29.7m	206m x 28.7m	262m x 31.7m
Speed	20kts	24kts	21kts	23kts	31kts
Armament	10 x 340mm	8 x 381mm	12 x 356mm	12 x 356mm	8 x 381mm
	22 x 138mm	14 x 152mm	14 x 127mm	20 x 140mm	12 x 140mm
Protection	250mm	330mm	340mm	305mm	305mm

Note: Dimensions, armament and protection are tabulated using the metric system to provide a comparison.

and a designed speed of 24 knots, while the battle-cruisers *Repulse* and *Renown* could make 30 knots. Even these ships were eclipsed in size and power by the latest American and Japanese super-dreadnoughts, which were armed with twelve 14in guns, and in 1918 the British launched the largest, fastest and most powerful warship in the world, the battlecruiser *Hood*, which would enter service in May 1920 (see table).

The *Courbet*s and the *Bretagne*s were not only inferior in size, power and speed to the latest foreign battleships but were of obsolescent design. Even with the advent of the 'all-big-gun' ship, the French persisted with the belief that 'decisive' battle range would be around 6000 metres, and that engagements between opposing battle lines were unlikely much beyond 8000 metres. The protection systems of the new battleships therefore continued to assume pre-dreadnought opponents armed with a multitude of calibres which included medium guns in the 165-240mm range, firing at relatively flat trajectories. Vertical protection was prioritised at the expense of horizontal protection, and little account was taken of plunging shell. The hull had a high, deep two-strake belt of thick cemented armour, with a strake of cemented armour of reduced thickness amidships; there was thick cemented armour on the turrets and the barbettes, and the casemate battery guns were in armoured 'redoubts', also with thick walls of cemented armour. The two light protected decks, which were composed of triple layers of thin steel plating, and the *entrepont cellulaire* between them, were intended simply to prevent the fragments of shells which broke up on the armoured belt from penetrating into the ship's vitals. The belt covered virtually the entire hull, and declined in thickness towards the bow

and the stern. In contrast the British had moved in the direction of heavier protection over the ship's vitals, other areas of the hull being armoured only sufficiently to keep out QF shell of 6in (150mm) calibre or below while the Americans, with their radical *Nevada* design of 1912, had accepted the logic of the all-big-gun ship and adopted an 'all-or-nothing' system in which the ship's vitals were protected by the heaviest possible armour, including a relatively thick armoured deck, while areas outside this 'citadel' remained virtually unprotected.

Because of the relatively short battle ranges envisaged, long range fire for the 305mm and 340mm main guns of the *Courbet* and *Bretagne* classes was considered unnecessary, so neither the turrets nor the fire control systems were designed with this in mind. The 12-degree elevation of the 305/45 and 340/45 guns, equivalent to maximum ranges of 13,500 and 14,500m respectively, was significantly less than in any of the other major navies.[3] The powerful secondary battery of twenty-two 138.6mm guns was to be used not only to repel torpedo-boat attacks but to pepper the superstructures of enemy battleships, disable the small-calibre guns mounted topsides, cause fires and general devastation, and bring about a crippling deterioration in fighting capability.

---

[3] The 28cm and 30.5cm guns of the Imperial German Navy could elevate to 16 degrees, the 12in and 14in guns of the US Navy to 15 degrees, while the Royal Navy began with 15 degrees for its 12in guns and raised this to 20 degrees for its 13.5in and 15in guns (maximum range for the latter two gun calibres was around 21,700 metres).

Grouped with the *Courbet* class as the *cuirassés de 23,500 tonnes*, the three 'super-dreadnoughts' of the *Bretagne* class had the same hull and dimensions as their immediate predecessors, the only major change being in the number and calibre of the main guns. In place of the twelve 305mm guns of the *Courbet* class there were ten 340mm guns in five twin centreline turrets. This is *Provence* shortly after her completion in 1915.

During the pre-dreadnought era the Marine Nationale had been well to the fore in the development of sophisticated fire control equipment, and both the *Courbet* and the *Bretagne* classes were fitted with a modern Le Comte-Aubry gunnery data transmission system which supplied bearing and elevation data directly to the guns, a Le Prieur graphical computer, and mechanical correctors for distance and deflection. However, the rangefinders initially supplied were British Barr & Stroud FT coincidence models with a base of only 2.74 metres (9 feet), and all aspects of fire control, including spotting the fall of shot, was exercised from the armoured conning tower. The rangefinders provided to the turrets for local control were 1.35-metre (5-foot) models mounted in a cupola at the after end. The heavy pole foremast had only a small platform – later slightly enlarged to form a crow's nest with canvas sides – and in the *Courbet* class was stepped directly abaft the first two funnels, thereby ensuring that it would be constantly shrouded in smoke during action. In contrast the British dreadnoughts used the foretop, which was generally supported by a sturdy tripod mast, as the primary spotting position, for which purpose it was equipped with binoculars on fixed pedestals to minimise the effects of vibration.

The Marine Nationale was sufficiently concerned about the long range fire control capabilities of these ships to stipulate in a note dated 25 April 1914 that the 2.74-metre rangefinders atop the conning tower be replaced by 15-foot (4.57-metre) models again purchased from the British company Barr & Stroud. These were duly fitted in a triplex tiered installation in the last two ships of the *Courbet* class while the latter were building, and were retrofitted in the first two ships in 1915. At the same time the 1.35-metre rangefinders on the turrets were replaced by two-metre B&S FT models. These modifications were applied to the *Bretagne* class from the outset.

However, the limited range of the guns themselves was to become a more pressing issue, as battle ranges in the early naval engagements of the Great War greatly surpassed what had previously been thought possible. In the Battle of the Falkland Islands (December 1914) the British battlecruisers *Invincible* and *Inflexible* opened fire at almost 15,000 metres, and the main action took place at 9000-13,000 metres. In January of the following year, at Dogger Bank, the action took place at ranges between 18,000 metres and 14,500 metres, while at Jutland fire in the early (daylight) phases was generally opened at ranges of 18-19,000 metres.

An early decision was made to increase the maximum angle of elevation of the guns from 12 to 18 degrees in the *Bretagne* class, thereby increasing the maximum range to 21,100m. However, the pressure of other more urgent maintenance work on the naval dockyards made this impossible in the short term. The after turret of *Lorraine* was modified in 1917, but work on her other turrets and on those of the other two ships of the class had to be postponed until after the war.

The other area in which the French had fallen behind was in anti-torpedo protection. The French dreadnoughts continued to rely on coal bunkers outboard of the machinery spaces with an internal reinforced holding bulkhead to absorb the worst effects of an exploding warhead, and there was little protection for magazines. The British and the Americans, on the other

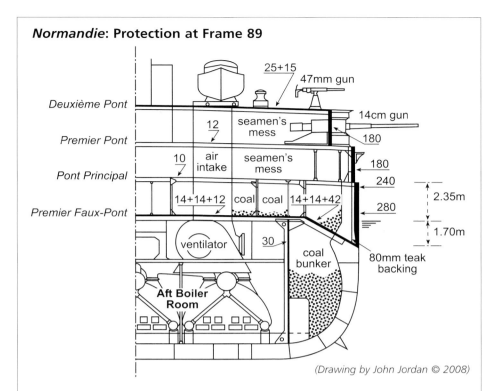

Normandie: Protection at Frame 89

(Drawing by John Jordan © 2008)

The half-section view of *Normandie* at Frame 89 shows the classic French dreadnought protection system, which was derived in turn from the pre-dreadnoughts of the *République/Liberté* and *Danton* classes. The main belt, which was of cemented armour, extended over virtually the entire length of the ship. It comprised two strakes of roughly equal height; the upper strake tapered slightly towards its upper edge and the lower strake tapered more sharply to 80/100mm below the waterline. The thickness of the plates was uniform amidships but was progressively reduced towards the ends of the ship. Immediately above the main armoured belt, between the Main Deck and the First Deck, there was an upper belt of cemented armour amidships. The battery-mounted secondary 138.6mm guns were housed within 'redoubts' protected by a mix of cemented and special steel plates with a thickness of 160-180mm: In the *Normandie* class these 'redoubts' partially incorporated the barbettes for the main guns: the forward redoubt was at the level of the Second Deck, the central redoubt (housing no fewer than twelve of the 14cm guns) on the First Deck, and the after redoubt on the Main Deck.

The main armoured deck was the First Platform Deck. Its primary purpose was to protect the magazines and machinery from shell fragments which managed to penetrate the main belt. French armoured decks of the period comprised multiple sheets of relatively thin mild steel (generally 12-15mm) riveted together. The central part of the main armoured deck in the *Normandie* class comprised three sheets of 14mm, 14mm and 12mm respectively. Although this added up to a total thickness of 40mm, a 'composite' deck of this type was far less effective in resisting penetration than a single thickness of 40mm; it did, however, permit the thickness of the deck to be graduated according to the importance of what was beneath it. The main armoured deck in the French dreadnoughts and pre-dreadnoughts extended from the steering gear at the stern to the bow, where it was angled down to form a sort of carapace. It was also sloped down at the sides to join the lower edge of the armoured belt, and these inclined sections were reinforced by a double row of plates of 42mm special steel to serve as a 'back-up' for the main belt.

Underwater protection in the *Normandie* was provided by a 30mm bulkhead, and there were coal bunkers to absorb the explosion of a torpedo warhead. Coal was also used as a 'filler' directly behind the main belt and in the typically French 'cellular layer' (*entrepont cellulaire*) between the First Platform Deck and the Main Deck. The outstanding features of French pre-dreadnought and dreadnought protection systems were their complexity and the extent of their coverage. It was envisaged that decisive battle ranges would be no more than 6000-8000m, at which large-calibre shell would have a relatively flat trajectory. The emphasis was therefore on thick vertical armour, with the lightly-protected decks intended only to keep out fragments of shells which succeeded in penetrating the main or upper belts. The lessons of the actions in the North Sea during the First World War were that capital ships now needed to be protected against plunging shell, which implied a major redistribution of armour from sides to decks. This was a key factor in the decision to send four of the five incomplete hulls of the *Normandie* class to the breakers.

hand, had developed elaborate torpedo protection systems by the late war period. The British had adopted the external torpedo 'bulge', with alternating void and liquid-filled compartments, and was fitting these to its most modern battleships and battlecruisers from 1917. They were also experimenting with sealed steel tubes designed to absorb the force of the explosion while at the same time minimising the flooding of side compartments. The US Navy was building similar torpedo protection systems using alternate void spaces and liquid loading into the design of its latest battleships. The cost in terms of both beam and speed would have been difficult for the French dreadnoughts to absorb, given that these ships were already relatively slow and had access to graving docks with limited dimensions.

FROM HERE TO MODERNITY

When the Great War ended the Marine Nationale faced some difficult decisions. The seven dreadnoughts, all except two of which had been completed during the conflict, now constituted the backbone of the battle fleet. However, these ships had so many obsolescent features built into their design that they were totally outclassed by the powerful modern units built or building for Britain, the United States and Japan. There was also the issue of whether, and with what modifications, the five battleships of the *Normandie* class should be completed. Four had been launched, their hulls and engines being generally 60-65 per cent complete; the fifth, *Béarn*, remained on the stocks at the private shipyard of Forges et Chantiers de la Méditerranée, La Seyne, and would be finally launched in April 1920. Despite their more powerful armament these ships as designed had the same dated features as the *Courbet* and *Bretagne* classes, particularly with respect to their horizontal and underwater protection, while the 'mixed' propulsion system was now considered a retrograde step which would need to be reconsidered

These were not the only issues facing the Marine Nationale. France was bankrupt, her finances exhausted by the war. The industrial North had been a battlefield, and the shipyards and naval dockyards had been denuded of skilled labour to service the more pressing needs of the Army. The entire naval infrastructure would have to be renewed before France was in a position to rebuild its battle fleet. Moreover, given the ambitious scope of the 1912 *Statut Naval*, it could be argued that battleship construction had suffered far less than other elements of the programme. Of the ten scout cruisers projected, not a single one had been laid down. The destroyer situation was in many respects just as bad. The standard 800-tonne destroyer built in the immediate prewar period had proved too small, too fragile and too short-legged to operate effectively with the battlefleet. The 1500-tonne *torpilleur d'escadre* envisaged in the 1912 programme, of which no fewer than thirty-two were to have been built, never materialised. Four 950-tonne torpedo-boats building for Argentina were requisitioned in August 1914 as the *Aventurier* class, but these and three 800-tonne torpedo-boats of the *Enseigne Roux* class were the only flotilla craft to be built in France during four years of war. In 1917, the situation was so desperate that twelve 'second class' destroyers of the *Kaba* class were ordered from Japan for anti-submarine duties in the Mediterranean.

In February 1919, Admiral de Bon, Chief of the Naval General Staff, established the construction priorities of the Marine Nationale as: first 'destroyers' (British terminology being adopted to denote the entire category of flotilla craft), and second light cruisers (to be employed as scouts); battleships came last. These were realistic priorities; even so it proved impossible to lay down a single light cruiser or destroyer until summer 1922.[4]

In the interim what money and dockyard labour was available could at least be used to bring the existing battleships up to modern standards. Even within this category of warship, however, priorities had to be established. The super-dreadnoughts of the *Bretagne* class, France's most modern battleships, would be the first to be taken in hand. Modernisation of the *Courbet* class would await a decision on the fate of the incomplete *Normandie*s. It was conceivable that should the latter be completed the older ships, which were outgunned by the latest foreign battleships, might be used for training or placed in reserve.

Bretagne was duly taken in hand at Toulon in 1919, with her sister *Lorraine* following in 1921 and the third ship, *Provence*, due to follow in 1922. All would have the elevation of the main guns increased from 12 to 18 degrees. A heavy tripod foremast would be fitted forward with a large fore-top for the gunnery officer, equipped with a 3.66-metre (12-foot) rangefinder in the *Bretagne*. *Bretagne* trialled a British Vickers fire control director; the other two units received a French Laurant-Paquelier model. The bridge structure was enlarged and the fore funnel raised. The four forward 138.6mm casemate guns were removed, as they could not be operated in a seaway, and four single 75mm HA guns were added topsides.

Meanwhile discussions proceeded as to whether the battleships of the *Normandie* class should be completed. Following her launch in 1920, *Béarn* was fitted with a temporary wooden flight deck and used for aviation trials. These were generally successful and led to proposals for the ship to be completed as an aircraft carrier. Factors in favour of her selection for conversion were her recent launch and her relatively incomplete state, which made conversion easier. As for her four sisters, consideration was given to new propulsion machinery capable of delivering 24-25 knots, but modifications would be costly; in addition to a new all-turbine plant with more than double the original horsepower (80,000shp against 32,000shp in the original design), the hull would need to be lengthened both to accommodate the new machinery and to secure a more favourable length to beam ratio. It was envisaged that the elevation of the main guns would be increased to 23 degrees, increasing gun range to 25-26,000 metres, and that a new tripod foremast similar to that currently being fitted in the *Bretagne* class, together with director

---

[4] At a meeting of the *Conseil Supérieur* on 30 September 1920, a programme was drawn up for the completion of eleven battleships of 40,000 tonnes and fifteen cruisers of 12,000 tonnes by 1940. The Naval General Staff, while at the same time acknowledging that it would be impossible to lay down any of these ships during the period 1921-1925, was anxious that technical developments abroad be closely monitored so that once the green light was given for the programme it could be embarked upon without delay. While these discussions were proceeding, a gun with a calibre of 450mm (17.7in) was being developed for testing at Gâvres.

fire control, would replace the original pole mast. Horizontal protection would be strengthened and one-metre bulges added at the waterline both to protect against torpedoes and to restore buoyancy. However, such extensive rebuilding would be both costly and labour-intensive, and by the time sufficient funding and dockyard capacity were available the basic design would be ten years old. There was an understandable reluctance by the civilian government to commit to such a major programme at a time of demobilisation and financial constraints.

THE WASHINGTON CONFERENCE

Invitations to attend a conference in Washington for the purpose of limiting naval armaments were received by each of the five leading naval powers in August 1921. Some of the more important items for discussion were flagged up well before the conference began. The French government was aware that overall tonnage restrictions would figure prominently on the agenda. It was also thought likely that a pause in new naval construction would be proposed, both for economic reasons and to defuse the new naval arms race developing between the United States, Japan and – belatedly – Britain. And it became clear that the British would press for the abolition of the submarine in the wake of the destructive 'unrestricted' campaign against British shipping by the German U-boats in the final two years of the war.

The French were not opposed in principle to overall tonnage limitations, although they naturally expected any differentiation in the totals accorded to each of the major powers to reflect status and need, with the worldwide French Empire – second only to that of Great Britain – weighing heavily in the balance. However, any suggestion of a 'naval holiday' was to be resolutely opposed, given the parlous state of the Marine Nationale with its ageing, obsolescent fleet units, as would any attempt to abolish the submarine, which the French saw as essential to defend its own coasts and the colonies.

On 12 November, Secretary of State Hughes (United States) opened the first plenary session of the conference with a proposal to freeze capital ship construction for ten years, and to agree future force strengths based on the total tonnage of 'capital ships' currently in service with the major navies. This sweeping proposal sent shock waves through all the delegations present. From the French standpoint the proposal was particularly uncomfortable. First, it established the capital ship as the primary unit of currency for the purpose of naval arms limitation – a move which favoured a 'battleship navy' such as the United States over the imperial navies of Britain and France, which had traditionally required large numbers of cruisers for 'policing' duties and commerce protection. Second, it attempted to impose a freeze on the construction of capital ships at a time when the Marine Nationale was looking to renewal for its salvation. And, third, it would leave France with a battle fleet older and less capable ship-for-ship than

The *Courbet* class underwent major refits during the early 1920s. The elevation of the main guns was increased from 12 degrees (13,500 metres range) to 23 degrees (26,300 metres). A heavy tripod foremast with a large British-style foretop was fitted and director fire control provided; the bridge structure was enlarged and the first and second funnels trunked together, changing their external appearance considerably. However, the protection system remained dated. This is *Courbet* in 1939, by which time she had been relegated to the role of gunnery training ship.

CAPITAL SHIPS TO BE RETAINED UNDER THE WASHINGTON TREATY

Class/type	Displacement	Main guns	Speed	Names	Completed	To be replaced	Age
Danton	18,890mt	4 – 305mm	19kts	*Condorcet*	1911	–	
		12 – 240mm		*Diderot*	1911	–	
				Voltaire	1911	–	
Courbet	23,500mt	12 – 305mm	20kts	*Courbet*	1913	1930	17yrs
				Jean Bart	1913	1930	17yrs
				France	1914	1932	18yrs
				Paris	1914	1934	20yrs
Bretagne	23,500mt	10 – 340mm	20kts	*Bretagne*	1915	1934	19yrs
				Provence	1915	1935	20yrs
				Lorraine	1916	1936	20yrs
Total	221,170mt (including three pre-dreadnoughts of 56,670mt)						

Note: Because none of her capital ship construction was recent, France was permitted to lay down two new ships each of 35,000 tons before the end of the ten-year 'battleship holiday' imposed on the three major contracting powers: one in 1927 and one in 1929. These would replace three of the four early dreadnoughts of the *Courbet* class. By 1931, the pre-dreadnoughts of the *Danton* class would be twenty years old, and of limited military value; they were not therefore included in the Washington schedule of replacements. Both France and Italy reserved the right to use their replacement tonnage as they saw fit to allow for a larger number of battleships below the 35,000-ton individual displacement limit.

that of any of the other three major powers.

In terms of its world status the Marine Nationale considered itself to be beneath the navies of the United States and Britain but at least on a par with that of Japan and certainly some way ahead of the Italian *Regia Marina*. However, for Britain and the United States the balance of power in the Western Pacific was seen as the key area for the deliberations of the conference. Tripartite negotiations between the latter two countries and the Japanese delegation quickly secured agreement on a 5:5:3 ratio for capital ships, but the French and the Italians were left outside these discussions; the balance of naval forces in Europe was considered to be a less pressing issue, and it was felt that decisions on the French and Italian capital ship allocations could be left for a later date.

French premier Briand, who viewed Washington as just one of a series of conferences about security and disarmament currently taking place under the broad umbrella of the League of Nations, was more concerned with resisting proposed cuts in France's land forces. He nevertheless recognised the parlous situation of the Marine Nationale and on 17 November instructed Admiral de Bon, the head of the naval delegation, not to accept a lower figure than that prescribed for Japan. On 24 November, having failed to obtain the security pact with the United States he had been hoping to achieve, Briand left the conference and returned to Paris. De Bon was left to negotiate a hoped-for figure of 350,000 tons (equivalent to ten battleships of the new 'standard' displacement of 35,000 tons), with a fall-back position of 280,000 tons (eight battleships). No quantitative limits were to be agreed on submarines, on which France was counting to offset the imbalance in capital ship force strengths between the Marine Nationale and the other major navies.

It was therefore with some consternation that Albert Sarraut, Minister for the Colonies, who now headed the French delegation in Washington in the absence of both Briand and President Viviani, learned from Secretary Hughes that France would receive a mere 175,000 tons of battleships (equivalent to five new-build ships), and that Italy would receive the same allocation. It was made clear that this figure was arrived at by taking into account current force strengths, as was the case with the tonnage allocation

for the other major naval powers attending the conference. No account could be taken either of the ambitious French capital ship programme of 1912, or of the incomplete hulls of the *Normandie* class – which, like the incomplete battleships of the US Navy and the Imperial Japanese Navy, were to be scrapped – or of France's status as a major imperial power.

The French government, despite its initial sense of shock and outrage, found itself obliged to accept this *fait accompli*. Taken together with French resistance to disarmament on land, an obstructive attitude towards naval disarmament would have led to France being held responsible for the failure of the conference and in consequence for undermining the entire world peace process. Moreover, Briand was well aware that French finances could neither fund nor sustain a fleet of new battleships without American financial assistance. He was therefore inclined to agree to the proposed 175,000-ton figure with the proviso that this same ratio should not also to be applied to light forces[5] and submarines. Indeed, the French position now became one of compensatory demands: by renouncing 'offensive' ships (ie capital ships) France should be permitted a *greater* number of 'defensive' units. Britain and the United States were quick to reject this linkage, but a French refusal to accept overall tonnage limits on 'auxiliary' vessels and submarines would mean that only limitations on capital ships and aircraft carriers could ultimately be agreed by the conference.

A meeting of the *Conseil Supérieur de la Défense Nationale* was held on 28 December 1921 to consider the overall implications of the Washington proposals. Briand was in the chair and all the major military figures were present. It was accepted that there was no money available for new battleship construction, and that given the increasing threat from the air it was by no means clear that this type of naval unit had a long-term future. Briand was of the opinion that France should opt for a purely defensive fleet, a view which was shared by certain of the naval officers present. Admiral Grasset suggested that for a sum of 500 million francs per year 330,000 tons of light surface ships and 90,000 tons of submarines could be built over ten years. It was

---

[5] Termed 'auxiliary vessels' in the language of the Conference.

agreed that all efforts be put into the construction of these two categories of ship, and the new programme was adopted by the French government the following day. These decisions served only to reinforce the obduracy of the French delegation at Washington when faced with proposals to limit submarines and 'auxiliary' surface warships. Wrong-footed by the US capital ship proposals, the French would now ensure that their broader naval interests were safeguarded.

Despite having been compelled to accept an unfavourable ratio in the capital ship category in the interests of disarmament and world peace, the French delegation would continue to fight its corner with regard to its right to modernise its ageing, obsolescent battle fleet. Improvements in the operational effectiveness of the battle fleet would undoubtedly flow from the construction of new scout cruisers and fleet torpedo boats – both unrestricted categories. Aircraft carriers operating reconnaissance and spotting aircraft would also enhance the general capabilities of the battle fleet, and the French delegation fought to secure a figure of 60,000 tons – 54,000 tons was the initial offer – to enable three ships of 20,000 tons to be built. The Marine Nationale also envisaged the construction of a new generation of fast 'fleet' submarines to accompany the battleships.

Moreover, the British delegation's insistence on being permitted to build two 'modern' capital ships of 35,000 tons as a counterweight to the latest US and Japanese ships created a negotiating lever which the French were not slow to exploit. If the British *Queen Elizabeth*s were not considered a match for the US *Tennessee* and *Maryland* classes or the Japanese *Hyuga* and *Nagato* classes, where did that leave the French with the *Courbet*s and the *Bretagne*s, the design of which dated from 1909? This legitimate complaint was to lead to two important concessions. The French – and the Italians, who were in a similar position – were permitted to submit their elderly dreadnoughts to a much more radical modernisation than the other treaty powers. For the three major powers the only modifications to existing capital ships permitted under Washington Treaty rules were 'defensive' in nature: a maximum of 3000 tons was allowed to improve horizontal protection (against bombs) and underwater protection (against torpedoes) and to increase anti-aircraft armaments. No alterations in side armour, in calibre, number or general type of mounting of main armament were permitted (Part III Section I clause [d]). However, paragraph 1 made an exception:

In the case of France and Italy, which countries within the limits allowed for bulge [ie 3000 tons] may increase their armour protection and the calibre of the guns now carried on their existing capital ships so as not to exceed 16 inches (406 millimetres)...

The other concession was that, in view of the age and obsolescent design of their dreadnought battleships, the French and the Italians would each be permitted to lay down one new battleship of 35,000 tons in 1927 (for completion 1930-1) and again in 1929 (for completion 1932-3), before the end of the ten-year 'battleship holiday' scheduled for 1931 to which the other major powers were bound. In return the French would be expected to scrap three ships of the *Courbet* class, and the Italians two of their own early dreadnoughts.

Because neither the Marine Nationale nor the *Regia Marina* was yet convinced of the need to move to battleships of 35,000-ton displacement – the existing French dreadnoughts displaced 23,500 tonnes, their Italian counterparts 22,500 tonnes – both powers reserved the right to employ their capital ship tonnage allocation as they saw fit, subject to Treaty limits. Thus the 70,000-ton allocation of 1927-9 could be used for two ships of 35,000 tons, three ships of 23,300 tons or for any combination of displacements which did not exceed this overall limit. This would become an important factor in the 'paper' designs of the 1920s which would culminate in *Dunkerque* and *Strasbourg*.

MODERNISING THE BATTLE FLEET

A radical reconstruction of the *Courbet* and *Bretagne* classes as permitted by the Washington Treaty was out of the question. The original design was extremely 'tight' in order to keep dimensions within the maximum which could be accommodated in existing graving docks. The superimposed turrets forward were unusually close to the bow, and their weight, together with the weight of the heavy bow armour, resulted in sea-keeping problems, particularly when operating in Atlantic waters.[6] Replacing their 305mm or 340mm guns by a smaller number of guns of 380mm or 406mm calibre would mean major reconstruction, and it was by no means clear what the optimum layout of the main guns would then be. Dimension and weight constraints also precluded horizontal protection on the scale currently being considered by the other major navies, while anti-torpedo bulges would have implications for maximum speed, which was already lower than that of the more modern foreign dreadnoughts. The fitting of bulges could be compensated only by lengthening the hull, which again would have major structural implications. Any one of these measures would be extremely costly and would impact on funding for infrastructure and for the new programme of cruisers, flotilla craft and submarines.

Although the French battle fleet was no longer in a position to contest the command of the seas with Britain or Japan – there was considered to be no risk of conflict with the US Navy – the Italian *Regia Marina* was another matter, and the Italian dreadnoughts were of similar vintage to those of the Marine Nationale. *Dante Alighieri*, the three ships of the *Cavour* class – *Leonardo da Vinci* had sunk in 1916 but had been salvaged and was still counted in Italy's Washington force strengths – and the two ships of the *Andrea Doria* class were armed with twelve/thirteen 12in/305mm guns, but these were British-pattern guns mounted in twin or triple turrets which permitted elevation to 20 degrees. The maximum theoretical range of the Italian 12in guns guns was 24,000 metres, almost double the range of the 305mm guns of the *Courbet* class, and substantially greater than the 21,000-metre range of the 340mm guns of the *Bretagne* class following their postwar modifications.

The modest reconstruction of the French dreadnoughts during the 1920s therefore focused on improving seaworthiness, gun range and fire control, and anti-aircraft defences; there was limited refurbishment of the propulsion machinery and no attempt was

---

[6] Each of the superimposed turrets in the *Courbet* class weighed 561 tonnes, of which 234 tonnes was armour.

RECONSTRUCTION OF THE *COURBET* AND *BRETAGNE* CLASSES 1918-31

Courbet class

	Name	Location	Began	Ended	Work done
First rebuild	*Paris*	Brest Dyd	25.10.22	25.11.23	main gun elevation 12° > 23°
	Courbet	FC Med	09.07.23	16.04.24	tripod foremast with foretop
	Jean Bart	Toulon Dyd	12.10.23	29.01.25	bow armour stripped
					No.1 BR > oil-fired
					4 x 75mm Mle 1918 HA + FC
Second rebuild	*Paris*	Toulon Dyd	16.08.27	15.01.29	Saint Chamond-Granat director FC
	Courbet	FC Med	15.01.27	12.01.31	new RF for main battery
	Jean Bart	Toulon Dyd	07.08.29	28.09.31	No.3 BR > oil-fired (not *Paris*)
					7 x 75mm Mle 1922 HA (not *Paris*)

Bretagne class

	Name	Location	Began	Ended	Work done
First rebuild	*Bretagne*	Toulon Dyd	12.06.19	18.10.20	main gun elevation 12° > 18°
	Lorraine	Toulon Dyd	10.11.21	04.12.22	tripod foremast with director FC
	Provence	Toulon Dyd	01.02.22	04.07.23	4 x 138mm (fwd) removed
					RF for secondary battery
					4 x 75mm Mle 1887 HA + FC
Second rebuild	*Bretagne*	Toulon Dyd	01.05.24	28.09.25	main gun elevation 18° > 23°
	Lorraine	Toulon Dyd	15.11.24	04.08.26	bow armour stripped
	Provence	Toulon Dyd	12.12.25	11.07.27	No. 6 BR > oil-fired
					new RF for main battery (not *Bretagne*)
Refit late 1920s	*Bretagne*	Toulon Dyd	15.11.27	12.05.28	Saint Chamond-Granat director FC
					new RF for main battery

made to remedy the ships' glaring deficiencies in horizontal and underwater protection, which would have proved both costly and labour-intensive.

The *Courbet* class underwent major refits which lasted between nine and fifteen months from 1922-5. The bow was stripped of its heavy armour and the elevation of the main guns increased from 12 degrees (13,500-metres range) to 23 degrees (26,300 metres). A heavy tripod foremast with a large British-style foretop was fitted; the bridge structure was enlarged and the first and second funnels trunked together.[7] The first of the five boiler rooms was changed to oil-firing, with four Du Temple boilers of modern design replacing the original coal-fired models. Four new 75mm Mle 1918 HA guns were fitted, together with new rangefinders for the secondary and AA batteries, and there were corresponding changes in the layout of the searchlight projectors and the boats. These ships now had a very different appearance and more than matched the Italian dreadnoughts, which apart from the addition of a few HA guns remained essentially unmodified.

Even before the first of these refits began the battleship *France* foundered in August of 1922. Under the provisions of the Washington Treaty she could have been replaced by a ship of similar displacement, but as France still had six operational dreadnoughts against the Italian five there was no urgency to do so.[8]

From 1924 to 1927, the three super-dreadnoughts of the *Bretagne* class would undergo a further modernisation to bring them up to the same standard as the

*Courbet*s. The angle of elevation of the main guns was again increased, this time to 23 degrees, which with the new Mle 1912-21 APC shell gave them a maximum range of 23,700 metres. The bow was stripped of its armour for improved seakeeping and one set of oil-fired boilers installed, as in the *Courbet* class. In *Lorraine* and *Provence* the Barr & Stroud 4.57-metre (15-foot) rangefinders from the original triplex installation were redistributed to the foretop and to new RF towers above the conning tower and around the mainmast for the main battery on the foretop and atop the conning tower, and a Zeiss stereo rangefinder with an 8.2-metre (27-foot) base was fitted to No.2 turret. New directors equipped with 2-metre Barr & Stroud FT Mle 1912-14 rangefinders for the secondary battery were also fitted.

Further modernisations of the *Courbet* and *Bretagne* classes would focus on fire control systems: a new Saint Chamond-Granat director control system of French design and manufacture was fitted in *Bretagne* and the *Courbet* class, which also received the same rangefinder upgrade as *Lorraine* and *Provence*. Proposals to extend oil-firing to the remaining boiler rooms had to be abandoned on grounds of cost, although *Courbet* and *Jean Bart* had a second boiler-room converted. By this time maximum speed was about 18 knots and all six ships were showing their age; reliability and availability had declined to a point at which retirement or a more radical modernisation would have to be considered.

In 1927, France's Mediterranean rival, the Italian *Regia Marina*, seriously considered scrapping all five of its elderly dreadnoughts. In the event, the four surviving vessels of the *Cavour* and *Andrea Doria* classes were retained primarily as 'bargaining chips' at the upcoming naval arms limitation conference to be held in London. In the same year both the French and Italians were permitted to lay down the first of two new capital ships each of a nominal 35,000 tons standard, and both countries gave serious consideration to this possibility.

---

[7] In *Paris*, the first ship to be modernised, the first funnel was simply moved aft to be adjacent to the second; this became a key distinguishing feature between the ships of the class.

[8] Following the Washington Conference the Italian *Regia Marina* made a decision not to rebuild *Leonardo da Vinci*; the salvaged hull was sold for scrap in March 1923.

CHAPTER 1

AFTER WASHINGTON: 1922-1931

FROM 1922 TO 1925, THE DESIGN TEAMS OF the *Service Technique des Constructions Navales* (STCN), the constructor's branch of the Marine Nationale, were almost fully occupied with designs for the new generation of cruisers, flotilla craft and submarines.

The Washington Treaty made a particular impact on cruiser design, with the maximum 10,000-ton (10,160 tonnes) displacement and 8in (203mm) gun calibre figures set to become the new standard for cruiser construction. To follow the three light cruisers of the *Duguay-Trouin* class, designed prior to the Washington Conference and armed with eight 155mm (6.1in) guns, France laid down her first two 'treaty' cruisers, *Duquesne* and *Tourville*, in October 1924 and April 1925 respectively, and this would elicit an immediate response from the Italian *Regia Marina* with its *Trento* and *Trieste*.

These early treaty cruisers were heavily armed with eight 203mm guns in twin turrets and were exceptionally fast; the two French ships attained 34 knots on trials while their Italian counterparts were even faster, with trial speeds in excess of 35 knots. Protection, however, was very light; the Italian designers managed to accommodate a 70mm armour belt with a 50mm deck over the magazines and machinery (at the cost of exceeding treaty limits by several hundred tonnes), but the French cruisers had only very light protection for their turrets and magazines, and relied largely on tight subdivision with reinforced bulkheads for their survival.

The British traded tactical speed for greater magazine protection for their own treaty cruisers of the 'County' class, envisaging that these ships would be used predominantly for commerce protection in distant waters. The US Navy wanted to use its new cruisers primarily for strategic scouting in the broad expanses of the Pacific, and initially found it difficult to secure a satisfactory compromise between armament, speed and protection. The new Japanese treaty cruisers were intended to supplement the battle line against the superior US battle fleet and sacrificed range for power, but the attempt to match their powerful armament and high speed with adequate protection resulted in ships that were grossly overweight.

France had two major security concerns regarding the foreign treaty cruisers. Like the British, they feared that the Japanese might use their large, powerful cruisers against French sea lines of communication in the Far East. However, the major concern was that Italy might employ its fast treaty cruisers against

French shipping in the western Mediterranean, thereby disrupting the vital communications between metropolitan France and the French colonies in North Africa. It was becoming increasingly clear that the *Regia Marina* saw its new cruisers not as an adjunct to the battle fleet, which it was making little attempt to modernise, but as a fast, independent strike force capable of lightning assaults on shipping, subsequently retiring to safety under the increasingly formidable air umbrella operating from 'aircraft carrier Italy'. It is therefore unsurprising that the Marine Nationale should have given serious consideration in 1926-7 to utilising the 70,000 tons of new capital ship construction due under the Washington Treaty in 1927 and 1929 not for ships intended to fight in the battle line, but for a new type of 'super-cruiser'.

THE *NAVIRE DE LIGNE DE 17 500T*

In 1926, Admiral Salaün, Chief of the Naval General Staff, requested from the STCN a study for a capital ship of 17,500 tons standard displacement with sufficient speed and gun power to hunt down and kill lightly protected treaty cruisers. The resulting ship would have had a length overall of 205 metres and a beam of 24.5 metres (corresponding figures for the cruiser *Duquesne* were 195 metres and 19.1 metres), and a speed of 35 knots. The main armament was to comprise eight 305mm 55-calibre guns, disposed in two quadruple turrets forward, and protection was to be sufficient to resist 203mm armour-piercing shells.

Trento and her sister *Trieste* were the first of Italy's 'treaty' cruisers. Fast, powerfully armed and lightly armoured, they attained more than 35 knots on trials. The threat that these cruisers posed to France's sea lines of communication with her North African colonies inspired a number of projects for small capital ships designed as 'cruiser-killers'.

Unfortunately, no sketch designs of this project have been found. However, a speed of 35 knots for a ship of this size suggests that power would need to be around 180,000shp, and that this was to be achieved by increasing the number of boilers (probably the same Guyot du Temple model fitted in *Duquesne* and the other French treaty cruisers) from eight to twelve.[1] In similar vein, although there is no detailed information

on the protection system, the stipulation that the ships be able to resist 203mm shell suggests an armoured belt in the region of 150-180mm, probably with a 75mm deck.

In effect these ships would have been strikingly similar in conception to the early 'battlecruisers' as originally envisaged by the British Admiral Fisher. The British *Invincible* of 1906 had a similar displacement (17,350 tons normal), a similar main armament (eight 12in/305mm guns – albeit disposed in a lozenge arrangement) and a similar level of protection (a main belt of 6in, equivalent to 150mm). When dispatched to the South Atlantic against the East Asiatic Squadron of

---

[1] This assumption appears to be borne out by the more detailed information we have on subsequent French capital ship designs – see the more detailed description of the 37,000-tonne 'battlecruiser' design of 1927-8.

Croiseur de Bataille de 37 000t (33kts):
Sketch profile and plan, dated May 1927
Characteristics:

Length oa:	254.5m
Length pp:	250m
Beam:	30.5m
Speed:	33 knots
Armament:	Twelve 305mm (3 x IV)
	Twelve 130mm (3 x IV)
	Eight 90mm (8 x I)
	Twelve 37mm (12 x I)

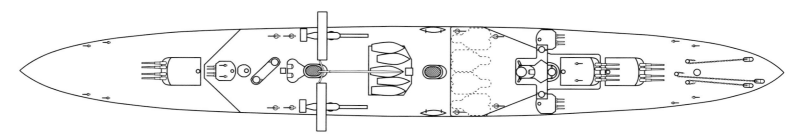

The collection of sketches of the 37,000-ton battlecruiser – six full plans plus a drawing of the master frame – that recently came to light in the Archives de l'Armement, Châtellerault, shows elements of three different variants designed during the period May 1927 to July 1928. The first, of which only relatively crude external profile and plan views survive, shows a 250-metre ship with a main armament of twelve 305mm guns in three quadruple turrets, a secondary armament of twelve 130mm guns (also in three quadruple turrets), and an AA armament of eight 90mm HA guns in the Mle 1926 CAS mounting and twelve 37mm CAS Mle 1925. There are triple banks of 550mm torpedo tubes in a recess in the side of the hull beneath a capacious full-width hangar for four reconnaissance seaplanes; a further two seaplanes could be carried on the catapults abeam the second funnel. The architectural style is very much that of the contemporary 10,000-ton 'treaty' cruisers of the *Suffren* class, with a doubling up of the propulsion plant of the latter to give a top speed of 33 knots. Unusually for a French capital ship, the design features a second, smaller conning tower aft.

All but one of the other drawings relate to a development of this project and appear to date from the period May-July 1928. Overall dimensions and the propulsion machinery are unchanged, and although the configuration of the 305mm – and probably the 130mm – turrets has been altered, armament is identical to that of the original project. The principal modifications are to the superstructures and masts. The bridge structure and foremast have been moved farther aft, and the tripod mainmast, which in the original design was stepped around the second funnel, has been relocated abaft the funnel to provide more elevated platforms for the after searchlight projectors and for the HA fire control directors. There is now a stand-alone crane amidships to handle boats

and aircraft. The after conning tower has been suppressed and the layout of the secondary and HA directors and the AA guns modified.

This later design appears to have progressed well beyond the initial sketch stage. Plans relating to this variant include: a detailed inboard profile; a set of fifteen section drawings, seven of which have been redrawn and are reproduced in this chapter; a section at the master frame showing the protection system and hull framing amidships, and plans of the lower decks showing the layout of the propulsion machinery. The external profile and plan views do not appear to have survived, and the drawings here have been pieced together from the other plans, using the inboard profile as the starting point.

The final drawing – numbered '4' in the collection – shows three deck plans (upper/main/first platform) of a slower, 27-knot variant armed with six 406mm guns in three twin turrets (only the first of these plans is reproduced here). The secondary battery features a fourth quad 130mm turret, the after pair of turrets being located side by side on the quarterdeck with the after 406mm turret superimposed above them. The hull is both shorter and fatter than the 33-knot variant, with a much fuller stern section, and the cross-section of each of the twin funnels is significantly smaller, suggesting a reduction from twelve boilers to eight. Protection may have been heavier in this variant, which is in many respects closer to the 'fast battleships' of the 1930s in its conception. However, the 'battlecruiser' classification is retained, and the ship has the same large complement of seaplanes. This variant appears to have been as well developed as the 33-knot design, as the deck plans show detailed compartmentation. No profile drawing has been found, but the superstructure plans suggest a broadly similar profile to the 33-knot type, albeit with slimmer funnels.

Admiral von Spee in December 1914, the battlecruisers *Invincible* and *Inflexible* would be pitted against armoured cruisers armed with 21cm guns – only just heavier than the 203mm guns of the treaty cruisers.

Because the Italian cruisers were high-speed units capable of running at 35 knots the French envisaged a stern chase in which their forward-mounted 305mm guns would have the advantage. The 55-calibre length of the proposed gun implied a high muzzle velocity; combined with a 45-degrees angle of elevation it would mean a maximum theoretical range of 43,000 metres. Mounting the guns in quadruple turrets forward would also effectively shorten the length of the armoured citadel, as in the latest British designs, with consequent savings in the weight of protection.

The 17,500-ton battleship was an attractive proposition for the Marine Nationale. Apart from the new 55-calibre 305mm guns and their mountings the design employed technology already developed for the new generation of French ships (Guyot du Temple small-watertube boilers, 90mm Mle 1926 HA guns and 37mm Mle 1925 AA guns, and presumably the new Saint Chamond-Granat director control system). Four could be built for 70,000 tons, two being ordered in 1927 for completion in 1930-1 and a further two in 1929 for completion 1932-3.

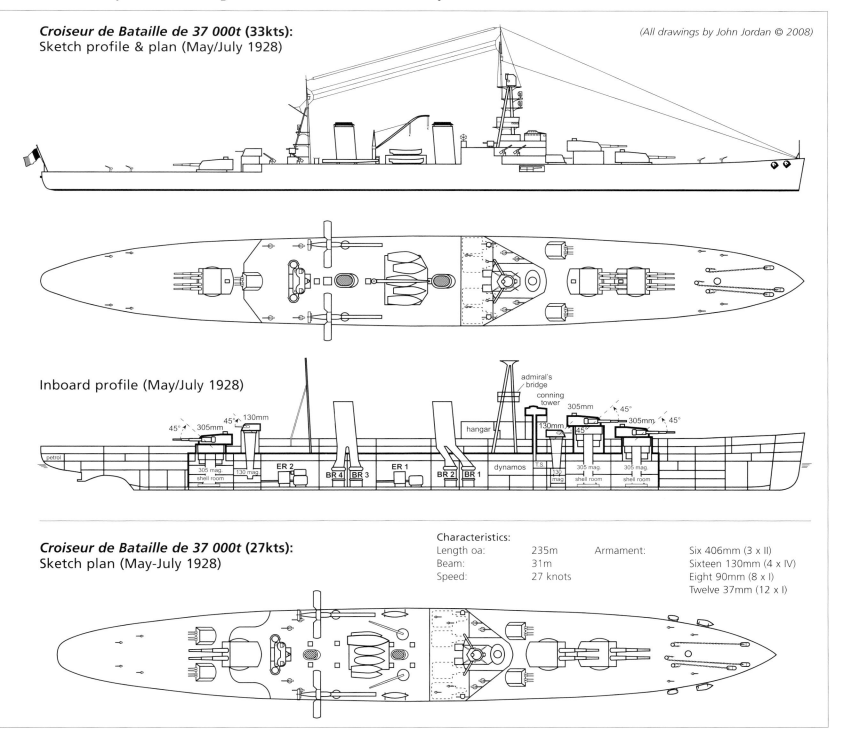

Croiseur de Bataille de 37 000t (33kts):
Sketch profile & plan (May/July 1928)

(All drawings by John Jordan © 2008)

Inboard profile (May/July 1928)

Croiseur de Bataille de 37 000t (27kts):
Sketch plan (May-July 1928)

Characteristics:

Length oa:	235m	Armament:	Six 406mm (3 x II)
Beam:	31m		Sixteen 130mm (4 x IV)
Speed:	27 knots		Eight 90mm (8 x I)
			Twelve 37mm (12 x I)

SKETCH DESIGNS 1926-31

	17,500t type	37,000t type A	37,000t type B	23,333t type	26,500t type
Date:	1926	1927-8	1928	1930	1932
Displacement:	17,500TW	37,000t^x	37,000t^x	23,333T^W	26,500TW
Dimensions:	205m x 24.5m	254m x 30.5m	235m x 31m	213m x 27.5m	215m x 31.1m
Speed (knots):	35	33	27	30	29.5
Armament:	8 x 305mm	12 x 305mm	6 x 406mm	8 x 305mm	8 x 330mm
		12 x 130mm LA	16 x 130mm LA	12 x 130mm DP	16 x 130mm DP
Protection:	150-180mm? belt	280-220mm belt	?mm belt	230-215mm belt	250mm belt
	?mm deck	75mm deck	?mm deck	130-100mm deck	140-130mm deck

Note: T^W denotes Washington standard displacement in long tons; t^x denotes normal(?) displacement in metric tonnes (see text).

The downside was the same as for the original battle-cruisers, as borne out strongly at Jutland in May 1916: although in terms of their armament they could stand in the battle line, the inadequacy of their protection against ships armed with guns of similar calibre made them vulnerable to catastrophic loss. However, given their 14-knot speed advantage (and 17,000m gun range advantage) over the elderly Italian dreadnoughts, the Marine Nationale felt that they could be used as strategic scouts for the superior (if equally elderly) French battle fleet with minimal risk.

In the end, it would not be considerations such as these that would kill the 17,500-ton *navire de ligne* but the emergence of a new 'prey' armed with guns considerably more powerful than the 203mm weapons of the Italian treaty cruisers: the German *Panzerschiffe* of the *Deutschland* class. However, in 1926-7 the threat of a commerce raider armed with 280mm (11in) guns was some way off.[2] Of greater concern to the French Naval Staff was how the new ships might fit into the overall scheme of things. Tempting as the idea of a fast 'cruiser-killer' might be, the allocation of 70,000 tons of the 175,000 tons Washington total to ships that could not fight in the battle line, leaving only 105,000 tons – the equivalent of only three battleships of 35,000 tons – for future capital ship construction was seen as being a major strategic risk, particularly as the Italian *Regia Marina* had yet to commit itself to new battleship designs. In December 1927, the *Conseil Supérieur de la Marine* – broadly equivalent to the British Admiralty Board – decreed that any new battleships should have a displacement that was an exact fraction of 175,000 tons, with the implication that the future French battle fleet would be made up of ships of broadly homogeneous displacement: that is, five ships of 35,000 tons, six ships of 29,160 tons, or seven ships of 25,000 tons.

During 1926-7, studies were undertaken of ships of the maximum displacement permitted by the Washington Treaty (35,000 tons), and in 1928, in response to the CSM decree of December 1927, Admiral Violette (Chief of the NGS) requested a study of a ship of 29,600 tonnes (equivalent to 29,135 'long' tons) with a speed of 27 knots. Until recently little information on these studies was available, but the Centre des Archives de l'Armement, Châtellerault, recently released detailed plans relating to a series of capital ship studies dating from 1927-8. The ships in question are both designated 'croiseur de bataille de 37 000T^x' (lit. '37,000-ton battlecruiser'), although the 27-knot variant would, with the benefit of hindsight, be more appropriately labelled a fast battleship. The displacement figure is a puzzle: it is almost certainly not Washington standard – normally abbreviated to 'tW' or 'TW' in French – as the imperial equivalent of 37,000 tonnes is 36,420 long tons, which exceeds the maximum permitted under the treaty. However, a 'normal' (or 'trial') displacement of 37,000 tonnes would give a Washington standard displacement in the region of 32,000-33,000 tons, ie intermediate between the 35,000-ton and the 29,160-ton types.

THE *CROISEUR DE BATAILLE DE 37 000T*

The earliest of the drawings is a profile and plan view of a 37,000-tonne battlecruiser of 33 knots. Drawn up under the supervision of Ingénieur Général du Génie Maritime Lejeune it is dated Paris, May 1927. It shows a ship that in its general configuration and layout is essentially an enlargement of the contemporary 10,000-ton cruisers of the *Suffren* class (see drawing). With a length between perpendiculars of 250 metres and a beam of 30.5 metres, the ship is armed with twelve 305mm guns in three quadruple turrets – two forward, one aft – and twelve 130mm,[3] also in three quadruple turrets, of which two are located abeam the bridge at the level of the upper deck with the third superimposed above No. 3 main turret aft. The midships section, as in the treaty cruisers, is dedicated to aviation arrangements. There is a capacious hangar capable of accommodating four large reconnaissance seaplanes with folded wings at the after end of the bridge structure, with twin trainable catapults abeam the second funnel. The tripod foremast and two widely spaced raked funnels are strongly reminiscent of *Suffren*, and there is a tripod mainmast forward of the second funnel supporting a single long-reach crane to handle both the boats (between the funnels) and the floatplanes. The fire control director for the main guns is atop the foremast, with a second director of similar size atop the conning tower. Directors for the secondary battery are located directly above the forward 130mm turrets at the ends of a platform projecting from the upper bridge.

The AA provision is similar to that of the cruisers *Colbert* and *Foch* (1926 and 1927 Estimates respec-

---

[2] The first of the *Panzerschiffe* was laid down only in February 1929.

[3] One drawing has one of these mountings labelled 120mm, but this is contradicted by other drawings. The 130mm calibre was the standard gun for the new destroyers, the *torpilleurs d'escadre* of the *Bourrasque* and *L'Adroit* classes. Although it was the standard destroyer gun in the *Regia Marina*, the 120mm was not a current French naval calibre.

tively). Eight single 90mm Mle 1926 HA guns are disposed port and starboard in four groups, the forward groups being mounted atop the hangar and the after groups on the shelter deck abaft the catapults. Twelve 37mm Mle 1925 single AA mountings (vs eight in the cruisers) are provided: four on the forecastle, four on the quarterdeck, with paired mountings on No. 2 305mm turret and the after 130mm quad turret. Fire control for the 90mm guns is provided by two HA fire control directors mounted *en echelon* atop a platform abaft the second funnel. Finally, as in the contemporary French treaty cruisers there are triple trainable torpedo tubes for 550mm torpedoes at upper deck level directly beneath the hangar.

The most important series of drawings dates from July 1928 and is attributed to Lejeune's successor as head of the STCN, Ing. Gén. François. Four of the plans relate to a modified variant of the 33-knot battlecruiser described above, while the fifth is of a 27-knot variant armed with six 406mm (16in) guns. Modifications to Lejeune's original design for the 33-knot ship focus primarily on the layout of the bridge, funnels and superstructures (see caption to drawings). However, of even more interest than the changes to the above-decks configuration is what these drawings tell us about the internal layout and protection system of the ship. The layout of the propulsion machinery, as one might suspect from the widely spaced funnels, is on the 'unit' principle, with two boiler rooms serving the forward engine room (turbines driving the outer shafts), and two boiler rooms serving the after engine room (turbines for the inner shafts). In effect the layout is identical to that of the cruisers *Duquesne* and *Tourville* except that each boiler room houses three boilers abreast. This strongly suggests a 50 per cent increase in power to 180,000shp, more than sufficient to drive a ship of this size at 33 knots.[4]

The protection system is similar in some respects to that of US battleships of the mid-war period (*Nevada* and *Pennsylvania* classes), with a heavy armour belt topped by a fairly thick deck intended to resist plunging shell. The sides above the belt are completely unarmoured, as in the US battleships, and as in the latter there is a 'splinter' deck below the main armoured deck covering the machinery spaces and magazines, the reinforced outboard section of the deck being inclined downwards to meet the bottom of the armour belt (see drawing of master frame). Unusually, the compartment thus formed behind the main belt was to be filled with coal, as in the contemporary cruisers of the *Suffren* class, suggesting that some of the boilers in the after BR may have been dual-fired to provide additional range at cruising speed – alternatively, as in the last two cruisers of the series, the coal

may have been intended simply to enhance the protection of the ship's vitals. Beneath the armoured 'box' formed by the external belt and the two armoured decks, there was to be a modern underwater protection system comprising a 50mm torpedo bulkhead flanked by two unarmoured bulkheads to create outer and inner void spaces, the compartment between the double bottom and the outer of the three internal bulkheads being 'liquid-loaded' with oil fuel. The double-banked coal and oil fuel protection extended only over the machinery compartments; abeam the magazines fore and aft these two spaces were left void, presumably because of fears that the oil and/or coal might combust and threaten the magazines themselves.

In the 33-knot battlecruiser design the main belt has a thickness of 280mm (11in) at the waterline and 220mm (8¾in) at its upper end; it is tapered below the waterline, and has the customary teak backing. The main armoured deck is 75mm on 15mm amidships, comparable to the 3in decks of the 'mid-war' American ships. It is not clear whether horizontal protection over the magazines was to be thicker.[5] The splinter deck

Croiseur de Bataille de 37 000t: Protection at Master Frame

(Drawing by John Jordan © 2008)

The protection system adopted for the *Croiseur de bataille de 37 000t* design is a curious mix of modern and traditional practice. Only the 'citadel' is armoured, and protection against shell is in the form of the now-standard armoured box, with the heavy side belt topped by a comparatively thick (75mm + 15mm) armoured deck at main deck level, backed up by a lighter splinter deck at the level of the first platform deck, which is inclined downwards outboard of the anti-torpedo bulkhead to join the lower edge of the belt. There is no side armour above the armoured belt and the ship's ends are unprotected. However, the thickness of the armoured belt and deck plating is not impressive by contemporary foreign standards – the British *Nelsons* had 13-14in inclined belts, a 4-inch deck over the machinery and 6 inches over the magazines. The belt is in two strakes and is similar in conception to that of the *Normandie* class of 1912 (see p.13). The thickest part of the lower armoured deck (PBI) is the incline behind the side belt, and coal protection has also been retained as backing for the belt, suggesting a continuing preoccupation with hits by heavy shell at comparatively short engagement ranges.

The battlecruiser design features a modern 'layered' underwater protection system using heavy oil fuel for the liquid loading component, but it lacks depth compared to contemporary foreign construction and the later *Dunkerques* – 4.25 metres from the outer hull plating to the anti-torpedo bulkhead as compared with more than 7 metres for *Dunkerque*. An unusual feature not repeated in later designs is the double thickness of 80mm teak bolted on to the outer side of the anti-torpedo bulkhead, which is presumably there to absorb steel fragments projected inboard by the explosion and which might otherwise penetrate the bulkhead, resulting in an ingress of water and oil fuel into the machinery spaces.

---

[4] The uncompleted Japanese battlecruisers of the *Amagi* class, which were virtually identical in dimensions to the French design, needed 131,200shp for their 30 knots. HMS *Hood*, which had a slightly larger hull (but with a similar length to beam ratio), required 144,000shp for 31 knots.

[5] The new British battleships of the *Nelson* class would have 3¼in on ½in over their machinery, but 6¼in on ½in over the magazines. Modernised battleships of the Royal Navy and the US Navy would also be given thicker armour over their magazines, albeit not on the scale of the *Nelsons*.

over the machinery is 25mm thick, with 40mm plating over 25mm on the inclined side sections – an arrangement derived from earlier French practice.

Annotations on the inboard profile of the ship reveal that the quadruple 130mm turrets, unlike the later dual-purpose mountings fitted in *Dunkerque* and *Strasbourg*, were to have a maximum elevation identical to that of the 305mm guns, 45 degrees, and could therefore be employed only against surface targets. High-altitude long-range fire was the domain of the 90mm Mle 1926 HA guns. The guns were to be disposed in four groups, as in the cruisers *Colbert* and *Foch*, and controlled by two HA directors. In the 1928 variant, the forward two groups were moved from the hangar to the forward angle of the bridge structure, where they enjoyed superior arcs on forward bearings.

The 27-knot 'fast battleship' variant is of broadly similar configuration to the 33-knot ship. The major difference lies in the main and secondary gun batteries. In place of the three quad 305mm turrets of the 33-knot design there are three twin 406mm turrets and the third of these is in the superimposed position aft, where it replaces the 130mm quad of the 33-knot ship. In place of the latter there are now two quad 130mm turrets aft to complement the two quads forward, and these are located side by side on the quarterdeck beneath the after 406mm turret. The 27-knot ship has a shorter, slightly broader hull, and the less favourable length to beam ratio, combined with a propulsion plant that probably delivered only two thirds of the power of the 33-knot ship, account for the lower maximum speed. However, in addition to the more substantial main and secondary batteries it may be that this variant also had thicker horizontal and vertical protection.

The 37,000-tonne battlecruiser plans constitute what might be termed a 'missing link' between the French battleship designs of 1909-14 and *Dunkerque* and *Strasbourg*. The adoption of quadruple turrets for the main and secondary armament is a distinctive feature. However, while the quadruple 130mm turret marks the rejection of the casemate gun in favour of the upper-deck trainable turret of the latest British capital ship designs, it is not yet the high-angle dual-purpose mounting of the *Dunkerque*. Other features of the British *Nelson*s are far less marked than they are in the later fast French battleships. In particular, the layout of propulsion machinery and aviation facilities is derived from the latest French cruisers of the 'treaty' type, and there is no attempt to minimise the length of the armoured 'citadel' in order to reduce the weight of – or alternatively increase the thickness of – protection. The protection system itself is influenced by American rather than British thinking, albeit with idiosyncratic 'national' preferences such as the continuing use of coal as backing for the main belt at the waterline. The armour belt is both deep and vertical, echoing traditional French concerns regarding shells plunging beneath the belt and penetrating the ship's vitals; the inclined armour belt pioneered by the British for the G3s, and for their successors of the *Nelson* class, would be adopted by the French only in their 1930s designs.

A REVERSION TO SMALLER BATTLESHIP DESIGNS

The detailed plans for the two major variants of the *Croiseur de Bataille de 37 000T*[x] make it clear that these were more than just 'preliminary sketches'. The Naval General Staff clearly felt the need to be in a position to proceed quickly with orders for the ships should the political situation demand it. In the event there were three primary reasons – one technical, one financial and one political – why the 35,000-ton capital ship was not pursued at this stage.

The technical reason, which also had financial implications, was that the necessary infrastructure was not in place to build ships of this size. In the immediate prewar period the French had embarked on major work in the two main dockyards, Brest and Toulon, to provide graving docks for ships up to 250 metres long. The two Laninon Docks (No. 8 and No. 9) at Brest, carved out of the granite shore-line of the inner harbour (the *Rade-Abri*), had been completed in 1916; dimensions were 250m by 36m. Even more impressive were the two Vauban *Grands Bassins* at Toulon, a massive engineering project that involved reclaimed land at the entrance to the *Petite Rade*, the anchorage just outside the dockyard. Two massive steel 'hulls' built at the nearby La Seyne shipyard were seated on an eight-metre thick masonry sill, and supporting beams and masonry quays with service cranes and associated equipment had then been built around them. The base had been in place by the outbreak of

Croiseur de Bataille de 37 000t:
Layout of Machinery

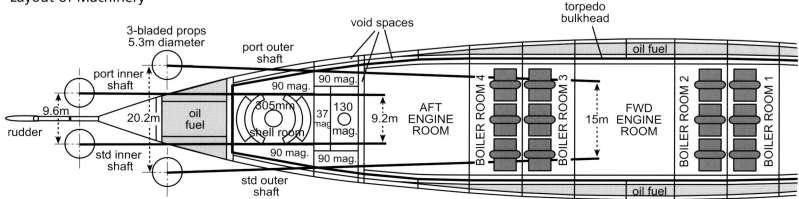

(Drawing by John Jordan © 2009)

Croiseur de Bataille de 37 000t:
Hull Sections

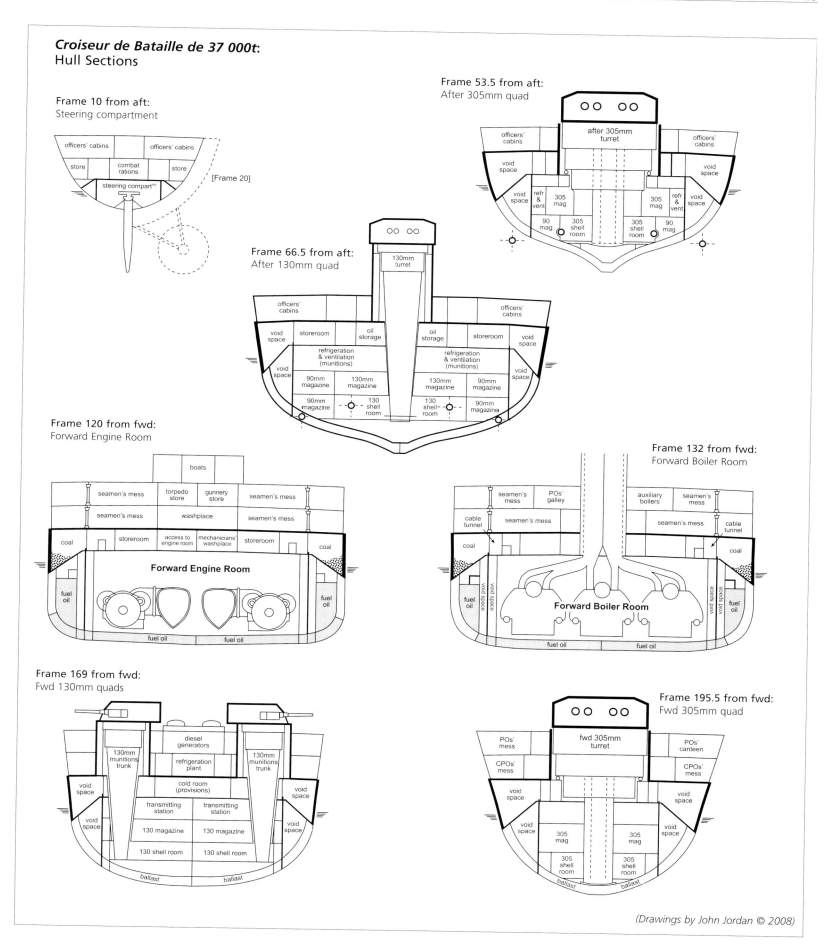

Frame 10 from aft:
Steering compartment

Frame 53.5 from aft:
After 305mm quad

Frame 66.5 from aft:
After 130mm quad

Frame 120 from fwd:
Forward Engine Room

Frame 132 from fwd:
Forward Boiler Room

Frame 169 from fwd:
Fwd 130mm quads

Frame 195.5 from fwd:
Fwd 305mm quad

(Drawings by John Jordan © 2008)

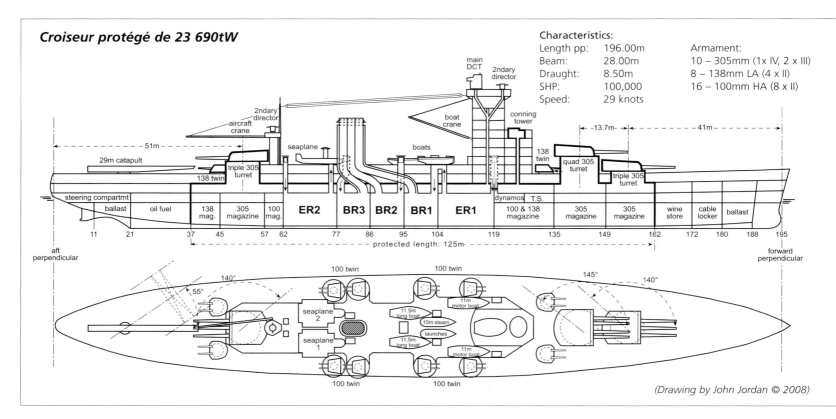

Croiseur protégé de 23 690tW

Characteristics:
Length pp: 196.00m
Beam: 28.00m
Draught: 8.50m
SHP: 100,000
Speed: 29 knots

Armament:
10 – 305mm (1x IV, 2 x III)
8 – 138mm LA (4 x II)
16 – 100mm HA (8 x II)

(Drawing by John Jordan © 2008)

war in 1914. Work had then been suspended; it was resumed in 1919 and the docks were finally completed in 1927.[6] They represented a huge advance on anything previously available to the Marine Nationale; dimensions were 422 metres by 40.7 metres for each of the two docks, and there were movable 'gates' that could be placed at 210 metres, 235 metres and 250 metres from the south-side entrance to enable ships to be docked simultaneously at both ends.[7]

However, the new docks were designed for refitting, not for building. Building required specialised slipways or building docks with steel-cutting sheds, boiler and engine shops and multiple heavy-lift cranes, and building ways of this size were simply not available to the Marine Nationale, neither in the naval dockyards nor in the private shipyards. The largest building facility at Brest, the Salou No. 4 Dock on the upper reaches of the River Penfeld, was just over 200 metres long. The private shipyards that had previously built battleships for the Navy were restricted to building hulls of similar length. The largest slipway available was that of Chantiers et Ateliers de Saint-Nazaire (Penhoët) at St. Nazaire, which would launch the 314-metre liner *Normandie* in 1932. A ship of 245-250 metres was out of the question unless there was major investment in the naval dockyards. An

STCN estimate of the cost in late 1930 was 130 million French francs – equivalent to the cost of two battleships.[8]

It would also be difficult to find the money for 35,000-ton battleships and their associated infrastructure without impacting on the large programme of cruisers, flotilla craft and submarines to which the Marine Nationale was already committed. By the late 1920s, this had translated itself into regular orders for one 10,000-ton cruiser, six large *contre-torpilleurs* and six fleet submarines per year. However, congestion in the shipyards and bottlenecks in the production of guns, rangefinders and machinery was already causing serious delays; ships due to be built under the 1928 Estimates had to be postponed by a year, with knock-on effects to the remainder of the programme. A 35,000-ton battleship would cost as much as four treaty cruisers. Thus in order to complete the current flotilla craft and submarine programme, it was unlikely that sufficient funding would be available for battleship construction until 1931 at the earliest.[9]

The third reason why the 35,000-ton battleship proposal was not pursued further at this time was political. At a time when France was at the forefront of moves towards global security underpinned by international law and was one of the primary instigators of the League of Nations Preparatory Commission for Disarmament,[10] which was to address not only naval issues but also that of land and air forces, it would

---

[6] The *Grands Bassins* were sufficiently complete for the *Normandie*-class battleship *Béarn*, during her reconstruction as an aircraft carrier, to be docked in 1924-5 for the installation of her shaft brackets and propellers.

[7] When completed in 1927, the Vauban *Grands Bassins* were the largest graving docks in the world; their nearest rivals were the Boston Dry Dock (357m – 1170ft), completed in 1920, and the St John Dock in Canada (350m – 1150ft), completed in 1923.

[8] *Dunkerque* would cost around 80 million French francs to build in 1938 currency.

[9] In the event, the first of the new generation of French battleships, *Dunkerque*, was the main item in the 1932 Estimates.

[10] The first meeting was on 18 May 1926 in Geneva.

This sketch design for a 'protected cruiser' of 23,690 tonnes standard – equivalent to 23,333 long tons – has recently been discovered at the Centre des Archives de l'Armement, Châtellerault. It is undated, but was probably drawn up around 1929. The design retains some features of the *Croiseur de bataille de 37 000t*, in particular the layout of the main and secondary turrets and the split secondary LA and tertiary HA batteries. However, the general layout is reminiscent not of the *Suffren* class cruisers, as was the case with the 'battlecruiser' of 1927-8, but of the later *Algérie*, which was designed in 1929 (and which was also initially classified *croiseur protégé*). In place of the conventional superstructures and tripod foremast there is a distinctive forward tower to carry the directors for the main and secondary guns combined with a short pole mainmast aft; the three boiler rooms are grouped together, the uptakes being combined in a single funnel; and the HA battery comprises eight twin 100mm guns – *Algérie* was the only other major French ship designed to carry this weapon. The major difference in the layout of the two ships is that in the 23,690-tonne design engine room No. 1 has been moved forward of the boiler rooms, placing the single funnel well abaft the forward tower and creating a balance in the profile of the ship which anticipates the later *Dunkerque*.

The adoption of a quad turret in 'B' position is perhaps surprising given that three triples would have been a neater and more logical solution, and that it implied the design of two separate turrets and revolving structures with quite different replenishment arrangements. If the design dates from 1929, this suggests a requirement for the maximum number of 305mm guns on a limited displacement – immediately before the London Conference of 1930, the British were pushing for a maximum displacement of 25,000 tons standard and a maximum gun calibre of 12in (305mm). The 138mm gun is probably the 50-calibre Mle 1929 under development for the *contre-torpilleurs* of the *Le Fantasque* class, but in a new (low-angle) twin armoured turret.

Despite the 'protected cruiser' designation, the design would have been classed as a capital ship under Washington. Rather the designation reflects the ship's intended purpose as a destroyer of 'treaty' cruisers, with the Italian *Trento* and *Zara* classes the anticipated adversaries. The 23,690-tonne ship is as fast as a British battlecruiser of the *Renown* class; later variants dating from 1930-1, including the initial design for *Dunkerque*, would be designated *croiseur de combat* (*Dunkerque* was referred to as 'CC1' in the initial proposals). No data are given for protection, but it seems reasonable to assume a belt of around 180-200mm and an armoured deck of 80mm, possibly increasing to 100mm over the magazines fore and aft. This would have been adequate against Italian 203mm (8in) shell, but not against the German 28cm (11in) shell of the new *Panzerschiffe*, the first of which had been laid down in February 1929. A major weakness of the design is the location of the single 29-metre catapult, which is exposed to the blast of the main and the secondary guns when firing on after bearings, and which is widely separated from the more sheltered stowage position of the two reconnaissance seaplanes, resulting in awkward handling arrangements which would have become impossible in heavy weather conditions. In the later, post-London 23,333-ton designs the main guns would be concentrated in two quadruple turrets forward, leaving the quarterdeck free for aircraft operations, and the secondary and tertiary batteries would be combined in a single 130mm DP battery.

This early variant of the 23,333-ton type appears to have been deliberately sized so that the hull could be constructed in one piece in the Salou No. 4 Dock at Brest. Later variants would have had to have been built minus the bow, as was *Dunkerque* herself.

have been very difficult for her to embark on a new generation of super-battleships that would then become the precursors of similar ships built by other nations once the 'naval holiday' expired in 1931, and effectively stoking up a new naval arms race. Moreover, there was little urgency from the point of view of 'national security'. The main threat to French naval hegemony in the key Mediterranean theatre was Mussolini's Italy, and the *Regia Marina* of the late 1920s seemed also to have little enthusiasm for a new generation of large and costly battleships.

These political considerations were reinforced by British moves prior to the London Conference of 1930, at which the extension and modification of the existing Washington Treaty was to be considered. The British were proposing a qualitative restriction on future battleship construction: a maximum displacement of 25,000 tons and a main gun calibre of 12in (305mm) were proposed as the basis for discussion. This would effectively lead the Marine Nationale to again consider smaller battleship designs.

THE LONDON CONFERENCE OF 1930

The London Conference began on 21 January 1930; it ended on 22 April of the same year with only a partial agreement. The French and Italian representatives signed up to four of the five parts of the treaty but were unable to agree quantitative limitations on cruisers, destroyers and submarines. The United States was predictably unhappy with the British proposal to reduce the qualitative limit for capital ships to 25,000 tons and 12in guns; however, there was little general enthusiasm for an imminent resumption of capital ship construction. It was therefore agreed that the ten-year 'battleship holiday' agreed at Washington be extended for a further five years, until 31 December 1936. It was further agreed that this was without prej-

udice to the Washington Treaty clause that permitted ships lost or destroyed to be replaced, a clause that could be invoked by both France (loss of the battleship *France* in 1922) and Italy (*Leonardo da Vinci*, a named ship despite her loss in 1916 and not subsequently rebuilt). A provision of Article 1 of the new treaty stated:

> France and Italy may, however, build the replacement tonnage which they were entitled to lay down in 1927 and 1929 in accordance with the provisions of the said [i.e. Washington] treaty.

There was a reduction in battleship numbers for the US Navy and Royal Navy to the fifteen ships implied by the 525,000-ton total allocation agreed at Washington, and for the Imperial Japanese Navy to nine ships, with additional elderly vessels (one per navy) demilitarised according to strict regulations to serve as training ships. It was clearly not thought worth the effort of negotiating comparable reductions in current force strengths for France and Italy. Italy by this time had only three of its original six dreadnoughts in service, with a fourth used for training. By 1927, France had relegated all three of her three elderly pre-dreadnoughts to training; only the three surviving dreadnoughts of the *Courbet* class and the three *Bretagne*s were still first-line units. By the time the conference convened in January 1930 the former were 17-18 years old, the latter 14-15 years old. All were now experiencing breakdowns followed by prolonged periods of unavailability, and it was evident that they could not continue in service without major refurbishment of their propulsion machinery.

For the Marine Nationale it was clear from the outcome of the London Treaty that new capital ship construction could not be delayed for much longer.

It was the laying down of the German *Panzerschiffe* of the *Deutschland* class that effectively killed off the French 17,500-ton and 23,333-ton capital ship projects. Although not as fast as the treaty cruisers, they were armed with six 28cm guns that had superior range and far superior armour penetration qualities to the Italian 203mm cruiser shell. They needed to be countered by a ship with higher speed (29-30 knots) but, even more importantly, superior protection to the early French interwar designs. The inevitable result was an increase in standard displacement to 26,000 tons. This is *Admiral Graf Spee* in 1936, shortly after her completion. (*L van Ginderen collection*)

Even if a new battleship were laid down in 1931 it could not be ready for service before 1935 at the earliest, by which time the *Bretagne* class would be twenty years old. In the same year that the new ship was completed a battleship of the *Courbet* class would have to be retired in accordance with the Washington Treaty (*France*, lost in 1922, was the obvious choice), and completion of a second new battleship (perhaps in the following year) would require the retirement of two further ships of the class.

There was little point in rebuilding the *Courbet* class given that two out of the three surviving ships would have to be retired by about 1936 – it would make sense to retain the third as a training ship to replace the elderly pre-dreadnoughts of the *Danton* class. The three ships of the *Bretagne* class would be generally refurbished: their original coal-fired boilers and turbine machinery were to be replaced, and they would receive an enhanced AA battery to make them more survivable against the increasing threat from land-based aircraft. Work would now begin in earnest on new battleship designs with a view to placing orders for two/three hulls before the international 'battleship holiday' expired on 31 December 1936.

THE 23,333 TONS AND 26,500 TONS DESIGNS
In the wake of the London Conference the Chief of the Naval General Staff instructed the STCN to prepare designs for battleships of a minimum displacement of 23,333 tons and a maximum of 25,000 tons standard, and advised that it envisaged laying down three such ships before the December 1936 deadline. The latter figure was the qualitative limit proposed by Britain prior to the conference, and despite US rejection of the proposal the British were sending out clear signals

that they would continue to press for a significant reduction in battleship size and gun calibre. This would make it politically difficult for France to exceed 25,000 tons and 12in/305mm guns for its new ships, as it would undermine British efforts to secure this reduction for the generation of battleships to be laid down after 1936. The figure of 23,333 tons standard, moreover, had the advantage of permitting three ships to be laid down before December 1936 without exceeding France's 70,000-ton 'exceptional allocation'.

In October 1930, following a series of meetings of the Conseil Supérieur, the Chief of the Naval General Staff had drawn up a new *projet de loi*, which included a *croiseur de bataille* to replace the battleship *France*. Political instability[11] led to further delay, but following a change of government in mid-December the project was re-submitted to the new Navy Minister Albert Sarraut, who agreed to submit a request for a single ship of 23,333 tons. At the same time the Navy was asked to justify its preference for a ship of 23,333 tons over a 35,000-ton ship. A joint submission from the STCN and the NGS in January reiterated the options available for use of the 70,000-ton allocation: two ships of 35,000 tons, three of 23,333 tons or four of 17,500 tons. The 35,000-ton ship was considered feasible only with considerable expenditure on infrastructure for building ways and quays, given that facilities currently available could not support a ship with a projected length of 245-250 metres; this was therefore the option that raised most technical difficulties. The 17,500-ton ship, on the other hand, was

---

[11] The period 1930-2 saw no fewer than nine changes of administration in France and five different navy ministers.

dismissed as too small to provide adequate protection. The Navy's preference for the 23,333-ton ship was based on studies that demonstrated that a battleship of this size would have the necessary military qualities, while at the same time such a ship could be built and maintained using existing infrastructure.

The protection issue was now paramount. In February 1929, Germany had laid down the first of its new *Panzerschiffe* (lit. 'armoured ships'), to be named *Deutschland*. The German Republic was forbidden by the Treaty of Versailles from building warships displacing in excess of 10,000 tons but no limit was placed on gun calibre, it being assumed that a ship of limited displacement armed with big guns would necessarily be slow, and therefore suitable for deployment only as a coast defence ship. The ingenuity of the *Deutschland* design lay in its combination of 28cm (11in) guns with the relatively high speed of 26 knots, using a combined diesel propulsion plant. Protection was only on a par with contemporary cruisers; however, this was considered sufficient to enable the *Panzerschiffe* to resist the shells of cruisers charged with defending convoys, while at the same time the cruisers, armed at best with 8in/203mm guns, would be heavily outgunned by the 28cm weapons of the German ship. The maximum speed of 26 knots was more than adequate to intercept a convoy and for outflanking manoeuvres against its escort. Reconnaissance aircraft, provided from the mid-1930s to facilitate location of possible mercantile targets, and the fuel economy of the ships' diesel engines would make these ships ideal for commerce raiding.

Further units of the *Deutschland* class were planned. Under the terms of the Treaty of Versailles, Germany was permitted to build six such ships as replacements for the elderly pre-dreadnoughts of the *Deutschland* and *Lothringen* types, all of which were more than twenty years old.

The impact of the *Panzerschiffe* abroad was considerable. The British acknowledged that although the presence of one of their older battleships with a convoy would provide security against attack, only the three battlecruisers *Renown, Repulse* and *Hood* were capable of hunting down the *Panzerschiffe*. The description by the French CNS of the proposed new French capital ship as a *croiseur de bataille* is therefore apposite; in order to counter the German commerce raiders both high speed and protection sufficient to resist 28cm shells would be required.

The characteristics of the 23,333-ton design are detailed in the accompanying table. Dimensions had by now grown to 213 metres length overall with a beam of 27.5 metres. The main armament was identical to that of the 17,500-ton design of 1926: eight 305/55 guns in an all-forward arrangement comprising two quadruple turrets. However, there was now a powerful secondary battery of twelve 130mm guns, also in quadruple turrets. The 130mm turrets were grouped together aft, and at this stage were probably of the dual-purpose model that would eventually be developed for the *Dunkerque*. Maximum speed was 30 knots, with a completely new propulsion plant using superheated steam. The weight allocated to protection was much greater than in the fast 'cruiser-killer' design: the belt was 230mm (9in) thick at the waterline, while the main armoured deck was thicker than that of the 37,000-tonne 'battlecruiser'

of 1927-8: 130mm (5in) over the magazines with 100mm (4in) over the machinery.

The Marine Nationale fully expected an order for the first of the new ships to follow. However, as part of the political fall-out from the London Conference, in January and February 1931 bilateral talks between France and Italy, with the active encouragement of Britain, took place in London and Paris with a view to establishing an agreed ceiling on new naval construction. A 'basis of agreement' dated 1 March stipulated that both countries would lay down two capital ships of 23,333 tons before the expiry of the Washington Treaty in December 1936. A new *projet de loi* was to be formulated to take this agreement into account, but when attempts to formalise the agreement with Italy came to nothing this had again to be reworded, and it was 4 May 1931 before the French cabinet gave its approval to the project. There then followed two months of debate in both the lower and upper houses of the French parliament during which there was much criticism of the low displacement of the proposed ships, which the new Navy Minister – the third in six months! – conspicuously failed to answer.

Eventually the Estimates were passed on 10 July, but the only funding allocated for the new capital ship was for further studies, with the proviso that the final characteristics should be subject to a thorough revision, and that those characteristics should then be submitted to parliament for approval before the Navy proceeded with orders. Following this the new Chief of the Naval Staff requested further studies from the STCN for a ship displacing between 23,333 tons and 28,000 tons. The STCN was to take note of recently established staff requirements that specified:

- a standard displacement of 25,000 tons
- a main armament of eight 330mm (13in) guns in two quad turrets forward
- a secondary armament of 130mm DP guns (number not specified)
- protection sufficient to resist 280mm shell and 500kg bombs released at 3000m
- underwater protection sufficient to resist a 300kg charge

It was estimated that an increase in main gun calibre from 305mm to 330mm was feasible if displacement were increased to 25,000 tons. However, the scaling up of the ship to accommodate this and other improvements had implications for other weights, and in particular for the weight of protection. A displacement of 26,000 tons standard now came to be regarded as the minimum, and this grew to 26,500 tons as the detail design progressed. The project was finally approved in early 1932, and on 27 April 1932 the STCN fixed the final characteristics as shown in the accompanying table.

By comparison with the 23,333-ton design, there was a 2-metre increase in length and an even more significant 2.5 metres in beam, resulting in a slight reduction in maximum speed to 29.5 knots. The 305/55 main gun – a feature of all the French capital ship projects of the 1920s – was replaced by a 330mm 52-calibre gun of new design. The three quad 130mm DP mountings aft were retained, but there were now additional twin mountings to cover the forward arcs; the former were in fully armoured turrets but the twin

By the end of the interwar period, the three ships of the *Bretagne* class were on their last legs. Despite the modifications made to the main guns, the fire control system and the propulsion machinery during the interwar period they remained vulnerable to large-calibre shell and to torpedoes. This vulnerability was cruelly exposed at Mers el-Kebir, when *Bretagne* and *Provence* were quickly disabled by British 15in shell (see Chapter 3). Seen here is the third ship, *Lorraine*, in 1938. Note the 100mm Mle 1931 twin HA mountings amidships; in 1940 these would be removed and mounted in *Richelieu* (see Chapter 4).

mountings were to have only light splinter protection. The 130mm DP guns were complemented by an impressive battery of close-in AA guns: eight 37mm in a new semi-automatic twin mounting Mle 1933 and thirty-two 13.2mm Hotchkiss MG Mle 1929 in eight quad mountings.[12] The main belt was increased in thickness from 230mm to 250mm, and the upper armoured deck from 130/100mm to 140/130mm, with a 45mm splinter deck below it. Protection was now on a scale that would make the ships invulnerable not only to German 28cm shell, but also to the 305mm shell of the older Italian battleships. This was a sound move, in that the Marine Nationale could employ the new ships both against the German *Panzerschiffe* in the North Atlantic and, should the situation arise, against the Italian battle fleet in the Mediterranean, where they would constitute a useful 'fast wing' to supplement the slow, 'heavy' ships of the *Bretagne* class.

The order for the first ship, *Dunkerque*, was placed with the Arsenal de Brest on 26 October 1932. The Marine Nationale wanted a second ship as soon as possible – by late 1932 the second and third *Panzerschiffe* had been laid down – and fought hard for its inclusion in the 1934 Estimates. The project was then thrown into disarray by an announcement by Mussolini on 26 May 1934 that Italy would use in full her 70,000-ton capital ship allocation and by a subsequent communiqué by the Stefani News Agency on 11 June stating that the *Regia Marina* would lay down two battleships of 35,000 tons standard armed with nine 381mm guns. With the vote on the 1934 Estimates imminent, the Marine Nationale was compelled to reconsider its position. However, the replacement of the future *Strasbourg* by a ship of 35,000-ton (or even 30,000-ton) displacement would mean new plans, the development, ordering and manufacture of new guns and machinery, and a consequent delay estimated at fifteen to eighteen months in getting the ship into service. Everything was in place for a second ship of the *Dunkerque* class; the name-ship had already been on the stocks for eighteen months and was due for launch the following year. At a meeting of the Conseil Supérieur on 25 June 1934, it was decided to proceed as planned, and to embark as quickly as possible on the construction of a second ship. There would be some 'beefing up' of vertical protection in the second *Dunkerque*, but the design would otherwise be unmodified. This would permit the design teams to focus on new studies for 35,000-ton ships to counter the new Italian units, the first of which was to be ordered before the expiry of the Washington Treaty

The order for *Strasbourg* was placed with the Ateliers et Chantiers de Saint-Nazaire (Penhoët) on 16 July 1934, and construction would begin in November of the same year.

---

12 The first installation of the Hotchkiss quad mounting was in the treaty cruiser *Dupleix*, completed in 1933.

CHAPTER 2

DUNKERQUE AND *STRASBOURG*:
Design and Characteristics

GENERAL CHARACTERISTICS AND LAYOUT

The design of *Dunkerque* and *Strasbourg* was heavily influenced by the latest British practice. The battleships *Nelson* and *Rodney*, scaled-down versions of the G3 battlecruiser design of 1922, entered service in August and November 1927 respectively and had a major impact on the thinking of other navies. They introduced a number of revolutionary design features: an all-forward main armament with the machinery aft, a secondary battery in trainable twin turrets above the weather deck, a tower structure to carry the main fire control directors, and an inclined 14/13in armour belt topped by an exceptionally heavy armoured deck. The all-forward main armament placed the turrets at the broadest part of the hull to maximise protection for the magazines from shells and torpedoes. Locating the machinery aft saved on shaft length and therefore on weight. The inclined armour belt was equivalent to a thicker vertical belt, and a shell striking at an oblique angle was more likely to be deflected or broken up. And the secondary turrets had better all-weather capability, superior firing arcs and greater range than casemate-mounted guns; they also benefited from replenishment systems similar to those of the main guns, which gave them a high sustained rate of fire.

Many of the key features of the *Nelson* design were focused on securing complete protection for the magazines and machinery. In particular, the length of the armoured citadel was reduced to a minimum in order to maximise armour thickness; this ran counter to accepted practice in other navies, notably the US Navy, which saw the armoured belt as a protector not only of the ship's vitals but also of its buoyancy and stability.

The French ships were by no means slavish copies of *Nelson* and *Rodney*, but the influence of the British ships on *Dunkerque* and *Strasbourg* and on their successors is readily apparent, particularly if the latter ships are compared with earlier French capital ship designs such as the 37,000-tonne battlecruisers (see Chapter 1). The all-forward main armament with the secondary guns in trainable turrets aft, the single funnel and heavy tower structure amidships, the inclined armour belt topped by a heavy armoured deck over the magazines and machinery, and the relatively short length of the armoured citadel (equivalent to approximately 58 per cent of length between perpen-

diculars);[1] all these features were characteristic of the latest British capital ship designs, and distinguish *Dunkerque* and *Strasbourg* from the 'paper' designs of the 1920s. In her general configuration and layout *Dunkerque* is as different from the 37,000-tonne battlecruiser as the last French treaty cruiser *Algérie* from the *Suffren* class.

However, there were also many important design differences between the British and the French ships, some of which relate to the relatively high speed of the French ships and others which result from *Dunkerque* being designed almost ten years later, when naval technology had moved on. The *Nelson*s had a two-shaft propulsion system with eight boilers and two sets of turbines delivering 45,000shp for their designed speed of 23 knots; *Dunkerque* and her sister had four shafts, six boilers and four sets of turbines delivering 107,000shp for 29.5 knots. Although the Indret boilers developed for *Dunkerque* were large high-pressure models and were housed side by side in pairs, the three boiler rooms were necessarily longer than those of the *Nelson*s. Moreover, the four-shaft propulsion system required two separate engine rooms, so the machinery spaces occupied a length of 53.5 metres as compared with 41.5 metres in the British ships. The French vessels, however, had only two main gun turrets because of the adoption of quadruple mountings, so the machinery spaces could be moved farther forward and occupied a more central position, with the forward engine room (housing the turbines for the wing shafts) in the broadest part of the hull amidships. As a result, the secondary quad turrets could be located abaft the superstructures – in the *Nelson*s these were abeam the superstructures – enjoying excellent arcs on after bearings.

The layout adopted for *Dunkerque* freed up the stern for comprehensive aviation facilities which included a trainable 22-metre catapult and a two-tier hangar on the centreline served by a lift. Three long-range reconnaissance aircraft could be carried, which was a particularly valuable resource when the ships were hunting down enemy commerce raiders. By locating the big guns forward and the aircraft facilities on the

---

[1] The armoured citadel of *Dunkerque* was 122 metres as compared with a length between perpendiculars of 209 metres. The figures for *Nelson* were 117 metres and 201 metres respectively – also 58 per cent.

quarterdeck, the risk of blast damage was eliminated, and the arrangement also had the advantage of placing the aircraft and the hangar close to the volatile aviation fuel, which in accordance with customary French practice was stowed in tanks isolated from the hull structure in the upper part of the stern.

Other novel features of the design included the mounting of fire control directors one above the other atop the forward tower and around the heavy pole mainmast. This arrangement was to have an unforeseen drawback (see Chapters 3 and 5), but it was certainly an ingenious way of economising on centre-line space, and it ensured clear, uninterrupted training arcs for the directors. Considerable attention was also given to 'passive' protection measures such as subdivision, the layout of the machinery spaces, and the design and location of the main gun turrets. Despite the single funnel a 'unit' machinery arrangement was adopted, with one boiler room forward and the other two between the two engine rooms. This had the disadvantage of extensive – and poorly protected – uptake trunking leading from the forward boiler room above the main armoured deck to the single funnel, but enabled the ship to continue to steam with two or even three adjacent machinery compartments flooded or otherwise out of action. The quadruple turrets were divided into two independent gunhouses by a central 40mm bulkhead which extended down into the

working chamber beneath the turret at a reduced thickness of 25mm. In order to minimise the risk of both turrets being disabled by a single shell or torpedo hit, they were separated by a distance of 28.5 metres – significantly greater than in the British *Nelson*s.[2]

MAIN AND SECONDARY ARMAMENT

The construction of the 330/52 Model 1931 gun, which was a new calibre for the Marine Nationale, was a mixture of modern and traditional methods. Drawings of the 330/52 gun have not been found, but it is thought that a loose auto-fretted liner and A tube were reinforced at the breech end by a single row of short hoops with an outer jacket (for a schematic drawing and detailed description of the similar 380/45 Mle 1935 gun, see Chapter 4). The breech mechanism comprised a Welin interrupted screw breech block, hydro-pneumatically powered and balanced by counterweights. Unusually, it opened upwards as the gun ran out after firing (see also Chapter 4).

The 330mm Mle 1935 shell weighed 570kg and muzzle velocity was 870m/s. In what constituted a departure from standard practice in other navies, the French had opted during the early years of the century

Dunkerque at anchor in 1939. The all-forward armament of these ships and the massive tower, topped by the directors for the main and secondary guns, is reminiscent of the British *Nelson*s. Note, however, the fine lines forward, indicative of the high speed for which *Dunkerque* and her sister *Strasbourg* were designed. (*J C Farjas collection*)

2 In the *Nelson* class, the distance between the axes of 'A' and 'B' turrets was only 19.5 metres; the distance between the axes of 'B' and 'C' turrets was 23 metres.

Dunkerque: Inboard Profile

Showing the principal operational
machinery spaces, magazines, fuel
bunkers and other liquid stowage.

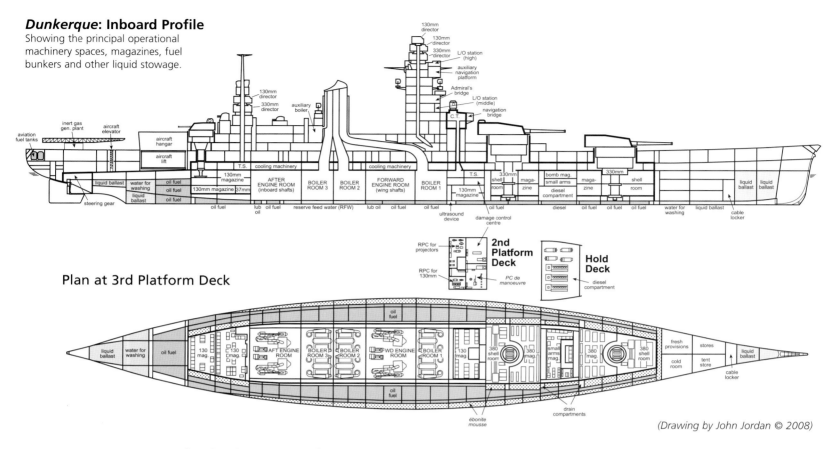

Plan at 3rd Platform Deck

(Drawing by John Jordan © 2008)

for the development of a single heavyweight omni-purpose shell, the *obus unique*, which could be used against both heavy armour and lighter plating. The 305mm Mle 1906 of the *Danton* class was the first gun to have the new shell, which combined the functions of earlier armour piercing (*obus de rupture*) and semi-armour piercing (*obus de semi rupture*) shell. The key to this development was a variable-delay base fuze, which appears to have proven effective in trials and operation.[3] The new shell was designated *Obus de Perforation de Rupture Coiffé* (abbreviated to OPf RC), a term which corresponded to the English armour piercing capped (APC). Although a 330mm high explosive shell, the OEA Mle 1935, was designed and probably tested for these guns, it appears not to have been put into production.

The 330mm OPfK Mle 1935 had an exceptionally large burster comprising 20.3kg of picric acid and dinitronaphthalene mix – equivalent to 3.6 per cent of

the weight of the shell. This was almost 50 per cent greater than for standard AP shell of the period and may reflect the intended target of the guns: the relatively lightly armoured *Panzerschiffe*. The weight of the burster in the later 380mm shell of the *Richelieus*, which was designed to penetrate the heavy armour of foreign battleships, was little more than this despite the much heavier shell (884kg against 570kg).

The quadruple turret was designed by Saint Chamond. Although each gun was in a separate cradle the relative movement of the guns in each pair was limited. The maximum angle of elevation was 35 degrees, at which the 330mm Mle 1931 had a theoretical range of 41,500 metres. The magazines and shell rooms for each pair of guns were on the same deck on opposite sides of the barbette and on two levels, with those for the left-sided pair of guns on the reinforced (30mm) inner bottom and for the right-sided pair on the deck directly above (see schematic drawings in

---

[3] Little is known about the 'double fuze' employed in the French shells. However, this was attempted – generally without success – by other navies. The technique generally employed was to use a fuze with a heavy sliding collar or bushing inside which would be moved forward under impact. If the deceleration was quite small and/or short, as it would be if the shell struck light plating, movement of the collar would be minimal and the expanding gases from the igniter would pass through a set of holes ('X') which created a certain delay ('Y'), usually short. If the impact was with a heavier plate, the deceleration would be greater and the collar would be displaced farther forward, covering the first set of holes and uncovering another set of holes ('A'), which led to a longer-delayed fuze train.

A different technique was used in the US Navy's Mark 11 base detonating fuze (BDF) introduced around 1937. This used a hollow needle which was thrown forward on impact and embedded itself into the black powder used as the delay element in combination with a firing pin which was cocked by its deceleration against a heavy spring and not released until resistance to penetration ceased. The higher the impact (i.e., against heavy armour) the deeper the needle embedded itself in the powder, resulting in a delay which went from 0.003 seconds (instant) to a maximum of 0.025 seconds. Reliability was an issue, particularly at oblique angles of impact, and the Mark 11 BDF was replaced during 1942 by the Mark 21, which had a fixed delay of 0.033 seconds.

Dunkerque: Hull Sections

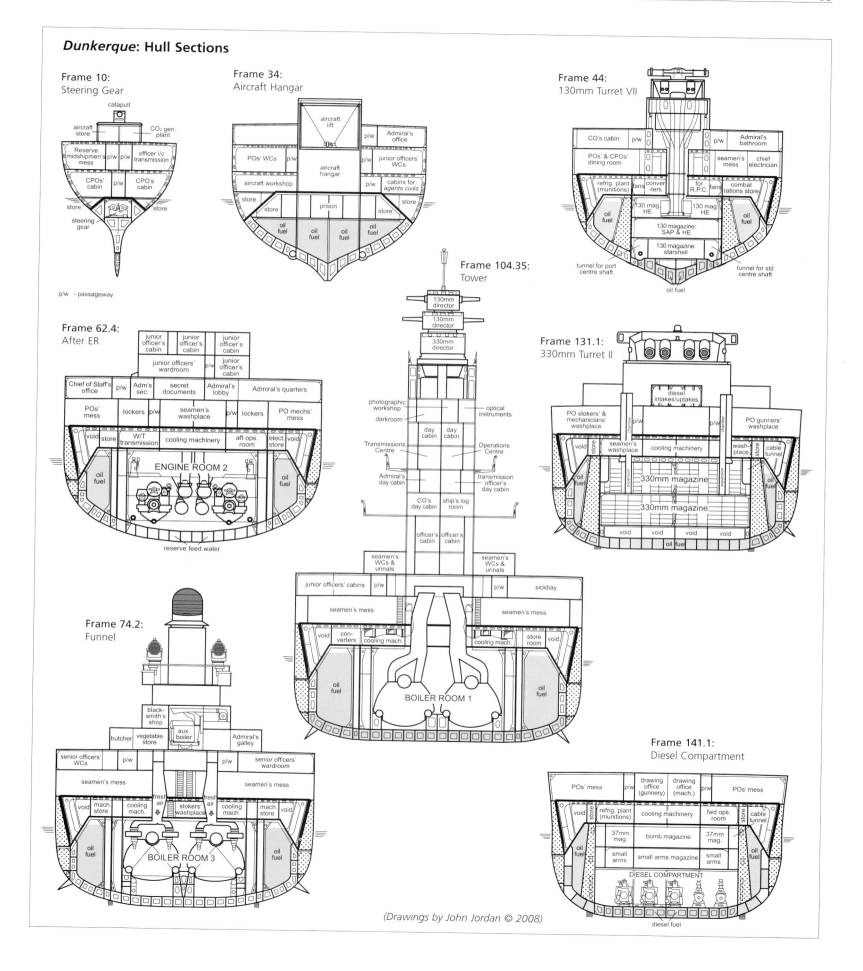

Frame 10:
Steering Gear

Frame 34:
Aircraft Hangar

Frame 44:
130mm Turret VII

Frame 62.4:
After ER

Frame 74.2:
Funnel

Frame 104.35:
Tower

Frame 131.1:
330mm Turret II

Frame 141.1:
Diesel Compartment

p/w - passageway

(Drawings by John Jordan © 2008)

The French 330mm Mle 1935 was a long-headed shell with a calibre radius head of 6crh. The length of the ballistic cap was almost half the total length of the projectile, and there were three copper driving bands. Although strictly an APC (armour-piercing, capped) shell as regards its construction the 330mm Mle 1935 was intended, like all French major-calibre shell since 1906, for use against both heavy armour and light plating, employing 'double-fuzing' in the base which used the deceleration of the shell on impact to determine the delay in detonation. The bursting charge in the 330mm shell was 20.3kg of picrid acid and dinitronaphthalene with a proportion close to 80/20. This was unusually large (3.6 per cent of shell weight) for an APC shell – almost on a par with that of the French 380mm Mle 1936, which was more than 50 per cent heavier. Campbell (*Naval Weapons of Word War Two*) has suggested that this was because the intended opponents of the *Dunkerque*s were the German *Panzerschiffe*, which were relatively lightly armoured. The large burster would inevitably have reduced the performance of the shell against very heavily armoured targets, because it would have been more likely to break up before full penetration.

The later OPfK variant of the Mle 1935 shell incorporated a dye bag and fuze in the ballistic cap (*dispositif* 'K') to colour not only shell splashes but hits, thereby facilitating spotting for ships operating in formation while in combat. The modified ballistic cap appears to have been in two parts (see also the drawing of the 380mm OPfK 1936; see p.106), the lower part being screwed directly onto the armoured cap of the shell, while the nose section containing the dye bag and the small-fuzed burster was secured to the lower section by pins or threaded screws. This presumably enabled the shells and the nose caps to be stored separately at support bases; shells could then be used by any ship of the class, the nose cap with its distinctive colorant being fitted prior to embarkation aboard ship. The authors have been unable to discover which colours were assigned to *Dunkerque* and *Strasbourg*. The later *Richelieu* was assigned yellow and her sister *Jean Bart* orange, so it seems likely that *Dunkerque* and *Strasbourg* fired red and green.

Campbell and others have stated that there was also an HE variant of the shell, designated OEA Mle 1935. Slightly shorter and lighter than the APC shell, it was otherwise similar in its external configuration. The burster was 60kg of *Mélinite* (picric acid) and there was a nose fuze. Campbell gives a total projectile weight of 522kg, a muzzle velocity of 865m/sec and a maximum range of 40,600 yards at 35 degrees elevation. The authors can find no reference to this shell in the wartime inventories of *Dunkerque* or *Strasbourg*, suggesting that this shell went no further than the project stage. The precise data figures given in Campbell and some French sources suggest that the shell may have been tested, but there is no evidence that it was subsequently ordered.

The SD propellant used for the bagged charges of the 330mm and the later 380mm guns was a 'solventless' propellant, which unlike the standard French BM 'strip' propellant was in single tube grain form. It was based on the German RP C/12, and had greater stability, reduced energy content, and burned at a lower temperature. Composition was 64-65 per cent nitrocellulose, 25 per cent nitroglycerine and 8-9 per cent centralite. The propellant for the 330mm Mle 1935 was designated SD19; that for the 380mm Mle 1936 was SD21. When *Richelieu* was at Dakar, SD19 charges stockpiled there for the *Strasbourg* were remanufactured using larger bags as a temporary measure (see p.126).

Sources: Campbell; and drawings and data published in various French gunnery manuals.

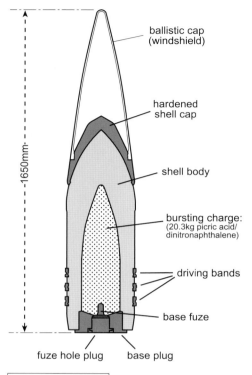

330mm Shell: OPf Mle 1935

- ballistic cap (windshield)
- hardened shell cap
- shell body
- bursting charge: (20.3kg picric acid/ dinitronaphthalene)
- driving bands
- base fuze

1650mm

fuze hole plug   base plug

shell weight: 570kg

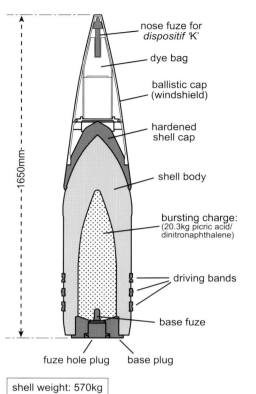

330mm Shell: OPfK Mle 1935

- nose fuze for *dispositif* 'K'
- dye bag
- ballistic cap (windshield)
- hardened shell cap
- shell body
- bursting charge: (20.3kg picric acid/ dinitronaphthalene)
- driving bands
- base fuze

1650mm

fuze hole plug   base plug

shell weight: 570kg

(Drawings by John Jordan © 2008)

A 330mm OPf Mle 1935 shell being brought on board *Dunkerque*. Note the three copper driving bands. The 330mm Mle 1935 had a slightly protruding base plug but lacked the distinctive aerodynamic 'boat tail' of the later 380mm Mle 1936. (*ECPAD*)

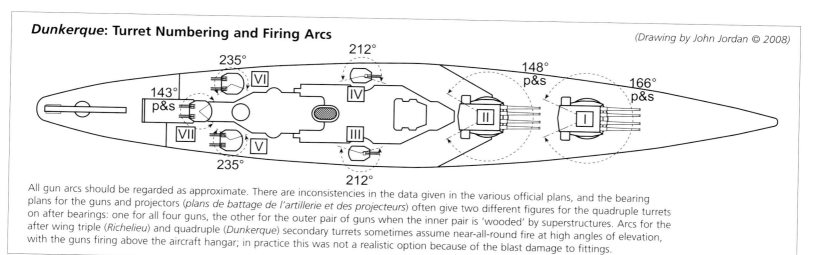

Dunkerque: Turret Numbering and Firing Arcs

(Drawing by John Jordan © 2008)

All gun arcs should be regarded as approximate. There are inconsistencies in the data given in the various official plans, and the bearing plans for the guns and projectors (*plans de battage de l'artillerie et des projecteurs*) often give two different figures for the quadruple turrets on after bearings: one for all four guns, the other for the outer pair of guns when the inner pair is 'wooded' by superstructures. Arcs for the after wing triple (*Richelieu*) and quadruple (*Dunkerque*) secondary turrets sometimes assume near-all-round fire at high angles of elevation, with the guns firing above the aircraft hangar; in practice this was not a realistic option because of the blast damage to fittings.

Chapter 4). A total of 456 shells (228 on each level) were provided for turret I, and 440 shells (220 per level) for turret II. The SD19 propellant charges were in quarters. Ammunition was fed by a shell and cartridge ring to a dredger hoist, one for each pair of guns, and transferred in the working chamber to the gun loading cages of the upper hoists, of which there was one for each gun. The cages had three compartments: the lower for the shell and the upper two for two quarter-charges each.

An important innovation of the Saint Chamond turret was its ability to load at all angles of elevation rather than at a fixed angle, which theoretically reduced loading times, thereby securing a faster firing

MAIN AND SECONDARY GUNS: CHARACTERISTICS

	330/52 Mle 1931	130/45 Mle 1932
Gun data		
Construction	'A' tube with hoops, jacket and liner	Monobloc autofretted barrel
Breech mechanism	Upward-opening Welin screw	Vertical sliding block
Weight of gun	70.5t	3.8t
Ammunition type	Separate	Fixed
Projectiles	OPf Mle 1935 (570kg)	OPfK Mle 1933 (33.4kg)
	OPfK Mle 1935 (570kg)	OEA Mle 1934 (29.5kg)
		OEcl Mle 1934 (30kg)
Propellant	SD19 in four quarter-charges (192kg)	BM9 (8.9kg)
Complete round		
Weight	–	53kg
Dimensions	–	1.35m x 0.18m (OPf)
		1.29m x 0.18m (OEA)
Muzzle velocity	870m/s (OPf)	800m/s (OPf)
		840m/s (OEA)
Max. range	41,500m (35°)	20,800m (45°)
Mounting data		
Designation	St Chamond Mle 1932	St Chamond quad Mle 1932
Weight of turret	1497t	200t
Distance apart gun axes	1.69m/2.54m	0.55m/2.45m
Protection	(see separate table)	(see separate table)
Loading angle	All angles	All angles
Elevation of guns	-5°/+35°	-10°/+75°
Max. training speed	5°/sec	12°/sec
Max. elevating speed	6°/sec	8°/sec
Firing cycle (per gun)	1.5-2rpm	10-12rpm

Notes:
All weights in metric tons (tonnes).
Speeds in metres/degrees per second.
OPf = *Obus de Perforation* (Armour Piercing Capped: APC)
OPfK = *Obus de Perforation* with red/green? '*K*' colorant.
OEA = *Obus Explosif en Acier* (High Explosive: HE)
OEcl = *Obus Eclairant* (starshell)
Distance apart gun axes: first figure for outer guns; second figure for inner guns; 130mm quad outer mountings in same sleeve.
St Chamond twin Mle 1932 weighed 81.2 tonnes; protection for the gunhouse was 20mm.

cycle. In order to facilitate this, an electric chain rammer was carried on an extension from each gun cradle, and the profile of the upper guide rails for the cage hoists was matched to the arc of the breech of the gun as the gun was elevated, with movement of the hoist synchronised with the elevating motors via a clutch and transmission system (see drawings in Chapter 4). In practice, problems were often experi-

enced with the shell becoming jammed in the breech at higher angles when the other guns in the mounting were fired, and reloading was generally carried out at 15 degrees elevation to avoid this.

The secondary armament comprised sixteen 130/45 Model 1932 guns, the three quad turrets mounted aft being supplemented by two twin mountings amidships to cover the forward arcs. These were the first French dual-purpose mountings; they had a vertical sliding breech and a maximum elevation of 75 degrees. In the anti-surface mode they fired a 33.4kg SAP shell with an initial velocity of 800m/s to a maximum range of 20,800 metres; against aircraft they fired a 29.5kg time-fuzed HE shell with an initial velocity of 840m/s. The fixed ammunition rounds weighed 53kg, which was close to the maximum weight that could be comfortably handled by a loader. Magazine capacity was about 6400 rounds (400 per gun), of which 2000 were SAP anti-surface rounds and the remainder time-fuzed HE and starshell.

Like the quadruple turrets of the main armament, the quad 130mm mounting was developed by Saint Chamond. The guns were paired in cast steel cradles, and there was a 20mm steel bulkhead dividing the turret into two independent halves. Each pair of guns was served by a double pusher hoist (one for anti-aircraft, the other for anti-surface rounds). The hoists for the centreline quad turret rose vertically from its two-level magazine, whereas the hoists for the beam quads were broken at the upper armoured deck. The upper hoists came up by the outer cradle trunnions of each pair of guns. A ready-use platform with a capacity of forty-eight rounds (thirty-two HE and sixteen SAP) was fixed to the upper section of the hoist, the rounds being stowed vertically by hand. The rounds were then passed to loading trays by a combination of hydraulically powered tilting and rotating trays and slide tracks. Pneumatic rammers were employed to ram the munitions home, following which the breech closed automatically.

The twin mounting resembled the quad half-mounting in layout, although the gun barrels were mounted farther apart. Whereas the quad mountings were fully armoured, the twins had only light 20mm plating. The twin mountings were 23 metres abaft their magazines, so that ammunition had to be transferred horizontally between the upper and lower armoured decks.

GENERAL CHARACTERISTICS (AS COMPLETED)

	Dunkerque	Strasbourg
Displacement		
Standard	26,500 tons	27,300 tons
Normal	30,750 tonnes	31,570 tonnes
Full load	35,500 tonnes	36,380 tonnes
Dimensions		
Length pp	209.00m	209.00m
Length oa	215.14m	215.50m
Beam	31.10m	31.10m
Draught (normal)	8.57m max.	8.73m max.
Draught (full load)	9.71m max.	9.89m max.

Machinery
Boilers	Six Indret small watertube boilers with superheating, 27kg/cm² (350°)
Turbines	Four-shaft Parsons geared steam turbines
Power	107,000shp for 29.5kts (designed)
Oil fuel	3700 tonnes
Endurance	7850nm at 15kts, 2450nm at 28kts
Generators	Four 900kW turbo-generators
	Three 400kW diesel generators
	Two emergency 100kW diesel generators

Armament
Main guns	Eight 330/52 Mle 1931 in two quadruple mountings Mle 1932 (896 AP rounds)
Secondary	Sixteen 130/45 Mle 1932 in three quadruple and two twin mountings Mle 1932 (2000 SAP rounds + 4400 HE and starshell)
Light AA	Ten(D)/eight(S) 37/50 Mle 1933 in four/five twin mountings
	Thirty-two 13.2/76 Mle 1929 Hotchkiss MG in eight quad mountings
Aircraft	Three Loire 130 seaplanes

Protection
Belt	225mm(D)/283mm(S)
Deck	115/125mm + 40mm
CT	270mm-130mm
330mm turrets	330mm-150mm(D)/360mm-160mm(S)
130mm turrets	135mm-80mm

Complement
Dunkerque (flag)	81 officers + 1300 men; total 1381
Strasbourg	32 officers + 1270 men; total 1302

Notes:
After Washington standard displacement in the Marine Nationale was generally given in long tons (Tonnes W or TW); other displacements were given in metric tonnes (tonnes – small-case 't')
Mle = Modèle (Model)

Breakdown of Weights

	Dunkerque	Strasbourg
Hull	7011t (22.8%)	7040t (22.3%)
Fittings	2767t (9.0%)	2809t (8.9%)
Armament	4858t (15.8%)	4858t (15.4%)
Protection		
Hull	8364t (27.2%)	8904t (28.2%)
Armament	2676t (8.7%)	2885t (9.1%)
Machinery	2214t (7.2%)	2214t (7.0%)
Oil Fuel (¾ load)	2860t (9.3%)	2860t (9.1%)
Total	30,750t (100%)	31,570t (100%)

Note: All weights in metric tons (tonnes).

FIRE CONTROL

Dunkerque was the first French battleship with a purpose-designed director control system for both the main and the secondary armament. Arrangements were particularly complete. The five main directors, each fitted with an OPL stereoscopic rangefinder, were mounted one above the other atop the forward tower structure and around the base of the pole mainmast. For the main armament there was a triplex 12-metre rangefinder (replaced in 1940 by a 14-metre model) in the lower director of the forward tower, a duplex 8-metre RF in the lower director of the after tower, and a duplex 12-metre RF in each of the two main turrets. For the secondary armament there were directors with integral 6-metre (middle) and 5-metre (upper) rangefinders on the forward tower, a director with a 6-metre RF on the after tower, and 6-metre rangefinders in each of the three quadruple turrets (see drawing and table).

Dunkerque returning to Brest following the Naval Review of May 1937. The quarterdeck is dominated by the aircraft facilities. Two of the after 130mm quads are abeam the hangar with the third above it. (*P du Cheyron collection*)

RANGEFINDERS

Main armament

One OPL 12-metre S (triplex)	Lower director fwd tower
One OPL 8-metre S (duplex)	Lower director after tower
Two OPL 12-metre S (duplex)	Turrets I and II

Secondary armament

Two OPL 6-metre S	Middle director fwd tower
	Upper director after tower
One OPL 5-metre S	Upper director fwd tower
Three OPL 6-metre S	Turrets V, VI and VII (quads)

Light AA

Four 1-metre	Two fwd tower, two on deckhouse aft

General use

One OPL 5-metre S	(D) atop conning tower (tactical)
	(S) atop admiral's bridge (tactical)
Two SOM 3-metre S	Directors either side of fwd tower (night vision)
Four 0.8-metre	Upper observation bridge (two per side)

Notes:
OPL *Optique de Précision Levallois-Perret*
SOM *Société d'Optique et de Méchanique de Haute Précision*
S Stereoscopic RF
C Coincidence RF

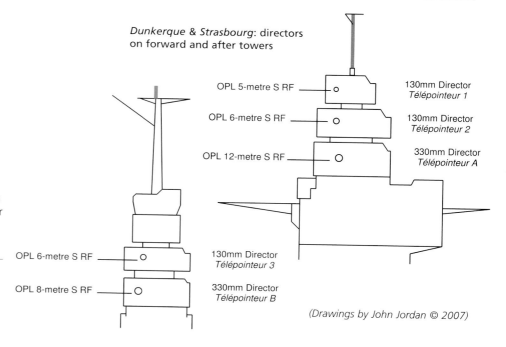

Dunkerque & Strasbourg: directors on forward and after towers

OPL 5-metre S RF — 130mm Director *Télépointeur 1*
OPL 6-metre S RF — 130mm Director *Télépointeur 2*
OPL 12-metre S RF — 330mm Director *Télépointeur A*

OPL 6-metre S RF — 130mm Director *Télépointeur 3*
OPL 8-metre S RF — 330mm Director *Télépointeur B*

(*Drawings by John Jordan © 2007*)

Opposite:
The 330mm guns of turret II
with the tower above them.
Note the concentration dials.
There were three of these on
the forward tower and one
on the after side of the
mainmast. The dials were
painted black with yellow
numbers and hands; the latter
were moved hydraulically.

Below:
Close-up of the port-side
director for night fire with its
3-metre SOM stereo
rangefinder. Note the white
painted RF arms. The photo
was taken aboard *Strasbourg*.
(ECPAD)

The location of the main directors atop the tower favoured accurate target discrimination at long range without smoke interference, and their position was deemed to give them virtual immunity to direct hits and shell bursts. These advantages were clearly considered sufficient to outweigh the high cost in topweight; the main FC director, which was 30 metres above the waterline, weighed 40 tonnes, the lower of the two 130mm directors 25 tonnes and the upper director 20 tonnes. The directors were gastight, and were fitted with light steel plating to protect them from the machine guns of strafing aircraft.

In addition to the main gunnery directors a stereoscopic OPL 5-metre tactical rangefinder was located atop the conning tower (in *Strasbourg* it was located atop the main tower), and stereoscopic SOM 3-metre rangefinders were mounted on the sides of the tower for night fire. Concentration dials (carried until removed in 1940) enabled the ship to transmit range data visually to another vessel in formation.

The directors provided target range, bearing and inclination data to a computer-equipped transmitting station located beneath the armoured decks, with continuous transmission to both the directors and the guns using the Granat system adopted during the 1920s. The transmitting station, which was essentially an enlarged version of the TS developed for the 10,000-ton cruisers, was equipped with the customary suite of tables, plotters and calculators and manned by twenty-four operators under the supervision of the deputy fire control officer (*directeur de tir adjoint*) and a petty officer *chef de poste*. It had facilities for firing at a target over the horizon with data supplied by another unit. There were also four-man computers in each of the main-battery turrets, and three nine-man anti-aircraft control posts for the 130mm DP guns. Data transfer was fully automated where possible to minimise time delay in transmission and to eliminate the possibility of human error. As in earlier French battleships, the action station of the fire control officer was in the heavily-armoured control tower.

Dunkerque was the first French battleship to have remote power control (RPC) for training and elevation. The turrets for the main and the secondary armament were powered by Léonard electric servo-motors with hydraulic drive. However, the Sautter-Harlé-Blondel RPC training gear proved unreliable; synchronisation between the turrets and the directors was poor, and manual intervention was needed for fine adjustment. Moreover, the servo-motors had insufficient power to cope with armoured turrets of this weight and size, resulting in slow tracking speeds and frequent breakdowns. Major problems were experienced on trials, and even following modification the system never worked properly.

For night firing there were seven 120cm searchlight projectors (six in *Strasbourg*): three grouped around the tower structure (two only in *Strasbourg*), and a further four on a raised platform around the after base of the single funnel. All were fitted with RPC, and could be controlled either using the 130mm directors or from four positions on the sides of the tower.

In the days before radar, target designation and tracking devices had to be cued by visual means. On *Dunkerque* and *Strasbourg*, there was an elaborate system of lookout posts on three levels linked by telephone to the *chef de veille* (officer of the watch), who had an overview of the surface and air situation on his side of the ship from a command post located on the navigation bridge.

At the lower level, which was at the level of the first deck abeam the bridge, there were three lookout positions port and starboard. Each lookout was provided with a pair of pedestal-mounted binoculars with an automatic dual-circuit Granat bearing transmitter; he could contact the *chef de veille* either by telephone or by using a bipolar switch which illuminated the signal lamp for his position. The middle lookout station was on platform 3 of the forward tower. There were five lookout posts on either side of the ship, each identically equipped to those at the lower level. The upper lookout station, which was on platform 8 of the tower, had posts for five lookouts on each side of the ship. Each pair of binoculars was fitted with a dual-circuit Granat transmitter for bearing plus a single-circuit Granat transmitter for elevation, the data being transmitted to one of two positions (port and starboard) manned by the *chef de défense* located on the same platform.

Target designation was exercised from the conning tower. In the upper part of the CT there were four periscopic glasses with dual-circuit Granat transmitters. Bearing – and, if applicable, elevation – data from either one the two *chefs de veille*, one of the two *chefs*

de défense or from the conning tower, were transmitted directly to the appropriate fire control director(s). In addition, the admiral's position in the conning tower was equipped with two sets of periscopic glasses with dual-circuit Granat transmitters, which enabled bearing data to be co-ordinated with two similarly equipped pairs of binoculars for an officer of the admiral's staff placed high in the tower. These binoculars could also transmit a bearing to the OPL 5-metre base rangefinder which was located atop the conning tower in *Dunkerque* and atop the superstructure tower in *Strasbourg*. Range data either from the 5-metre RF or from the transmitting station for the 330mm guns could be received and read in the conning tower.

The target designation circuits were completed by sets of indicator lamps in the various directors which could be illuminated from the two stations of the *chefs de veille*.

LIGHT AA WEAPONS

For close-in air defence, *Dunkerque* was originally to have had four 37mm Model 1933 twin semi-automatic mountings and eight quadruple 13.2mm Hotchkiss MG mountings. The 37mm Model 1933, although still to enter service when *Dunkerque* was laid down, was based on the single mounting Model 1925 fitted in the treaty cruisers and the *contre-torpilleurs*. It had a conventional sliding breech and was fed from boxes of six cartridges, which resulted in a maximum (theoretical) rate of fire of only 30-40rpm per barrel. It was quickly recognised that this was insufficient against modern high-performance aircraft, so the Marine Nationale opted for the development of an advanced twin fully automatic weapon with RPC, the 37mm ACAD[4] Model 1935, designed for an unprecedented 200rpm per barrel. This was adopted from February 1935 for *Dunkerque* and *Strasbourg*, for the contemporary *contre-torpilleurs Mogador* and *Volta*, and for the new *torpilleurs d'escadre* of the *Le Hardi* class. It still features in the official plans of *Dunkerque* dated Brest 1 March 1939, which show two mountings on the upper deck abeam turret II, a further pair on either side of the deckhouse between the funnel and the mainmast, and a fifth mounting on the centreline aft above the after 130mm quad turret – these locations were in part determined by the requirement for an

---

[4] ACAD = *Automatique Contre-Avions Double* (automatic AA twin).

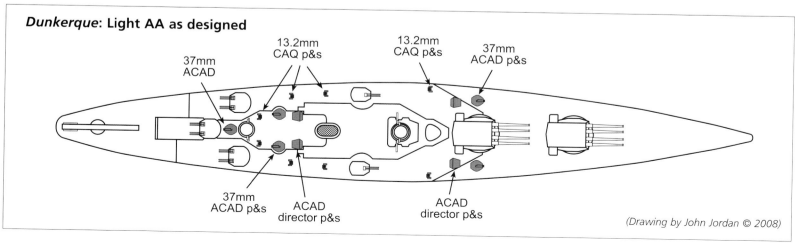

***Dunkerque*: Light AA as designed**

37mm ACAD

13.2mm CAQ p&s

13.2mm CAQ p&s

37mm ACAD p&s

37mm ACAD p&s

ACAD director p&s

ACAD director p&s

(Drawing by John Jordan © 2008)

Right:
Close-up of the starboard-side 130mm DP quad of *Strasbourg*. The centreline mounting can be seen atop the hangar on the far right of the photograph.

ammunition lobby directly beneath the gun mounting. There were to be four associated directors with integral 2-metre rangefinders and RPC: two at the forward end of the shelter deck above the forward pair of mountings, and two on either side of the deckhouse between the funnel and the mainmast (see drawing).

Unfortunately the complexity of the new mounting resulted in protracted development: the first prototype was ready only in spring 1939, and it was envisaged that the delivery of production models would be possible only from late 1940. In the interim, *Dunkerque* would be fitted as a temporary measure with six single 37mm Model 1925 guns (two abeam turret II and four on the after superstructure); from early 1939 these would be replaced by five twin Model 1933 mountings, disposed as in the original plans.

LIGHT ANTI-AIRCRAFT GUNS: CHARACTERISTICS

	37/50 Mle 1933	13.2/76 Mle 1929
Gun data		
Weight of gun	300kg	30kg
Ammunition type	Fixed	Fixed
Projectiles	OEA Mle 1925 (0.73kg)	Solid bullet (50gm)
	OI Mle 1924 (0.73kg)	
Propellant	BM2 in cartridge (0.2kg)	52g
Complete round		
Weight	2.8kg	122g
Dimensions	408mm x 61mm	135mm x ??
Muzzle velocity	810m/s	800m/s
Max. range	8000m theoretical	3500m theoretical
	5000m effective	2500m effective
Mounting data		
Mounting designation	CAD Mle 1933	CAQ Mle 1929
Weight of mounting	N/A	1.16t
Elevation of guns	-15°/+80°	-15°/+90°
Firing cycle (per gun)	30rpm theoretical	450rpm theoretical
	15-21rpm practical	250rpm practical

Notes:

CAS	*Contre-Avions Simple*	AA single mounting
CAD	*Contre-Avions Double*	AA twin mounting
CAQ	*Contre-Avions Quadruple*	AA quad mounting
Mle	*Modèle*	Model
OEA	*Obus Explosif en Acier*	High Explosive (HE)
OI	*Obus Incendiaire*	Incendiary

INSTALLATION OF LIGHT AA GUNS 1937-40

Dunkerque		
May 1937	6 x 37mm CAS Mle 1925	2 abeam fwd tower (02/03 decks)
		4 on deckhouse abaft funnel
Oct. 1937	6 x 13.2mm CAQ Mle 1929	02 deck amidships and abeam tower
May 1937	[6 x 37mm CAS disembarked]	
	2 x 13.2mm CAQ Mle 1929	Deckhouse abaft funnel
Feb. 1939	4 x 37mm CAD Mle 1933	2 abeam turret II (01 deck)
		2 on deckhouse abaft funnel
	[2 x CAQ abeam tower moved from 02 deck to sides of bridge]	
Aug.1939	1 x 37mm CAD Mle 1933	Centreline abaft mainmast
Feb. 1940	[2 x 37mm CAD moved from 01 deck fwd to 02 deck]	
Strasbourg		
Dec. 1938	5 x 13.2mm CAQ Mle 1929	4 on 02 deck amidships
		1 on front face fwd tower
Early 1939	4 x 37mm CAD Mle 1933	2 abeam turret II (01 deck)
		2 on deckhouse abaft funnel
	2 x 13.2mm CAQ Mle 1929	Deckhouse abaft funnel
Aug. 1939	1 x 13.2mm CAQ Mle 1929	Centreline abaft mainmast

Strasbourg would receive only four – all except the centreline mounting aft, which was replaced by a 13.2mm quad mounting shortly before the outbreak of war (see table for the fitting of the light AA 1937-40).

The 37mm Mle 1933 guns were disposed in two groups fore and aft for control purposes, four one-metre rangefinders being provided. As with the forward 130mm mountings, the forward 37mm guns were some way abaft their magazines, and the hoists (at frames 145 and 114 respectively following the relocation of the mountings to the superstructure deck in early 1940) were broken at the main deck, the ammunition cases being transferred horizontally on trolleys. The hoists for the after mountings (frame 58) were just forward of the magazines and raised the cases directly to the roof of the after deckhouse.

The 13.2mm MG were divided into three groups: after, amidships, and forward. The munitions for these guns were stowed in the small arms magazine forward (there was a separate magazine for tracer). The forward 37mm hoists were used to bring the munitions cases up to the main deck; they were then transported manually to the gun mountings.

PROTECTION

The armour belt, which was inclined 11°30 in *Dunkerque* and 11°50 in *Strasbourg*, extended from frame 41.60,[5] immediately abaft the 130mm magazines, to frame 167.35, which marked the forward end of the 330mm magazines, and was closed by armoured transverse bulkheads. The belt comprised a single strake of cemented armour the upper edge of which

5 Frames on French ships were numbered according to the distance in metres from the after perpendicular.

Dunkerque: Decks of Forward Tower

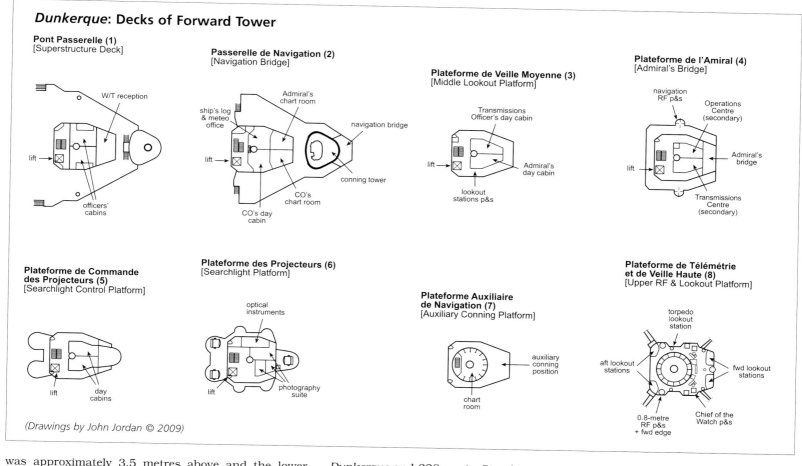

(Drawings by John Jordan © 2009)

was approximately 3.5 metres above and the lower edge 2 metres below the waterline at normal displacement. Each of the forty plates that made up the belt on each side was approximately 5.75 metres high, with widths varying between 2.4 metres and 3.6 metres. Each plate was of a constant thickness at and above the waterline – 225mm in *Dunkerque*, increased to 283mm in *Strasbourg* – and extended over two/three frames. A rebate in the upper edge of the plates provided the seating for the upper armoured deck. The armour belt was tapered below the waterline and had a teak backing 60mm thick; the plates were secured by armour bolts 60mm in diameter above the waterline and by 45mm diameter bolts below.

The forward transverse bulkhead extended from the upper armoured deck to the 30mm floor of the munitions magazines; the plates were 210mm thick in *Dunkerque* and 228mm in *Strasbourg*. The after bulkhead had plates 180mm thick (210mm in *Strasbourg*) where it enclosed the two armoured decks but only 80mm below, the reduced thickness made possible by the extension of the lower armoured deck aft above the shafts and the heavy armoured box over the steering compartment (see drawings).

The upper armoured deck (PBS or *Pont Blindé Supérieur*), which was at main deck level and rested on the upper edges of the belt at its outer edges, comprised non-cemented armour plates fixed to a 15mm steel deck. The plates were laid lengthways (see drawing) and were 115mm thick over the machinery and after magazines (frames 41.60 to 121.55), increasing to 125mm over the forward magazines (frames 121.55 to 167.35). These thicknesses were the same in both ships.

The lower armoured deck (PBI or *Pont Blindé*

AMMUNITION ABOARD STRASBOURG 8 NOVEMBER 1941

Gun calibre	330	130		37		13.2	
Shell Type	OPfK Mle 35	OPfK Mle 33	OEA Mle 34	OEA Mle 25	OI Mle 24	perf./tracer	ord.
No. of shells	800	1498 D	3149 D	6018 D	1997 N	96,090	6000
		498 N	999 N				
No. of charges	2400+	(fixed ammunition)		(fixed ammunition)		(fixed ammunition)	

Notes:
OPfK = <u>O</u>bus de <u>P</u>er<u>f</u>oration (APC/SAPC) with red/green? 'K' colorant.
OEA = <u>O</u>bus <u>E</u>xplosif en <u>A</u>cier (HE: contact or time-fuzed AA).
OI = <u>O</u>bus <u>I</u>ncendiaire (incendiary).
D = day rounds; N = night rounds.
For the 130mm rounds, 2000 could have the RVG contact fuze fitted in place of the standard time fuze; this would naturally bring about a corresponding decrease in the number of AA rounds available.

Source: Inventory from *Devis de Campagne* of CV Seguin (23.08.40-08.11.41)

Dunkerque: Protection

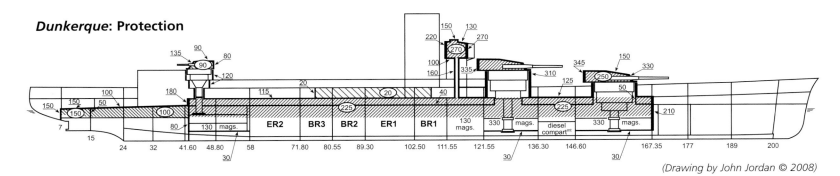

(Drawing by John Jordan © 2008)

Inférieur), which was on the level of the first platform deck, was of similar composition but at a much-reduced thickness: 40mm on the broader horizontal section and the same thickness on the inclined sides that joined the lower armoured deck to the lower edge of the armour belt (in *Strasbourg*, the inclined plates were increased in thickness to 50mm).

Abaft the after transverse armoured bulkhead the first platform deck was inclined downwards towards the stern. An armoured deck with inclined sides

100mm thick in the form of a carapace covered the shafts in this area, and connected the main armoured citadel to the box over the steering gear, which extended from frame 7 to frame 15. The plates over the steering gear were 150mm (100mm + 50mm) thick, and the after bulkhead comprised a single plate of the same thickness. At its inboard end, the 'box' was closed by a 50mm bulkhead.

Some internal bulkheads were reinforced to 20mm to provide splinter protection. There were longitudinal bulkheads of 20mm steel abeam the steering gear (frames 7 to 24). Similar protection was applied to the longitudinal bulkhead inboard of the armour belt between the upper and lower armoured decks, as part of the *entrepont cellulaire*, and there was a box of similar thickness to protect the funnel uptakes above the level of the main deck (frames 76.10 to 107).

The following internal bulkheads were reinforced to 18mm thickness: the transverse bulkhead at frame 24 at the forward end of the steering gear compartment; the bulkheads enclosing the citadel (frames 41.60 and 167.35); the bulkheads enclosing each of the two 330mm magazines (frames 121.55, 136.30, and 146.60); the after bulkhead for the machinery spaces (frames 58.00); and the bulkhead dividing the machinery spaces into two independent units (frame 89.30).

Conning tower and superstructures

The heavily armoured conning tower was on two levels with a raised position at its after end. The upper level housed the command station (*Poste de Commande-ment* – forward section) and the operations centre (*PC Opérations* – after section); the lower level housed the conning station (*Poste de Manoeuvre* – forward section) and the transmissions centre (*PC Transmissions*). The raised position in the *PC Opérations* was for the use of the admiral if embarked.

The face and sides of the tower were protected by five vertical plates of cemented armour 270mm thick. The rear wall was protected by two 220mm vertical plates of cemented armour. The plates were fixed to a base comprising a double thickness (2 x 15mm) of 50kg construction steel. Access to the two levels was via two gastight doors of 220mm special steel set into the starboard side of the after wall. The raised position was protected by a band of three 270mm plates of special steel on the face and sides, a single plate of 220mm forming the rear wall. The roof of the main body of the conning tower was formed by four 130mm plates of cemented armour on a double thickness (2 x 15mm) of 50kg construction steel, while the roof of the raised position was a single 150mm plate of cemented armour (see drawing).

PROTECTION

Armour Belt

Height of upper edge of belt above the waterline at trials displacement.	Frames 41.60-121.55	3.415m
	Frames 121.55-167.35	3.425m
Depth of lower edge of belt beneath the waterline at trials displacement.	Frame 41.60	1.840m
	At mid-point	2.240m
	Frame 167.35	2.050m

	Dunkerque	*Strasbourg*
Vertical protection		
Main belt	225mm	283mm
Forward bulkhead	210mm	228mm
After bulkhead above PBI	180mm	210mm
Bulkhead abaft steering gear	150mm	150mm
Horizontal protection		
PBS over magazines	125mm	(as *Dunkerque* except
PBS over machinery	115mm	50mm inclines on PBI)
Lower armoured deck (PBI)	40mm	
Over shafts	100mm	
Over steering gear	150mm	
Conning tower		
Face and sides	270mm	(as *Dunkerque*)
Rear	220mm	
Roof	150mm/130mm	
Communications tube	160mm	
330mm turrets		
Turret face	330mm	360mm
Turret sides	250mm	250mm
Turret roof	150mm	160mm
Turret rear	345mm (I)	352mm (I)
	335mm (II)	342mm (II)
Barbette above PBS	310mm	340mm
Barbette below PBS	50mm	50mm
130mm quad turrets		
Turret face	135mm	(as *Dunkerque*)
Turret sides	90mm	
Turret roof	90mm	
Turret rear	80mm	
Barbette	120mm	

Dunkerque: Conning Tower

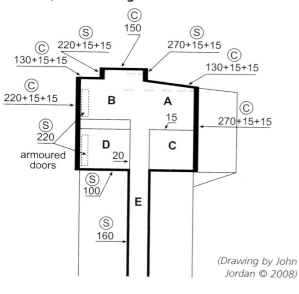

(Drawing by John Jordan © 2008)

Ⓒ cemented armour   Ⓢ special steel

A Command Station (*Poste de Commandement*)
B Operations Centre (*PC Opérations*)
C Conning Station (*Poste de Manoeuvre*)
D Transmissions Centre (*PC Transmissions*)
E Communications Tube (*Tube de transmission d'ordre*)

There were nine embrasures in the main body of the conning tower, and a further three in the raised section, all of which could be protected by thick gastight glass panels. The floor of the two-level conning tower was of 100mm special steel, and the communications tube linking the conning tower with the transmitting station beneath the main armoured deck was of 160mm special steel and was 900mm in diameter.

As protection against strafing the outer skin of the forward tower was sheathed in plates of 10mm hardened steel, the plates being laid vertically. The directors atop the forward tower and around the mainmast were protected by plating 20mm thick, as was the tube in the centre of the forward tower which served as the trunk for the director cabling.

Main turrets

The main turrets were protected by a carapace composed of heavy plates of cemented armour resting on a steel framework and secured to one another with butt straps of 40mm special steel and armour bolts. The roof plates could be removed individually to give access to the guns. The face of each turret comprised five plates of 330mm angled at 30 degrees to the vertical, the sides walls each of two plates 250mm thick, and the roof twelve plates of 150mm (in *Strasbourg* these plates were 360mm, 250mm and 160mm respectively). The rear wall of the turrets was protected by two plates of 60kg special steel: 345mm for turret I, 335 for turret II (increased in *Strasbourg* – see table).

The floor of the firing chamber was of 50mm/60kg special steel, and this was reinforced at the front and sides where it projected from the turret walls to form a glacis by 100mm of 80kg special steel, and at the rear, where the turret overhung the barbette, by a

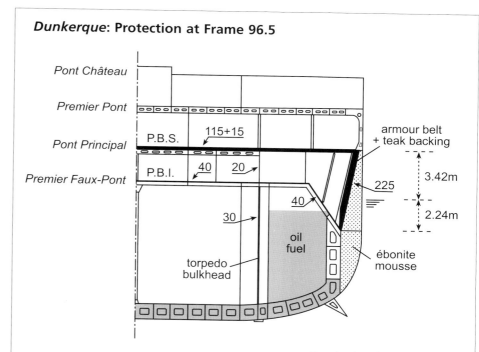

(Drawing by John Jordan © 2009)

In comparison with earlier French protection systems, that for *Dunkerque* was very advanced. It had most of the features of the battleships built for the US Navy following the First World War and of the British *Nelson*s, while incorporating some novel features of French conception.

As in the British ships, the main armour belt was inclined (11°30 in *Dunkerque*) and internal; it comprised a single strake of rectangular plates laid vertically (see armour plan on p.47). The thick armoured deck, which rested on the top edges of the belt, was backed up by a 40mm 'splinter deck' above the machinery on the American pattern. Interestingly, the French retained the traditional *entrepont cellulaire* between the armoured decks, using longitudinal bulkheads of 20mm thickness to divide up the space.

The underwater protection system, a major weakness in earlier French designs, was remarkably well developed. It comprised the now-standard 'sandwich' with void spaces, light bulkheads, liquid loading and a heavy internal holding bulkhead of high-tensile steel to absorb the explosion of a torpedo warhead; the depth of the system at the point of greatest beam was just under 7.5 metres – a remarkable figure for the period. A particular French innovation was the filling of the compartments outside the inclined belt with a rubber-based water-excluding compound (*ébonite mousse*) to absorb the initial impact and to prevent uncontrolled flooding of the side compartments.

double thickness of 60kg steel. There were protective caps of 150mm nickel-chrome steel for the ends of the 12-metre rangefinders incorporated into the rear end of the turrets, and 100mm hoods of the same material to protect the periscopic sights for the turret commander and trainer on the roof of the turret and the sights for the gunlayers on the turret sides. The gun embrasures were protected by 80mm steel masks of 80kg special steel.

The barbettes for the main turrets were protected above the level of the main deck (PBS) by 310mm plates (340mm in *Strasbourg*) of cemented armour bolted onto a double layer of 15mm plating of 60kg steel. There was a single armoured band comprising twelve plates for turret I, and a double band each of twelve plates for turret II. Beneath the upper armoured deck, protection was reduced to 50mm of 60kg steel; the diameter for turret I was 11.5 metres; for turret II it was 7.2 metres.

Secondary turrets

The quadruple secondary 130mm turrets were

Dunkerque: Disposition of Armour Plates

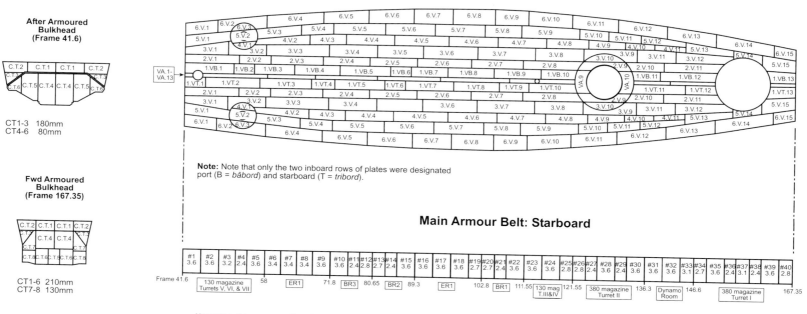

Upper Armoured Deck (*P.B.S.*)

After Armoured Bulkhead (Frame 41.6)

CT1-3   180mm
CT4-6   80mm

Fwd Armoured Bulkhead (Frame 167.35)

CT1-6   210mm
CT7-8   130mm

Note: Note that only the two inboard rows of plates were designated port (B = *bâbord*) and starboard (T = *tribord*).

Main Armour Belt: Starboard

Note: The plates were numbered 1-40 beginning at the after transverse bulkhead. Approximate plate widths are given in metres.

(Drawing by John Jordan © 2008)

protected by plates of 80kg nickel-chrome steel secured to one another with butt straps as in the main turrets, without a steel backing. The frontal plate, angled at 65 degrees to the vertical, was 135mm thick, and the single plates of the side walls 90mm. The hemicylindrical rear wall comprised two plates 80mm thick. The roof comprised three plates with a uniform thickness of 90mm: for the forward section, which was removable and was angled down towards the turret face, there was a single transverse plate, while two plates formed the horizontal after section. At the after extremity of each turret was a hood of 80mm nickel steel in which the 6-metre base rangefinder and the sight for the turret commander were housed. The turret floor was of 30mm 60kg steel, and as with the main turrets was reinforced where it protruded at the front and sides by 80kg special steel 75mm thick to form a glacis. The sights for the gunlayers and trainers were located at the base of the front plate between the guns, the housing being of 120mm nickel steel. All the sights could be closed by hinged protective covers. The twin masks for the gun embrasures were of 80kg special steel 50mm thick.

The fixed barbette armour for the secondary turrets was of 80kg nickel-chrome or special steel with a uniform thickness of 120mm. The plates were assembled with riveted joints; there was no steel plating to form a backing. The upper band (four plates) had an interior diameter of 7 metres, the lower band (four plates) a diameter of 5.3 metres and for the centreline turret, positioned one deck higher than the wing turrets, there was a third, smaller band of 2.15 metres diameter (three plates). The trunk for the hoists was fitted internally with a diaphragm of 80kg nickel-chrome steel 70mm thick at the level of the main armoured deck; the diaphragm was pierced only where strictly necessary to permit the passage of the munitions hoists. The tube for the centreline turret had a

second diaphragm 40mm thick where it passed through the lower armoured deck.

Protection for the forward twin 130mm turrets was on a much-reduced scale. The gunhouse was protected only by 20mm plating of 80kg nickel-chrome steel. The barbettes had 20mm nickel-chrome plating on a double layer of thick steel plating (20mm + 20mm) above the level of the main armoured deck. There was also a diaphragm of 80kg special steel 120mm thick inside the munitions trunk where the hoists passed through the main armoured deck.

Underwater protection

The underwater protection system of *Dunkerque* was in line with the latest thinking, employing a 'sandwich' comprising void spaces, light bulkheads, liquid loading and a heavy internal holding bulkhead of special steel to absorb the explosion of a torpedo warhead. The major innovation in the French ships was the filling of the compartment outboard of the inclined armour belt, which had a maximum depth of 1.5 metres, with a rubber-based water-excluding compound (*ébonite mousse*) to absorb the initial impact and to prevent uncontrolled flooding of the side compartments. Inboard of this compartment there was a 16mm bulkhead enclosing a void compartment 0.9 metres deep, followed by an oil fuel bunker 3.9 metres deep, followed by a 10mm bulkhead enclosing a void compartment 0.7 metres deep, backed by a 30mm torpedo bulkhead of special steel. The compartment between the torpedo bulkhead and the bulkhead enclosing the machinery spaces was used for electrical cabling runs. The total depth of the underwater protection system from the outer skin to the inner face of the torpedo bulkhead at the widest point of the hull was almost 7.5 metres, an impressive figure by any standards (most contemporary foreign systems had a depth of around 5 metres).

The tower of *Strasbourg* seen from the forecastle during 1939. Note the sub-calibre 90mm guns mounted on the sides of the turrets. There were numerous detail differences in the towers of the two ships, notably the number and location of the searchlight projectors. *Strasbourg* had her 5-metre tactical RF mounted atop the Admiral's bridge, whereas in *Dunkerque* it was mounted on the conning tower (see photo p.33).

(H Landais collection)

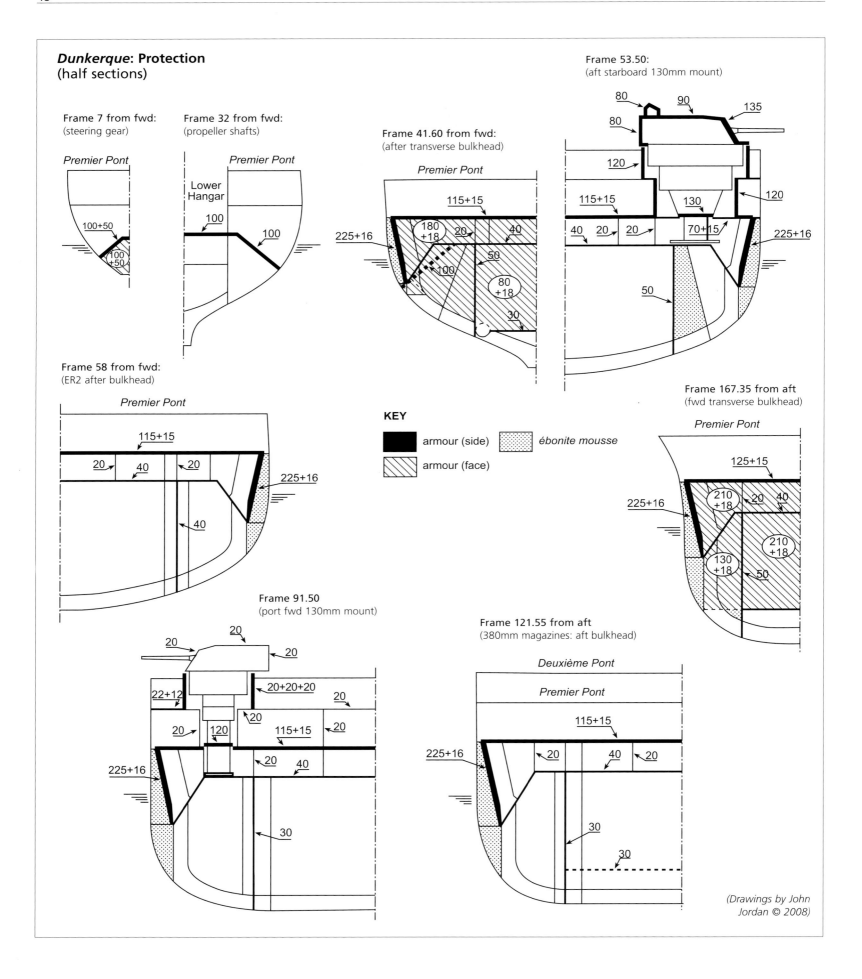

Dunkerque: Protection
(half sections)

Frame 7 from fwd:
(steering gear)

Frame 32 from fwd:
(propeller shafts)

Frame 41.60 from fwd:
(after transverse bulkhead)

Frame 53.50:
(aft starboard 130mm mount)

Frame 58 from fwd:
(ER2 after bulkhead)

Frame 167.35 from aft
(fwd transverse bulkhead)

Frame 91.50
(port fwd 130mm mount)

Frame 121.55 from aft
(380mm magazines: aft bulkhead)

KEY

armour (side)

armour (face)

ébonite mousse

(Drawings by John
Jordan © 2008)

The underwater protection system covered the same area as the main armoured belt. Abeam the magazines fore and aft the thickness of the torpedo bulkhead was increased first to 40mm then to 50mm to compensate for the reduction in depth, and the internal bulkhead enclosing the fuel bunkers was angled outboard (see section drawings) to increase the depth of the space between the fuel oil and the torpedo bulkheads, which was filled with *ébonite mousse*; abeam the forward 330mm magazines (frames 146.60 to 167.35) the fuel bunker was dispensed with altogether in favour of a single compartment with an *ébonite mousse* filling.

In order to provide protection against mines the floors of the 330mm and 130mm magazines were raised clear of the double bottom. These platform decks were of 30mm special steel, the plates being laid longitudinally beneath the magazines for the 130mm guns and for turret II, and transversely beneath the magazine of turret I. The plates were secured to one another by double welded butt-straps to provide the same level of watertight protection as for the torpedo bulkhead.

Hull protection in *Dunkerque* accounted for fully 27.2 per cent of normal displacement (28.2 per cent in *Strasbourg*), while the protection of the main and secondary armament accounted for a further 8.7 per cent (9.1 per cent in *Strasbourg*). The total of 36 per cent was claimed to be higher than in any earlier battleship.

PROPULSION

The propulsion machinery, in which the latest high-pressure boilers were combined with lightweight geared steam turbines, was remarkably compact for its power rating and accounted for only 7.2 per cent of displacement, with oil fuel (three quarters load at trials displacement) accounting for a further 9.3 per cent.

Six Indret small-tube boilers with superheating were paired in three boiler rooms: the first was located directly beneath the tower, which necessitated substantial angled uptake trunking above the armoured deck; the other two boiler rooms were adjacent to one another directly beneath the funnel. Between the forward and after boiler rooms was the forward engine room, housing the turbine sets for the two wing shafts. The after engine room, with the turbines for the centre shafts, was directly abaft the midships boiler rooms.

The 'unit machinery' layout, effectively dividing the machinery into two independent systems, was in line with the latest cruiser practice, and was considered essential for these relatively lightly-armoured ships to enable them to continue operating following action damage. *Dunkerque* was the first battleship to incorporate this layout; even the most recent British and American battleship designs, including the postwar

The damage control centre of *Strasbourg*, showing the main display panels and the counter-flooding controls. (*ECPAD*)

INDRET BOILERS: CHARACTERISTICS

Type	Small-tube vertical with superheaters
Pressure rating	27kg/cm^2
Temperature rating	350° C
Dimensions	
Length	5.325m
Width	6.500m
Height	5.335m
Burners	8 Hugé du Temple

MACHINERY TRIALS (SELECTED)[1]

Dunkerque

Date	Nature of trial	Displacement	SHP (Max.)	Speed (max.)
15.05.36	1H[2] acceptance	30,550t/30,150t[3]	94,170shp	29.40kts
28.05.36	8H max. power	30,870t/30,115t	114,050shp	30.37kts
	2H with forcing		135,585shp	31.06kts
09.10.36	2H at 80,000shp	30,585t/30,235t	81,540shp	28.30kts
	3H at max. power[4]		113,420shp	30.38kts

Strasbourg

Date	Nature of trial	Displacement	SHP (Max.)	Speed (max.)
21.06.38	1H acceptance	30,097t/29,724t	105,920shp	29.76kts
21.07.38	8H max. power trial	31,607t/30,959t	115,620shp	30.16kts
	2H with forcing		131,960shp	30.90kts
11.01.39	2H at 80,000shp	31,297t/31,103t	80,000shp	28.21kts
	1H at max. power		115,250shp	30.10kts

Notes:

[1] Trials not recorded here are preliminary, endurance/fuel consumption, and initial trials at 13,500shp/27,000shp/53,500shp following inspection of the machinery.

[2] H = hour.

[3] Displacement was measured at the start and end of the trial.

[4] Final trial followed dismantling and inspection of machinery.

Nelson class, had their boilers grouped together with the turbine machinery abaft the boiler rooms.

The Indret small-tube boilers operated at a pressure of 27kg/cm^2 (350° C). Those for *Dunkerque* were built by Indret, while those for *Strasbourg* were manufactured under licence by the shipbuilder, Penhoët. They were located side by side in each of the three boiler rooms: Nos 11 and 12 were in the forward boiler room, Nos 21 and 22 in the centre boiler room, and Nos 31 and 32 in the after boiler room.

There were four sets of Parsons geared turbines, each with its own independent condensers and lubrication pumps, and each driving a three-bladed propeller with a diameter of 4.2 metres (four-bladed 4.045 metres in *Strasbourg*). Each set comprised two HP (27kg/cm^2) turbines, one MP (8.5kg/cm^2) turbine, and LP forward and reverse turbines, which were linked in series with HP1 as a cruise turbine. The ships could steam 15.5 knots on two shafts and 20 knots on four at one quarter power, HP2 being engaged at between 0.34 and 0.5 maximum power. Designed horsepower was 107,000shp for 29.5 knots, but *Dunkerque* attained 31.06 knots with 135,585shp on trials (see table).

The maximum fuel load for peace-time cruising was 4500-5000 tonnes, but this figure was reduced to 3700 tonnes in wartime in order to maximise the effectiveness of the underwater protection system – filling the liquid loading compartments to the brim meant that instead of the fuel oil absorbing the pressure of the explosion it created additional pressure on the internal bulkheads. The lower figure gave an estimated range of 2450nm at 28.5 knots, 6300nm at 20 knots, and 7850nm at 15 knots.

The single counterbalanced rudder was normally driven by one of two main electric servo-motors. Each of the motors could be controlled from the conning tower, from the secondary conning position in turret II, or from the steering compartment itself. The rudder could in theory be turned from 0 degrees to a maximum angle of 32 degrees by either of the main motors, but there was a tendency for the rudder to jam above 25 degrees; it took twenty seconds to turn the rudder from 0 degrees to 25 degrees when steaming ahead. An emergency motor, which again could be controlled from either of the main conning positions, could turn the rudder 0 degrees to 15 degrees in one minute provided the speed of the ship was below 19 knots; at 24 knots, 7 degrees was the maximum rudder angle. The changeover from main to emergency motor took approximately one minute.

In the event of a complete power failure, the ship could be steered manually from the auxiliary steering compartment; there were six spoked hand wheels attached to a central shaft crewed by up to twenty-four men, the time taken to turn the rudder 0 degrees to 15 degrees was three minutes (19 knots maximum ship speed). It took approximately thirty seconds to change over from the emergency motor to manual steering.

To provide the ship with the necessary electrical power there were four turbo-generators each of 900kW distributed between the engine rooms; the turbo-generators were paired and could be coupled together. To provide power when alongside there were three diesel generators each of 400kW located low in the ship between the magazines for the main guns; these could produce 480kW on overload for one hour and 550kW for half an hour. Two emergency diesel genera-

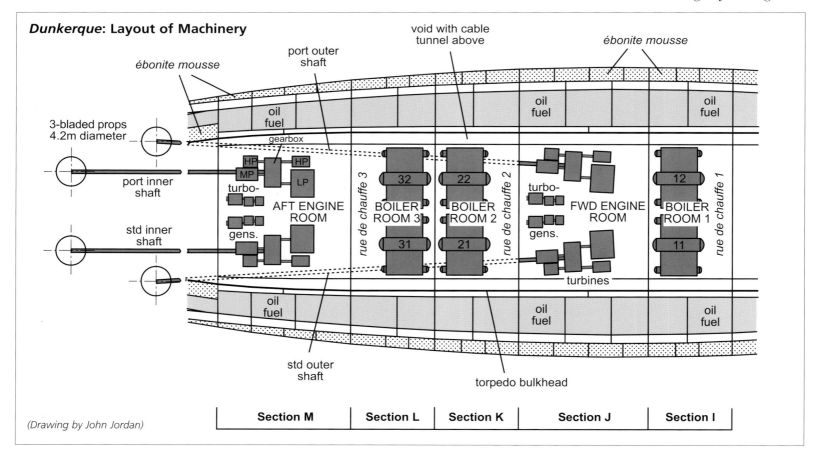

Dunkerque: Layout of Machinery

void with cable tunnel above

port outer shaft

ébonite mousse

ébonite mousse

3-bladed props 4.2m diameter

oil fuel

oil fuel

oil fuel

gearbox

port inner shaft

HP

HP

MP

LP

turbo-

32

22

turbo-

12

AFT ENGINE ROOM

BOILER ROOM 3

BOILER ROOM 2

FWD ENGINE ROOM

BOILER ROOM 1

std inner shaft

gens.

31

21

gens.

11

rue de chauffe 3

rue de chauffe 2

rue de chauffe 1

turbines

oil fuel

oil fuel

oil fuel

std outer shaft

torpedo bulkhead

(Drawing by John Jordan)

| Section M | Section L | Section K | Section J | Section I |

tors were mounted high in the ship directly beneath the tower; each was rated at 100kW (120kW for one hour). These figures were remarkable for the period and reflected the number of powered-operated gun and control systems installed in the ships. By way of comparison, the British battlecruiser *Hood* had a total generating capacity of 1400kW, while the *Nelson*s had a capacity of 1800kW.

AVIATION FACILITIES

Aviation facilities comprised a trainable catapult, a two-tier hangar with an internal lift, and a crane for recovery of the aircraft. The hangar had adjoining workshops for maintenance and repair of the aircraft, and there was a system of rails and an elevator set into the quarterdeck to raise the aircraft to the level of the catapult beam.

By the 1920s, aircraft were increasingly seen as important both for scouting in broad expanses of ocean for enemy fleet units or commerce raiders, and for spotting fall of shot at the longer ranges now anticipated for gunnery engagement. However, they were vulnerable to damage from the firing of the big guns, and the stowage of the exceptionally volatile aviation fuel close to their catapults was a potential fire hazard; ships generally stowed their aviation fuel in specially constructed tanks located in the bow or the stern, so for those with their catapults amidships the vulnera-

bility of the lengthy fuel lines was an additional safety issue. Ideally, the aircraft needed to be accommodated in a hangar when not in use to protect them from blast damage and corrosion, and the aviation fuel tanks needed to be isolated from the ship's structure, with inert gas (generally CO_2) being used both for pumping and to replace the fuel in the tanks and the fuel lines when emptied.

The aviation arrangements on *Dunkerque* and her battleship successors of the *Richelieu* class were particularly complete and well designed, and were a major advance on the extemporised facilities installed in the older battleships during the 1920s. The single trainable catapult was located on the centreline aft. It was 22 metres long, operated by compressed air and could launch a 3500kg aircraft at a speed of 103km/h. When atop the catapult on its launch trolley, the aircraft was almost 9 metres above the waterline, so it was not only well-protected against the blast of the guns but also from heavy seas.[6]

The upper bay of the two-tier hangar was at upper-

---

[6] The British battlecruiser *Hood*, which had a catapult fitted above her stern in 1929, experienced real difficulties in this respect because of the lack of freeboard aft. The catapult was frequently awash in the heavy seas experienced in the North Atlantic, and was removed in 1932.

The quarterdeck of *Strasbourg* in 1939, with a Loire 130 reconnaissance seaplane at the forward end of the single catapult. The shuttered door of the two-tier hangar is slightly raised. (*H Landais collection*)

LOIRE 130 SEAPLANE

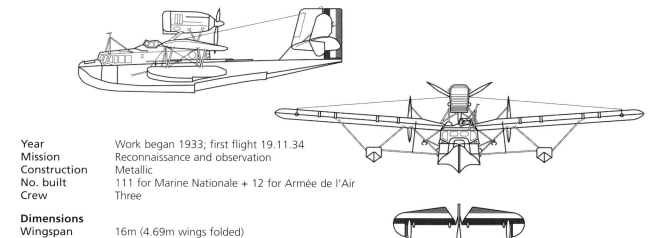

Year	Work began 1933; first flight 19.11.34
Mission	Reconnaissance and observation
Construction	Metallic
No. built	111 for Marine Nationale + 12 for Armée de l'Air
Crew	Three

Dimensions

Wingspan	16m (4.69m wings folded)
Length	11.25m
Height	3.85m

Engine

Type	Hispano-Suiza 12-cylinder ('X' config.) liquid-cooled
Power	720hp

Performance

Max. speed	210km/h at 2100m altitude
Cruise speed	165km/h at 1300m altitude
Climb	12 minutes to 3000m
Ceiling	6000m
Endurance	7h30 at 150km/h and 500m altitude

Weight

Empty	2050kg
At catapult load	3260kg
Max. load	3500kg

Armament

Machine guns	Two Darne 7.5mm (one in nose, one dorsal aft-facing)
Bombs	Two 75kg G2 type

(Drawing by John Jordan © 2008)

A Loire 130 seaplane is manoeuvred onto the catapult aboard *Dunkerque* during 1939. Initial trials of the catapult took place using a Gourdou-Leseurre Type 111 folding-wing floatplane; the first Loire 130 was embarked in April 1937. The Loire 130 was to have been complemented by the Loire 210 float fighter in 1940, but the latter aircraft experienced structural problems during its prolonged development and was abandoned following trials.

deck level; the lower bay extended down almost to the first platform deck. Inside the outer body of the hangar was a lift cage with two platforms, which, when in the lowered position, constituted the two floors of the hangar. The hangar could accommodate two large reconnaissance seaplanes of the Loire 130 type, which was under development when *Dunkerque* was being built. The first test flight was in November 1934 and the aircraft entered service with the Marine Nationale in 1937. The Loire 130 had a height of 3.85 metres, which effectively dictated the configuration of

AVIATION

Catapult

Length	22.085m
Width	1.394m
Height above deck	3.38m
Width of trolley	1.44m
Height of aircraft above deck	3.835m
Height above waterline	8.89m
Max. launch weight	3300kg
Max. launch speed (3500kg)	103km/h
Air pressure in accumulators	275kg
Air pressure in launch cylinder	78kg

the two-tier hangar. Had a double, side-by-side hangar of the type adopted for the contemporary light cruisers of the *La Galissonnière* class been fitted it would have impacted on the firing arcs of the wing 130mm quad turrets on after bearings. Adjacent to the hangar on the first platform deck there were aircraft workshops for repair and maintenance, and there was a magazine to stow the 75kg bombs carried by these aircraft abaft the 330mm magazines in the forward part of the ship.

The aircraft were moved to and from the hangar on their launch trolleys. Rails set into each of the hangar floors extended onto the quarterdeck and terminated atop an elevator set into the deck (see drawing Chapter 4); each aircraft was manhandled from the hangar to the elevator, where the wings were deployed. With the catapult trained aft (180 degrees) the elevator was raised until it was level with the top of the catapult; the aircraft, still on its launch trolley, was then positioned on the catapult using the catapult winch and prepared for launch. At the end of its

mission the Loire 130 landed on the surface of the sea and then taxied alongside. It was lifted aboard by a recovery crane with a capacity of 4.5 tonnes; wings were then folded and it was again stowed in the hangar. When not in use the articulated crane, which was mounted to port of the hangar, was stowed flat on the quarterdeck.

The aviation fuel was stowed in three tanks with a total capacity of 11,400 litres, located within the upper part of the stern. The fuel tanks incorporated a number of safety features, including the replacement of used fuel by an inert gas, and refrigeration and sprinkler systems. The fuel could quickly be pumped over the side by remote control if threatened by a fire in or on the quarterdeck.

APPEARANCE
General

From their entry into service until January 1940 (*Strasbourg*) and February 1940 (*Dunkerque*) both ships were painted light grey except for:

A Loire 130 on the catapult of *Strasbourg* in late 1940. Following the Armistice these aircraft carried a distinctive high-visibility livery for recognition purposes. The upper part of the hull was painted blue with a yellow stripe running along the sides of the fuselage; both the vertical and the horizontal tail surfaces were painted with alternate red and yellow stripes. (*H Landais collection*)

– rangefinders: painted white to reflect the heat, thereby minimising distortion;
– upper deck and superstructure deck: teak planking except for the forecastle forward of the first break-water, which was painted steel grey;
– funnel cowling, anchors and chains, waterline: black.

There were brief attempts at camouflage with the primary aim of disrupting enemy rangefinders. From April until September 1939, *Dunkerque* had a black spiral painted on her mainmast, and during October-November 1939, *Strasbourg* had a more elaborate scheme with two black rings around the mainmast together with two wide black vertical stripes on the after side of the tower. The trials appear to have been unsuccessful and the markings were painted out.

From early 1940, the light grey livery was replaced by a darker grey more appropriate to operations in the North Atlantic. From October 1940, following her

The forward quadruple 330mm turrets and the tower of *Dunkerque* viewed from the forecastle in late 1939. Note the tiered directors atop the tower: the lower director with its 12-metre RF for the main guns, the middle director with its 6-metre RF for the secondary guns in the anti-surface mode, and the upper director with its 5-metre RF for the latter in the anti-aircraft mode. (*ECPAD*)

return to Toulon, *Strasbourg* was again painted light grey.

Boats
The ships' boats had a black keel with light/dark grey upperworks. The interior of the launches was matt white. The smaller 9-metre motor boats had mahogany cabins, while those of the larger motor boats were grey. The only exceptions were those belonging to the admiral and the CO: the admiral's barge was painted white and had a mahogany cabin with a white roof; the CO's motor boat was royal blue, also with a mahogany cabin.

Markings
White bands denoting the *1ᵉ Division de ligne* (First Battle Division) were painted on the funnels in March 1939: a single band for the *Dunkerque* as division flagship, two for *Strasbourg*. These were painted out in August 1940 when the division was dissolved.

Tricolore identification bands were painted on turrets II (330mm) and VII (130mm, centreline) in November 1940 for *Strasbourg* and February 1942 for *Dunkerque*. The latter ship was still in her dark grey 'Atlantic' livery at this time.

MODIFICATIONS FOLLOWING COMPLETION: *DUNKERQUE*
15 August – 18 October 1937
– 90cm projector originally fitted on platform above admiral's bridge replaced by seventh 120cm model.
– screens at sides of admiral's bridge extended aft.
– roof of admiral's bridge extended forward by rounded platform with screen.
– concentration dials fitted.
– installation of rangefinders and radio antennae completed.
– six 13.2mm Hotchkiss CAQ installed on superstructure deck.

12 March – 2 May 1938
– funnel cowling fitted.
– all 37mm CAS Mle 1925 landed.
– two 13.2mm Hotchkiss CAQ installed on deckhouse abaft funnel.
(Ship officially entered service with the fleet on 1 September 1938.)

29 November 1938 – 27 February 1939
– four 37mm CAD Mle 1933 installed together with four one-metre RF.
– sides of navigation bridge modified to accommodate two 13.2mm Hotchkiss CAQ (moved from abeam tower on superstructure deck).
– modifications to deflectors around admiral's bridge.

July – August 1939
– fifth 37mm CAD Mle 1933 installed on cylindrical structure abaft mainmast.

4 January – 12 February 1940
– all four 47mm saluting guns disembarked.
– minor modifications to bridge wings and platforms.
– 12-metre stereo RF in lower director on tower replaced by 14-metre model.
– two forward 37mm CAD Mle 1933 moved from forecastle to forward end of shelter deck.

Strasbourg returning to Brest in 1939. The hull and superstructures are medium light grey; the funnel cap and anchors are picked out in black. The two white rings on her funnel mark her out as the second ship of the *1re Division de Ligne*. (ECPAD)

The funnel and after structure of *Strasbourg* are seen in close-up in this 1941 view. The lower of the two directors is the auxiliary director for the main armament and is fitted with an 8-metre RF; the upper director is for the secondary armament and has a 6-metre RF. Note that the arms of the rangefinders are painted white to reflect the heat and minimise distortion. (P Caresse collection)

MISCELLANEOUS EQUIPMENT

Anchors
Forward
Three 9-tonne Guérigny type anchors in hawsepipes with 82mm chains: a single anchor to port and to starboard and a third set into the bow.

Aft
A single centreline stern anchor as above; Guérigny-type 3-tonne anchor with 48mm chain.
(Also two 1.5-tonne kedge anchors.)

Boats
Dunkerque (as flagship)
Four 11-metre motor boats
Two 10.8-metre motor boats
Two 9-metre motor boats
Two 11-metre motor launches
Two 13-metre long boats
One 13-metre motor pinnace
Two 7-metre whalers
One 5-metre dinghy
Two 3.5-metre flat-bottom boats

The larger boats were stowed on crutches forward of and abeam the funnel. The remainder were grouped around the base of the tower on crutches or trolleys; those on trolleys could be moved aft on rails set into the deck to enable them to be handled by the two boat cranes, which were located at the after foot of the tower.

Strasbourg
From her completion until she became flagship of the Forces de Haute Mer (FHM), Strasbourg had two 11-metre motor launches in place of two of the 11-metre motor boats.

Radio Equipment
Transmitters	Power	Range
One medium-wave transmitter	6kW	1000nm
One medium-wave transmitter	2kW	200nm
One medium-wave transmitter	600W	300nm
Two short-wave transmitters	75W	300nm
One short-wave transmitter	2500W	2000nm
One short-wave transmitter	500W	1000nm
One emergency transmitter		100nm

Aerials
– main antenna: six horizontal strands strung between the signal yards of the forward tower and the forward arms of the mainmast starfish.
– 350mm diameter prism between port forward arm of mainmast starfish and after deckhouse.
– two 400mm prisms eight metres long on mainmast.

– black leather blast bags fitted to guns in main turrets.
(Last two measures undertaken as a result of experience in the North Atlantic, where green seas frequently washed over the forecastle because of insufficient buoyancy in the bow.)

February – November 1942: *modifications executed or planned*
The repair and reconstruction of Dunkerque following her repatriation from Mers el-Kebir was beset by material difficulties. A particular difficulty was that the French steel industry was located in the Occupied Zone. In the light of these problems the following measures were proposed by the STCN following liaison with the ship's CO:

– hull repairs, especially to sections E/F/G/H, which had been seriously damaged by British shellfire on 6 July 1940;
– rebuilding of the protection in these sections;
– repairs to the propulsion machinery, to include

collector No. 1 (badly corroded and unable to withstand $27kg/m^2$ pressure), the upper steam drum of boiler 21, and the turbine joints (at the same time advantage would be taken for a full overhaul of the remaining machinery);
– repair and replacement of the electrical cabling, which had given persistent problems due to the combustible nature of the insulation sheathing and the lack of watertightness of the bulkhead seals;
– removal of the remote power control (RPC) systems for the main and secondary guns, which had never worked properly;
– an increase in the number of light AA guns (it was envisaged that the aviation facilities would be removed and replaced by additional 37mm CAD Mle 1933);
– two of the three 130mm control stations to be repaired, and the two night-time directors to be refurbished;
– review of damage control arrangements, with particular consideration given to more powerful pumps fore and aft of the armoured citadel and remedying

the defective installation of the armoured machinery access panels;
- more powerful and robust converters for the training and elevation of the main and the secondary guns; also for the rudder, which had been subject to regular failures;
- consideration to be given to the reconstruction of the bow, which had insufficient freeboard and flare.

MODIFICATIONS FOLLOWING COMPLETION: STRASBOURG

15 September – 15 December 1938
- funnel cowling fitted.
- five 13.2mm Hotchkiss CAQ installed.

First half 1939
- four 37mm CAD Mle 1933 installed.

August 1939
- one 13.2mm Hotchkiss CAQ installed abaft the mainmast.

29 November 1939 – 9 January 1940
- screen fitted to searchlight platform on forward tower (this also provided protection for 13.2mm gun crew).
- degaussing cable fitted around upper part of hull to provide protection against German magnetic mines.

14 August – 11 September 1940
- light AA mountings atop after deckhouse protected against strafing by screen of hardened steel.

November – December 1940
- upper part of the tower modified to provide an admiral's bridge and equipped with four signal projectors. (From this time onwards *Strasbourg* became flagship of the *Forces de Haute Mer*.)
- waterproof leather seals between the turret and the barbette modified to improve watertightness; blast bags of canvas and black leather fitted and the original masks removed; these modifications were made initially to turret I and then to turret II.

31 January – 25 April 1942
- 5-metre RF atop the admiral's bridge landed, and all concentration dials removed.
- admiral's bridge and upper bridge fitted with deflectors similar to those in *Richelieu* and a steel screen fitted around the radio cabin located atop the after director.
- forward pair of 37mm CAD Mle 1933 relocated from the forecastle to the forward end of the shelter deck (as in *Dunkerque* 1940), and three 13.2mm CAS Browning MG installed (one on the quarterdeck, the other two forward on the shelter deck, slightly abaft the 37mm CAD).
- radar of French design and manufacture (*Détecteur Electro-Magnétique* or DEM) installed; the four small rectangular antennae were fitted atop the main yards projecting at 45 degrees from the tower; the starboard forward and port after antennae were for transmission, the opposite pair for reception; the ME 140 transmitter and MR 126[7] receiver were

developed and manufactured by the Sadir Company; trials were cut short by events, but early tests indicated a detection range against aircraft of 50km with a bearing accuracy of ±1 degree and a range accuracy of ±50 metres under favourable conditions.

A close-up of the funnel and tower of *Dunkerque* taken while the ship was at anchor in the *Rade-Abri* at Brest in 1937. The six searchlight projectors (two on the after side of the tower, four on the funnel platform – there was a seventh on the forward side of the tower) are particularly prominent, as are the remote control positions for the searchlights mounted on the sides of the tower at the same level. On the superstructure deck just abaft the funnel, two of the six 37mm single mountings Mle 1925 mounted as a temporary measure are at full elevation. Note the white-painted arms of the rangefinders in the directors for the main and secondary batteries. *(Collection H. Landais)*

---

[7] The 'E' was for *émetteur* = transmitter; the 'R' for *récepteur* = receiver.

CHAPTER 3

DUNKERQUE AND *STRASBOURG:* 1932-1942

D*UNKERQUE* WAS LAID DOWN AT THE Arsenal de Brest in December 1932. The main body of the hull was built in the Le Salou No. 4 dock, the only large building facility available in the dockyard. Even so, when launched on 2 October 1935 she was missing the first 17 metres of her bow, and this was subsequently fitted in one of the 250-metre Laninon graving docks. She was then towed to the fitting-out quay (the *Quai d'Armement*) for completion, commissioning in December of the following year. Trials and work-up of this new and complex ship would take a further twenty months. *Dunkerque* would finally enter service with the Atlantic Squadron (*Escadre de l'Atlantique*) on 1 September 1938.

TRIALS AND WORK-UP

Dunkerque went to sea for the first time at 1500 on 18 April 1936 to begin a long series of trials. Her super-structures were as yet incomplete and many of her secondary and light AA guns were not yet in place. After this preliminary trial, *Dunkerque* returned to Brest at 0800 on 20 April and moored at the Laninon fitting-out quay for an inspection of her machinery.

Further sea trials took place during 4-5 May. On 15 May, the ship attained 29.43 knots with 94,170shp.

The attainment of this first hurdle allowed *Dunkerque* to embark on her official trials, which took place from 22 May to 9 October. These were inter-rupted by two comparatively lengthy stays in the dock-yard. Final trials to check that all machinery was oper-ating correctly took place on 9 October, and *Dunkerque* then returned to the dockyard for further work.

Dunkerque was moved from the fitting-out quay to the anchorage at Brest, the *Rade-Abri*, on 3 February 1937 and weighed anchor at 0600 the following day

with Vice-Admiral Morris, Rear-Admiral Rivet of the Trials Commission and two senators of the Navy Commission on board. Firing trials with the secondary armament took place as planned off Ouessant and the ship returned to Brest that afternoon. However, trials of the main armament projected for 8 February had to be cancelled due to stormy weather. These finally took place during 11-14 February and were considered generally satisfactory.

The next gunnery trials, which took place on 3 March, were witnessed by Vice-Admiral Darlan, who was conducting a general inspection of Brest in his current role as Chief of the Naval General Staff. The following day *Dunkerque* was docked at Laninon, where she remained until 25 April. The Trials Commission, the *Commission Permanente des Essais* (CPE), was on board for the next round of gunnery trials, which took place off Ouessant 26 April. On 11 May, with the help of tugs from the port, *Dunkerque* calibrated her gyro-compasses in the anchorage.

On 15 May, Vice-Admiral Devin, *Préfet maritime de la 2e région*,[1] raised his flag on *Dunkerque*. As the newest and most prestigious unit, the battleship would repre-

---

[1] In the same way that France itself was divided into regions called *Départements* headed by a 'Prefect' appointed by the central civil government, the coasts of France and North Africa were divided up into four-five *Régions Maritimes* administered by a *Préfet Maritime*, a vice-admiral appointed by the Navy to be responsible for the naval dockyards, the training establishments and the coastal waters of that area. The First Region was centred on Cherbourg, the Second on Brest, the Third on Toulon and the Fourth on Bizerta (Algeria); in 1939, a Fifth Region based on Lorient would be created.

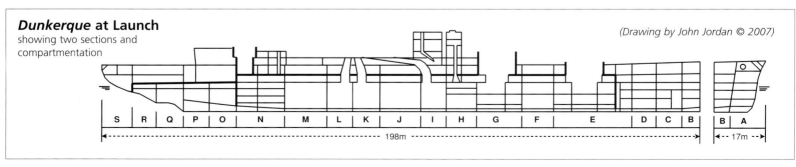

Dunkerque at Launch
showing two sections and compartmentation

(Drawing by John Jordan © 2007)

sent France at the Naval Review of 1937 due to take place at Spithead, Portsmouth, to mark the coronation of King George VI. *Dunkerque* left Brest on 17 May and returned on 23 May, having made a very strong impression at the review.

A further review took place on 27 May off the Isle of Sein, where the Mediterranean and Atlantic squadrons were assembled following combined exercises. On this occasion *Dunkerque* hosted not only Darlan, but Navy Minister Gasnier Duparc and several parliamentary representatives. While conducting the review the ship was accompanied by the *contre-torpilleur Milan*, with the press aboard.

Further sorties for gunnery trials continued virtually on a daily basis until mid-June, when *Dunkerque* was again moored at the fitting-out quay at Brest for work which lasted until the end of July. After further trials she was in the dockyard from 15 August until 14 October for final inspection of her machinery and other equipment. Gunnery trials off Ouessant then continued until the end of the year, by which time it had become apparent that both the main and secondary guns were over-complex and prone to breakdown.

The crew of *Dunkerque* spent the first part of January 1938 preparing for her 'endurance cruise' (TLD – see table for explanation), which would take her to the French West Indies and to Dakar in West Africa. The ship left Brest at 1500 on 20 January and arrived at Fort-de-France on 31 January, remaining there until 4 February. She then proceeded to the Saintes Islands. She left on 15 February, pausing for a brief port call at Fort-de-France on 16 February, and then headed east for Senegal. After a short stay in the Bay of Rufisque during 22-25 February, she entered the port of Dakar on 25 February. She left for France on 1 March, and arrived back in Brest on 6

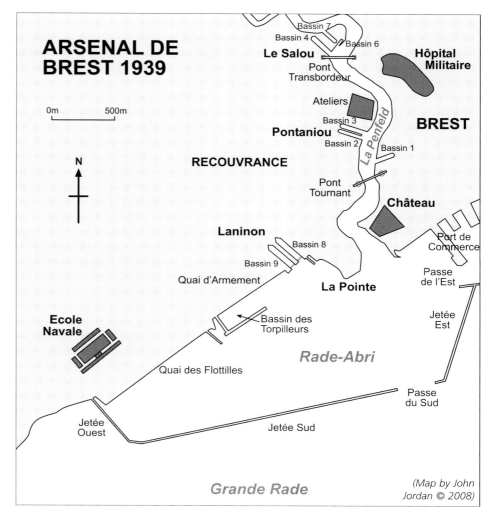

CONSTRUCTION DATES

Name	Estimates	Builder	Laid down	Launch	Trials	Acc. trials	Commiss'd	Completion	In Service
Dunkerque	1931	Arsenal de Brest	24.12.32	02.10.35	01.02.36	15.05.36	31.12.36	09.06.38	01.09.38
Strasbourg	1934	Ateliers et Chantiers de Saint-Nazaire (Penhoët)	25.11.34	12.12.36	02.04.38	21.06.38	15.09.38	06.04.39	24.04.39

Notes:

The different stages of construction of warships were defined by decrees published in the *Bulletin Officiel* (BO). The baseline publication was that of 17 June 1925, subsequently modified on 19 August 1929, 10 July 1933 and 13 March 1937. An explanation follows:

Mise sur cale (laying down): date first steel laid on building way (prefabrication of material will normally have already begun).

Lancement (launch): date of launch – or floating out; followed by *achèvement* (fitting out).

Armement pour essais (trials): initial trials of machinery, both alongside and at sea; command of the ship at this point passes from the builder to the Navy and its nominated CO.

Présentation en recette (acceptance trials): the official acceptance trials; the turbines and gearing, together with other items of auxiliary machinery are partially dismantled towards the end of this stage and all components inspected (*les démontages*).

Armement définitif (commissioned): from this date the vessel is fully provisioned and receives her full complement; this is effected during the period of inspection of the machinery and before reassembly prior to the final machinery trials (*les essais de bon fonctionnement*), conducted to ensure that all machinery is in fully working order. (After 13 March 1937 this would become the completion date – *date d'achèvement* – in order to conform to the provisions of the London Treaty of 25 March 1936.)

Clôture de l'armement (completion): follows successful completion of the *essais de bon fonctionnement*; it is generally marked by a visit from the Trials Commission, the *Commission supérieure d'armement*. (Before 10 July 1933, this was also the official completion date – see above.) The *Clôture de l'armement* was followed by an endurance cruise, which had to be for a minimum of four days for large surface warships, called the *traversée de longue durée* (TLD).

Admission au service actif (in service): the subject of an official pronouncement by the Navy Minister, this date often coincides with the attachment of the ship to a specific squadron/division/flotilla. (Before 10 July 1933, the date of 'entry into service' was that of the *Clôture de l'armement*; between 10 July 1933 and 13 March 1937 it was the date of *Armement définitif*; from 13 March 1937 it became a date in its own right.)

Source: Unpublished study by Jean Moulin, dated 14 February 1999.

A stern quarter view of *Dunkerque* at anchor taken in 1937. (*H Landais collection*)

March; the cruise had lasted almost seven weeks.

Following gunnery trials on 11 March, *Dunkerque* entered dry dock for machinery inspection following her endurance cruise. This work was completed at the beginning of May, and from 3 May *Dunkerque* was again conducting gunnery trials both off Brest and in the Morgat area. There was a visit to Dunkirk (the town in northern France to which she was affiliated) during 1-4 July, followed by a visit to Saint Vaast-La-Hougue on the Cotentin Peninsula on 4-5 July. She returned to Brest the following day.

Dunkerque again left Brest, on 16 July, this time for Boulogne, where King George VI and the Queen were making an official visit. A squadron of French warships was assembled for the occasion, commanded by the local *Préfet maritime*, Vice-Admiral Rivet, in the torpedo-boat *Branlebas*. Besides *Dunkerque*, the 4th Cruiser Division (*Georges Leygues*, *Montcalm* and *Gloire*) was present, together with the *Emile Bertin* and

the 10th DCT[2] (*Le Fantasque*, *L'Audacieux* and *Le Terrible*). *Dunkerque* left Boulogne on 22 July for Calais, where she anchored the same day ready to salute the departure of the British Royal Family.

Finally, on 1 September 1938, *Dunkerque* officially entered service and became flagship of the Atlantic Squadron, flying the flag of C-in-C Vice-Admiral Gensoul. The composition of the Atlantic Squadron can be seen in the accompanying table.

STRASBOURG

Strasbourg was laid down at Ateliers & Chantiers de Saint-Nazaire (Penhoët) in November 1934, almost two years after her sister. The No. 1 slipway of the private yard, which two years previously had launched the 313-metre liner *Normandie*, was large enough to accommodate the full length of the hull.

---
[2] DCT – *Division de contre-torpilleurs.*

Dunkerque at anchor off Spithead, Portsmouth, in May 1937, on the occasion of the Naval Review that marked the coronation of King George VI.

The French Navy Minister, Gasnier Duparc, reviews the combined French Atlantic and Mediterranean squadrons from *Dunkerque* off Ile de Sein on 27 May 1937.
(*P du Cheyron collection*)

Launched in December 1936, *Strasbourg* was towed to the fitting-out quay for completion. She left St. Nazaire for Brest on 15 June 1938, conducting a short speed trial en route and arriving the following day. She was at sea again on 21 June, the first day of her official acceptance trials, returning to be docked the following day for further fitting-out work which was completed on 30 June.

Sea trials continued throughout July, followed by gunnery trials off Ouessant on 24-25 August. Commissioning took place on 15 September. On the same day, the ship was again docked for inspection of the machinery, and following this work resumed her sea trials on 15 December. Gunnery trials and work-up followed with a view to speeding her entry into

service in a rapidly deteriorating international situation. *Strasbourg* entered service with the Atlantic Fleet (formerly 'Squadron') on 24 April 1939, barely eight months after her sistership *Dunkerque*; together the two ships now formed the First Battle Division (*1re Division de ligne* or 1re DL).

PREWAR SERVICE

Following her entry into service on 1 September 1938, *Dunkerque* continued her individual work-up programme but now also participated in exercises with other ships of the Atlantic Squadron. There were exercises during 18-20 October with the carrier *Béarn*, the torpedo boats *Boulonnais* and *Foudroyant* and the sloop *Somme* off the coast of Brittany. *Dunkerque* again

Dunkerque in the *Rade-Abri* at Brest with elements of the Atlantic and Mediterranean squadrons in spring 1937. *Dunkerque* is on the left with the cruiser *Algérie* in the centre; other cruisers can be seen moored to the jetty on the right of the picture.

Above:
Strasbourg in the early stages of fitting out at the Penhoët shipyard, St. Nazaire. (*C Picard collection*)

Left:
Embarkation of one of the 330mm guns during fitting out. (*C Picard collection*)

Below:
Strasbourg alongside in the Bassin de Penhoët at St. Nazaire. She is now virtually complete and ready for sea trials. (*C Picard collection*)

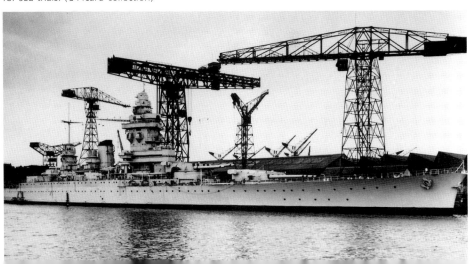

ESCADRE DE L'ATLANTIQUE, 1 SEPTEMBER 1938

Flagship: *Dunkerque* (VA Gensoul)

2e Division de ligne	4e Division de croiseurs	Aircraft-carrier: *Béarn*
Lorraine (CA Vallée)	*Georges Leygues*	
Provence	(CA Godfroy)	
Bretagne	*Montcalm*	
	Gloire	

2e Escadre légère: *Mogador* (CA Lacroix)[1]

8e Division de contre-torpilleurs:	10e Division de contre-torpilleurs:	Note:
L'Indomptable	*Le Fantasque*	[1] Problems with *Mogador* were to delay her arrival from Lorient until 6 November 1938; in the interim VA Lacroix flew his flag in *L'Audacieux*.
Le Malin	*L'Audacieux*	
Le Triomphant	*Le Terrible*	

2e Flottille de torpilleurs: *Bison* (CA Brohan)

2e Division de torpilleurs:	4e Division de torpilleurs:	5e Division de torpilleurs:
Fougueux	*Bourrasque*	*Brestois*
Frondeur	*Orage*	*Foudroyant*
L'Adroit	*Ouragan*	*Boulonnais*

6e Division de torpilleurs:	7e Division de torpilleurs:	8e Division de torpilleurs:
Cyclone	*Tramontane*	*Bordelais*
Siroco	*Typhon*	*Trombe*
Mistral	*Tornade*	*L'Alcyon*

2e Flottille de sous-marins: *Jules Verne* (CA Cayol)

Surcouf	2e Escadrille:	4e Escadrille:
	2e, 4e and 6e Divisions de sous-marins (*1500 tonnes*)	12e, 14e, and 16e Divisions de sous-marins (*600 tonnes*)

Notes:
VAE	*Vice-amiral d'escadre*	DCT	*Division de contre-torpilleurs*
CA	*Contre-amiral*	DT	*Division de torpilleurs*
DL	*Division de ligne*	ESM	*Escadrille de sous-marins*
DC	*Division de croiseurs*	DSM	*Division de sous-marins*

left Brest on 8 November in company with the *Béarn* and the cruisers of the 4th Cruiser Division and was at Cherbourg the following day for celebrations marking the 20th anniversary of the Armistice of 1918. Group exercises followed, and the ship returned to Brest on 17 November. After gunnery practice against the hulk of the old battleship *Voltaire*, *Dunkerque* was moored at the fitting-out quay at Brest for further work which lasted until 27 February 1939.

On 28 February, *Dunkerque* sailed with the Atlantic Squadron for exercises off the south coast of Brittany. She was then docked from 17 March to 3 April for further modifications. This was followed by extensive gunnery practice, again south of Brittany, and the ship returned to Brest on 7 April.

The crisis in the Sudetenland then came to a head and led the French Admiralty to detach *Dunkerque* and other elements of the Atlantic Squadron to the Azores during 14-16 April to cover the return from the French West Indies of the training cruiser *Jeanne d'Arc*. This

Overhead of *Dunkerque* underway during 1939.

measure was dictated by the presence off the coasts of Spain of a large German squadron led by the *Panzerschiff Graf Spee*.[3] *Dunkerque* made a further sortie with elements of the Atlantic Squadron for exercises during 25-29 April.

Dunkerque's sister, *Strasbourg*, had officially joined

[3] The squadron, making an official visit to Spain following the end of the Civil War, comprised *Graf Spee* (flag of the German C-in-C Admiral Boehm), the light cruisers *Köln*, *Leipzig* and *Nürnberg*, and seven destroyers, as well as U-boats and support ships.

THE *FORCE DE RAID*, 1 OCTOBER 1939

1re Escadre: (VAE Gensoul)

1re Division de ligne	4e Division de croiseurs
Dunkerque (VAE Gensoul)	Georges Leygues
Strasbourg	(CA Godfroy)
	Montcalm
	Gloire

2e Escadre légère
(CA Lacroix)

6e Division de contre-torpilleurs	8e Division de contre-torpilleurs	10e Division de contre-torpilleurs
Mogador (CA Lacroix)	L'Indomptable	Le Fantasque
Volta	Le Malin	L'Audacieux
	Le Triomphant	Le Terrible

the Atlantic Squadron on 24 April, and the two ships sortied together for the first time on 1 May, arriving in Lisbon (Portugal) on 3 May for commemorations of the anniversary of the discovery of Brazil by the explorer Alvares Cabral. They left the Portuguese capital the following day and re-entered Brest on 7 May, where they entertained a visiting British squadron.

On 23 May, the future *Force de Raid* (the 1st DL, the 4th DC and the 2nd EL) left Brest for exercises off the British coast. The two battleships visited Liverpool (25-30 May), Oban (31 May-4 June), Staffa (4 June), Loch Ewe (5-7 June), Scapa Flow (8 June), Rosyth (9-14 June), and Le Havre (16-20 June), returning to Brest on 21 June. There were further exercises off the coast of Brittany during July and early August.

By the time that war was declared on 3 September, both ships were considered to be fully worked up and combat-ready. There had been extensive liaison with the British Admiralty during August, and the lines of responsibility of the respective fleets had been drawn. At a meeting that took place in Portsmouth on 8 August the French took primary responsibility for protecting the Allied trade routes from the Gulf of Guinea to the Channel, including the waters off the North African and Portuguese coasts and the Bay of Biscay. Protection of these trade routes was to be ensured on the one hand by the escort of convoys – under the *Forces Maritimes de l'Ouest* (FMO) command – and, on the other hand, by the active pursuit and destruction of enemy surface raiders operating in the zone. For the latter role the French formed the *Force de Raid*, an élite force based on Brest and comprising the two fast battleships of the

Left:
Dunkerque with the flag of
VAE Gensoul, commander of
the Atlantic Squadron, at the
masthead. The photo almost
certainly dates from the
Autumn of 1938, when the
ship entered service. She does
not as yet have the single
white funnel band which
would later mark her out as
the lead ship of the *1re
Division de ligne*; this was
painted in March 1939,
shortly before the entry into
service of her sister
Strasbourg. (*ECPAD*)

Right:
Strasbourg moored with her
sister *Dunkerque* in the
background during a visit to a
port on the Atlantic coast
during 1939.
(*ECPAD Marine 80*)

Below:
Dunkerque at anchor during
1939. (*H Landais collection*)

Dunkerque class, three modern light cruisers of the 7600-tonne type, and the eight most modern and powerful *contre-torpilleurs* of the *Le Fantasque* and *Mogador* classes (see table); the latter ships were all capable of 35 knots in formation. The *Force de Raid* was to operate east of a line running from Ouessant through the Azores to the Cape Verde Islands.

Anti-aircraft firing practice aboard *Dunkerque* using the port-side 130mm guns during 1939. The 130mm quad proved less successful than hoped. The fixed ammunition was on the light side for the anti-destroyer role, while the complex reloading mechanism was fragile and the training speed of the heavily armoured turret was too slow to be effective against modern high-performance aircraft. (*H Landais collection*)

HUNTING THE GERMAN RAIDERS 1939-40

On the eve of the outbreak of war, the French were informed by the British that German *Panzerschiffe* had sailed for the Atlantic and that contact had since been lost. Fearing an attack on shipping off West Africa, the French Admiralty mobilised the *Force de Raid*, which sailed from Brest at 2000 on 2 September, escorted into open waters by the 2nd and the 5th Torpedo-boat Divisions (DT). When informed that the German ships were still in the North Sea, Gensoul ordered the squadron to return to Brest after picking up the liner *Flandre*, which was at Horta in the Azores; the captain of the latter ship feared the presence of U-boats and was happy to have such a powerful escort available in the area. The *Force de Raid* returned to Brest on 6 September, and was escorted in by the 2nd and 4th DT.

At the beginning of hostilities, the French and British Admiralties created hunting groups charged with seeking out and destroying German surface raiders. From this point *Dunkerque* and *Strasbourg* often operated separately, generally in conjunction with units of the Royal Navy. *Strasbourg*, with half of the *Force de Raid*, was to be allocated to a new tactical grouping designated Force X, which was also to comprise the cruisers *Algérie* and *Dupleix*, detached from the Mediterranean Fleet, and the British carrier *Hermes*, under the command of VAE[4] Duplat in the *Algérie*. *Strasbourg* left Brest on 7 October with *Volta* and the 10th DCT. The French ships joined up with *Hermes* off Camaret the same day, and the combined

Aerial view of *Dunkerque*, possibly taken during the visit of the two ships to Liverpool during late May 1939. The single white funnel band marks her out as the lead ship of the 1re *Division de Ligne*. (*H Landais collection*)

force then headed south to rendezvous with *Algérie* and *Dupleix* off Casablanca. Now at its full strength,[5] Force X arrived at Dakar, its future base, on 14 October.

From 23 to 29 October, Force X undertook a sweep between Dakar and a point 5°N 34°W, capturing the German cargo ship *Santa Fe* on 25 October. A second sortie took place during 7-13 November, the group being joined by the flying boat *Mouneyrès* (Latécoère 302 type) of E4 Squadron. The patrol zone was to the west of the Cape Verde islands. During a search operation, four German nationals were found aboard the Belgian liner *Piriapolis* and taken prisoner.

On 21 November, having been relieved by other units, *Strasbourg*, *Algérie* and the 10th DCT left Dakar for metropolitan France. Shortly before *Strasbourg* and the 10th DCT were due to enter Brest, the port was closed following an air alert, as a result of which it was feared that mines had been laid in the harbour approaches. The ships were diverted to Quiberon, entering Brest only at midday on 29 November after the 'all-clear' had been given.

Meanwhile, on 22 October, *Dunkerque* left Brest accompanied by the cruisers *Georges Leygues* and *Montcalm* and the 8th DCT to escort convoy KJ3 from Kingston in Jamaica on the home leg of its Atlantic crossing, returning on 25 October. Exactly one month later, *Dunkerque*, with the same two cruisers but with the newly reunited 6th DCT, joined the British battlecruiser HMS *Hood* for a sweep that aimed to intercept the German *Scharnhorst* and *Gneisenau*, which had just sunk the armed merchant cruiser *Rawalpindi* south of Iceland. The French ships joined up with *Hood* off the south coast of Ireland, the combined force being under the command of Admiral Gensoul, and then headed north. As they were approaching Iceland, a huge storm blew up. *Dunkerque* took a battering, her bow being constantly submerged in the heavy seas, and the ship was forced to reduce to 10 knots to avoid further damage.[6] By this time, it was clear that the enemy had reversed course, and the French ships returned to Brest on 3 December. *Dunkerque* was immediately docked for repairs; the combination of the lack of freeboard forward and the fine lines and light construction of the bow was from this moment recog-

nised as a serious design defect that would be difficult to remedy and would result in regular damage in heavy weather.

In the last sortie of 1939, *Dunkerque*, accompanied by the cruiser *Gloire*, left for Canada at 1715 on 11 December loaded with cases of gold from the Bank of France. For the first two days, escort was provided by *contre-torpilleurs* of the 2nd EL (*Mogador*, *Volta*, *Le Triomphant*, *Le Terrible*) plus *Valmy* (FMO). The weather was unusually clement for the time of year, permitting a sustained speed of 18 knots, which was increased to 20 knots once the escort was dismissed. *Dunkerque* and *Gloire* entered Halifax at 1330 GMT on 17 December. On their return they bolstered the escort of convoy TC2, comprising seven transports with Canadian troops aboard and the battleship HMS *Revenge*. They left Halifax on 22 December and were met by the 6th and 10th DCT from Belfast on 29 December. The French ships then left the convoy and returned to Brest at 1530 on the following day. *Dunkerque* was again docked from 4 January to 6 February for repairs, subsequently being moved to the fitting-out quay for further modifications, which were completed on 12 February. From 21 February to 23 March, she conducted individual and group exercises off the south coast of Brittany. In some of these exercises she was joined by her sistership, which was otherwise engaged in convoy escort duties.

NORWAY AND THE MEDITERRANEAN APRIL-JUNE 1940

By early spring 1940, the threat from German surface raiders had diminished with the destruction of *Graf Spee*. However, the situation in the Mediterranean was becoming more precarious, and it was feared that Italy

Strasbourg during a firing practice. The 330mm quad mounting was effectively two half-turrets, and it was standard practice to fire the pair of guns in each half-turret together, as illustrated in the photo. This facilitated replenishment and reloading and maximised rate of fire, but resulted in dispersion problems due to the close proximity of the shells as they left the barrels. (*ECPAD*)

---

4 VAE – *Vice-amiral d'escadre*. Vice-Admiral was the highest rank in the sea-going Navy; a 'Squadron Vice-Admiral' commanded either a Fleet, or a Squadron (*escadre*) within a fleet. In September 1940 VAE Duplat commanded the 3e Escadre of the Mediterranean Fleet, the 'fast' squadron with two divisions of heavy cruisers and four divisions of *contre-torpilleurs*. The 'heavy' squadron of the Mediterranean Fleet, comprising the older battleships and the 1st Torpedo-boat Flotilla, was commanded by VAE Ollive. The Italian *Regia Marina* was organised in similar fashion.

5 With the exception of *Volta*, which had to return to Brest with machinery problems.

6 An eyewitness account of one of the gunners, Guillaume Pailler, published in Le Hir, *Mers el-Kébir & Catapult: les marins de l'oubli*, Marines 2005, states:

At the bow the anchor had been forced through the hull plating. The turrets were full of water, we had had to reduce our speed in the heavy seas. When we returned from our mission, the bow was reinforced with a second breakwater.

The *1ʳᵉ Division de Ligne* in the anchorage at Mers el-Kebir in June 1940. *Strasbourg* (two white funnel bands) is the ship nearest the camera. Note that both ships have retained their 'Atlantic' colour scheme.

might soon enter the war on the side of Hitler's Germany. It was therefore decided to despatch the *Force de Raid* to Mers el-Kebir and Algiers, from which ports it could operate against either the *Regia Marina* in the western Mediterranean or German raiders in the Atlantic.

The bulk of the *Force de Raid* (the 1st DL with *Dunkerque* and *Strasbourg*, the 4th DC with *Gloire* and *Montcalm* and the 2nd EL with *Mogador*,

L'*Indomptable*, *Le Malin*, *Le Triomphant* and *Le Terrible*) left Brest at 1600 on 2 April. It arrived at Mers el-Kebir at 1900 on 5 April, but its stay was brief because it was subsequently decided that a joint operation with the British would be mounted against Norway in order to block German imports of iron ore. The *Force de Raid*, minus *Le Terrible*, which was immobilised with machinery problems, returned to Brest 9-12 April and prepared to escort convoys of troops and supplies to Norwegian waters.

However, with the situation in the Mediterranean more menacing by the day, the *Force de Raid* was again despatched to Mers el-Kebir. The flagship *Dunkerque* left Brest at 1600 on 24 April, followed by *Strasbourg*, *Gloire*, *Georges Leygues*, *Mogador*, *Le Terrible* and *L'Audacieux*; the cruiser *Montcalm* and the 8th DCT remained behind (*Montcalm* replaced *Emile Bertin*, which had been damaged by a German bomb on 19 April) to take part in the Norwegian operation. The main force arrived at Mers el-Kebir at 1600 on 27 April.

The two battleships, accompanied by the two cruisers of the 4th DC and the Mediterranean-based cruisers *Jean de Vienne* and *La Galissonnière* (3rd DC) sortied for exercises on 9 May, being joined in the evening by *Mogador*, *L'Audacieux* and *Le Terrible*. They returned to harbour the following day.

On 10 June 1940, Italy entered the war. The *Force de Raid* was by this time at full strength, and had been joined in the western Mediterranean by the Second Squadron of the Mediterranean Fleet, comprising the elderly battleships *Bretagne* and *Provence* and the 4th DCT (*Tigre*, *Panthère* and *Lynx*), and by the 3rd DC (*Marseillaise*, *Jean de Vienne* and *La Galissonnière*). The big ships were at Mers el-Kebir, while most of the cruisers and *contre-torpilleurs* were at Oran and Algiers.

The Battle of France, now entering its decisive phase, must have seemed far away. Here was the mass of the French Fleet, trained and ready for action, preparing to take on the Italian *Regia Marina*. It was at this moment that information was received suggesting

THE *FLOTTE DE L'ATLANTIQUE* 11 JUNE 1940

1ère Escadre (VAE Gensoul)
Force de Raid

1ère DL (VAE Gensoul)	3e DC (CA Marquis)	4e DC (CA Bourragué)
Dunkerque (fl)	*Marseillaise* (fl)	*Georges Leygues* (fl)
Strasbourg	*Jean de Vienne*	*Montcalm*
	La Galissonnière	*Gloire*

2e Escadre Légère (CA Lacroix)

6e DCT	8e DCT	10e DCT
Mogador (fl)	*L'Indomptable*	*Le Fantasque*
Volta	*Le Malin*	*L'Audacieux*
		Le Terrible

2e Escadre

2e DL (CA Bouxin)	4e DCT
Provence (fl)	*Tigre*
Bretagne	*Lynx*

Tactical Groups

Groupe *Dunkerque*	Groupe *Provence*	Groupe *Marseillaise*	Groupe *G Leygues*
1ère DL	2e DL	3e DC	4e DC
+	+	+	+
6e DCT	4e DCT	8e DCT	10e DCT

that the *Kriegsmarine* was about to force the Strait of Gibraltar with a force of battleships with a view to reinforcing the Italians. A general sortie by the French ships took place on 12 June, the fleet of no fewer than twenty-three major warships assembling south of Cartagena at dawn on 13 June and heading west to intercept the German ships at a speed of 18 knots. Pulses quickened when at 0540 a reconnaissance aircraft reported a large force of warships to the south-west heading for Gibraltar. This could only be an Italian squadron attempting to rendezvous with the German units, and speed was increased to 24 knots (the older battleships excepted) in order to make the interception. However, disappointment soon followed when at 0600, following a more careful study of relative positions, it was concluded that it was the French fleet that had been spotted by the aircraft. The fleet had effectively been chasing its own shadow. After receiving confirmation that there were no other ships in the operational zone, the ships returned to their respective bases, again reducing speed to 18 knots. This phantom battle would subsequently be christened 'la bataille de l'armoire à glace' (lit. 'Battle of the Mirror Wardrobe'). It would be the last war sortie by *Dunkerque* and *Strasbourg*.

OPERATION 'CATAPULT'

The background to Operation 'Catapult' is confused and controversial. It took place in the wake of the catastrophic – and unexpected – defeat of the French Army on land, the occupation of much of France by the Germans, and a Franco-German Armistice the terms of which were still being interpreted, negotiated and firmed up long after the ink had dried on the signatures appended to it on 22 June. In late March, the French Prime Minister, Paul Reynaud, with the chiefs of the French armed forces as his witnesses, had promised that France would fight to the end alongside her British allies and would not sue for a separate peace. However, when the scale of the French defeat on land became apparent the British RAF, anticipating a total French military collapse, successfully resisted appeals to release the twenty-five fighter squadrons earmarked for the defence of Britain to support what remained of the French armies. There was therefore a heartfelt sense of betrayal in both camps, leading inevitably to a lack of mutual trust.

During this turbulent period, Admiral of the Fleet Darlan made repeated assurances to the British by private communiqué that (i) the French Fleet would under no circumstances be 'handed over' to the Germans and that, (ii) any attempt by the Germans to seize French ships by force would be met by the implementation of sabotage measures already in place. However, British trust in Darlan was weakened once he agreed to join the new Pétain administration. Although a French naval delegation headed by Vice-Admiral (VAE) Odend'hal remained in the UK, communications with the French Admiralty were difficult because the French government was continually in transit, having left first Paris and then Bordeaux for the provincial town of Vichy.

The terms of the Armistice were available to the British War Cabinet from 23 June. For Churchill, Alexander (First Lord of the Admiralty) and Admiral Pound (First Sea Lord) the key clause was Article 8, which stated:

An overhead view of *Dunkerque* and *Strasbourg* taken at the same time. Note the Loire 130 seaplane on *Dunkerque*'s catapult, which is trained ready for launch.

The French fleet, with the exception of that part left at the disposition of the Government to safeguard French interests in its colonial empire, will be assembled *in ports to be determined* and is to be demobilised and disarmed under German or Italian *supervision*. The designation of these ports will be made *according to the ships' home ports in peacetime*. The German Government solemnly declares that it has no intention to use during the war, for its own purposes, that part of the French fleet stationed in German-occupied ports, with the exception of the *units necessary for coastal patrol and minesweeping*. It further declares solemnly and expressly that it has no intention of making claims on the French fleet after the war ends. With the exception of that part of the French fleet, yet to be determined, which is to be tasked with safeguarding French interests in her colonial empire, *all warships currently outside her territorial waters must be recalled to France.* (The translation and the italics are the authors'; there was of course no 'official' English version.)

Although most of the key points were clear, there remained ambiguities which were to be resolved by further negotiation. In particular the phrase 'according to the ships' home ports in peacetime', which the Germans saw as the base line for negotiation, conflicts with the phrase 'in ports to be determined', which reflects French concerns regarding the return of ships to ports in Occupied France.

A crucial ambiguity lay in the use of the French word *contrôle*, which was (wilfully?) mistranslated. Pound, Churchill and the English press[7] interpreted it as meaning that the ships would be under German and Italian 'control' – a key point in the subsequent discussions by the British War Cabinet – whereas the context makes it clear that the word refers to the process by

---

[7] Cf. *The Times*, 24 June: 'The French Fleet is to be concentrated in ports to be indicated and demobilized and disarmed under the *control* of Italy and Germany' (authors' italics).

which the deactivation of the ships would be verified and monitored, and it is therefore more appropriately translated as 'supervision'.[8] In agreeing this clause the French were accepting that German and Italian officials would be charged with monitoring the state of readiness of French ships and any proposed deployment of the few vessels permitted to remain active for exercises, the rotation of those deployed overseas, etc. Indeed, this would be one of the primary functions of the Italo-German Armistice Commission over the next two and a half years. However, the idea that the Germans and Italians would exercise 'control' over the modern, powerful French fleet was an emotive concept that Churchill readily grasped and used for his own purposes. Churchill became obsessed by the idea that once the fleet was safely repatriated to metropolitan France the Germans would seize the ships by force, thereby threatening the dominance of the Royal Navy in the European theatre. And when preparing the House of Commons for the aggressive pre-emptive action on which the War Cabinet had effectively already decided, Churchill of course did not fail to draw attention to Hitler's past record with regard to formal declarations of intent and treaty guarantees.

With the benefit of hindsight it is clear that Churchill and the British War Cabinet misread the situation. There is little evidence that Hitler was interested in the French fleet except insofar as he was particularly anxious that it should not fall into the hands of the British. He was quite content to have occupied the Atlantic seaboard of France, which together with the recent acquisition of Norway presented an exceptional opportunity for the growing fleet of German U-boats, to which would be added a powerful flotilla of Italian ocean-going submarines. The *Kriegsmarine* was already experiencing manning problems due to its rapid expansion from what in 1935 had been a comparatively low base. The acquisition of the French fleet, numerically the fourth largest in the world, would have imposed immense strains on manpower and training, and these would have been further exacerbated by the serious logistic problems inherent in operating ships with different calibre guns, different fire control equipment, and different machinery. Whilst these problems could be overcome relatively easily for small patrol craft, for a large and complex piece of machinery such as a battleship they were of a totally different order. Pound's estimate that following a German seizure of *Dunkerque* and *Strasbourg* the ships could be fully operational within two months was undoubtedly well wide of the mark; it would take the *Kriegsmarine* eight to nine months to bring their own new battleship *Bismarck* to operational status after her completion in August 1940.

Perhaps the key piece of evidence for the absence of any firm design on the French fleet is the comparative ease with which the French managed to secure German agreement during the seven days which followed the signing of the Armistice for the repatriation of French warships to ports *outside* of the Occupied Zone. According to an agreement reached with the Germans and the Italians on 29 June the incomplete *Richelieu* and *Jean Bart* would return to

Toulon; *Dunkerque* and *Strasbourg* would remain at Mers el-Kebir, while the three old battleships of the *Bretagne* class would be demobilised at Bizerta. Only five cruisers, six torpedo-boats and fourteen submarines would be kept in commission. Once implemented this agreement would take the French fleet out of reach of the British, while at the same time the location of major vessels armed with large-calibre guns in the colonial ports of Mediterranean North Africa would hopefully serve to deter any British 'adventures' which aimed to take advantage of French military weakness. Subsequently the Germans would even veto the repatriation of *Richelieu* and *Jean Bart* to Toulon, for fear that the ships would be seized by the Royal Navy while attempting to transit the Strait of Gibraltar.

THE BRITISH PLAN IS FORMULATED

Even while these negotiations were proceeding, the future of the French fleet was the focus of urgent and heated discussion by the British. Time was of the essence: although at present the bulk of the fleet was in North Africa it could be a matter of days before the ships were returned at the insistence of the Germans to French metropolitan ports. On 25 June, French merchant ships in British-held ports were impounded, and those naval vessels in the UK or at Alexandria were forbidden from leaving. On the same day, the Royal Navy imposed a blockade on the Strait of Gibraltar to prevent any of the French ships currently in the Mediterranean from returning to their bases in the Occupied Zone. And on 27 June, the War Cabinet, goaded by an impatient Churchill, unanimously agreed that the French fleet currently based at Mers el-Kebir and Oran should be coerced into continuing the war alongside its former allies or sunk by aggressive action.

The measures taken by the British on 25 June put the French in a difficult position. The precise terms of the Armistice were still being negotiated, and the Germans suspected Darlan of double dealing. Any move to comply with British demands could prejudice the Armistice itself, to the great detriment of France. Article 10 clearly stated:

The French Government pledges not to undertake in the future any hostile action against the German Reich with *any part of the armed forces which remain under its command*, nor in any other way.

The French Government will also *prevent members of the French armed forces from leaving French territory* and will ensure that neither arms, nor any other equipment, *nor ships*, nor planes, etc., *will be transferred to England or abroad*.

The French Government will *forbid French citizens from fighting against Germany in the service of states with which Germany remains at war*. French nationals who do not conform to this decree will be treated by German troops as insurgents. (Authors' translation and italics)

The Article aimed to forestall the transfer of any part of the French fleet to Britain. From this point on, the fleet, intact, undefeated, and located in the main in North African ports became an important bargaining counter for the new French government, currently in the process of moving to Vichy. The British were desperate to get their hands on it, the Germans equally

---

[8] The word 'control' in the French sense of the word survives in English only in phrases like 'passport' or 'border controls': formal checks and verification.

desperate to keep it out of British hands. This strengthened Darlan's hand in the negotiations for the repatriation of the fleet. By playing on German fears that ships returning to ports in Occupied France might be intercepted by the British and compelled to sail to England, Darlan was able to secure agreement on 29 June that the fleet would be demobilised in Toulon, Mers el-Kebir and Bizerta, where the ships would be safe from German seizure.

This agreement was instantly communicated to the British in London via Admiral Odend'hal. Darlan was confident that the new arrangements, which continued to be backed up by preparations for sabotage which were to be kept secret from the Germans and the Italians, would suffice to reassure the British that no French warship would fall into enemy hands. However, the agreement was too late; Churchill's mind had been made up,[9] the War Cabinet had decided, and the necessary preparations were already being put in hand for Operation 'Catapult', which was to be executed on 5 July.[10] French ships in British ports and in Alexandria would be seized by force, and an ultimatum given to the French fleet at Mers el-Kebir.

The selection of an admiral to command the force tasked with the seizure or destruction of the French fleet at Mers el-Kebir was problematic. The Admiralty required someone of similar rank to his French counterpart, Vice-Admiral (VAE) Gensoul, but all the current serving fleet commanders had fought alongside the French and were known to be opposed to any act of aggression against their former allies. In the end the command of a newly formed Force H (Atlantic Fleet, based on Gibraltar) was given to Vice-Admiral James Somerville, who following early retirement through illness in 1939 had been recalled to supervise the development of naval radar. If Somerville was delighted to receive this new and prestigious command, he was less happy when he opened the envelope containing his instructions. Selected in part for his diplomatic skills, Somerville would be seconded by Captain Holland of *Ark Royal*, ex-naval attaché in Paris and a fluent French speaker. Under his command he would have the battlecruiser *Hood* (his flagship), the battleships *Valiant*, *Resolution* and *Nelson*,[11] the aircraft-carrier *Ark Royal*, two cruisers and eleven destroyers. Somerville was to sail for Gibraltar from Spithead, Portsmouth, on board the light cruiser *Arethusa* on 28 June; besides the admiral this ship would be carrying a special consignment of magnetic mines, to be laid in the pass of Mers el-Kebir to block the escape of the French ships.

MERS EL-KEBIR

Since the turn of the century the major French naval base in North Africa had been Bizerta in Tunisia. Popularly referred to as *le Toulon africain*, it had initially been developed as a forward base for torpedo

OPERATION 'CATAPULT': MERS EL-KEBIR

Force H (V-Ad Somerville)

Battleships:	Aircraft-carrier:	Light cruisers:
Hood (fl)	*Ark Royal* (VA Wells)	*Arethusa*
Valiant	30 Swordfish, 24 Skua	*Enterprise*
Resolution		

8th Flotilla	13th Flotilla	Attached submarines:
Faulknor (L)	*Keppel* (L)	*Proteus*
Foxhound	*Active*	*Pandora*
Fearless	*Wrestler*	
Forester	*Vidette*	
Foresight	*Vortigern*	
Escort		

Flotte de l'Atlantique (VAE Gensoul)

1ère DL (VAE Gensoul)	6e DCT (CA Lacroix)	Aviation Transport:
Dunkerque (fl)	*Mogador* (fl)	*Commandant Teste*
Strasbourg	*Volta*	

2e DL (CA Bouxin)	4e DCT	Detached CT:
Provence (fl)	*Tigre*	*Le Terrible*
Bretagne	*Lynx*	*Kersaint*

boats with a view to threatening British sea lines of communication passing through the central Mediterranean. Major expenditure was authorised in 1901 to equip the base to support a major part of the French Mediterranean Fleet, with basins and graving docks capable of the simultaneous refit and repair of six battleships and six cruisers, and much of this infrastructure was in place before the outbreak of war in 1914.

By the early 1930s, however, it was becoming more likely that France's potential enemy in a future Mediterranean conflict would be Italy, and Bizerta was too close to Italian airfields to serve as anything more than a forward base for light forces.[12] Moreover, with Italy the enemy, even the major French Mediterranean base at Toulon was vulnerable to air attack. In 1934 it was therefore proposed to build a major North African base for the French fleet at Mers el-Kebir, a comparatively sheltered anchorage six kilometres west of the port of Oran. Construction work began on the proposed 2000-metre jetty in 1936, and the ambitious plans featured new coast defence guns for the existing forts, underground command bunkers, batteries of medium and light AA guns, piers, quays and dry docks, fuel tanks and munitions stocks (see map and caption).

Little of this was in place by June 1940; Mers el-Kebir remained an empty shell. Only a 900-metre stretch of the main jetty had been completed, with work still in progress on the remaining 1100 metres.

---

9 Churchill chose not to reveal the new basing agreement to the War Cabinet, presumably for fear of weakening its resolution in favour of draconian action.

10 It was subsequently decided to bring the operation forward by two days in order to free up participating ships to meet a possible invasion of Britain.

11 *Nelson* was ultimately withdrawn from the operation because of fears of an imminent German invasion.

---

12 From 1 October 1939, Bizerta was the base for the *Forces légères d'attaque*, comprising the 3rd (light) Cruiser Division and three two-three-ship divisions of *contre-torpilleurs* under CA Decoux.

There were minefields to protect the approaches of the anchorage from attack by torpedo craft, and there was a net across the harbour entrance to bar access to hostile submarines. For anti-aircraft defence there were four batteries of 75mm HA guns ashore together with three sections of 8mm and 13.2mm MG on the jetty itself. The coast defence battery of four 194mm guns in the old Santon Fort, located on the heights overlooking the bay, had a theoretical range of around 20,000 metres. The other long-range battery, comprising three 240mm guns (range 23,000 metres), was at Cape Canastel, three kilometres on the far side of Oran. There was no public transport between Mers el-Kebir and Oran, and of the ships gathered in the anchorage in June 1940, only the flagship, *Dunkerque*, was connected to the shore by land telephone line.

Mers el-Kebir: Project of 1936

The project for a major naval base in the bay to the west of Oran, approved by the French parliament in 1936, was ambitious. It would have involved the construction of two jetties (1) to enclose the anchorage, the northernmost of which would have been fully two kilometres long on completion. In the northwestern corner, close to the village of Mers el-Kebir, quays were to be built to accommodate cruisers and flotilla craft; (2) To the south of the quays, in front of the village of Saint André, a large replenishment base was to have been built on reclaimed land. Two large moles of trapezoid configuration, angled towards the harbour entrance, and a smaller triangular mole were to have enclosed two deepwater (nine-metres plus) basins where ships could take on fuel and stores. (3) Finally, in the southeastern corner of the anchorage, close to the village of Sainte Clotilde, a repair facility (*Port de Travaux*) was to be constructed, again on reclaimed land, enclosing a larger and a smaller basin with a slipway for the maintenance of smaller craft. (4) The depth of water in the larger of the two basins was eight metres on the northern side and six metres on the southern side. There was to be a small floating dock (90 metres) and a larger pontoon dock (120 metres) capable of accommodating submarines and flotilla craft, but major ships would still have had to return to Toulon for docking. In addition to the port facilities, an underground command centre with the latest communications would have been installed, and the existing heavy coast defence and AA batteries upgraded.

In July 1940, little of this was in place. Only the first 1000 metres of the *Jetée Nord* had been completed, together with some of the planned quays between Mers el-Kebir and Saint André. Work was still proceeding on the *Jetée Nord*, but had yet to begin on either the replenishment base or the maintenance base. The command bunkers had not been excavated, the elderly coast defence guns had yet to be upgraded, and the only usable part of the base in the northwestern corner close to Mers el-Kebir was connected to Oran only by the coastal road, with a single telephone line.

(Map by John Jordan © 2008)

The situation of the French fleet at Mers el-Kebir prior to 'Catapult' was particularly unfavourable in a number of respects. The battleships were securely moored at 120-metre intervals facing the shore with their sterns 60 metres off the jetty. For *Dunkerque* and *Strasbourg*, with their all-forward main armament, this meant that they were unable to train their guns towards the open sea from their moorings. The difficulties posed by the long, narrow anchorage, which was only 800 metres at its widest point, meant that in normal circumstances it would take a ship around thirty minutes to reach open waters.

The terms of the Armistice effectively removed from the fleet other customary means of self-defence. The breeches of the guns at Fort Santon and Canastel had in the last few days been removed and placed in storage under the terms of the Armistice. There was a division of 600-tonne coastal submarines at Oran, but the firing pistols had been removed from the warheads of their torpedoes and the compressed air chambers emptied. There was a fighter squadron at nearby La Senia but many of its aircraft had been grounded by the lack of spare parts and munitions. The situation for the bombers of the Armée de l'Air, which could have deterred an attack by hostile ships, was even worse. Fearing that crews would defect by flying to Gibraltar, their commanding officer had ordered that fuel tanks be drained and tyres deflated. Flight crews had either been demobilised or were untrained for missions over the sea. Even reconnaissance flights were prohibited by the Armistice, which meant that the approach of Force H went undetected.

Finally, the French Atlantic Fleet was no longer a fleet at war. Reservists, who accounted for about 20 per cent of the crews of *Dunkerque* and *Strasbourg* and about a third of the crews of the older battleships *Provence* and *Bretagne*, were already looking forward to their imminent demobilisation. Of the regular personnel there were some who would have welcomed an order from their superior officers to continue the war on the side of their former allies, but equally there were many who were less enthusiastic. Many of the regular seamen were from Brittany, a traditional recruiting area for the Marine Nationale. They had received no letters from home since the German occupation of the west coast; some feared reprisals against their families if they were to continue the fight alongside the British. The flag staff and the ships' officers were very conscious of these internal tensions, which they attempted to dissipate by ensuring that the crews were 'kept busy'. Besides the standard ship maintenance tasks there were organised hikes ashore in the mountainous hinterland. Many men were ashore when Force H arrived off Mers el-Kebir, and had to be hastily recalled.

THE ULTIMATUM

The arrival of the British destroyer *Foxhound* at the mouth of the anchorage just before 0800 (GMT + 1[13]) on 3 July and the subsequent appearance at 0900 of the battleships of Force H, cruising at the limit of visibility – 15,000-16,000 metres – to the northwest of the anchorage, caused a considerable stir among the crews of the French ships; in the hearts of some they raised hopes, but for most there was only anxiety, and

---

[13] The French ships were on British Summer Time (i.e., GMT + 1). This time is used in all French accounts of the action.

The French fleet at Mers el-Kebir seen from the Santon heights shortly before the British attack. Moored with their sterns to the jetty are (left to right) the battleships *Dunkerque*, *Provence*, *Strasbourg* and *Bretagne*, and the aviation transport *Commandant Teste*; in the foreground are the six *contre-torpilleurs*. Note the darker 'Atlantic' grey of the two modern battleships.

Strasbourg in the anchorage at Mers el-Kebir in June-July 1940. One of her Loire 130 seaplanes is taxiing alongside. The planes were normally launched using the catapult but recovered by crane. (*H Landais collection*)

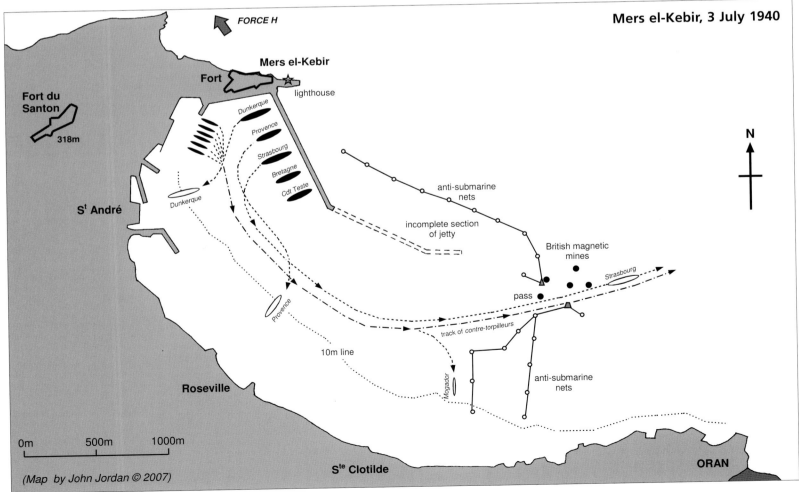

Mers el-Kebir, 3 July 1940

FORCE H

Mers el-Kebir

Fort

lighthouse

Fort du Santon

318m

Dunkerque

Provence

Strasbourg

Bretagne

Cdt Teste

S¹ André

Dunkerque

anti-submarine nets

incomplete section of jetty

British magnetic mines

pass

Strasbourg

track of *contre-torpilleurs*

Provence

10m line

Mogador

anti-submarine nets

Roseville

0m   500m   1000m

(*Map by John Jordan © 2007*)

Ste Clotilde

ORAN

N

on some ships mutinous groups of reservists gathered on deck and had to be dispersed by their officers.

Negotiations proved even more difficult than the British had anticipated. The French Admiral Gensoul initially refused to engage in talks for fear of violating the terms of the Armistice, and then demanded that any negotiation in which he was to be personally involved be conducted with an officer of equal rank – effectively Somerville, who was tied to his flagship for the execution of the operation. Captain Holland, charged with the delicate negotiations, was compelled to conduct them initially through the intermediary of a junior officer of the admiral's staff, then with Gensoul's flag captain. Gensoul, an authoritarian officer who was in the habit of consulting only the other flag officers of his fleet before taking his decisions, was particularly incensed to see the British ships openly signal their invitation to his ships to rejoin the fight, effectively appealing to the French crews over the heads of their commanding officers.

The French admiral was presented with the following ultimatum from Somerville:

It is impossible for us, your comrades up to now, to allow your fine ships to fall into the power of the German enemy. We are determined to fight on until the end, and if we win, as we think we shall, we shall never forget that France was our Ally, that our interests are the same as hers, and that our common enemy is Germany. Should we conquer we solemnly declare that we shall restore the greatness and territory of France. For this purpose we must make sure that the best ships of the French Navy are not used against us by the common foe. In these circumstances, His Majesty's Government have instructed me to demand that the French Fleet now at Mers el Kebir and Oran shall act in accordance with one of the following alternatives;

(a) Sail with us and continue the fight until victory against the Germans.

(b) Sail with reduced crews under our control to a British port. The reduced crews would be repatriated at the earliest moment.

If either of these courses is adopted by you we will restore your ships to France at the conclusion of the war or pay full compensation if they are damaged meanwhile.

(c) Alternatively if you feel bound to stipulate that your ships should not be used against the Germans lest they break the Armistice, then sail them with us with reduced crews to some French port in the West Indies – Martinique for instance – where they can be demilitarised to our satisfaction, or perhaps be entrusted to the United States and remain safe until the end of the war, the crews being repatriated.

If you refuse these fair offers, I must with profound regret require you to sink your ships within 6 hours. Finally, failing the above, I have the orders from His Majesty's Government to use whatever force may be necessary to prevent your ships from falling into German hands.

Gensoul responded by ordering his fleet to prepare to break out and fight and by attempting to contact Darlan for advice. He was well aware of the likely content of any reply but needed to play for time to prepare his fleet for action; there was even the (admittedly optimistic) possibility that the negotiations might be prolonged into the late afternoon, when a thick heat haze often descended and restricted visibility, or even to nightfall, when the fleet might escape under cover of darkness. However, during the time that the French ships were engaged in furling awnings, raising the steam pressure in their boilers, getting their absent personnel back on board, readying their guns and loosening their moorings, Force H continued its relentless pacing back and forwards to the northwest, often hidden from view by the old fort, its guns trained on the anchorage. Walrus and Swordfish spotting aircraft overflew the anchorage, and at 1305 Swordfish from *Ark Royal* dropped five magnetic mines in the narrow pass. The French AA gunners were ordered not to fire on the aircraft to ensure that the responsibility for any act of aggression would fall clearly on the British.

TIME RUNS OUT

Negotiations were protracted. The difficulties of conducting talks via intermediaries and the delays attendant on that process, Gensoul's desperate playing for time, Somerville's willingness to explore every possible avenue rather than open what he knew would be a devastating fire on a former ally, and the precarious state of communications between the French flagship and the French Admiralty, ensured that they dragged on into the late afternoon. Had either of the admirals been given a completely free hand, a satisfactory compromise might have been reached on the basis of a demobilisation and deactivation of the French ships at Mers el-Kebir. However, Darlan could not be reached and the only advice Gensoul received from his deputy, Le Luc, was to 'meet force with force'. Somerville likewise received little support; the Admiralty dismissed Gensoul's final proposal as unacceptable and insisted that Somerville carry out his instructions to the letter. The French ships went to action stations at 1725.

At 1755, the flashes of the first four-gun salvo from *Hood* were seen and Gensoul gave the orders simultaneously to cast off and open fire. Four of the French *contre-torpilleurs* had already moved out towards the pass. They were to be followed by *Strasbourg*, then the flagship *Dunkerque*, then the older, slower *Bretagne* and *Provence*.

For the British battleships firing on stationary targets, it was like a gunnery practice. The first salvo was short; the second struck the jetty, hurling shell splinters and chunks of masonry over the anchorage; the third struck the French ships with devastating effect. *Strasbourg* was quickly away from her moorings; she turned slowly under a hail of flying debris and headed for the pass. The other three French battleships were less fortunate. *Dunkerque* and *Provence* opened fire immediately on the British squadron, but due to failures in command which were subsequently the subject of an official enquiry[14] *Dunkerque* was still securely moored to the jetty four minutes after the action had started. With the help of a tug she then got free, but was promptly hit by four

---

[14] The deck parties fore and aft responsible for casting off had either gone to action stations within the ship or had fled for cover once the ship's guns had opened up and the first British shells started to fall.

Mers el-Kebir 3 July 1940: *Strasbourg* has just slipped her moorings. In the foreground is the old battleship *Provence*, her main guns trained on the British squadron. She will be crippled in the British attack. In the background the *Bretagne* has just cast off; she will be lost to a magazine explosion. The photo was taken from the tower of *Dunkerque*, which despite Admiral Gensoul's instructions remained firmly secured to the jetty. *(ECPAD)*

15in shells, two of which penetrated her 225mm main armour belt amidships and exploded in the ship's vitals, causing the ship to lose speed and all electrical power. She was beached in shallow water opposite her moorings facing the village of Saint-André (see map).

Both the older battleships were sunk or disabled. As *Bretagne* cast off from her moorings and began her turn she was struck by two 15in shells aft which penetrated the main 340mm magazines. The resulting explosion devastated the after part of the ship and water poured in. Settling by the stern, and struck amidships by a further two 15in shells which detonated the 138mm magazines, she rolled over and sank within minutes, taking with her more than a thousand men. Her sister, *Provence*, almost suffered a similar fate when she was likewise struck by a 15in shell aft. Fortunately the crew was able to flood the magazines in time to prevent an explosion, but the ingress of water was sufficient to ensure that the ship would not make open water, and she was beached, like *Dunkerque*, facing the shore 1000 metres farther down the anchorage.

The final casualty of the British bombardment was the *Mogador*, flagship of CA Lacroix, which was leading the *contre-torpilleurs* towards open waters. As she approached the pass an unlucky hit aft caused the sixteen 250kg depth charges to explode, obliterating her stern as far as the after engine room bulkhead. Fortunately the explosion failed to set off the after magazines and the engine room bulkhead held,

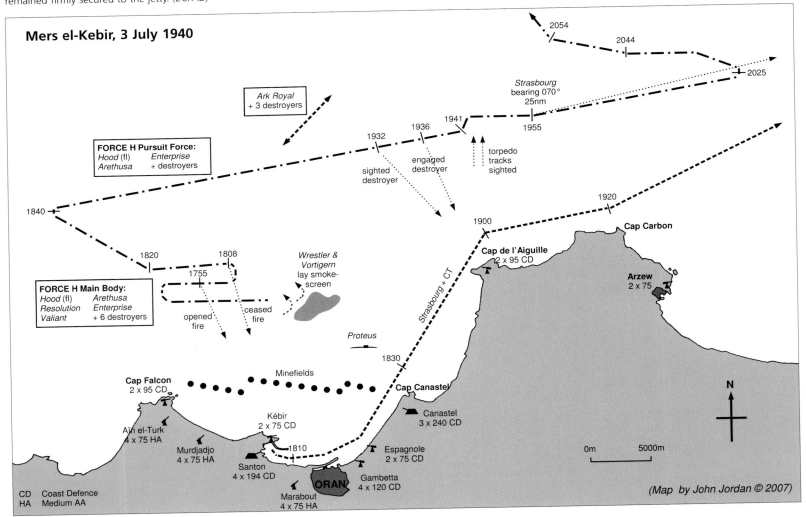

Mers el-Kebir, 3 July 1940

(Map by John Jordan © 2007)

allowing the ship to be beached close to the pass. The other four *contre-torpilleurs*, led by *Volta* and *Le Terrible*, with *Lynx* and *Tigre* bringing up the rear,[15] steamed past her and engaged British destroyers before taking up a protective disposition on the port flank of *Strasbourg* as she made her way past the coast defence battery at Canastel.

The action was over as suddenly as it began. In little over ten minutes the British had sunk one battleship, disabled two others and crippled the *Mogador*. The degree of devastation was readily apparent to Somerville, who saw no need to inflict further unnecessary casualties. The entire anchorage was shrouded in thick smoke, and he was as yet unaware that *Strasbourg*, identified in his instructions as one of the two ships which under no cicumstances should be permitted to escape, had been able to flee the carnage.

THE DAMAGE TO *DUNKERQUE*[16]

The first of the four 15in shells which struck *Dunkerque* impacted on the forward (angled) section of the roof of turret II. *Dunkerque* had already fired several 330mm salvos at HMS *Hood*, and at the time of the hit both turrets were trained to starboard in the direction of the British squadron at an angle of about 100 degrees. The shell struck directly above No. 8 gun (outer starboard) at an angle of 20 degrees to the armour plate. It pushed in the plate as it ricocheted and continued on its course without any appreciable deviation. It did not explode and landed ashore some 2000 metres from the ship and at a height of about 150 metres above the village of Sainte-Clotilde.[17]

The plate of cemented armour was pushed in at its

centre producing a crescent-shaped opening and punching out plugs of armour beneath the hardened face with a maximum thickness of 10-12cm, which were found on the floor of the firing chamber. These demolished the run-out cylinder, then part of the gunlayer's position on the right side and the azimetric sight. A fragment of the base of the shell was found on the floor of the firing chamber.

The report stated that one of the armour fragments, or more probably the fragment of shell found on the

British 15in shells fall on the far side of the jetty as *Strasbourg* slips her moorings and makes for the pass. To the left of the picture, *Provence* has still not left her berth. (*H Landais collection*)

Strasbourg turns to port to clear the anchorage. She is passing ahead of *Bretagne*, which is on fire and sinking.

---

15 The sixth ship, *Kersaint*, could only operate on one shaft and followed later.

16 This account is based on the official report of ingéneur des I.N. Tessier du Cros (member of armour committee) dated 01.10.40.

17 A large fragment is also reported to have struck the fire control top of the battleship *Provence*, fatally wounding the gunnery officer and causing that ship to cease fire.

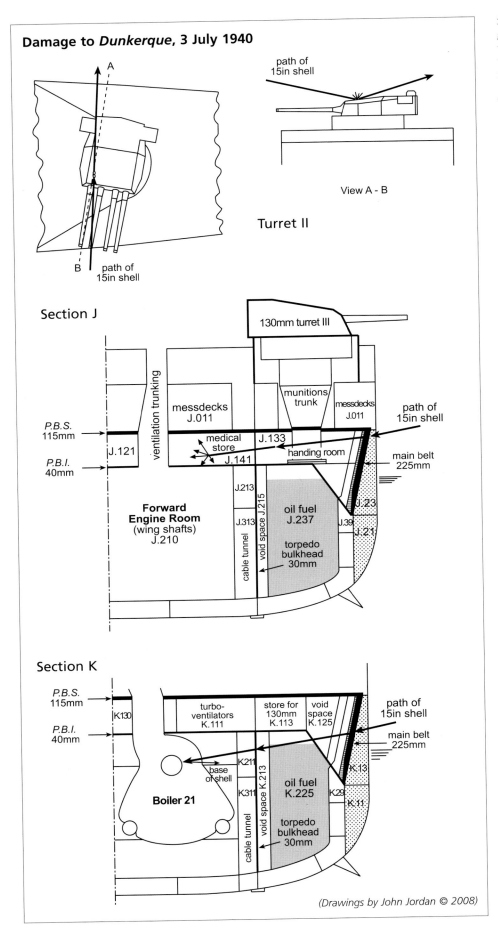

Damage to *Dunkerque*, 3 July 1940

path of 15in shell

A

B | path of 15in shell

View A - B

Turret II

Section J

130mm turret III

ventilation trunking

munitions trunk

messdecks J.011

messdecks J.011

path of 15in shell

P.B.S. 115mm

J.121

medical store

J.133

handing room

main belt 225mm

P.B.I. 40mm

J.141

Forward Engine Room (wing shafts) J.210

J.213

void space J.215

J.313

cable tunnel

oil fuel J.237

J.39

J.23

J.21

torpedo bulkhead 30mm

Section K

P.B.S. 115mm

K130

turbo-ventilators K.111

store for 130mm K.113

void space K.125

path of 15in shell

P.B.I. 40mm

K211

base of shell

void space K.213

main belt 225mm

K311

oil fuel K.225

K29

K13

Boiler 21

cable tunnel

torpedo bulkhead 30mm

K.11

(Drawings by John Jordan © 2008)

floor of the firing chamber between No. 7 and No. 8 guns, was propelled across the chamber, scraping the underside of the turret roof directly above the well for the gun loading cages. It ricocheted towards the spanning tray of No. 8 gun where it set fire to the first pair of charges which were in the process of being loaded. The fire from the charges asphyxiated the gun crew of the right-hand firing chamber and also slightly affected the personnel in the turret command station, the rangefinder position and the auxiliary position. However, it did not spread into the left-hand turret chamber, nor to the working chamber, or to the cages themselves. The latter were nevertheless in position to load the last two charges for gun No. 8 and the first two for gun No. 7, but their anti-flash doors, which were still closed, were fully effective. There was no fire in the electrical fittings of the turret (motors, cables, etc.).

After the impact and the fire among the bagged charges, turret II was in the following state:

– replenishment hoists/cages: working for all four guns
– traverse mechanism: good working order
– elevation: full working order for left side of turret (guns 5 and 6); No. 7 gun could be elevated, No. 8 gun could easily be decoupled

Three guns were therefore able to fire provided the gun crew for the right side of the turret was replaced and the electrical firing transmission restored to No. 7 gun.

The second shell struck aft, in the unarmoured part of the ship. It passed through the lower hangar, pierced the main deck and exited through the port side of the hull without exploding. A towering shell splash flooded the quarterdeck. As the Loire seaplanes had been disembarked prior to the action and the aviation fuel tanks emptied, damage should have been minimal. Unfortunately during its passage through the ship the shell sliced through the electrical cabling for the rudder; as a result the 35,000-tonne *Dunkerque*, still in the process of manoeuvring off the jetty, had to be steered manually using an emergency four horsepower Renault motor.

These two shell hits were inconvenient, but not disabling. However, the two which followed were devastating. Both were amidships, and both passed straight through the 225mm main armoured belt, which had been designed to resist German 28cm not British 15in (381mm) shell, exploding deep in the ship's vitals.

Just after 1800, a third 15in shell struck *Dunkerque* to starboard, above the waterline in section J,[18] 1.20 metres forward of transverse bulkhead JK and 0.40 metres beneath the upper edge of the armour belt. It passed through the armour belt and penetrated the handing room J133 of turret III (twin 130mm to starboard), where it carried away part of the rotating trunk and started a serious fire among the cartridges, causing at least two 130mm shells to explode. It passed through the 20mm bulkhead which was an upward continuation of the torpedo bulkhead, and finally burst in the medical store J141 (see drawing). Shell splinters

18 Whereas frames were numbered from the stern to the bow in French warships, compartments were designated by letter beginning at the bow. The central machinery compartments in *Dunkerque* were I (BR1), J (ER1), K (BR2), L (BR3) and M (ER2) – see drawing.

and the blast destroyed and carried away several light bulkheads and part of the ventilation trunking, and tore open the 20mm bulkhead which separated the medical store J141 from the longitudinal compartment J110 containing the air-cooling plant for the turbines in the forward engine room (ER1).

Shell splinters destroyed the starboard ventilation duct and the blast blew away an inspection door for the ventilation trunking in the engine room, opening up a large hole through which poured smoke and fumes produced by the explosion of the shells and the fires burning among the 130mm cartridges. Thick yellow smoke and a few flames penetrated into the machinery spaces via the funnel gratings of the lower armoured deck. This invasion of smoke, exacerbated by the loss of ventilation, quickly made the forward engine room uninhabitable. The personnel tried to escape, but was prevented from doing so because the armoured doors could not be opened. Only a dozen managed to escape using the ladders at the forward end, the after doors being blocked by steel debris. The main electrical switchboard was disabled, causing all power throughout the ship to be lost.

The explosion of this shell was followed on the evening of 3 July by several spaced explosions. An examination of the refrigeration space and the hoists feeding turrets III and IV revealed that five or six 130mm shells in the starboard hoists had exploded in that compartment, showering the ventilation trunking and the associated equipment with more shell splinters. These explosions were accompanied by a serious fire in the electrical cabling which spread from the after to the forward end of the compartment.

Less than one hour after the battle, the personnel in the handing room for turret IV (port-side twin 130mm) reported that smoke from the magazine hoist was invading their space. They secured the safety door and the order to flood the corresponding magazine (section H) was given. Up to that point the handing room personnel had not noticed anything untoward; they evacuated having secured all the safety doors.

Shortly after a petty officer reported the destruction and fire in the handing room of turret III, the corresponding magazine (also section H) was also flooded. The magazine personnel, who had reported seeing in the darkness a bright glow coming from the hoist at the time of the explosion, secured the safety doors and evacuated. It was not possible to control the fires in the handing room of Turret III and the refrigeration space.

The fourth 15in shell struck *Dunkerque* at the waterline to starboard in the adjacent section L, 0.30 metre abaft transverse bulkhead KL and 2.50 metres beneath the upper edge of the armour belt. It passed through the watertight bulkhead behind the armour belt and bulkhead KL above the angle of the lower armoured deck and projected fragments from these bulkheads above the armoured deck into compartments K113 and L113 (see drawing).

It passed through the inclined part of the lower armoured deck in section I and penetrated into fuel bunker K225 which was almost full (one metre from ceiling). Its passage opened up large breaches in bulkhead KL (between K225 and L215) and in the longitudinal bulkhead of the void compartment. The shell passed through the torpedo bulkhead and the watertight bulkhead behind it, severing a number of cables in tunnel K211, and then penetrated into boiler

room 2. In this compartment it severed steam collector 1, which connected boiler 21 with the forward group (BR1 + the wing turbines), then smashed into collector 2 (saturated steam) and the exhaust collector of the auxiliaries. It went on to penetrate the starboard casing and the upper steam drum of boiler 21 and the broken remains – three fragments of the shell body and the entire base of the projectile (weight: 350-400kg) – rolled back along the roof of the boiler containment box.[19]

Fuel oil entered the boiler room via the breach made by the shell. Scalding steam from boilers 11, 12 and 21, which were at $27kg/cm^2$, quickly escaped into boiler room 2 through the holes in boiler 21 and steam collector 1. Boilers 22, 31 and 32 emptied more slowly through the holes in collector 2. The personnel in boiler room 3 attempted to stem the leaks by raising the temperature.

Boiler room 2 seems to have suddenly been put under enormous pressure, and whether by static pressure or by dynamic effect, the uptakes of the two boilers collapsed. The personnel, who were either killed or incapacitated by the sudden failure of the boiler, were unable to put out the boiler fires, so that for some time afterwards the hot gases of the two boilers were partially escaping into the compartment. This deadly combination of combustion gases and scalding steam passed directly into the hydraulics control station K112 via the ventilation trunking; the personnel were asphyxiated or burned, and with the failure of the pressurised oil system the armoured doors throughout the ship could no longer be operated automatically.[20]

The escape of hot gases and the steam also dramatically increased the temperature of bulkhead KL separating the two boiler rooms. As a result of the failure of the ventilation system, the air in BR3 quickly became unbreathable and the captain ordered the evacuation of all personnel. However, later inspection revealed that the installations in BR3 had sustained no damage, and that in BR2 boiler 22 and all the auxiliaries were in full working order. In particular, all the delicate parts, including small-diameter pipework, pressure gauges, etc. appeared to be intact.

CONCLUSIONS

The two shells which hit amidships, piercing the main 225mm armour belt, were decisive. Within seconds, *Dunkerque* could neither fight nor run; beaching was the only possible outcome. The devastation these shells wrought in the ship's vitals was testimony to the

---

[19] It was standard practice in the latest French ships fitted with high-pressure steam machinery to fit a containment box around each boiler or, as on *Dunkerque*, each pair of boilers. This made for more pleasant working conditions for the boiler room personnel, for whom a transverse walkway called a *rue de chauffe* was provided, giving access to the front of the boiler together with all controls. In *Dunkerque* the *rues de chauffe* for the two central boiler rooms (BR2 and BR3) were at the forward and after ends of the boiler rooms respectively, the four boilers (21/22 and 31/32) being located back-to-back with their uptakes directly beneath the single funnel (see drawing).

[20] The Royal Navy and the US Navy used either counterweights or torsional springs to raise the heavy armoured hatches; these were less vulnerable to action damage than hydraulic systems.

effectiveness of the 15in armour-piercing shell, the successors of the 'Greenboys' developed by the British in the wake of the failures at Jutland; they worked exactly as designed, piercing a relatively thick inclined armour belt at an oblique angle and penetrating deep inside the hull before exploding. The penetration of the hull amidships resulted in an ingress of 700 tonnes of water, which had to be compensated by admitting a further 150 tonnes into the port-side tanks.

However, despite the rapidity with which *Dunkerque* was disabled, and despite the heavy casualties among engine room and boiler room personnel caused by escaping steam and the invasion of the spaces by noxious fumes, the ship was not seriously damaged. Repairs to the hull, the broken steam collectors and the electrical cabling would begin as soon as the dead and the injured were evacuated. Admiral Gensoul still hoped to return to Toulon for proper repairs within a few days. The turbines were undamaged and could be made fully operational, and it was hoped to have five out of the six boilers on line. In some respects *Dunkerque* was fortunate to have been in harbour when attacked; had she been struck by 15in shells and similarly disabled when at sea there can be little doubt that she would have been sunk, just as *Bismarck* and *Scharnhorst* would be once their own fire control and electrical systems were disabled.

THE ESCAPE OF *STRASBOURG*

The escape of *Strasbourg*, which served to boost French morale and to infuriate Churchill, was little short of miraculous in the circumstances. Unhampered by having an admiral and his flag staff aboard to interfere with proceedings,[21] Captain Collinet's crew quickly loosed their moorings and Collinet then set about turning his ship on the spot by putting her port engines into reverse (100rpm then 120rpm) and going ahead on starboard engines (150rpm). Debris from the shattered jetty and the first hits on the other battleships were hammering down on *Strasbourg*'s decks; the hull was punctured and dented, and the wooden deck planking was smouldering in several places. As the ship was turning at 1800 a 15in salvo fell where her stern had been one minute previously. *Strasbourg* then headed for the pass, gaining speed all the time. Abaft there were spectacular explosions on *Bretagne*, which was burning furiously and sinking by the stern to port. Keeping to

---

21 French sources suggest that the tensions between Gensoul and his flag staff on the one hand, and Captain Seguin and his senior officers on the other hand, appear to have been a significant factor in *Dunkerque*'s failure to cast off when the British began firing.

STRASBOURG: REPORT OF CV COLLINET AFTER ACTION AT MERS EL-KEBIR, 3-4 JULY 1940, BASED ON *JOURNAL D'OPÉRATIONS*

3 July 1940
Time (BST)　Events in chronological order
Situation at 0800:

	Moored to jetty, bow 250°, in following order (north to south): *Dunkerque*, *Provence*, *Strasbourg*, *Bretagne*, *Commandant Teste*. To the west of them six *contre-torpilleurs*, all with boilers unlit and at six hours notice.
	At about 0830 a British destroyer moors outside the anchorage requesting an interview with the Admiral.
0850	Receive order to prepare for Action Stations; one boiler lit.
0900	Three English battleships visible out to sea, including the *Hood*, a battleship of the 'R' class and a modified *Warspite*, accompanied by *Ark Royal*, two cruisers and nine destroyers. These ships would criss-cross from east to west at 6-7nm from the Bay of Oran until fire opened.
0955	Receive the order to raise steam in all boilers as quickly as possible.
1010	Received from C-in-C: 'English fleet has proposed unacceptable armistice. Be prepared to answer force with force' 0900.
1020	Watch stations manned; guns replenished.
1042	Received from C-in-C: 'Lower one floatplane onto buoy – stop – Mission: spotting for guns' 0930.
1128	Received from C-in-C: 'Lower second floatplane onto buoy – stop – Second floatplane of *Dunkerque* to spot for *Provence*, second floatplane of *Strasbourg* to spot for *Bretagne* – stop – Instructions re. wavelength to follow in sealed envelope' 1005.
1245	Boilers fired up; signal C-in-C: 'Situation *Strasbourg* – stop – Machinery ready and steam for 30 minutes – stop – I will not cast off without a new order from you – stop – Ship ready for action – stop – Watch stations manned' 1155.
1330	Five British planes flying at low altitude lay mines in the gateway of the anti-submarine net barrier.
1340	Received from C-in-C: 'When casting off the two anchor chains will be separated on deck to save time – stop – The two chains are to be broken at the sixth link and held by a joining shackle with a removable pin under tension – stop – Have blow-torches ready to cut the lateral hawsers aft' 1235.
1408	British destroyer approaches and signals by projector: 'If you accept our conditions, hoist a square flag at the mainmast – if not I open fire.'
1410	Ship to Action Stations (signalled by C-in-C), cut through two lateral hawsers aft. *Strasbourg* now secured to jetty only by centre-line hawser, which is ready to be cast off. *Strasbourg* trains her guns 90° to starboard.
1448	Received from C-in-C: 'Am sending a tug to your port quarter to angle you towards *Bretagne* at the first discharge of the guns'. The tug arrives and takes a line aboard. It will not be used (see later).
1510	The *Mogador* casts off and moors near the pass. The *Volta* and another *contre-torpilleur* cast off but return immediately to their previous moorings.
1520	Received from C-in-C: 'Turrets to be trained fore and aft' 1410.
1522	Received from C-in-C: 'I am receiving an English delegation for discussions' 1410.
1530	A British motor boat brings officers who are received on board *Dunkerque*. Crew stood down from Action Stations; snacks distributed.
1720	Intercept message from *Hood*: 'If proposals not accepted by 1730 I must sink your ships.'
1722	British delegation leaves *Dunkerque*.
1727	Received from C-in-C: 'Sound Action Stations'.
1740	Received from C-in-C: 'Let go axial anchor chain'. *Volta*, *Lynx* and *Le Terrible* cast off .
1745	Received from C-in-C: 'If the order to cast off is given, departure in the order: 1st DL [*Dunkerque*, *Strasbourg*], 2nd DL [*Provence*, *Bretagne*], *Commandant Teste* – stop – Keep close to the south side of the pass.'
1755	The British ships open fire, firing above Fort Mers el-Kebir. They cannot be seen from the *Strasbourg*. First salvo correct in range to the east of the jetty. Simultaneously: – cast off aft – let go port anchor chain – starboard engines ahead 60rpm, then 120rpm – rudder hard to port
1758	Received from C-in-C: 'Cast off without waiting for further signal. Open fire.' The second [British] salvo falls on the jetty. One or two shells from the third salvo strike close to the after turrets of *Bretagne*; magazine explosion. Several shell splinters strike *Strasbourg*. Ship underway; port turbines in reverse 100rpm then 120rpm, then

the south side of the pass *Strasbourg* then passed *Mogador*, her stern wrecked by a 15in shell.

Strasbourg had recently been fitted with a degaussing cable, so Collinet was confident that she would not detonate the British magnetic mines laid in the pass. In fact, when the ship returned to Toulon an inspection revealed that the equipment had been incorrectly installed and tested, and in places the polarity was wrong. By rights the ship should have detonated one or other of the mines; only by keeping close to the buoy marking the southern limit of the pass had the ship avoided disaster. In the event the psychological effect of the mines was greater on Somerville, who refused to believe an early Swordfish report that a *Dunkerque* class battleship was making her escape.

As she emerged from the pass, *Strasbourg* was preceded by what remained of the two divisions of *contre-torpilleurs*, *Volta* and *Le Terrible* followed by *Lynx* and *Tigre*. The latter were engaging the British destroyer *Wrestler*, which was tasked with monitoring the exit to the pass and now turned away to lay a smokescreen to protect the British battleships. *Strasbourg* was now increasing speed from 15 knots to 28 knots, but was hampered by damage to an air intake on the funnel, which had been blocked by a piece of flying masonry from the jetty. The result was a huge plume of black smoke from the ship, which in good weather conditions would have been visible up to twenty miles away.

Strasbourg now headed for the gap in the protective minefield off Cape Canastel (see map), where she would be under the protection of the powerful 240mm coastal battery. Collinet still feared that a determined attempt by Somerville in the *Hood* would cut off his escape before he was able to round the Cap de l'Aiguille and head east along the coast of French North Africa. At 1840, following a submarine alert which resulted in the depth-charging of HMS *Proteus* by *Tigre* and *Lynx*, Collinet glimpsed through his binoculars a large ship thought to be *Hood* on a bearing of 290 degrees, but before she could be engaged she disappeared into the murk.

Strasbourg, with black smoke still pouring from her funnel, was now following the line of the coast with the 4th DCT (*Tigre* and *Lynx*) scouting ahead and *Volta* and *Le Terrible* providing protection on the 'engaged' side. Three torpedo-boats from Oran, *La Poursuivante*, *Bordelais* and *Trombe*, covered her stern. At 1900, *Strasbourg* turned away to starboard (course 080 degrees) as she passed Cap de l'Aiguille, and twenty minutes later she turned to port (course 060 degrees), keeping close to Cap Carbon. Collinet was still concerned about the distinctive plume of black smoke

	starboard turbines ahead 150rpm; we begin to move off. *Dunkerque* is firing. *Strasbourg* struck by shell splinters and debris.
1800	British salvo falls in wake of *Strasbourg*, exactly where the ship was one minute before. *Dunkerque* and *Provence* are hit. Salvoes are falling in the pass.
1805	*Bretagne* capsizes.
1809	Pass through the gateway in the barrier net keeping a few metres away from the south side – pass *Mogador*, which has lost her stern and is on fire. Once into the pass speed increased to 28 knots. The British battleships are cloaked by thick smoke screens and are invisible. Only target visible: destroyer at one end of the smoke screen. Ahead of us the *contre-torpilleurs* are heavily engaged [with the British destroyers]. Head for the swept channel close to Cap Canastel.
1840	Submarine alert from *Tigre*, which together with *Lynx* is making depth charge attack.
1845	Open fire on four enemy aircraft. Signal to *Volta* and *Terrible* to take up protective station on port beam, and to the 4th DCT to scout ahead.
1852	Signal to HS25 (Loire 130) which is in signal range: 'Scout for me until nightfall, then make for Arzew.'
1900	Change course to 80° to round Cap de l'Aiguille.
1905	HS25 signals by radio three large ships bearing 350°, heading 90°.
1920	Change course to 60° keeping close to Cap Carbon.
1945	Attacked by two aircraft; bomb 200m to starboard; open fire.
1950-54	More planes; respond with AA fire; no attack.
2000	Received from HS25: 'Three large ships plus destroyers 10nm from Arzew bearing 330°, course 70°. 1855. Position of *Strasbourg*: 3nm bearing 300° from Cap Ivi.
2010	Received from C-in-C by W/T: 'Concentrate forces at daybreak and head for Toulon – stop – Rendez-vous to be fixed by Admiral [in] *Marseillaise*.'
2015	Sun setting; planes in view in that direction; open fire. Open fire at plane in distance.
2055	Signal to *Volta*, *Terrible*, *Tigre*, *Lynx*: 'For now: heading 60° – stop – At midnight (BST) without any signal from me change course to north – stop – Speed 28 knots – stop – At night *Volta*, *Terrible* in position off starboard bow; *Tigre*, *Lynx* port bow – stop – Keep a lookout for

	French cruisers which have left Algiers for Oran.'
2057	Signal to [sloop] *Poursuivante*: 'At midnight (BST) I will turn to a northerly course without signalling, speed 28 knots – stop – Headed for Toulon – stop – If you do not have sufficient fuel replenish at Algiers.'
2112	Almost night; enemy plane at low altitude from direction of land; rudder hard over to port; bomb falls 25m away on port quarter.
2130	Crew stood down; supper; normal rotation of watches.

4 July 1940

0000	Course 70°, head towards San Pietro.
0215	Receive rendez-vous from Admiral *Marseillaise* 0400 east of Menorca; given impossibility of making this rendez-vous and my wish to maintain radio silence I take no action and continue on the same course.
0400	At daybreak again increase speed to 28 knots; note that *Lynx* has lost us during the night and replaced by [fleet torpedo boat] *Bordelais*.
0518	Signal to *Volta*: 'Take station straight ahead (*Le Terrible* starboard bow, *Tigre* port bow, *Bordelais* astern).'
0854	*Bordelais* having signalled unable to sustain 28 knots because of fuel situation, given freedom of manoeuvre; heads directly for Toulon at 25 knots.
1000	At 60nm from San Pietro change heading to 10°.
1120	Five land planes in close formation in sight on port quarter; crew to Action Stations. Planes clearly Italian heading for Cagliari.
1300	With the headland revealing that we are twelve miles closer than estimated, decide to head directly for Toulon to arrive 2100: R342.
1625	Having received a report from the submarine *Iris* of a surfaced submarine 45nm to the WNW of us, increase speed slightly, begin zigzagging and warn escorts to look out for submarines.
1900	Two French aircraft fly over us as escort.
2045	*Contre-torpilleurs* given freedom of manoeuvre.
2110	Pass jetties; make our entrance to the cheers of all the ships in the anchorage.

CV Collinet
CO, *Strasbourg*

emanating from the funnel, but was informed by the chief engineering officer that the problem could be fixed only by shutting down boiler room No. 2, effectively reducing speed to 20 knots. With the 31-knot *Hood* in pursuit this was not an option.[22]

Meanwhile Somerville, who had initially headed northwest after ordering his battle squadron to cease fire at about 1805 and had subsequently refused to believe the initial reports of *Strasbourg*'s escape from the anchorage, was now embarked on a stern chase with *Hood*, the two light cruisers and the destroyers in company, and had ordered Wells to launch Swordfish attacks from *Ark Royal* with a view to slowing the French ship. One six-plane flight armed with 250lb bombs was already in the air, and a second was now armed with torpedoes and prepared for take-off. The first attack went in at 1945. The aircraft were heavily engaged by the 130mm guns of *Strasbourg* and the light AA of the *contre-torpilleurs*; no hits were scored and two of the aircraft were downed.

At 2025, a French reconnaissance aircraft from Arzew reported that *Hood* had reversed course and was now making off to the northwest.[23] Twenty minutes later the final Swordfish attack came in. Again no hits were scored, possibly as a result of failure of the magnetic warheads of the torpedoes. Soon it was nightfall and *Strasbourg* could safely reduce her speed to 20 knots to enable the armoured hatches to boiler room no.2 to be opened. Inside the boilers were found to be operating at their full designed pressure of 27kg/cm[2] while all thirty of the boiler room personnel were lying unconscious, overcome by the heat and the toxic fumes; five were subsequently found to have died. Repairs to the ventilation trunking were relatively straightforward, and within an hour the boilers could again be lit.

Uncertain as to whether the British had abandoned the chase Collinet, rather than risk the direct route to Toulon, headed for the south of Sardinia, keeping strict radio silence. At 1000 the following morning, sixty miles from San Pietro Island, *Strasbourg* changed course to the north for Toulon. At 2110, she entered the harbour with her crew lining the decks, to be greeted with the cheers of the crews and bands playing the 'Marseillaise' aboard the heavy cruisers of the 1st Division: *Algérie*, *Foch*, *Colbert* and *Dupleix*. *Strasbourg* duly took her place in the anchorage.

THE SECOND ATTACK ON *DUNKERQUE*

At 2000 on the evening of 3 July, Admiral Gensoul ordered the evacuation of all crew not involved in damage control measures, and the recovery of the dead and wounded from turret II and the machinery spaces. At 2030, he informed Somerville of this evacuation, only to receive a strong rebuke from Admiral Le Luc for 'parleying with the enemy'. Some 800 crewmen were disembarked from *Dunkerque*, to be accommodated in particularly unpleasant and cramped conditions on the liners *Champollion* and *Mariette Pacha* moored at Oran. Only 360 men remained on board.

The ship was beached for some 30 metres of her bow. She had taken on 700 tonnes of water to starboard, and 150 tonnes of water had been admitted into the port ballast tanks to stabilise the list. Fires were still raging in the trunk of turret III and in the oil pumping station, and the forward part of the ship was still without power. By the following day, however, the fires had been extinguished, the dead and wounded evacuated to the hospital at Saint-André, and work was proceeding on sealing the breaches in the hull, pumping out the water, restoring power and repairing the steam lines and collector drums. Gensoul was optimistic that the ship would be able to undertake an anticipated return to Toulon, where she could be docked for full repairs and refurbishment, within a matter of days, and informed the French Admiralty and Admiral Esteva (*Amiral Sud*, Bizerta) accordingly. Esteva then proceeded to issue an unfortunate communiqué to the Algerian press in which he made light of the damage to *Dunkerque* and boasted that she would soon be able to return to Toulon under her own power.

The impact of this communiqué on Churchill and the British Admiralty was such that Somerville promptly received instructions to take Force H to sea again to 'finish the job' at Mers el-Kebir. Following negotiation between the Admiralty and Somerville, who was anxious not to cause unnecessary civilian casualties now that *Dunkerque* was beached only 50m from the shore facing the village of Saint-André, it was agreed that the attack would be mounted using torpedo planes from *Ark Royal*. Twelve Swordfish, armed with torpedoes fitted with special deflectors to enable them to be launched in shallow water, were to attack at dawn on 6 July in one wave of six and two waves of three, each of the last two waves having an escort of three Skua fighters to counter an anticipated aerial response from French shore-based fighters.

In order to launch their torpedoes in these shallow waters the Swordfish needed to make their approach only just above the surface, which made them particularly vulnerable to anti-aircraft fire. However Gensoul, in order to make it appear that the ship had been abandoned, insisted that the light AA should not be manned.[24] Both he and the ship's captain, Seguin, had agreed that the ship's working parties would be evacuated in the event of an air attack. However, this could only happen if sufficient warning of such an attack was received, and aerial reconnaissance was still patchy and poorly organised. The three small patrol boats assigned to evacuating the crew were now moored alongside: *Terre-Neuve* was moored on the starboard side abeam the main turrets, and *Sétoise* and *Grouin du Cou* were to port next to the after gangway. Not only were these patrol boats stacked with depth charges, many of which were still primed, but also raising sufficient pressure in their coal-fired boilers to get underway would take around thirty minutes. As if to compound these serious errors of judgement Seguin had not thought to surround his

---

22 There is no evidence that *Hood* made more than 27 knots in her pursuit of *Strasbourg*, even after Somerville dispensed with the services of the two older battleships. Although she made 31 knots in her prime, *Hood* was in serious need of a major overhaul.

23 Somerville was concerned that any further advance to the east risked a night engagement with the French light forces despatched from Algiers. His two older battleships had also been left without protection.

---

24 The 130mm guns could not be operated because there was no power for the turrets or the directors.

ship with torpedo nets, even though the French must have been aware that an aerial torpedo attack was a possibility.

When the first wave of Swordfish appeared at 0615 on 6 July and started its approach the foredeck of *Dunkerque* was packed with crewmen sleeping in the open air, AA guns were unmanned, there were no torpedo nets and there was no fighter cover. However, the difficulties posed by a torpedo launch in shallow water were considerable, even at point-blank range against a stationary target. One torpedo hit the patrol boat *Terre-Neuve* amidships, causing her to sink by the stern, but the warhead failed to explode; the others porpoised and ran wide. Similar problems were experienced by the second and third waves, none of which managed to secure a hit on *Dunkerque* herself. However, one of the torpedoes from the second wave exploded against the hull of *Terre-Neuve*, breaking the ship in half and causing panic and many casualties among the crew members of *Dunkerque* endeavouring to escape the ship; and one of the torpedoes of the third wave sank the tug *Esterel*, manoeuvring 70 metres off the port side of the battleship.

Some minutes after the torpedo struck *Terre-Neuve*, there was a massive explosion, which ripped apart the starboard side of *Dunkerque*'s bow, distorting the decks and the internal bulkheads and even dislodging two of the massive armour plates of the main belt. A column of blackish water rose 100 metres into the air and fell back onto the foredeck and the bridge platforms. In the subsequent investigation, it was determined that no fewer than fourteen of the forty-four depth charges carried by *Terre-Neuve* had exploded – equivalent to 1400kg of TNT; it is thought that at least one of the charges known to have been primed may have been set off by the water pressure following the patrol boat's sinking. Fortunately, the main 330mm magazines had been flooded on the orders of Captain Seguin as soon as the first Swordfish appeared: there

can be little doubt that they would otherwise have exploded, resulting in the total loss of the ship.

The Commission which subsequently inspected the damage reported that the ship's outer hull, double bottom and the 40/50mm torpedo bulkhead had been distorted over a length of 40 metres, with numerous breaches in the area of bulkhead FG, the centre of the explosion (see drawing). The explosion opened up a hole 18 metres by 12 metres abeam the 330mm magazines, causing an ingress of 20,000 tonnes of water and causing the bow to settle deeper into the surrounding mud. A 5-degree list had been halted by counter-flooding. With the waterline now above the level of the lower armoured deck, the machinery spaces and the transmitting station, damage control station, etc. were flooded. The forward plates of the armour belt were pushed in, and the armoured decks

View of the breach in the hull of *Dunkerque* made by the explosion of the depth charges alongside. It was this damage, rather than the shell damage sustained on 3 July, that crippled the ship and effectively precluded her repatriation for repair until February 1942. (*ECPAD*)

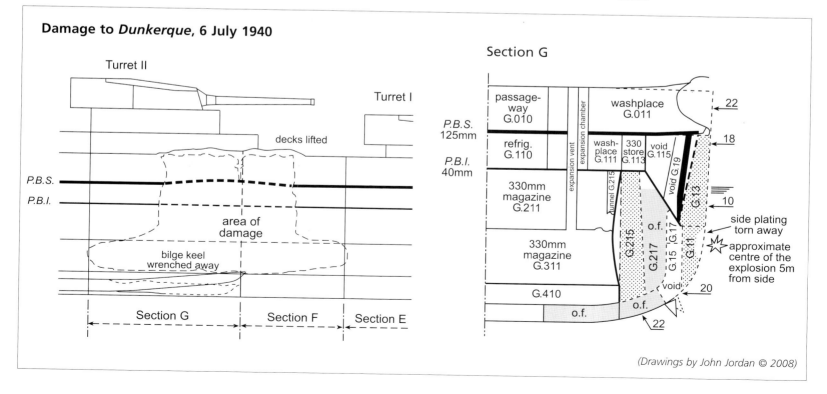

Damage to *Dunkerque*, 6 July 1940

Turret II

Turret I

decks lifted

P.B.S.

P.B.I.

area of damage

bilge keel wrenched away

Section G   Section F   Section E

Section G

P.B.S. 125mm

P.B.I. 40mm

passage-way G.010

washplace G.011

22

refrig. G.110

wash-place G.111

330 store G.113

void G.115

18

void G.19

330mm magazine G.211

expansion vent

expansion chamber

tunnel G.215

G.13

G.11

10

330mm magazine G.311

G.215

o.f.

G.217

G.15

G.17

side plating torn away

approximate centre of the explosion 5m from side

G.410

o.f.

void

20

o.f.

o.f.

22

(Drawings by John Jordan © 2008)

had been lifted. The shock had also unseated the main fire control directors from their ball races.[25]

Dunkerque was now clearly out of action for the foreseeable future. The explosion of *Terre-Neuve*'s depth charges had a far greater effect on her watertight integrity than all four of the 15in shell hits sustained on 3 July, and the damage would be far more difficult to repair. The estimated figure of 1400kg of TNT was the equivalent of eight air-launched torpedo warheads,[26] and it would certainly have taken a number of torpedo hits from *Ark Royal*'s aircraft to achieve a comparable result.

Much of the blame for this sad affair can be laid at the door of Admiral Gensoul, and Captain Seguin cannot be entirely exonerated. Although it is clear that there was little love lost between them, this does not explain or excuse some of the poor decisions taken between 3 and 6 July: the failure to cast off moorings on 3 July, the decision not to man the light AA guns, the inability to recognise the dangers inherent in mooring patrol boats packed with primed depth charges alongside, and the failure to surround the grounded hull with anti-torpedo nets. These were serious errors of judgement which reflected badly on

both men and cast a dark shadow over the performance of the Marine Nationale in a period otherwise illuminated by the courage and professionalism shown by the officers and men who ran the gauntlet of fire at Mers el-Kebir. Had they been serving in the contemporary Royal Navy, it is hard to imagine that the subsequent careers of Gensoul and Seguin would have been so little affected. It is a measure of the desperate depths of despondency into which France had fallen by early July 1940 that their loyalty to the government of Marshal Pétain counted for more than their questionable performance in the execution of their duties.[27]

For Gensoul this reprieve was of relatively short duration. Snubbed by Darlan on his return to Toulon, he would be conspicuously overlooked for the post of C-in-C when in the autumn the main body of the French fleet was reorganised as the *Forces de Haute Mer* under Admiral Jean de Laborde.[28] However, Seguin would

Dunkerque grounded opposite the village of Saint André following the damage sustained in early July 1940. The ship has now – belatedly – been surrounded by torpedo nets. Rising behind her can be seen the Santon heights, on which the fort of the same name with its battery of four 194mm coast defence guns was located. To the right is the village of Mers el-Kebir with its fort.

25 These may have been unseated by the whiplash effect on the masts around which they were mounted.
26 The standard British Mk XII torpedo was fitted with a 388lb (175kg) TNT warhead.

27 Seguin and Gensoul were members of a group of officers who were known as the 'ADD' (*Amis De Darlan*). This had undoubtedly helped Seguin's career to recover after the grounding of the fleet torpedo boat *Mistral* in July 1930 while under his command; the ship had sustained extensive damage to her hull and repairs spanned three years.
28 Gensoul was nevertheless subsequently accorded his fifth star as a reward for his loyalty, becoming a full admiral.

Turret I of *Strasbourg* is trained to starboard in this photo taken during 1941. Note the blast bags of canvas and black leather fitted during the same year.

TEMPORARY REPAIRS AND REPATRIATION

The second attack on *Dunkerque* caused the deaths of a further 30 officers and men. The total number killed in the actions of 3 and 6 July was now 210 (nine officers, thirty-two petty officers and 169 men). After the removal of the bodies and the evacuation of the wounded, work restarted on repairing the ship, although the scale and nature of the damage to the forward part was beyond the expertise of the crew and, in the absence of docking facilities for a ship of this size, beyond the capacity of the dockyard at Oran. Engineers were despatched from Toulon, and a full inspection of the damage was conducted during 11-12 July.

The first priority was to seal the breach in the hull. A steel panel measuring 22.6 metres by 11.8 metres was fabricated, and at the same time the torn plating of the hull was 'cleaned up' ready to receive it. The panel was delivered and put in place during 19-23 August and over the following eight days was secured by threaded bolts. From 31 August to 11 September the breach was sealed with 200 cubic metres of concrete (weight: 450 tonnes).

Once the concrete had set work commenced on draining the hull using pumps. The ship was floated at 1800 on 27 September. She was then towed to a new mooring perpendicular to the quay of the port of Saint-André. She was surrounded by torpedo nets and all her anti-aircraft guns readied for firing and manned.

During November, boiler rooms 1 and 3 were repaired, together with engine room No. 2. Unfortunately on 5 December a welding torch caused a serious fire in the electrical cabling tunnel between sections K and F. Numerous other small fires would break out during repairs in parts of the ship where oil fuel had impregnated the rubberised *ébonite mousse* filling which formed part of the ship's protection.

During April 1941, *Dunkerque* conducted trials of equipment and machinery while at her moorings. She was crewed from 19 May, and placed in care and maintenance[29] under the terms of the Armistice on 28 June. She was ready to sail for Toulon by July, but this operation was delayed because of the intense naval activity in the western Mediterranean at this time. Meanwhile work on the ship continued.

On 25 January 1942, the ship again suffered a serious fire in her cabling, this time in compartment H210. The fire was caused by a short circuit and destroyed the cabling to the conning tower. After temporary repairs preparations were made in the greatest secrecy for the ship's return to Toulon. The rear-admiral commanding at Oran was on board to supervise the operation. At 0430 on 19 February *Dunkerque* slipped through the pass at Mers el-Kebir and was joined by an escort comprising the 5th DCT (*Kersaint*, *Tartu*, and *Vauquelin*) from Toulon and the 2nd DT (*Fougueux* and *Frondeur*). Substantial air cover was provided for the operation:

Naval Aviation
1st Fighter Flotilla (Squadrons 1AC, 2AC): twenty-three aircraft
4th Bomber Flotilla (Squadrons 6B, 7B): eleven aircraft

---

[29] The correct term was *en gardiennage d'Armistice*. Ships in this category were laid up with skeleton crews and were subject to inspection by the Armistice Commission.

Strasbourg at Salins d'Hyères in 1941. Training sorties by the *Forces de Haute Mer* (FHM) were permitted twice per month by the Italo-German Armistice Commission during this period. (*C Picard collection*)

Torpedo Squadron 2T: five aircraft
Air Force
Fighter Group 3/3: nineteen aircraft
Bomber Group 1/11: seven aircraft
Reconnaissance Group 2/52

Dunkerque sustained a steady speed of 18 knots throughout the transit and entered Toulon at 2300 on 20 February. She was again placed *en gardiennage d'Armistice* on 1 March, and on 22 June entered the more southwesterly of the large Vauban graving docks for reconstruction and refurbishment (see p.91).

STRASBOURG AND THE FORCES DE HAUTE MER

On 6 July, the day that *Dunkerque* was disabled by British Swordfish torpedo-bombers, VAE Gensoul was recalled to Toulon. That same evening, he raised his flag on *Strasbourg*. The ship had received only minor damage during her escape from Mers el-Kebir and was quickly repaired.[30]

Following the Armistice there would be a major restructuring of the French fleet to take into account both the new regulations and the effective abolition of the Atlantic Theatre. Ministerial Instruction 1497 FMF3 of 8 August outlined the new provisional organisation of French naval forces. The 1st DL was dissolved on 8 August and the Atlantic Squadron on 12 August. Gensoul left *Strasbourg* on 10 August and the ship was now attached to the 3rd (Mediterranean) Squadron as a

---

[30] There were four small holes above the waterline in the unarmoured after part of the ship to starboard, and two small deformations of the hull amidships (compartment M), caused by shell fragments and debris.

private ship. She was docked from 14 August to 11 September, when screens of hardened steel were fitted on either side of the deckhouse abaft the funnel to protect the gun crews of the light AA weapons.

On 25 September, the *Forces de Haute Mer* (FHM, lit. 'High Sea Forces') were created, and *Strasbourg* became the flagship of the newly-appointed C-in-C, Admiral Jean de Laborde. On 5 November, accompanied by the cruisers *Dupleix*, *Foch*, *La Galissonnière* and *Marseillaise* and the *contre-torpilleurs* of the 5th DCT, she sortied to meet the battleship *Provence*, refloated after the damage received at Mers el-Kebir and now returning to Toulon.[31] The latter was escorted by the

Strasbourg in heavy weather in 1941. The turrets are trained aft to prevent ingress of water. Note the tricolore identification bands on turret II (*ECPAD*)

---

[31] The ship was refloated on 26 July, and temporary repairs were carried out at Oran from 23 August.

THE *FORCES DE HAUTE MER* 25 SEPTEMBER 1940

FLAGSHIP: *STRASBOURG* (Amiral de Laborde)

1ère Escadre de croiseurs (CA Bouxin)

1ère DC (CA Bouxin)	**3e DC** (CA Barnaud)
Algérie (fl)	*Marseillaise* (fl)
Foch	*La Galissonnière*
Dupleix	

3e Escadre Légère *Aigle* (CA Jardel)

3e DCT	7e DCT	10e DCT
Guépard	*Vautour*	*L'Indomptable*
Valmy	*Albatros*	*Volta*
Cassard	*Gerfaut*	

Note: All other ships in Toulon were placed *en gardiennage d'Armistice*, with skeleton crews. There was regular rotation of units between the active units and those *en gardiennage* to enable active ships to undergo refit, but the basic structure of the *Forces de Haute Mer* always remained the same: *Strasbourg* as flagship; a cruiser squadron comprising a 10,000-ton flagship together with two two-ship cruiser divisions, one of 10,000-ton cruisers, the other of 7600-ton cruisers; and a 'light' squadron comprising a flagship plus three two/three-ship divisions of *contre-torpilleurs*. When the new fleet-torpedo-boats of the *Le Hardi* class returned to Toulon in November a three-ship division was permitted to remain active.

COMMANDING OFFICERS AND FLAG OFFICERS

Commanding Officers

Dunkerque

CV Fenard	01.02.36 – 01.09.38
CV Negadelle	01.09.38 – 31.10.39
CV Seguin	31.10.39 – 19.08.40
(CF Tanguy	19.08.40 – 23.08.40)[1]
CV Tanguy	23.08.40 – 05.03.42
CV Amiel	05.03.42 – 27.11.42

Strasbourg

CV Bouxin	02.04.38 – 16.11.39
CV Collinet	16.11.39 – 12.08.40
(CF Amiel	12.08.40 – 23.08.40)[1]
CV Seguin	23.08.40 – 08.11.41
CV Seyeux	08.11.41 – 27.11.42

Notes:

CF	*Capitaine de frégate*	(RN equivalent rank: commander)
CV	*Capitaine de vaisseau*	(RN equivalent rank: captain)

Note: [1] These were temporary appointments in which the Executive Officer was given command of the ship.

Flag Officers

Dunkerque

VA Devin	16.05.37 – 24.05.37
VAE Gensoul	01.09.38 – 06.07.40

Strasbourg

VAE Gensoul	06.07.40 – 10.08.40
Amiral de Laborde	25.09.40 – 27.11.42

Smoke billows up from the *Strasbourg*, moored at the Milhaud finger piers during the scuttling of the French fleet 27 November 1942. (*H. Landais collection*)

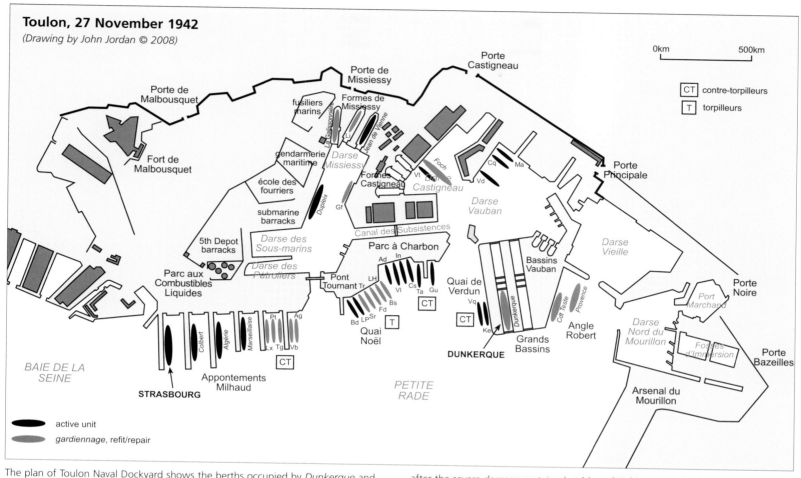

Toulon, 27 November 1942
(Drawing by John Jordan © 2008)

0km   500km

CT contre-torpilleurs

T torpilleurs

Porte de Malbousquet

Porte de Missiessy

Porte Castigneau

Fort de Malbousquet

fusiliers marins

Formes de Missiessy

Porte Principale

gendarmerie maritime

Darse Missiessy

Formes Castigneau

Darse Vauban

Porte Noire

école des fourriers

Duplerx

Gf

Foch

Vd

Cq

Ma

submarine barracks

Canal des Subsistences

Darse Vieille

5th Depot barracks

Darse des Sous-marins

Parc à Charbon

Bassins Vauban

Port Marchand

Parc aux Combustibles Liquides

Darse des Pétroliers

Pont Tournant

Ad In

LH

Vl Cs Ta Gu

Quai de Verdun

Darse Nord du Mourillon

Fosses d'Immersion

Porte Bazeilles

Tr

Bs

Vq

Cdt Teste

Provence

CT

Bd LP Sr Fd

Quai Noël

T

Dunkerque

Angle Robert

Pt Ag

CT

DUNKERQUE

Ke

STRASBOURG

Colbert

Algérie

Marseillaise

Lx Tg Vb

CT

Grands Bassins

Arsenal du Mourillon

BAIE DE LA SEINE

Appontements Milhaud

PETITE RADE

● active unit

◗ *gardiennage*, refit/repair

The plan of Toulon Naval Dockyard shows the berths occupied by *Dunkerque* and *Strasbourg* when the French fleet was sabotaged in response to the German invasion of the Unoccupied Zone. *Strasbourg*, currently the flagship of the *Forces de Haute Mer* (FHM), was moored at the first of the finger piers of the *Appontements Milhaud*. The three westernmost piers, each of which was 320 metres long with a water depth of 12 metres, were to have been fitted out to handle the new generation of 35,000-ton battleships (see Chapter 7). *Dunkerque*, still under repair

after the severe damage sustained at Mers el-Kebir, was docked in the westernmost of the two *Grands Bassins Vauban*. Her sabotage involved the admission of 50,000 cubic metres of water into the dock, a process that took three hours.

Not shown in the plan are the many submarines, training ships, auxiliaries and service craft present at the time. Four submarines escaped to open waters, but virtually all the other craft were lost, posing immense infrastructure problems for what remained of the navy from 1942 until the early 1950s.

brand-new fleet torpedo-boats *Le Hardi*, *Epée*, *Fleuret*, *Lansquenet* and *Mameluk*. The two forces joined up off the Balearics and entered Toulon on 8 November.

The year 1941 was largely uneventful. Apart from being docked for maintenance 15 April to 3 May and a four-day visit to Marseille in December, *Strasbourg* made only brief training sorties to the anchorage at Salins d'Hyères (a maximum of two sorties per month was permitted by the Armistice Commission).

On 31 January 1942, *Strasbourg* was docked for a major refit. Modifications were made to the light AA (see p.57) and radar installed. Throughout this refit *Strasbourg* was maintained at four days readiness. The refit was completed on 25 April and the ship became operational two days later. A gearing problem with the rudder servo-motors led to a five day break in service in mid-July; otherwise training at Salins d'Hyères continued to follow the normal pattern.

THE SCUTTLING OF THE FLEET

At 0530 on 27 November 1942, with the arrival of the tanks of the German 7th Panzer Division imminent, Admiral de Laborde broadcast from *Strasbourg* the order to scuttle the fleet. Since early morning the sabotage teams had been working to ensure that when the

order was given, following the evacuation of the crews, all the required measures were in place. The barrels of each of the main guns were stuffed with 8kg of *Mélinite* (picric acid) explosive; there were smaller charges for the 130mm guns and all the detonators were in place. Teams were circulating through the ship armed with sledge-hammers destroying rangefinders, searchlight projectors, gyroscopic compasses, machinery dials, radio sets, and all other delicate apparatus that might be of value to the enemy. Mechanicians and stokers were sabotaging the reduction gearing and the

Strasbourg scuttled and on fire at her moorings. The breeches of her guns and her propulsion machinery have been destroyed using explosive charges.
(H Landais collection)

Left:
Strasbourg, in the aftermath of the scuttling. She has settled on an even keel, which makes her look deceptively intact. She would be refloated by the Italians on 17 July 1943, but damage was so extensive that scrapping began immediately. Note the collar of black oil just below the anchor hawsepipes and the prominent degaussing cable along the upper part of the hull. *(H. Landais collection)*

Below:
Dunkerque, scuttled in the Vauban graving dock in which she was under repair. The sluice gates had to be opened in order to flood the ship. The photo shows *Dunkerque* some time after the scuttling, when the water had again been drained from the dock. *(P Caresse collection)*

Following the salvage of *Strasbourg's* hull, the ship is towed into one of the Vauban graving docks. She would subsequently be sunk in the shallow waters of the Bay of Lazaret in August 1944. (*P Caresse collection*)

turbines and lighting the boilers while turning off the water feeds.

When the German tanks arrived at 0550 and Major Heilbronn, commanding the detachment, confronted de Laborde with an order to hand over the ship intact the admiral, standing calmly on the quarterdeck of *Strasbourg*, informed him that his ship was already sunk. At first the Germans were uncomprehending; the ship appeared undamaged, and with her tricolore ensign at the stern and the five-star flag of the admiral flapping at the topmast of the tower appeared to be on the point of getting underway. However, by this time the sea-cocks had been opened and the ship was slowly settling on an even keel on the shallow bottom alongside the pier.

At 0620, with only the fifty-strong sabotage team remaining on board, de Laborde authorised the setting off of the charges. The warning klaxon sounded and was followed by a series of explosions; smoke and flames poured from all corners of the ship. De Laborde remained on deck while the colours were struck for the last time.

The sabotage of *Dunkerque* posed a different problem. Charges were in place, but the ship was still in dry dock. The only possible solution was to open the stop-cocks and to flood the dock. It would take two to three hours to admit the 50,000 cubic metres of water required to effect this. However, as the Vauban docks were on the far side of the dockyard it took until 0700 before the German troops arrived. In the general confusion, no attempt was made to stop the ingress of water into the dock, or to cut the detonators for the charges, which shortly afterwards exploded and effectively wrecked the ship.

After the scuttling of the French fleet, it was the Italians who showed most interest in salvaging what they could – their allocation of tonnage was 212,559 tonnes as compared with only 24,490 tonnes for Germany. An organisation with the name *Ente Recuperi Italiani a Tolone* ('Italian Recovery Agency at Toulon') was set up in the port in January 1943 with the brief of recovering as many vessels as possible for service with the *Regia Marina*. Those ships found to be too badly damaged to be recoverable would be scrapped and the steel shipped back to Italy by train.

When the Italian company drained the dock in which *Dunkerque* was located it found the damage too extensive to justify recovery and she was scrapped on the spot. The same decision was taken when her sister *Strasbourg* was refloated on 17 July. This work ceased when, in the wake of the Italian capitulation of 8 September, the port was taken over by the Germans. The bow of *Dunkerque* was amputated during 1944 so that the hull could be floated out, thereby freeing up the dock. On 18 August of the same year, *Strasbourg*, now in a 'state of conservation', was sunk in the shallow waters of the Bay of Lazaret by American bombers. The two hulks survived into the postwar period, and were finally stricken 15 September 1955 and 22 March 1955 respectively and sold for scrap.

CHAPTER 4

RICHELIEU AND JEAN BART:
Design and Characteristics

THE ANNOUNCEMENT BY THE ITALIAN STEFANI Press Agency on 11 June that two new battleships of 35,000 tons were to be ordered shattered all previous assumptions regarding the likely course of capital ship development among the Mediterranean powers, and had a much wider international impact. At Washington, in 1922, Italy had supported France in reserving the right to build capital ships with a displacement below the maximum permissible figure of 35,000 tons, giving both navies the option of trading unit displacement for numbers. The *Regia Marina* had subsequently followed the same course as its French counterpart, commissioning from its constructors a series of smaller designs, of which the most note-worthy was a fast battleship of 23,000 tons armed with six 381mm (15in) guns in twin turrets and with a speed of 28-9 knots, the intention being to build a class of three to utilise to the full Italy's 70,000-ton allocation for modernisation of her battle fleet.

With the increasing demands on capital ship design, which included high tactical speed to keep pace with the new Treaty cruisers, the need to accommodate and launch aircraft for spotting and reconnaissance, and the requirement for powerful batteries of anti-aircraft guns with good arcs, it was becoming more difficult to produce an effective design for a small battleship. The *Regia Marina* was not entirely happy with the 23,000-ton proposal, which, although ingenious, was riddled with compromises; six main guns were considered by most contemporary navies too few for effective salvo fire, and the aviation arrangements amidships were particularly cramped. Moreover, naval funding in Italy was still tied up in the large cruiser programme embarked upon during the late 1920s. The *Regia Marina* therefore decided to wait upon developments abroad, including possible new restrictions on the size of future battleships which might be agreed by the London Conference of 1930.

The order for *Dunkerque* forced the Italians' hand. Although the stated purpose of the new ships was to

A COMPARISON BETWEEN THE NEW ITALIAN BATTLESHIPS AND *RICHELIEU*

	Littorio	*Richelieu*
Displacement[1]	35,000 tons	35,000 tons
Dimensions	237.7m x 32.9m	248m x 33m
Propulsion		
Type	4-shaft gst	4-shaft gst
SHP	130,000	155,000
Speed	30 knots	32 knots
Armament		
Main	9 – 381/50 (3 x III)	8 – 380/45 (2 x IV)
Secondary	12 – 152/55 (4 x III)	15 – 152/55 DP (5 x III) [2]
Heavy AA	12 – 90/50 HA (12 x I)	
Light AA	20 – 37/54 (8 x II, 4 x I)	12 x 37/70 (6 x II)[2]
Aircraft	three	four
Protection		
Belt	70 + 280mm	330mm
Decks	36mm + 150/100mm[3]	170/150mm + 40mm
Turrets	380mm max.	430mm max.
CT	255mm max.	340mm max.
Complement	1866	1570

Notes:
[1] Both ships exceeded their designed displacement, the *Littorio*s by a wide margin.
[2] AA for *Richelieu* as originally designed.
[3] In the Italian ships the weather deck was armoured as a 'bomb deck' with the main armoured deck below; the French persisted with the heavy armoured main deck backed by a lower 'splinter deck' introduced in *Dunkerque*.

counter the German *Panzerschiffe*, the new French battleship effectively outgunned and outclassed all of the older Italian capital ships, and therefore had to be opposed by new construction. The modernisation of the two battleships of the *Cavour* class, taken in hand in October 1933 for a radical reconstruction that was to take almost four years, was a direct response to the laying down of *Dunkerque* by the French. However, modernisation of Italy's older battleships could only be a temporary measure to correct a projected imbalance in naval forces in the Mediterranean during the late 1930s. Serious consideration was now given to building two new battleships of the maximum displacement permitted by the Washington Treaty. Ships of this size and power would not only trump the French *Dunkerque* and her projected sistership, but would also enable the *Regia Marina* to stand up to the 15in-gun battleships of the British Mediterranean Fleet, a possible future opponent as Mussolini's Italy pursued its dream of an extensive colonial empire in North and East Africa.

The two battleships of the *Littorio* class laid down in October 1934 had a main armament of nine 381mm (15in) guns in three triple turrets, a secondary battery of twelve 152mm (6in) guns also in triple turrets, a powerful two-tier anti-aircraft armament of 90mm HA and 37/20mm light AA guns, an armoured belt 350mm thick and a maximum speed of 30 knots (see table). It was they, rather than the French *Dunkerque*, that would set the standard for the new generation of fast battleships that would be laid down following the expiry of the Washington Treaty on 31 December 1936. The orders for these two ships effectively ended any chance of British success in reducing the maximum displacement of future battleships, and even the limited British success in securing agreement on a maximum gun calibre of 14in (356mm) at the London Conference of 1935 was to prove something of a pyrrhic victory. Britain would be the only country to build ships armed with guns of a calibre inferior to 15in (381mm) in the build-up to the Second World War; all the other major European powers would opt for 380/381mm guns for their new battleships while the US Navy, suspecting that the new Japanese battleships were to be armed with 16in (406mm) guns,[1] duly invoked the 'escalator' clause in the London 1936 Treaty[2] and accordingly up-gunned the two ships of the *North Carolina* class.

THE FIRST SKETCH DESIGNS

The French response to Italy's declaration of intent was immediate. On 24 July 1934, less than two weeks after the characteristics of the new Italian battleships were announced and only eight days after the order for *Strasbourg* was placed with the Ateliers et Chantiers de Saint Nazaire (Penhoët), the Conseil Supérieur de la Marine defined the characteristics of the new French battleships as follows:

- displacement: 35,000 tons standard
- main armament: eight/nine guns of 380/406mm calibre
- secondary armament: to be capable of fire against

surface targets and long-range anti-aircraft fire
- speed: 29.5-30 knots
- protection: belt 360mm; PBS 160mm; PBI 40mm; underwater protection as *Dunkerque*

The Chief of the Naval Staff, Admiral Durand-Viel, was particularly keen that there should be continuity between the design of *Dunkerque* and the new ships in order to reduce to a minimum planning and construction delays and to create homogeneous combat groups. It was therefore envisaged that an all-forward main armament of either eight 380/406mm in two quad turrets as in *Dunkerque*, or nine 380mm in three triple turrets might be adopted as the basis of the design, and that the secondary dual-purpose armament would comprise four or five of the quadruple 130mm mountings developed for *Dunkerque* and her sister.

Preliminary calculations by the STCN constructors quickly established that the 406mm calibre was a non-starter given the other requirements. The 380mm calibre was judged the maximum that could be accommodated successfully in a quadruple turret, and alternative three-turret arrangements using 406mm guns all came out at well over 35,000 tons. The six preliminary designs submitted to the Conseil Supérieur for consideration on 27 November (see drawings) all featured ships with eight or nine 380mm guns.

Project 1 was essentially an enlargement of the *Dunkerque*. The design was considered generally satisfactory but was 350 tons overweight. *Projects 2, 3* and *4* were similar, but with three turrets forward as in the British *Nelson* class. *Project 2* had eight 380mm in one twin and two triple mountings; *Project 3* had eight 380mm in one quad and two twin mountings, the quad mounting being superimposed; and *Project 4* had nine 380mm in three triple mountings. The secondary armament was as in *Project 1*.

The cost of a third main gun turret was significant. The length of the machinery spaces had to be compressed, and this resulted in substantially reduced horsepower (110,000shp) and the loss of two knots in speed (29.5 knots). Moreover, each of these designs was seriously overweight: 550 tons for *Project 2*, 450 tons for *Project 3*, and 1150 tons for the triple-turret design, *Project 4*.

Projects 5 and *5 bis* were based on an idea of the Italian Admiral de Feo. The two quadruple 380mm mountings were just forward of amidships, turret I being located abaft the tower structure with turret II superimposed above it. The secondary armament, comprising three quad 130mm mountings in *Project 5* and three quad plus two twin sided mountings in *Project 5 bis* (see drawings), was disposed on the centreline fore and aft. This arrangement had a number of advantages: in particular, the magazines for the main guns were located in the broadest part of the hull and could therefore be accorded the deepest protection, and the dual-purpose secondary battery enjoyed excellent arcs when firing against both surface and aerial targets. Horsepower and speed were as in *Project 1*. Overweight was 50 tons in *Project 5* and 350 tons in *Project 5 bis*.

Projects 5 and *5 bis* were quickly rejected because the main guns could fire only on the beam, and the arcs on both forward and after bearings were poor. There was a 'blind' arc of almost 90 degrees forward and 50 degrees aft for turret I, although the figures for

---

[1] The battleships of the *Yamato* class would in the event be completed with 46cm (18.1in) guns.

[2] Article 4(2).

Richelieu: **Preliminary Design Studies**

All of these projects had the following characteristics in common:

Displacement: 35,000TW (baseline – but see 'Overweight:' below)
Dimensions: 247m x 33m
Protection: 360mm belt
               160mm + 40mm decks

Project 1
Armament: 8 x 380mm (2 x IV)
             20 x 130mm (5 x IV)
SHP: 150,000
Speed: 31.5 knots
Overweight: +350 tons

Project 2
Armament: 8 x 380mm (2 x III, 1 x II)
             20 x 130mm (5 x IV)
SHP: 110,000
Speed: 29.5 knots
Overweight: +550 tons

Project 3
Armament: 8 x 380mm (1 x IV, 2 x II)
             20 x 130mm (5 x IV)
SHP: 110,000
Speed: 29.5 knots
Overweight: +450 tons

Project 4
Armament: 9 x 380mm (3 x III)
             20 x 130mm (5 x IV)
SHP: 110,000
Speed: 29.5 knots
Overweight: +1150 tons

Project 5
Armament: 8 x 380mm (2 x IV)
             12 x 130mm (3 x IV)
SHP: 150,000
Speed: 31.5 knots
Overweight: +50 tons

Project 5 bis
Armament: 8 x 380mm (2 x IV)
             16 x 130mm (3 x IV, 2 x II)
SHP: 150,000
Speed: 31.5 knots
Overweight: +350 tons

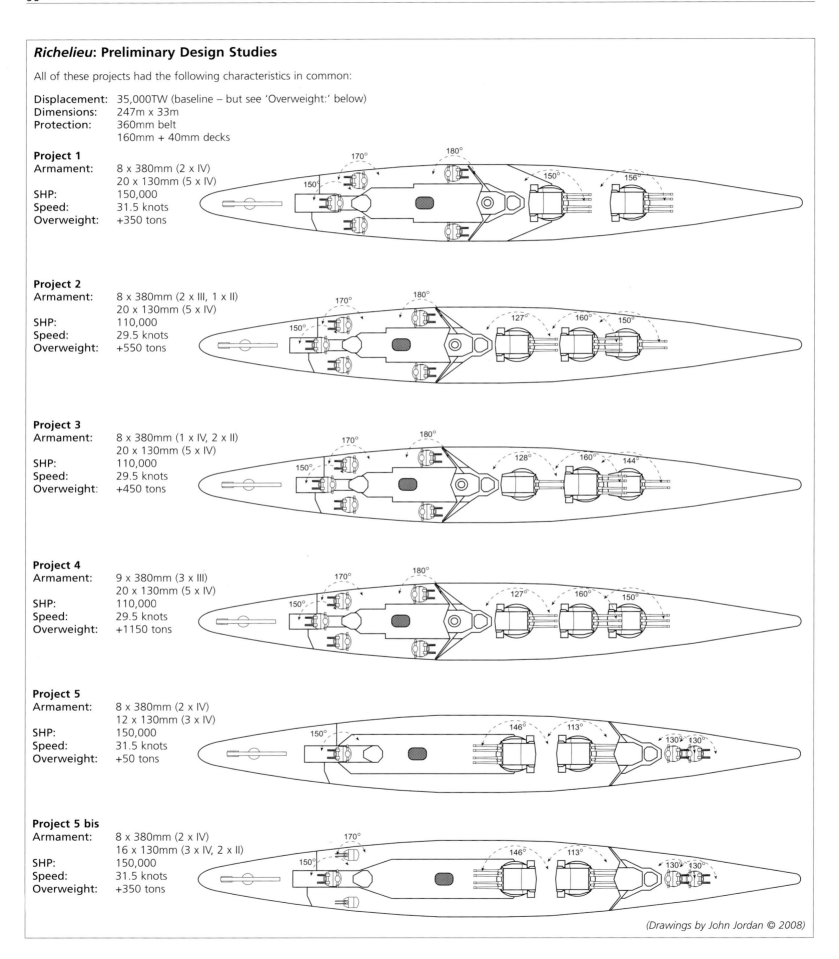

(Drawings by John Jordan © 2008)

turret II were somewhat better. Ingénieur Général Charpentier, Head of the STCN, was asked to advise on the relative merits of the other designs. He expressed a clear preference for *Project 1*, which he considered provided the best combination of offensive power, speed and protection on the displacement. The three-turret designs with eight guns (*Projects 2* and *3*) were heavier, and the loss of two knots was not felt to be compensated by the limited benefits of distributing the main armament over a greater length (+20 per cent) of the ship. Moreover the design with three triple turrets (*Project 4*), in which the loss of two knots was compensated by an increase in offensive power, was 1150 tons over the permitted Washington displacement.

After careful consideration of these projects, the CSM opted for *Project 1*. However, concerns were expressed that the 130mm calibre of the secondary guns was on the weak side for a ship of this size. The British *Nelson* and *Rodney*, which had set the standard for future 35,000-ton battleships, had a secondary armament of twelve 6in (152mm) guns in twin turrets, and the new Italian battleships would be similarly armed; even the elderly 23,500-tonne battleships of the *Courbet* and *Bretagne* classes had a secondary battery of 138.6mm guns, heavy enough to penetrate the armour of a light cruiser or to stop a destroyer. The STCN was therefore requested to undertake studies for a ship with a secondary armament of 152mm guns to investigate the number which could be accommodated and their proposed location.

Further STCN studies led to two proposed solutions:

– five triple 152mm turrets disposed as in *Project 1*, with a separate high-angle armament comprising six single 75mm guns in open mountings (in tubs).
– four triple 152mm turrets, either with the centreline mounting aft eliminated or with two superimposed mountings on the centreline aft to complement the two sided turrets amidships; the HA armament would be boosted to eight single 75mm guns.

The solution of dividing the uniform secondary battery into low-angle and high-angle components would be a feature of the new battleships under construction for the Italian and German navies. It posed the problem of locating HA guns (generally in open mountings) in close proximity to heavy turret-mounted secondary guns, where the gun crews and delicate sights of the HA weapons were vulnerable to blast from the heavier weapons. The Germans resolved this problem by locating the HA guns at a higher level than the secondary guns, the Italians by moving the secondary turrets to the four 'corners' of the upper deck, thereby leaving space amidships for the HA guns, which were also in fully enclosed mountings.

Neither of these two solutions was available to the STCN; the German arrangement was precluded by the relatively high position of the secondary turrets, two/four of which were located on the raised shelter deck amidships (the centreline turret/s aft were even higher), and the all-forward main armament effectively precluded the Italian arrangement of the secondary turrets. However, the major problem for the STCN constructors was that the split-battery solution further increased weights, which were already 350 tons above treaty limits. The 75mm HA gun had to be abandoned in favour of a proposal that the triple 152mm turrets

would have a dual-purpose function: they would be used both against surface targets and for long-range AA fire. This was accepted by the Conseil Supérieur at a meeting 14 April 1935, when it was also decided to fix the number of turrets at five, located as the quad 130mm in the original *Project 1* design.

At the same time as these studies were taking place, the STCN constructors attempted to resolve the over-weight problem with a view to keeping design displacement within the permitted 35,000 tons. It was found that by adopting a new-model boiler – the designation Sural was for Suralimenté (pressure-fired) – the length of the machinery spaces could be reduced. The Sural boilers provided similar power to the Indret model on reduced dimensions, and the greater beam of the new battleships (33 metres against 31 metres for *Dunkerque* and *Strasbourg*) meant that three boilers could be accommodated side by side, thereby reducing the number of boiler rooms from three to two. This effectively reduced the length of the armoured citadel by 4.85 metres for a substantial saving in weight.

Other weight-reduction measures were as follows: the armoured belt was reduced from 360mm in the original sketch designs to 330mm, the angle of inclination being increased from 11°03 to 15°24 to compensate for the reduction in thickness; small reductions were also made in the thickness of the armour on the main transverse bulkheads, the conning tower, and the turrets and barbettes of the 152mm guns.

With the weight and secondary armament issues resolved, attention now turned to the light AA guns. The position of the midships 152mm turrets made it difficult to find a satisfactory solution for the proposed 37mm guns, particularly as both the existing Mle 1925 CAS and projected Mle 1933 CAD were in open mountings. This prompted the development of a new advanced twin weapon in a fully enclosed mounting, the 37mm Mle 1935 (ACAD). The mounting for the new gun, which was fully automatic in operation and fitted with RPC for training, was designed for an unprecedented 200rpm per barrel. There was an ammunition lobby immediately beneath the mounting, making it well-suited to installation on the upper decks of a battleship.

According to the modified plans drawn up in 1935, six of the new twin mountings were to be provided: two at the level of the forecastle deck on each side of turret II and four abeam the after structure. All were well clear of the secondary wing turrets, and the midships mountings were located as close as possible to the superstructures to protect them from blast. They were to be complemented by 13.2mm Hotchkiss quad MG in open mountings located high in the superstructures fore and aft.

Unfortunately the complexity of the new ACAD mounting resulted in protracted development: the first prototype was ready only in spring 1939, and it was envisaged that the delivery of production models would be possible only in late 1940. This was to lead to a fundamental revision of the secondary armament and AA provision in *Richelieu* and *Jean Bart*, because it was not feasible simply to substitute the Mle 1933 in open mountings for the fully enclosed Mle 1935.

The final changes made in the design concerned the aviation arrangements. It was found that there was sufficient space on the quarterdeck for a second catapult, and the necessary adjustments were made to the positioning of the catapults (now offset *en echelon* to port and to starboard), the handling crane and the service rails leading from the two-tier hangar. Four aircraft could now be embarked (two in the hangar and two on the catapults) for reconnaissance and spotting, and there was sufficient space atop the hangar for a fifth.

ORDERS FOR TWO SHIPS

The definitive plans were submitted to the Navy Minister and accepted on 14 August 1935. The contract for the first ship was placed with the Arsenal de Brest on 31 August. The main body of the hull was to be constructed in the Le Salou No. 4 building dock, currently occupied by the hull of *Dunkerque*, which would be launched only on 2 October. Whereas the latter ship had been built minus a 17-metre section of her bow (added in dry dock following launch), an even more radical solution had to be adopted in order to construct the hull of the new battleship, which had a length overall of 248 metres (against 215 metres for *Dunkerque*). Not only would *Richelieu* be launched without the first 43 metres of her bow, but she would also be missing the last eight metres of her stern; this brought the main body of the hull down to a manageable 197 metres.

The keel was laid on 22 October 1935, which technically placed the French in breach of their treaty obligations. France was permitted to lay down capital ship tonnage up to a maximum of 70,000 tons standard before the expiry of the Washington Treaty on 31 December. She had now laid down *Dunkerque* and *Strasbourg*, each of 26,500 tons, and *Richelieu* of 35,000 tons, for a total of 88,000 tons. With the laying down of the second ship, *Jean Bart*, on 12 December 1936 – admittedly less than three weeks from the expiry date of the treaty – this total rose to 123,000 tons.

Although the French government had failed to ratify the London Treaty of 1930 that extended the Washington 'battleship holiday' by five years, the relevant part of the treaty (Part I) had been signed by the then-Foreign Minister Aristide Briand and the Navy Minister Jacques-Louis Dumesnil. France was therefore under a moral obligation to conform to the provisions of this section of the treaty.[3] However, the French had been incensed by the Anglo-German Naval Agreement of 18 June 1935, which effectively buried the Treaty of Versailles, permitted the *Kriegsmarine* to build up to 35 per cent of Royal Navy strength, and in political terms left the Marine Nationale exposed to a conflict in which it might be opposed by both the Italian and the German fleets. Given that the British had shown such a cavalier attitude to their obligations under the Treaty of Versailles, the French felt fully justified in laying down the two new battleships in breach of their own treaty obligations; after all, *Dunkerque* and *Strasbourg* were now needed to counter the two new '*Panzerschiffe* of 26,000 tons with 280mm guns', which were the central element of the German naval programme published in the wake of the Anglo-German Naval Agreement,[4] while the two new 35,000-ton battleships were essential to counter the Italian *Littorio*s. Although the British would make clear their dissatisfaction with France's 'escalatory' actions, their protests were undermined by their unilateral concessions to Hitler's Germany.

The order for *Jean Bart* was placed with the Ateliers et Chantiers de Saint-Nazaire (Penhoët) on 27 May 1936, and the ship was laid down on 12 December, the same day that *Strasbourg* was launched. Whereas the latter ship had been laid down on the No. 1 slipway of the Penhoët shipyard, the keel of *Jean Bart* would be laid in the construction dock of the revolutionary new

---

[3] The British would lay down the first two ships of the *King George V* class on 1 January 1937, the day after the treaty expired. The first of the new generation of US and Japanese battleships would be laid down only in October 1937. The Italians, who were in the same legal position as the French having signed Part I of the London Treaty but failed to ratify it, would restrict new construction during the treaty period to the two *Littorio*s.

[4] These became *Scharnhorst* and *Gneisenau*; displacement when completed was close to 32,000 tons standard.

Richelieu: **Inboard Profile**

Showing the principal operational and machinery spaces, magazines, fuel bunkers and other liquid stowage. The plans on which this drawing is based show the ship as originally designed; the forward 152mm magazines would become the magazines for the 100mm HA guns.

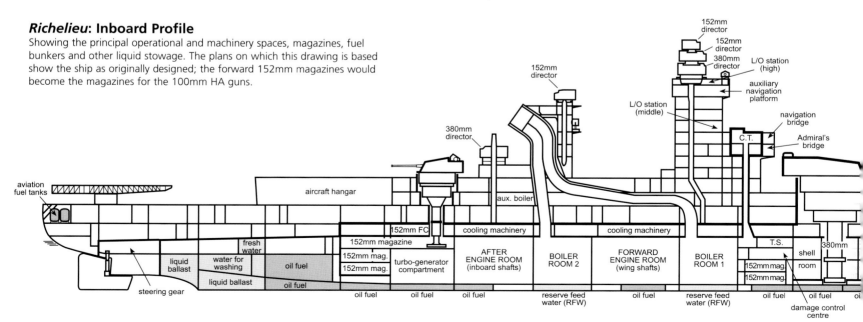

facility designed by the civil engineer Albert Caquot for the adjoining Loire shipyard (see Chapter 6). Workers from both shipyards participated in the construction of the hull, which could only begin in earnest when the Penhoët workforce was released from their work on the hull of *Strasbourg*.

GENERAL CHARACTERISTICS AND LAYOUT

Richelieu was essentially an enlarged *Dunkerque*. She had a virtually identical hull form and a broadly similar layout in which the 330mm quadruple turrets were upgunned to 380mm, and the 130mm dual-purpose quad/twin secondary turrets of *Dunkerque* were replaced by 152mm D-P guns in uniform triple turrets. Other features, from the distinctive tower structure with its stacked directors down to the arrangements for stowing and handling the ships' boats, are further evidence of the close relationship between the two designs.

There were, however, some important modifications, most of which were made possible by the elimination of the third boiler room and the consequent reduction in the length of the machinery spaces. The single funnel incorporating the boiler uptakes was in the same position relative to the forward tower structure as in *Dunkerque*. However, the shortening of the main machinery spaces enabled the centreline 152mm mounting to be moved farther forward. The after turbo-generators of *Richelieu* were housed in a separate dynamo room abaft the after engine room – in *Dunkerque* both sets of turbo-generators were accommodated in the engine rooms – but this space was neither as wide nor as high as the main machinery spaces, which permitted the magazine and shell rooms for the centreline 152mm turret to be fitted in beneath the armoured deck with the magazines for the close-range 37mm AA to the sides. The lateral after 152mm turrets remained in the same position as the 130mm quad mountings of *Dunkerque*, their magazines being worked in abaft the generator room.

Moving the 152mm axial turret farther forward in turn enabled the aviation hangar to be lengthened, so

GENERAL CHARACTERISTICS (*RICHELIEU* AS COMPLETED)

Displacement

Standard	37,250 tons
Normal	40,927 tonnes
Full load	44,698 tonnes

Dimensions

Length pp	242.00m
Length oa	247.85m
Beam	33.08m
Draught (normal)	9.22m max.
Draught (full load)	9.90m max.

Machinery

Boilers	Six Sural small watertube boilers with superheating, 27kg/cm^2 (350° C)
Turbines	Four-shaft Parsons geared steam turbines
Power	155,000shp for 32 knots (designed)
Oil fuel	5866 tonnes
Endurance	9500nm at 15 knots, 3450nm at 30 knots
Generators	Four 1500kW turbo-generators Three 1000kW diesel generators Two emergency 140kW diesel generators

Armament

Main guns	Eight 380/45 Mle 1935 in two quadruple mountings Mle 1935 (832 AP rounds)
Secondary	Nine 152/55 Mle 1930 in three triple mountings Mle 1936 (3600 SAP/HE rounds)
HA guns	Twelve 100mm/45 Mle 1930 in six twin mountings Mle 1931 (6000 rounds incl. 120 SAP and 500 starshell)
Light AA	Eight 37mm/50 Mle 1933 in four twin mountings Twenty 13.2mm/76 Mle 1929 Hotchkiss MG in four quad and two twin mountings
Aircraft	Four Loire 130 seaplanes

Protection

Belt	330mm
Deck	150/170mm + 40mm
CT	340-170mm
380mm turrets	430mm-170mm
152mm turrets	130mm-60mm

Complement

Wartime	total 1569

Notes:
After Washington standard displacement in the Marine Nationale was generally given in long tons (Tonnes W or TW); other displacements were given in metric tonnes (tonnes – lower-case 't')
Mle = *Modèle* (Model)

Breakdown of Weights (designed)

Hull	8276t (20.2%)
Fittings	4706t (11.5%)
Armament	6130t (15.0%)
Protection	
Hull	11,910t (29.1%)
Armament	4135t (10.1%)
Machinery	2865t (7.0%)
Oil Fuel (½ load)	2905t (7.1%)
Total	**40,927t (100%)**

Notes:
All weights in metric tons (tonnes).
The percentages here are broadly comparable to those of *Strasbourg* (see p.38). However, the calculations for *Dunkerque* and *Strasbourg* were based on a normal displacement which included ¾ fuel load.

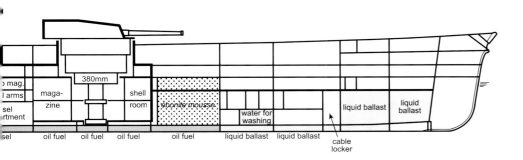

(Drawing by John Jordan © 2008)

Richelieu: Hull Sections

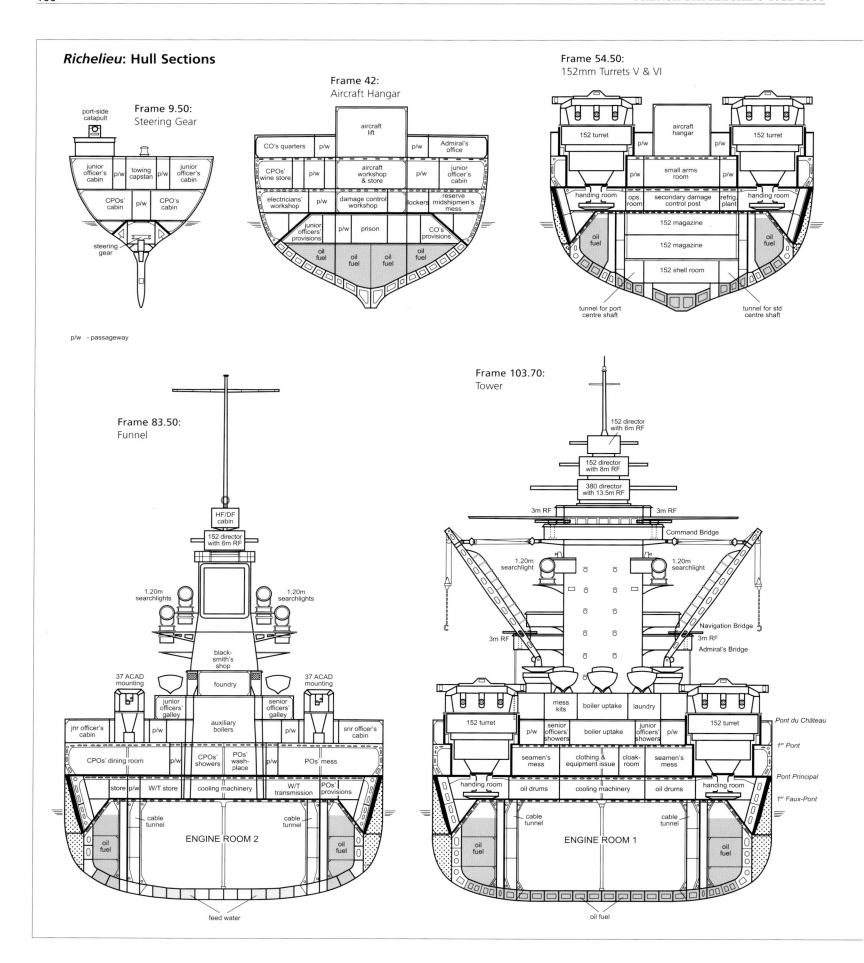

Frame 9.50:
Steering Gear

port-side catapult

junior officer's cabin | p/w | towing capstan | junior officer's cabin

CPOs' cabin | p/w | CPO's cabin

steering gear

Frame 42:
Aircraft Hangar

aircraft lift

CO's quarters | p/w | p/w | Admiral's office

CPOs' wine store | p/w | aircraft workshop & store | p/w | junior officer's cabin

electricians' workshop | p/w | damage control workshop | lockers | reserve midshipmen's mess

junior officers' provisions | p/w | prison | CO's provisions

oil fuel | oil fuel | oil fuel | oil fuel

Frame 54.50:
152mm Turrets V & VI

152 turret | aircraft hangar | 152 turret

152 turret | p/w | p/w | 152 turret

p/w | small arms room | p/w

handing room | ops. room | secondary damage control post | refrig. plant | handing room

oil fuel | 152 magazine | oil fuel

152 magazine

152 shell room

tunnel for port centre shaft | tunnel for std centre shaft

p/w - passageway

Frame 83.50:
Funnel

HF/DF cabin

152 director with 6m RF

1.20m searchlights | 1.20m searchlights

blacksmith's shop

37 ACAD mounting | foundry | 37 ACAD mounting

junior officers' galley | senior officers' galley

jnr officer's cabin | auxiliary boilers | snr officer's cabin

p/w | p/w

CPOs' dining room | p/w | CPOs' showers | POs' wash-place | p/w | POs' mess

store | p/w | W/T store | cooling machinery | W/T transmission | POs' provisions

oil fuel | cable tunnel | cable tunnel | oil fuel

ENGINE ROOM 2

feed water

Frame 103.70:
Tower

152 director with 6m RF

152 director with 8m RF

380 director with 13.5m RF

3m RF | 3m RF

Command Bridge

1.20m searchlight | 1.20m searchlight

3m RF | Navigation Bridge | 3m RF

Admiral's Bridge

mess kits | boiler uptake | laundry

152 turret | p/w | senior officers' showers | boiler uptake | junior officers' showers | p/w | 152 turret | *Pont du Château*

seamen's mess | clothing & equipment issue | cloak-room | seamen's mess | *1er Pont*

handing room | oil drums | cooling machinery | oil drums | handing room | *Pont Principal*

cable tunnel | cable tunnel | *1er Faux-Pont*

oil fuel | ENGINE ROOM 1 | oil fuel

oil fuel

Frame 68.85:
Turret VII

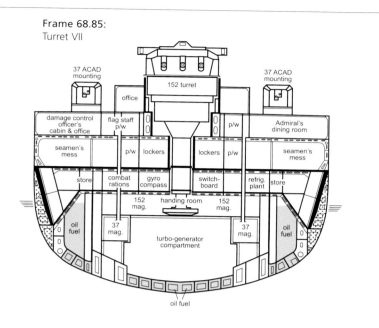

Frame 140.55:
380mm Turret II

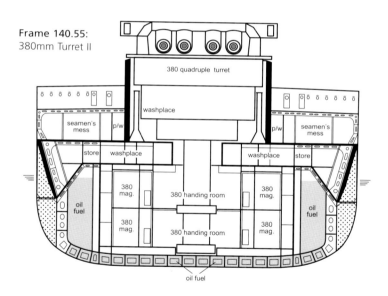

Frame 102.91:
Bow Section

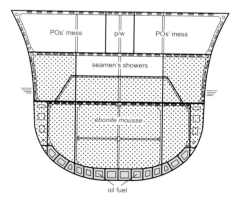

(Drawings by John Jordan © 2008)

that two aircraft could now be stowed in line on the upper deck. The two-tier aircraft lift could now be dispensed with, reducing the complexity of the aircraft handling arrangements and simultaneously eliminating the lift opening in the upper deck, which in theory weakened the hull girder. Lengthening the hangar also permitted the embarkation of a fifth aircraft, which was to be stowed (wings folded) at the after end of the hangar roof.[5]

The centreline 152mm turret now effectively displaced the prominent pole mainmast of *Dunkerque*, around the base of which were seated the after directors for the main and secondary guns. The designers of *Richelieu* and her sister devised the ingenious solution of combining the mainmast with the funnel in a precursor to the 'mack' (combined <u>ma</u>st and <u>stack</u>) widely adopted for US missile frigates of the 1960s – designs in which centreline space was likewise at a premium. The funnel uptakes were angled out from a lightly constructed after superstructure carrying the after director for the secondary guns with a tall mainmast for the W/T aerials. Directly beneath the angled funnel and located atop a short deckhouse was the auxiliary director for the main guns. The compactness of the superstructures was in marked contrast to those of *Dunkerque* and *Strasbourg*, and gave the new battleships a distinctive, altogether 'heavier' appearance.

MAIN AND SECONDARY ARMAMENT

The 380/45 Model 1935 gun was the most powerful ever mounted in a French battleship. It was a built-up gun similar in construction to the 330/52 fitted in *Dunkerque* and *Strasbourg*. Published drawings show an A tube and loose liner inside a double row of overlapping hoops at the breech end.[6] Later guns had fewer components (see schematic drawing and caption). The configuration and operation of the Welin interrupted screw breech block were essentially unchanged from the 330/52.

The 380mm Mle 1936 APC[7] shell weighed 884kg and had an initial velocity of 830m/s. The ballistic cap housed a dye bag which served to colour the shell splashes in order to facilitate spotting when operating in company with other ships; a small burster and nose fuze ensured dispersion.[8] The shells supplied to *Richelieu* contained a yellow dye; *Jean Bart* was assigned orange.

The quadruple turret was designed by Saint Chamond and was a development of the earlier 330mm model, the principal difference being that conical rollers were used in place of ball bearings for training. Like the 330mm turret, it was divided into two separate gunhouses by a central bulkhead, which

---

[5] In the event, only three Loire 130 reconnaissance seaplanes were assigned to *Richelieu*, and the proposed arrangement would certainly have exposed the fifth aircraft to an unacceptable level of blast when the after secondary guns were fired.

[6] Campbell, *Naval Weapons of World War Two*, p.283.

[7] There was no HE shell. For an explanation of French heavy shell development see Chapter 2.

[8] This technology, termed *dispositif K* in the Marine Nationale, was offered to the British in 1939 as part of a two-way transfer which on the British side included Asdic. It was subsequently adopted by the British for their own heavy shells.

MAIN AND SECONDARY GUNS: CHARACTERISTICS

	380/45 Mle 1935	152/55 Mle 1930
Gun data		
Construction	'A' tube with hoops, jacket and liner	Auto-fretted jacket and 'A' tube with loose liner
Breech mechanism	Upward-opening Welin screw	Vertical sliding block
Weight of gun	94.1t	7.8t
Ammunition type	Separate	Separate
Projectiles	OPfK Mle 1936 (884kg)	OPfK Mle 1931 (56.0kg)
		OPfK Mle 1937 (57.1kg)
		OEA Mle 1936 (54.7kg)
		OEA Mle 1937 (49.3kg)
		OEcl Mle 1936 (47kg)
Propellant	SD21 in four quarter-charges (288kg)	BM11 (17.1kg) BM7 (8.7kg) for OEA Mle 1936 and OEcl Mle 1936
Muzzle velocity	830m/s	870m/s
Max. range	41,500m (35°) theoretical 37,800m practical	26,500m (45°)
Mounting data		
Designation	St Chamond Mle 1935	St Chamond Mle 1936
Weight of turret	2476t	228t
Distance apart gun axes	1.95m/2.95m	1.85m
Protection	(see separate table)	(see separate table)
Loading angle	All angles	All angles (designed – but see text)
Elevation of guns	-5°/+35°	-6°50 (V/VI), -8°10 (VII)/+90°
Max. training speed	5°/sec	12°/sec
Max. elevating speed	5.5°/sec	8°/sec
Firing cycle (per gun)	1.3-2rpm	5-6rpm

Notes:

All weights in metric tons (tonnes).

Speeds in metres/degrees per second.

OPf = *Obus de Perforation*; both the 380mm and 152mm shells were armour piercing capped (APC); the K extension denoted a shell with colorant; this was yellow for *Richelieu*, and orange for *Jean Bart*.

OEA = *Obus Explosif en Acier* (high explosive: HE); figures for the Mle 1936 are for the contact-fuzed variant; those for the Mle 1937 for the time-fuzed (AA) variant.

OEcl = *Obus Eclairant* (starshell); note that the OEcl Mle 1936 originally slated for these guns was effectively replaced by the OEcl Mle 1928 provided for the 100mm Mle 1930 guns fitted in place of turrets III and IV in 1940.

Distance apart gun axes (380mm only): first figure for outer guns / second figure for inner guns.

in the *Richelieu* class was increased to 45mm thickness. The guns were in pairs, and although each gun was in a separate cradle the relative movement of the guns in each pair was again limited. The guns could be loaded at any angle, and the maximum angle of elevation was 35 degrees, at which the 380mm Mle 1935 had a theoretical range of 41,500 metres. Training and elevation were powered by Léonard circuit electric motors with hydraulic drive, each pair of guns having a single elevating motor with individual drive gear. RPC was to have been fitted for both training and elevation; however, the failure of the Sautter-Harlé-Blondel system fitted in *Dunkerque* and *Strasbourg* (see p.40) resulted in a loss of confidence in the application of this technology to heavy armoured turrets, and it was never fitted.

The magazine layout and the loading/replenishment arrangements were modelled on those of the 330mm turrets (see drawings). A total of 832 AP shells were provided – slightly fewer than in *Dunkerque* and *Strasbourg* (896 rounds). As with the 330/52 gun, the propellant charges were in quarters, which for a gun of this calibre made them unusually heavy. The overall replenishment cycle proved slower than anticipated, and during gunnery trials in spring 1940 the big guns

Above:
One of *Richelieu*'s 380mm guns preserved and on public display at Brest Naval Dockyard, close to the Tourville Basin. The gun, numbered R 1938-5, was captured at Ruelle in 1940, despatched by the Germans to Octeville as part of the Atlantic Wall coast defences, and installed in turret I in 1950. (*Net Marine*)

Left:
View from the forecastle of *Richelieu* at Dakar in 1941. The 380mm quad turrets were simply a scaled-up version of the 330mm turrets of *Dunkerque* and *Strasbourg*, with the guns of each half-turret closely spaced and a dividing partition of 45mm steel.

Richelieu as designed: Turret Numbering & Firing Arcs

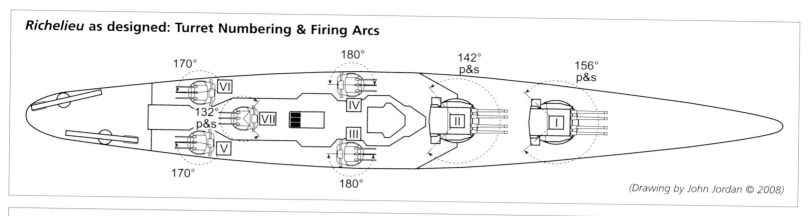

(Drawing by John Jordan © 2008)

French gun construction

The construction of the French 330/52 and 380/45 guns was a mixture of modern and traditional methods. The guns were of built-up construction, with complicated assembly and many more component parts than contemporary British and US major-calibre guns. They were built by the Fonderies de Ruelle, the establishment near Angoulême responsible for the design and construction of all French naval guns and shells.

Early French naval guns dating from before the Great War were built up using large numbers of ring-shaped hoops for strength to compensate for the inferior steels available – the special (HLE) steels had elasticity values of only 35–45 per cent, well below those available to the other major navies, which meant that the gun could withstand a maximum internal pressure of only 2700kg/cm². It was a French engineer, Malaval, who in 1912 proposed auto-fretting as a means of increasing the strength of the barrel while reducing the number of component parts. During the assembly process the hoops were heated to high temperatures, slipped over the gun tube and allowed to cool. As they cooled they contracted, until at the end of the process they were squeezing the gun tube inside with a pressure of many thousands of kilos per square centimetre. By using this 'pre-stressing' technique it was possible to make a gun barrel more resistant to internal pressure. An experimental 100mm gun built using these techniques was found to be able to sustain an internal pressure of 5000kg/cm².

All French naval guns built from 1922 were auto-fretted, and improvements in the quality of French high-tensile steels (to 60–70 per cent elasticity) made possible further reductions in the number of components.

A document recently discovered at the Archives de l'Armement at Châtellerault makes it clear that there were two variants of the 380/45 gun:

– a Mle 1935 C/35 with 31 components: an A tube, a breech bush, twenty hoops, a breech ring, four tubes to the muzzle ending in the muzzle bush, and a locking ring. The 'stepped' loose liner with the rifling was held in place by a ring screwed into the breech end of the A tube.
– a Mle 1936 C/35 with only 20 components: the number of hoops was reduced from twenty to ten and the number of tubes to the muzzle from four to three.

Construction of a 380mm Mle 1935 Gun

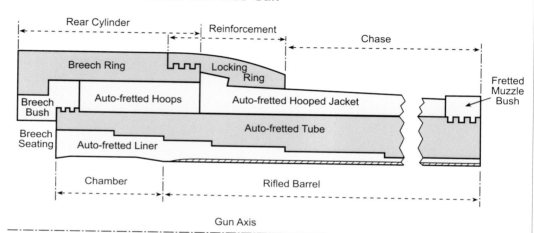

Note: The drawing, which was adapted from a drawing in a French gunnery manual, is not to scale: length has been considerably compressed in relation to the height. The construction of the gun has also been considerably simplified (see caption left).

Breech Block of 380mm Mle 1935

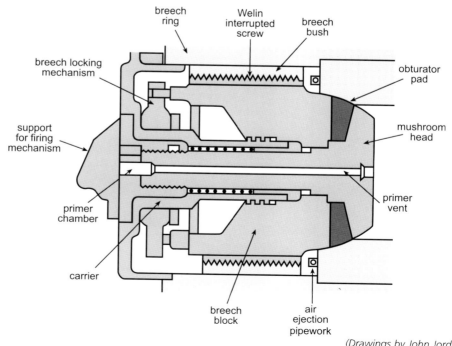

(Drawings by John Jordan © 2008)

380MM GUNS BUILT PREWAR

Number of Gun	Destination	Fate
R 1936-1	Ruelle	Captured 1940; to Norway; preserved Ecole Navale Lanvéoc Poulmic
R 1936-2	*Richelieu* TI	Retained 1943; relined and to TII 1950; preserved Ruelle
R 1936-3	Gâvres	Captured 1940; to Norway
R 1936-4	*Richelieu* TI	Retained 1943; relined and to TII 1950
R 1937-1	*Jean Bart* TI	To *Richelieu* TII 1943
R 1937-2	*Richelieu* TI	Retained 1943; relined and to TII 1950
R 1937-3	*Jean Bart* TI	To *Richelieu* TII 1943
R 1937-4	*Jean Bart* TI	Retained 1949
R 1937-5	*Richelieu* TI	Retained 1943; relined and to TII 1950
R 1937-6	*Richelieu* TII	Explosion in barrel Dakar Sept. 1940
R 1937-7	*Jean Bart* TI	To *Richelieu* TII 1943
R 1937-8	Gâvres	Captured 1940; to Meppen; to *Richelieu* TI 1950
R 1937-9	*Richelieu* TII	Retained 1943; discarded postwar
R 1937-10	Gâvres	Preserved Gâvres
R 1938-1	*Richelieu* TII	Explosion in barrel Dakar Sept. 1940
R 1938-2	*Jean Bart* TII	Captured Ruelle 1940; to Hanover
R 1938-3	*Richelieu* TII	Explosion in barrel Dakar Sept. 1940
R 1938-4	*Jean Bart* TII	Lost on freighter *Mécanicien Principal Lestin* off the Gironde June 1940
R 1938-5	Ruelle	Captured Ruelle 1940; to Octeville; to *Richelieu* TI 1950; preserved Brest
R 1938-6	*Jean Bart* TII	Captured St Nazaire 1940; to Norway; to Richelieu TI 1950
R 1938-7	*Jean Bart* TII	Captured between Ruelle and St Nazaire 1940; to Essen (Krupp)

Notes:
1. The 'R' in the designation stands for Ruelle; the date is the year of manufacture, while the final digit denotes the number of the gun within the sequence. Sixteen guns were constructed for *Richelieu* and *Jean Bart*, while five were retained at Ruelle and Gâvres (testing ground).
2. All except one of the guns fitted in *Jean Bart* when rebuilt during the late 1940s were of postwar construction; only R 1937-4 was retained (see Chapter 9 for a full listing).
3. The three guns which were transported to Norway were to be installed in a coast defence battery at Vardås, guarding the approaches to Oslo. The battery remained incomplete at war's end, and the guns were exchanged for three German 38cm guns from the Todt Battery in the Pas-de-Calais. Following prolonged negotiations and an impressive engineering effort, the guns were brought back to France aboard the oil tanker *Gascogne* in August 1949, and were subsequently refurbished at Ruelle.

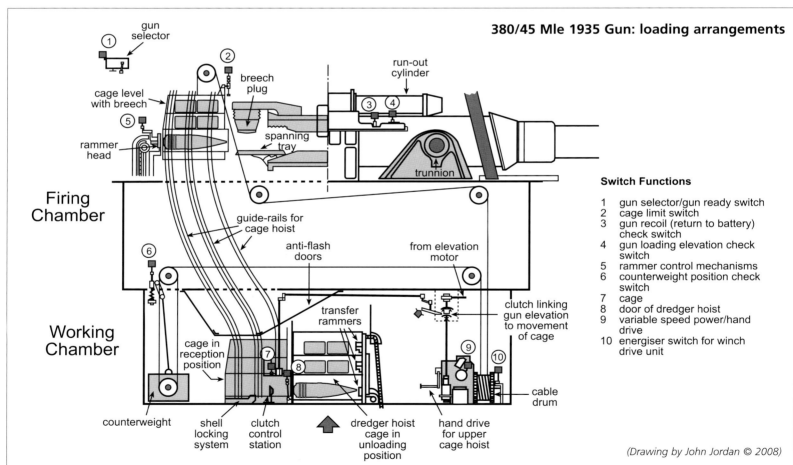

380/45 Mle 1935 Gun: loading arrangements

Switch Functions

1. gun selector/gun ready switch
2. cage limit switch
3. gun recoil (return to battery) check switch
4. gun loading elevation check switch
5. rammer control mechanisms
6. counterweight position check switch
7. cage
8. door of dredger hoist
9. variable speed power/hand drive
10. energiser switch for winch drive unit

(Drawing by John Jordan © 2008)

The Welin 'interrupted screw' breech block opened upwards automatically when the gun ran out. It was hydro-pneumatically powered and was balanced by counterweights. Opening and closing times are given as 3.5 seconds. An automatic lock with a magazine for ten electric tubes was fitted.

The propellant charges were in quarters, and both the dredger hoist cages and the upper cage hoists had three compartments, each of the upper two housing a pair of charges with the Mle 1936 shell in the lower compartment. The guide rails for the upper cage hoists had a distinctive curved profile to enable loading to take place at any angle of elevation, the electric chain rammers being carried on an extension from each of the gun cradles. (In practice, the guns were generally reloaded at 15 degrees elevation to avoid the shell becoming jammed in the breech when the other guns were fired.) Maximum elevation for the gun was 35 degrees. A spanning tray to protect the screw threads of the breech cavity ran in and out automatically, and the complete ramming time was 13.5 seconds.

GUNS MOUNTED IN *RICHELIEU* AND *JEAN BART* 1940-3

Richelieu 1940

Turret I	Turret II
R 1936-2	R 1937-6
R 1936-4	R 1937-9
R 1937-2	R 1938-1
R 1937-5	R 1938-3

Jean Bart 1940

Turret I	Turret II
R 1937-1	R 1938-2
R 1937-3	R 1938-4
R 1937-4	R 1938-6
R 1937-7	R 1938-7

Note: The guns for turret II were not fitted (see notes above).

Richelieu 1943

Turret I	Turret II
R 1936-2	R 1937-1 (ex-*JB*)
R 1936-4	R 1937-9
R 1937-2	R 1938-3 (ex-*JB*)
R 1937-5	R 1938-7 (ex-*JB*)

Note: The serial numbers listed for the guns in each of the quadruple turrets (see also Chapter 9) are in numerical sequence; the position in the list does not reflect the position of the gun in the turret.

330/52 Mle 1931 and 380/45 Mle 1935: replenishment arrangements

(Drawing by John Jordan © 2008)

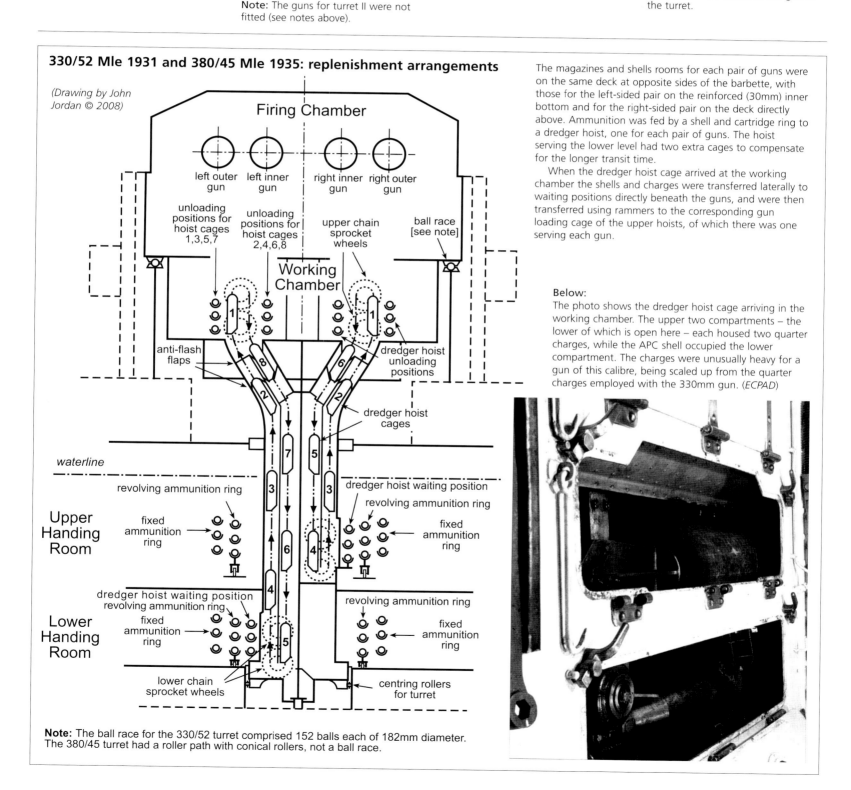

The magazines and shells rooms for each pair of guns were on the same deck at opposite sides of the barbette, with those for the left-sided pair on the reinforced (30mm) inner bottom and for the right-sided pair on the deck directly above. Ammunition was fed by a shell and cartridge ring to a dredger hoist, one for each pair of guns. The hoist serving the lower level had two extra cages to compensate for the longer transit time.

When the dredger hoist cage arrived at the working chamber the shells and charges were transferred laterally to waiting positions directly beneath the guns, and were then transferred using rammers to the corresponding gun loading cage of the upper hoists, of which there was one serving each gun.

Below:
The photo shows the dredger hoist cage arriving in the working chamber. The upper two compartments – the lower of which is open here – each housed two quarter charges, while the APC shell occupied the lower compartment. The charges were unusually heavy for a gun of this calibre, being scaled up from the quarter charges employed with the 330mm gun. (*ECPAD*)

Note: The ball race for the 330/52 turret comprised 152 balls each of 182mm diameter. The 380/45 turret had a roller path with conical rollers, not a ball race.

achieved a rate of fire of only 1.3 rounds per minute.

The secondary armament as designed comprised fifteen 152/55 Model 1930 guns in a new high-angle triple mounting Model 1936 with a theoretical maximum elevation of +90 degrees. The 152mm Mle 1930 had initially been installed in a triple low-angle mounting in the minelaying cruiser *Emile Bertin* and then in the six 7600-tonne cruisers of the *La Galissonnière* class. The low-angle Mle 1930 mounting, which had a maximum elevation of 45 degrees, was to prove highly satisfactory. However, the design of a dual-purpose mounting intended to fire two different types of shell with high-speed loading at all angles was a challenge of a different order. The Mle 1936 mounting fitted in the new battleships was larger, heavier and altogether more complex than its low-angle counterpart (see drawing). Although designed for a maximum elevation of 90 degrees with loading at any angle, the gun proved difficult to load and prone to jamming at angles greater than 45 degrees. This, together with the relatively slow training and elevating speeds, which made it difficult to track fast-moving aerial targets, limited its use to long-range barrage fire against low-flying torpedo planes.

In anti-surface mode the 152/55 fired the modified

The port-side 152mm triple mounting of *Richelieu*, seen here in 1953. (*ECPAD*)

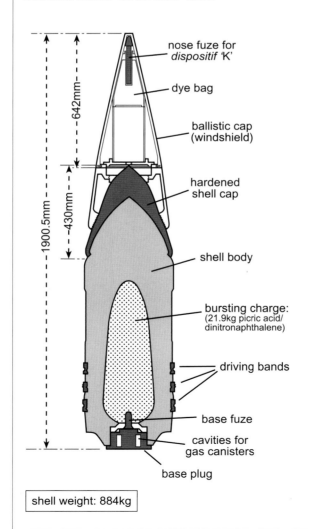

380mm Shell: OPfK Mle 1936

- nose fuze for *dispositif* 'K'
- dye bag
- ballistic cap (windshield)
- hardened shell cap
- shell body
- bursting charge: (21.9kg picric acid/ dinitronaphthalene)
- driving bands
- base fuze
- cavities for gas canisters
- base plug

642mm
430mm
1900.5mm

shell weight: 884kg

The French 380mm Mle 1936 was similar in conception to the 330mm Mle 1935. It had a long, tapered ballistic cap and three copper driving bands. The distinctive moulded base formed a 'boat tail' which assisted in keeping the shell stable in flight. A disadvantage of this configuration was that shells could not be safely balanced on their base and had to be stowed and moved horizontally from magazine to shell hoist. The bursting charge was 21.9kg of picrid acid and dinitronaphthalene, little heavier than that of the 330mm Mle 1935 and at 2.5 per cent of shell weight more in line with the practice of the other major navies. The 380mm Mle 1936 was designed from the outset to accommodate a dye bag and nose fuze (*dispositif* 'K') to colour shell splashes and hits, and the split ballistic cap resembles that of the later OPfK variant of the 330mm shell (see p.36). The shells for *Richelieu* contained a yellow dye, while the colorant for *Jean Bart* was orange.

The 380mm Mle 1936, like the 330mm Mle 1935, used the solventless SD propellant. The bagged charges were designated SD21. Due to a shortage of these charges when *Richelieu* arrived at Dakar in June 1940, SD19 charges stockpiled there for the *Strasbourg* were remanufactured using larger bags as a temporary measure (see p.126). These were generally satisfactory when used against the attempted British landings of September 1940, but they proved underpowered, which upset the initial ballistic calculations and caused many shells to fall well short of their targets.

The base plug of the 380mm Mle 1936 differed from that of the 330mm Mle 1935 in having four cavities for the possible insertion of cylindrical gas canisters. These were never used, and the screw caps which covered them proved unable to withstand the highest gas pressures when the SD21 charges were detonated in the breech of the gun. This was to result in severe damage to three gun barrels at Dakar in September 1940 (see Chapter 5). The cavities were eliminated altogether in the American Crucible Steel shell patterned on the Mle 1936 and ordered in 1943 (see Chapter 8).

Sources: Campbell, and Sarnet and Le Vaillant; drawings and data published in various French gunnery manuals.

(Drawing by John Jordan © 2008)

152mm OPfK Mle 1931 Shell

152mm OEA Mle 1937 Shell

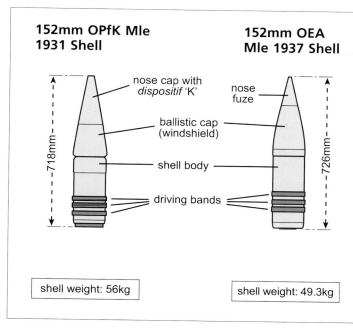

shell weight: 56kg

shell weight: 49.3kg

The 152mm Mle 1931 was the standard anti-surface armour-piercing shell for the 152mm Mle 1930 gun developed for the French light cruisers of the 1930s, and remained in the inventory of French warships armed with this gun into the mid-1950s. The modification with *dispositif* 'K' (referred to in one source as Mle 1936) entered service during the late 1930s, and was embarked on *Richelieu* from the outset. The OPfK Mle 1931 shell was complemented by a purpose-designed 'K' variant, Mle 1937, which was slightly longer (726mm) and heavier (57.1kg). As for the main guns the 'K' colorant was yellow for *Richelieu*, orange for *Jean Bart*.

An HE shell was developed, primarily for use in the triple Mle 1936 DP mounting against aircraft and lightly built flotilla craft. The 54.5-55kg OEA Mle 1936 appears to have been used only with a reduced (8.7kg) charge. It was quickly followed into service by the lighter OEA Mle 1937 (depicted here). Both models of shell had alternative contact, delayed-action and time fuzes.

The propellant was of the standard BM type: nitrocellulose in strip form with a small quantity of diphenylamine as stabiliser. The single 17.3kg BM11 charge was in an aluminium bronze cartridge case just over one metre long.

Sources: Campbell; drawings and data from the Archives de l'Armement, Châtellerault.

(Drawings by John Jordan © 2008)

OPfK Mle 1931 SAP shell or the heavier Mle 1937 (see drawing), which was designed from the outset to accommodate a dye bag in its nose to colour splashes; the maximum theoretical range was 26,500 metres. Against aircraft it fired time-fuzed shells (OEA Mle 1936/1937). Unlike the 130/45 Mle 1932 gun fitted in *Dunkerque* and *Strasbourg*, the 152/55 used separate ammunition, the propellant charge being 17kg of BM11. Magazine capacity for the three mountings fitted was 3600 rounds (roughly 400 rounds per gun). With the fitting of the twin 100mm Mle 1931 mountings in place of the two midships 152mm turrets (see below), the remaining 152mm magazine capacity was weighted towards SAP shell for use in the anti-surface mode.

The guns were in separate cradles; they were driven together by the elevating gear with differentials for individual correction between the hydraulic drive and the elevating worms. Full RPC was fitted. The low-angle cruiser mountings had catapult rammers for the shells and a chain rammer for the cartridges, but for the dual-purpose mountings hydro-pneumatic chain rammers on extensions from the cradles, as in the main 380mm guns, were adopted. There were separate pusher hoists for AA and SAP shells which came up to the left of the gun, while the pusher hoists for the cartridges emerged on the right. For reasons of alignment the hoists for the lateral mountings were broken between the armour decks, where rotating transfer mechanisms were installed. The two forward turrets, had they been installed, would have been 28 metres from their magazine, which was directly abaft the magazines for the main guns, and would have required a lengthy horizontal transfer at the level of the lower armoured deck.

FIRE CONTROL

The director control system adopted for *Richelieu* and *Jean Bart* was closely modelled on that developed for *Dunkerque*. Three of the five main directors, each fitted with a multiple OPL stereoscopic range-finder, were mounted one above the other atop the forward tower structure; the after directors for the main and

152mm OEcl Mle 1936 Shell

Prior to the invention of radar, 'starshell' was necessary to illuminate the target at night or in conditions of poor visibility. The drawing shows the *Obus Eclairant* Mle 1936 designed for the dual-purpose Mle 1936 triple mounting to be fitted in *Richelieu* and *Jean Bart*.

The outer body of the shell closely resembles that of the OEA Mles 1936 & 1937, but the large explosive burster of the latter is replaced by an illuminant and a parachute, which are housed within an inner cylindrical sheath. At a predetermined distance from the firing ship, the time fuze in the nose operates, and a detonator of black powder projects the inner casing through the base of the shell, the circular plug of which is only lightly secured with pins. The illuminant burns brightly while its casing is suspended from the deployed parachute.

The 152mm shell would have had the advantage over smaller-calibre models of greater range and a longer 'burn' time due to the greater capacity of the illuminant chamber. However, when the French opted to land two of the original five triple 152mm turrets on *Richelieu* and replace them with six twin 100mm HA mountings, the latter were used in preference for target illumination, presumably because the Navy wished to maximise anti-ship and anti-aircraft ammunition stocks for the remaining secondary guns. Although *Richelieu* as originally designed was to have carried 656 of these shells, it is not clear whether this provision survived the decision to suppress the two midships 152mm turrets, or even whether the OEcl Mle 1936 went into production; significantly, the shell does not feature in the *Richelieu* ammunition inventory dated 1943 (*qv*).

Sources: ETNCAN, *Cours d'Artillerie Tome II bis: Pyrotechnie* (1946), p. 17.

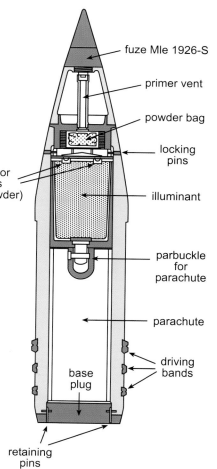

fuze Mle 1926-S

primer vent

powder bag

locking pins

detonator pellets (black powder)

illuminant

parbuckle for parachute

parachute

driving bands

base plug

retaining pins

(Drawing by John Jordan © 2008)

secondary batteries were mounted as described in a previous section. For the main armament there was a triplex 14-metre rangefinder in the lower director of the forward tower, a duplex 8-metre RF in the after director located beneath the funnel, and a duplex 14-metre RF in each of the two main turrets. For the secondary armament there were directors with integral 8-metre (middle) and 6-metre (upper) rangefinders on the forward tower, a director with a 6-metre RF atop the after tower, and 8-metre rangefinders in each of the five – later three – triple turrets (see drawing and

table). All of these directors were gastight, and they were fitted with light steel plating to protect them from the machine guns of strafing aircraft.

In addition to the main gunnery directors two stereo-scopic OPL 3-metre (subsequently 4-metre) range-finders were provided for the flag staff; they were initially to have been fitted in the wings of the admiral's bridge, which in the *Richelieu* was at the upper level of the conning tower, but were eventually mounted on sponsons projecting from the lower sides of the tower (see below). There was also a stereoscopic

152mm Mle 1930 in triple Mle 1936 mounting

The triple Mle 1936 mounting was designed to load at higher angles of elevation to provide the high rate of fire necessary for effective AA performance. Pusher hoists for the 17.3kg charge came up to right of each gun level with the trunnions, with the projectile hoists emerging on the left in the same position. Projectiles and shells were then transferred via intermediate tubes running on either side of the gun to their respective loading trays. The hydro-pneumatic chain rammers were carried on an extension of the cradle, as in the main guns. The loaders stood on platforms between the guns which rose and fell with the angle of elevation.

The 152mm Mle 1936 proved to be a complex, fragile mounting with training and elevation speeds which were too slow to cope with modern aircraft. Loading was difficult beyond 45 degrees, and firing at angles above 75 degrees resulted in regular jams, although postwar improvements would make 85 degrees possible. Once *Richelieu* was fitted with the British Type 285 radar her 152mm guns were capable of effective barrage fire against aircraft flying at medium and low altitudes, but war experience showed the wisdom of replacing the midship Mle 1936 mountings with the more responsive 100mm Mle 1930, which was altogether more robust and effective in the anti-aircraft role.

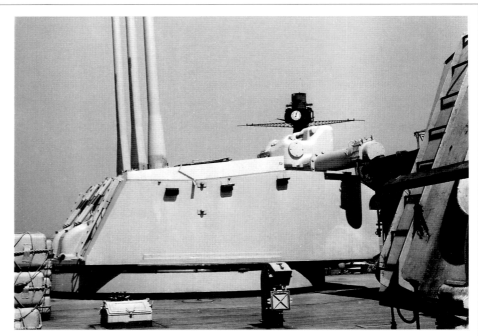

A postwar view of the 152mm guns at maximum elevation. In the background is the foremast of the old battleship *Paris*, towed from Plymouth to Brest in August 1945 to subsequently become base ship for the flotilla craft of the 2e Région Maritime (HQ Brest). (*ECPAD*)

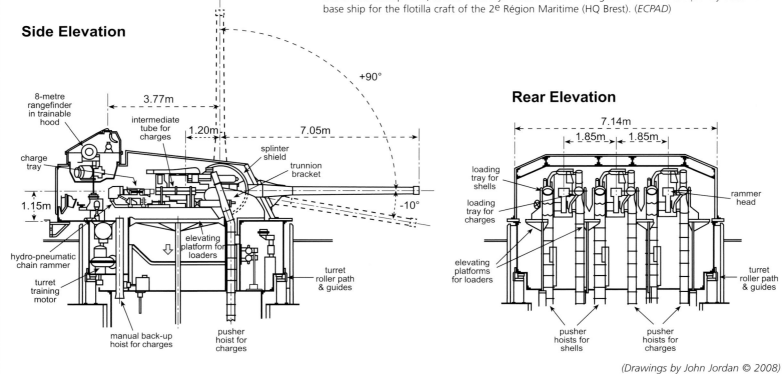

(*Drawings by John Jordan © 2008*)

SOM 3-metre 'tactical' rangefinder atop the bridge.

As in *Dunkerque* and *Strasbourg*, the directors provided raw target data to the transmitting station located beneath the armoured decks, with continuous transmission to both the director and the guns. Concentration dials were originally to have been fitted, but these would be removed from *Dunkerque* and *Strasbourg* during 1940 and *Richelieu* was completed without them.

For night firing there were five 120cm searchlight projectors: one atop the admiral's bridge on the forward tower, with two on either side of the funnel structure. All were fitted with RPC, and could be controlled either using the 152mm directors or from positions on the tower.

Lookout and target designation facilities were similar in principle to those in *Dunkerque* (detailed on p.40). However, there was a degree of reorganisation and simplification of the arrangements – as there had been in *Strasbourg*. The lower lookout station (*veille basse* = low-level surveillance) was on platform 3 of the tower (vs first deck) and was for close-range contacts. The middle level (now designated *veille éloignée* = long-range surveillance) was for both surface and aerial contacts and was on platform 6 of the tower (vs platform 3). And the upper lookout station (*veille haute* = high-level surveillance) was primarily for spotting torpedoes and mines.

Target designation, as in *Dunkerque* and *Strasbourg*, was exercised from the conning tower or the bridge, which were similarly equipped with sets of periscopic binoculars with automatic transmission of bearing and elevation.

LIGHT AA WEAPONS

For close-in air defence *Richelieu* was originally to have had six 37mm Mle 1935 twin automatic (ACAD) mountings. These were to have been divided into two groups: two mountings on the forecastle deck abeam turret II, and four mountings at shelter deck level abeam the after funnel structure. The fully enclosed base-ring mountings were electrically powered with Sautter-Harlé RPC for training but not for elevation. Replenishment was by pusher hoist; one was provided for each gun, the six-round magazines being fed from an ammunition lobby directly beneath the mounting (see Chapter 7). There were to be four associated directors with integral 2-metre rangefinders and RPC: two at the forward end of the shelter deck above the forward pair of mountings, and two on projecting platforms on either side of the auxiliary director for the main guns, just above the after group (see drawing).

When in November 1939 it became clear that the new ACAD mounting would not be ready in time for the ship's completion, it was decided that the secondary and anti-aircraft batteries would need to be radically revised. The two midships 152mm triple turrets were reallocated to the third ship, *Clemenceau*, and replaced by twelve 100mm Mle 1930 HA guns in six open twin mountings Mle 1931. This was the same mounting fitted in the last of France's Treaty cruisers, *Algérie*, and in the old battleship *Lorraine*, which had undergone a radical (and final) reconstruction during 1934-5. In order to facilitate this change without delaying *Richelieu*'s completion the four twin mountings originally fitted in *Lorraine* were disembarked at Toulon and transported to Brest, together with two additional

RANGEFINDERS (AS FITTED IN *RICHELIEU*)

Main armament

One OPL 14-metre S (triplex)	Lower director fwd tower
One OPL 8-metre S (duplex)	Director abaft after tower
Two OPL 14-metre S (duplex)	Turrets I and II

Secondary armament

One OPL 8-metre S	Middle director fwd tower
Two OPL 6-metre S	Upper director fwd tower
	Director after tower
Three OPL 8-metre S	Turrets V, VI and VII

100mm guns

Two OPL 4-metre S	Directors bridge wings

Light AA

Four OPL 1.5-metre	Two on shelter deck forward
	Two on superstructure deck aft
Four OPL 1-metre	Two atop fwd tower (platform 8)
	Two after superstructure

General use

One SOM 3-metre S	Atop navigation bridge (navigation/tactical)
Two OPL 4-metre S	Lower sides of fwd tower (flag staff)
Two OPL 1-metre	Lower sides of tower (navigation)

Notes:
OPL   *Optique de Précision Levallois-Perret*
SOM   *Société d'Optique et de Méchanique de Haute Précision*
S   Stereoscopic RF
C   Coincidence RF

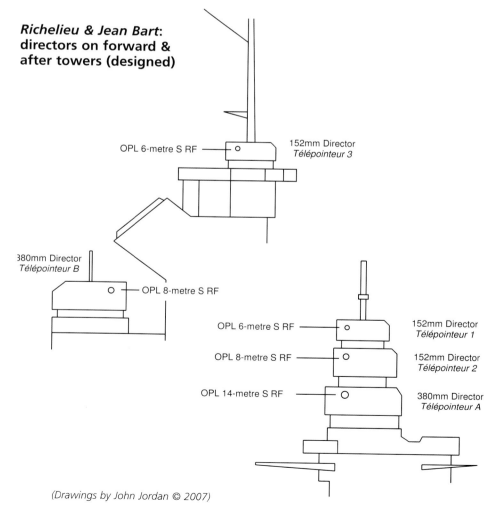

Richelieu & Jean Bart: directors on forward & after towers (designed)

OPL 6-metre S RF — 152mm Director *Télépointeur 3*

380mm Director *Télépointeur B* — OPL 8-metre S RF

OPL 6-metre S RF — 152mm Director *Télépointeur 1*

OPL 8-metre S RF — 152mm Director *Télépointeur 2*

OPL 14-metre S RF — 380mm Director *Télépointeur A*

(Drawings by John Jordan © 2007)

INSTALLATION OF LIGHT AA GUNS *RICHELIEU* 1940-2

Apr.-June 1940	4 x 37mm CAD Mle 1933	Abeam after tower (02 deck)
	4 x 13.2mm CAQ Mle 1929	Upper corners of tower
	2 x 13.2mm CAD Mle 1929	Abeam turret II (02 deck)
July 1940	(2 x 13.2mm CAD Mle 1929	Moved atop hangar
Nov. 1940	2 x 37mm CAD Mle 1933[1]	Abeam tower (03 deck)
Dec. 1940	1 x 13.2mm CAS Browning[1]	Atop after tower (std aft)
Feb. 1941	1 x 13.2mm CAQ Mle 1929	Atop after tower (port fwd)
June 1941	3 x 13.2mm CAS Browning	Two abeam tower (02 deck)
		One quarterdeck
July 1941	2 x 37mm CAD Mle 1933	Atop hangar (*en echelon*)
	(2 x 13.2mm CAD Mle 1929	Moved abeam turret II (02 deck)

Note: [1] Removed from *L'Audacieux*

mountings from the Niolon Battery near Marseille.[9] Three of these mountings (port No. 3 and starboard Nos 2 and 3) were duly embarked on 11 April 1940, and the remaining three during late May. The barbette and other infrastructure for the 152mm turrets remained in place, although no armour was fitted.

The guns were in a common cradle and loading was by spring rammers. In the anti-aircraft rôle the 100mm Mle 1930 fired a time-fuzed 13.5kg shell (OEA Mle 1928) with an initial velocity of 780m/s. The weight of the fixed ammunition was 22.7kg, so manual loading was relatively straightforward. There was also an SAP shell (OPf Mle 1928) with a contact fuze, but relatively few of these shells were generally embarked (ten per gun) because the powerful secondary armament of *Richelieu* meant that the 100mm guns would be used primarily as AA weapons. Illuminating shell (*Obus Eclairant* Mle 1928) was also provided. The ammunition was stowed in double cases of either duralumin or brass, depending on the type of round, in the magazines intended for the midships 152mm mountings. These were located forward at a considerable distance from the mountings, and the ammunition boxes had to be transferred laterally between the two armoured decks before they could be hoisted directly to the reception position for the guns. A substantial quantity of ready-use ammunition was therefore stowed in lockers close to the mountings.

[9] They were replaced aboard *Lorraine* by eight single shielded 75mm Mle 1922 guns, six of which were earmarked for auxiliary cruisers.

ANTI-AIRCRAFT GUNS: CHARACTERISTICS

100/45 Mle 1930

Gun data

Construction	Monobloc auto-fretted barrel
Breech mechanism	SA concentric ring
Weight of gun	1670kg
Ammunition type	Fixed
Projectiles	OPf Mle 1928 (15kg)
	OEA Mle 1928 (13.5kg)
	OEcl Mle 1928
Propellant	BM7 (3.9kg)
Complete round	
Weight	24.2kg (OPf), 22.7kg (OEA)
Dimensions	1.01m x 0.15m
Muzzle velocity	765m/s (OPf)
	780m/s (OEA)
Max. range	15,800m
Ceiling	10,000m

Mounting data

Mounting designation	CAD Mle 1931
Weight of mounting	13.5t
Elevation of guns	-10°/+80°
Firing cycle (per gun)	10rpm

Notes:

CAD	*Contre-Avions Double*	AA twin mounting
Mle	*Modèle*	Model
OPf	*Obus de Perforation*	SAP
OEA	*Obus Explosif en Acier*	High Explosive (HE)
OEcl	*Obus Eclairant*	Starshell

For data on the 37mm CAD Mle 1933 and 13.2mm CAQ/CAD Mle 1929, see Chapter 2. For data on the 37mm ACAD Mle 1935, see Chapter 7.

Fire control directors for the 100mm mountings were provided on extensions from the bridge wings abeam the tower, effectively displacing the rangefinders provided for the flag staff, which were moved to a lower level. Each of the directors was fitted with a stereoscopic OPL rangefinder with a 4-metre base.

The 37mm ACAD was to have been replaced, as in *Dunkerque* and *Strasbourg*, by the semi-automatic 37mm CAD Mle 1933, but the demand for these mountings was so great that production could not keep pace. When *Richelieu* left Brest for North Africa on 18 June 1940 only four twin mountings were in place. These were located on the shelter deck abeam the after funnel structure in the same positions reserved for the ACAD mountings; however, as the Mle 1933 twins were in open, unshielded mountings they

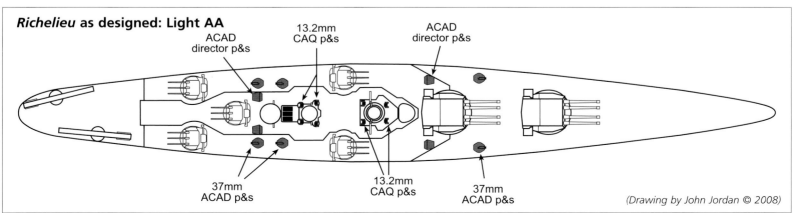

Richelieu **as designed: Light AA**

ACAD director p&s — 13.2mm CAQ p&s — ACAD director p&s — 37mm ACAD p&s — 13.2mm CAQ p&s — 37mm ACAD p&s

(Drawing by John Jordan © 2008)

Richelieu: Protection

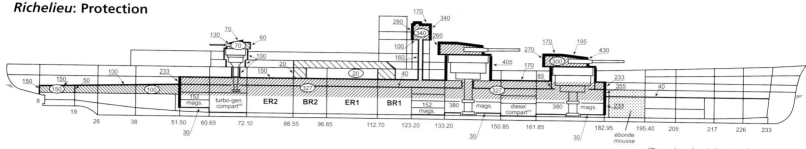

(Drawing by John Jordan © 2008)

were mounted inside a steel screen which provided some protection from spray and blast.

The 37mm CAD mountings were to be complemented by six (later eight) 13.2mm Hotchkiss quadruple MG mountings, mounted on the upper platforms of the forward and after towers. When *Richelieu* sailed for North Africa four CAQ mountings were mounted at the upper corners of the forward tower, and there were two twin (CAD) mountings at the forward end of the shelter deck, abeam turret II, in place of the projected 37mm CAD mountings. Further additions to the close-range AA would be made during the ship's stay at Dakar as mountings became available (see table).

When *Jean Bart* left St. Nazaire for Casablanca, she was many months from completion and very few of her guns and directors had been installed. Because of the anticipated threat from German bombers, as many close-range AA weapons as were available were hurriedly installed, but they were simply bolted on, and the position chosen in no way reflected the original plans. A full description of *Jean Bart*'s initial outfit follows in Chapter 6.

PROTECTION

The protection system of *Richelieu* and *Jean Bart* was essentially the same as that of *Dunkerque* and *Strasbourg* but with the armour plating of the citadel, the conning tower and the main turrets substantially 'beefed up' in order to resist 381mm (15in) shellfire. Outside the citadel the only significant modification was the addition of a 40mm 'splinter deck' forward at the level of the second platform deck, which extended from the forward main transverse bulkhead almost to the bow and covered the refrigeration plant, the cold stowage and the wine store. This had the additional benefit of strengthening the bow section, which in *Dunkerque* and *Strasbourg* was to prove fragile and prone to sea damage.

The armour belt, which was inclined at 15°24, extended from frame 51.50, immediately abaft the 152mm magazines, to frame 182.95, which marked the forward end of the 380mm magazines, and was closed by armoured transverse bulkheads. The belt comprised a single strake 6.25 metres high which extended about 2.5 metres below the waterline (see table). Each plate was of a consistent thickness of 327mm tapering to 177mm at its lower edge, and extended over two frames, the width of each plate varying between 2.5 metres and 3.05 metres. The armour belt had a teak backing 60mm thick; the plates were secured by armour bolts 60mm in diameter above the waterline and by 45mm diameter bolts below. Each plate had a 52mm wedge of 80kg non-cemented armour steel of the same depth as the main armoured deck welded to its upper edge (see drawings).

The forward transverse bulkhead extended, as in *Dunkerque* and *Strasbourg*, from the upper armoured deck (PBS or *Pont Blindé Supérieur*) to the 30mm floor of the munitions magazines. The thickest plates were between the first and second platform decks, where they were 355mm cemented on 18mm plating. Above the first platform deck (PBI or *Pont Blindé Inférieur*) the thickness of the plates was reduced to 233mm, the main armoured bulkhead being backed by 85mm armour plating which was a downward continuation of the barbette between the armoured decks (see drawing). Beneath the second platform deck plate thickness was likewise reduced to 233mm. Outboard of the torpedo bulkhead the thickness of the plates was further reduced to 165mm.

PROTECTION: COMPARISON BETWEEN *RICHELIEU* AND *STRASBOURG*

	Richelieu / Jean Bart	Strasbourg
Vertical protection		
Main belt	330mm	283mm
Forward bulkhead	355mm	228mm
After bulkhead above PBI	233mm	210mm
Bulkhead abaft steering gear	150mm	150mm
Horizontal protection		
PBS over magazines	170mm	125mm
PBS over machinery	150mm	115mm
Lower armoured deck (PBI)	40/50mm	40/50mm
Over shafts	100mm	100mm
Over steering gear	150mm	150mm
Conning tower		
Face and sides	340mm	270mm
Rear	280mm	220mm
Roof	170mm	150mm/130mm
Communications tube	160mm	160mm
Main turrets		
Turret face	430mm	360mm
Turret sides	300mm	250mm
Turret roof	170/195mm	160mm
Turret rear	270mm (I)[1]	352mm (I)
	260mm (II)[1]	342mm (II)
Barbette above PBS	405mm	340mm
Barbette below PBS	80mm	50mm
Secondary turrets		
Turret face	130mm[2]	135mm
Turret sides	70mm	90mm
Turret roof	70mm	90mm
Turret rear	60mm	80mm
Barbette	100mm	120mm

Notes:
[1] Thinner plates of cemented armour were used; the plates on *Strasbourg* were of special steel.
[2] Although the thickness of the armour plating on the secondary turrets was reduced, all five of the original turrets were to have uniform protection, whereas the two twin 130mm turrets of *Strasbourg* had only light plating.

The after bulkhead also extended from the upper armoured deck (PBS) to the 30mm floor of the munitions magazines. The bulkhead was 233mm throughout its centre section, reducing to 165mm outboard of the torpedo bulkheads. All bulkhead plating was secured by 49mm and 80mm bolts, but there was increasing use of welding where the plates met the decks and side plating.

The upper armoured deck (PBS), which was at main deck level, comprised thick non-cemented armour plates without a backing (see drawing p.116). The plates were laid lengthways and were 150mm thick over the machinery (frames 51.50 to 130.00), increasing to 170mm over the forward magazines (frames 130.00 to 182.95).

The lower armoured deck (PBI), which was on the level of the first platform deck, was of similar composition but at a much-reduced thickness: 40mm on the broader horizontal section and 50mm on the inclined sides which joined the lower armoured deck to the lower edge of the armour belt.

The new armoured deck forward of the citadel was at the level of the second platform deck and was composed of plates of non-cemented armour 40mm thick. It extended from the forward transverse bulkhead (frame 182.95) to the forward end of Section B (frame 233.00).

The armour protection abaft the after transverse armoured bulkhead was as in *Dunkerque* and *Strasbourg*. At the level of the first platform deck there was an armoured deck with angled sides 100mm thick in the form of a carapace to protect the shafts. It was inclined downwards towards the stern, thereby connecting the main armoured citadel to the box over the steering gear, which extended from frame 8 to frame 19. The plates over the steering gear were 150mm thick, and the after bulkhead comprised a

PROTECTION: ARMOUR BELT

Height of upper edge of belt above the waterline at trials displacement.	Frames 51.50-182.95	3.380m
Depth of lower edge of belt beneath the waterline at trials displacement.	Frame 51.50	2.220m
	At mid-point	2.580m
	Frame 167.35	2.420m

Richelieu: Protection at Master Frame

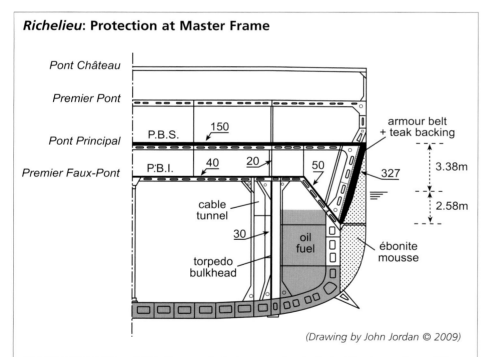

(Drawing by John Jordan © 2009)

The protection system of *Richelieu* was similar in conception to that of *Dunkerque* (see p.45) but there were some detail differences. The armour belt, which for the first time in a French battleship tapered inboard instead of outboard at its base, was inclined at a much steeper angle – 15°24. Both the belt and the main armoured deck (PBS) were significantly 'beefed up', while the incline of the lower armoured deck (PBI) was increased in thickness to 50mm, as in *Strasbourg*. Because of the need to accommodate three of the new Sural boilers side by side in the two boiler rooms the depth of the underwater protection system was slightly reduced as compared to the *Dunkerque*s, from just under 7.5 metres to about 7 metres.

The main difference in the protection system of the two classes lay forward of the armoured citadel, where *Richelieu* had a reinforced deck 40mm thick at the level of the second platform deck and a compartment beneath filled with the water-excluding compound *ébonite mousse* (see longitudinal and section drawings). This arrangement had the effect of strengthening the long, unarmoured bow section and of extending the protected waterline by reducing the potential for uncontrolled flooding in this part of the ship.

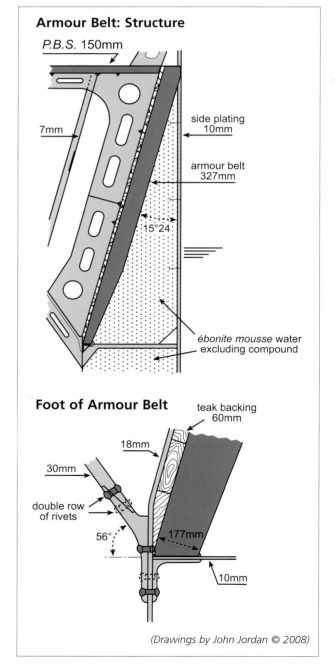

Armour Belt: Structure

Foot of Armour Belt

(Drawings by John Jordan © 2008)

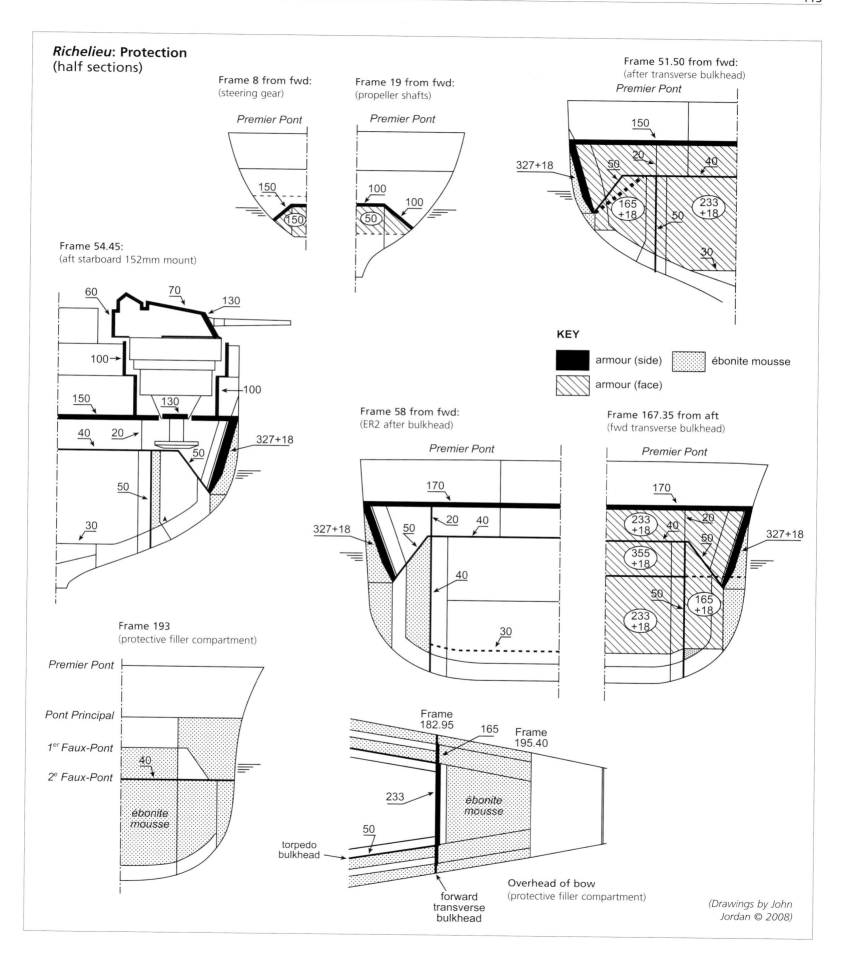

Richelieu: Protection
(half sections)

Frame 8 from fwd:
(steering gear)

Frame 19 from fwd:
(propeller shafts)

Frame 51.50 from fwd:
(after transverse bulkhead)

Frame 54.45:
(aft starboard 152mm mount)

Frame 58 from fwd:
(ER2 after bulkhead)

Frame 167.35 from aft
(fwd transverse bulkhead)

Frame 193
(protective filler compartment)

KEY

armour (side)

armour (face)

ébonite mousse

Overhead of bow
(protective filler compartment)

(Drawings by John
Jordan © 2008)

single plate of the same thickness. At its inboard end the 'box' was closed by a 50mm bulkhead.

Some bulkheads were reinforced to 20mm to provide splinter protection. There were longitudinal bulkheads of 20mm steel abeam the steering gear (frames 8 to 26). Similar protection was applied to the longitudinal bulkhead inboard of the armour belt between the upper and lower armoured decks, as part of the *entrepont cellulaire*, and there was a box of similar thickness to protect the funnel uptakes above the level of the main deck (frames 86.35 to 118.00).

The following internal bulkheads were reinforced to 18mm thickness: the transverse bulkhead at frame 26 at the forward end of the steering compartment; the bulkheads enclosing the citadel (frames 51.50 and 182.95); the bulkheads enclosing each of the two 380mm magazines (frames 133.20, 150.85, and 161.85); the after bulkhead for the machinery spaces (frames 72.10); and the bulkhead dividing the machinery spaces into two independent units (frame 96.85). Some of these bulkheads were reinforced to 30mm at their base up to a height of one metre.

CONNING TOWER AND SUPERSTRUCTURES

The heavily armoured conning tower was on two levels with a raised position at its after end, arranged as in *Dunkerque*.

The face and sides of the tower were protected by five vertical plates of cemented armour 340mm thick. The rear wall was protected two vertical 280mm plates of cemented armour. The plates were fixed to a base of 50kg standard construction steel with a single thickness of 20mm. Access to the two levels was via two gastight doors of 280mm special steel set into the star-

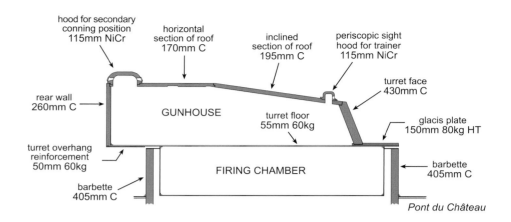

Key:
C   cemented armour
NiCr   nickel-chrome steel
HT   high-tensile steel

Turret II: Protection
(Drawing by John Jordan © 2008)

board side of the after wall. They were opened and closed manually using hand-wheels from inside or outside the conning tower. The raised position was protected by a band of three 340mm plates of cemented armour. The roof of the main body of the conning tower was formed by three 170mm plates of cemented armour on a single thickness of 20mm 50kg construction steel, while the roof of the raised position was a single 170mm plate of cemented armour.

There were seven embrasures in the main body of the conning tower, and a further five in the raised section, all of which could be protected by thick

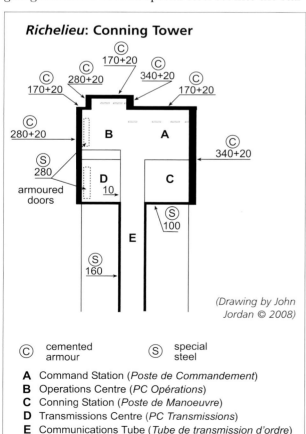

Richelieu: Conning Tower

(Drawing by John Jordan © 2008)

Ⓒ cemented armour   Ⓢ special steel

A Command Station (*Poste de Commandement*)
B Operations Centre (*PC Opérations*)
C Conning Station (*Poste de Manoeuvre*)
D Transmissions Centre (*PC Transmissions*)
E Communications Tube (*Tube de transmission d'ordre*)

The tower of *Richelieu* photographed at Dakar in 1940. Note the three large superimposed directors: the lower one, fitted with a 14-metre stereo RF, was for the main guns; the middle director, with an 8-metre RF, was for the 152mm DP guns in the anti-surface role; and the upper director, fitted with a 6-metre RF, was originally to control AA fire for the 152mm guns. It was never fully fitted out, and was removed during *Richelieu's* reconstruction in the United States in 1943. Note the director for control of the 100mm guns mounted in the bridge wings, equipped with an OPL 4-metre stereo RF. Beneath it is a second OPL stereo rangefinder for tactical use by the flag staff. (*ECPAD*)

gastight glass panels. The floor of the two-level conning tower was of 100mm special steel, and the communications tube linking the conning tower with the transmitting station beneath the main armoured deck was of 160mm special steel and was 900mm in diameter.

As protection against strafing the outer skin of the forward tower was sheathed in plates of 10mm hardened steel, the plates being laid vertically. The directors atop the forward tower and around the mainmast were protected by plating 20mm thick, as was the tube in the centre of the forward tower which served as the trunk for the director cabling.

MAIN TURRETS

The main turrets were protected by a carapace composed of heavy plates of cemented armour on a steel framework secured to one another with butt straps. The face of each turret comprised five plates of 430mm angled at 30 degrees to the vertical and the sides walls each of three plates 300mm thick. The plates of the inclined forward section of the roof were 195mm thick, those of the horizontal after section 170mm thick. The plates directly above the guns were designed for easy removal. The rear wall of the turrets was protected by two plates: 270mm for turret I, 260mm for turret II.

The floor of the firing chamber was of 55mm 60kg steel, and this was reinforced at the front and sides where it projected from the turret walls to form a glacis by 150mm of 80kg special steel, and at the rear, where the turret overhung the barbette, by 50mm of 60kg steel. There were protective caps of 170mm nickel-chrome steel for the ends of the 14-metre rangefinders incorporated into the rear end of the turrets, and 115mm hoods of the same material to protect the periscopic sights for the turret commander and trainer on the roof of the turret and the sights for the gunlayers on the turret sides.

The barbettes for the main turrets were protected above the level of the main deck (PBS) by 405mm plates of cemented armour bolted onto a single thickness of 20mm construction steel. There was a single armoured band comprising sixteen plates for turret I, and a double band each of sixteen plates for turret II. Beneath the upper armoured deck protection was reduced to 85mm of 60kg HT steel.

SECONDARY TURRETS

The secondary 152mm turrets were protected by plates of 80kg nickel-chrome steel secured to one another with butt straps as in the main turrets, without a steel backing. The frontal plate, angled at 45 degrees to the vertical, was 130mm thick, and the single plates of the side walls 70mm. The vertical rear wall comprised a single plate 60mm thick. The roof comprised two removable central plates 70mm thick inclined downwards towards the turret face, two inclined side plates of the same thickness, and a flat lower after section which formed a sort of redan for the 8-metre rangefinder, comprising a single plate of 70mm thickness with a 60mm vertical wall at its forward end. The rangefinder was in a rotating hood which incorporated the sight for the turret commander. All the optical sights were gastight, as was the gunhouse itself.

The turret floor was of 30mm 60kg steel, and as with the main turrets was reinforced where it protruded at the front and sides by 80kg special steel 65mm thick

Richelieu: Decks of Forward Tower (as designed, 1936-7)

Pont Passerelle (1)
[Superstructure Deck]

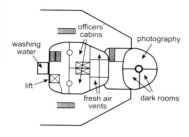

Plateforme Intermédiaire (2)
[Intermediate Platform]

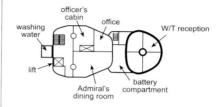

Passerelle de l'Amiral (3)
[Admiral's Bridge]

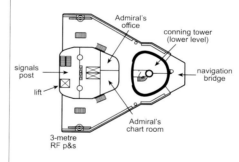

Passerelle de Navigation (4)
[Navigation Bridge]

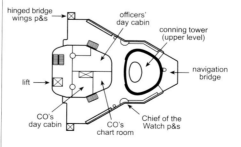

Plateforme de Veille Moyenne (5)
[Middle Lookout Platform]

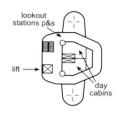

Plateforme des projecteurs de 120 (6)
[120mm Searchlight Platform]

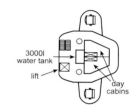

Plateforme du P.C. Réduit (7)
[Auxiliary Command Platform]

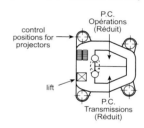

Passerelle Auxiliaire de Manoeuvre et de Commandement (8)
[Auxiliary Command Deck]

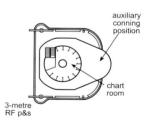

Plateforme de Télémétrie et de Veille Haute (9)
[Upper RF & Lookout Platform]

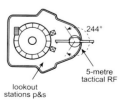

Note: The source of these drawings is a plan dated 9 June 1936, but with modifications up to February 1937 included. The principal differences to the ship as completed were that directors incorporating 4-metre stereo rangefinders for the new 100mm HA battery were located in the wings of the Admiral's bridge in place of the planned 3-metre open rangefinders for the flag staff, which were replaced by 4-metre models installed on the lower sides of the tower. The planned 5-metre base tactical rangefinder on platform 9 was replaced by a 3-metre model installed, as in *Dunkerque*, atop the navigation bridge. (*Drawings by John Jordan © 2009*)

to form a glacis. The sights for the gunlayers and trainers were located at the base of the front plate between the guns, the housing being of 115mm nickel steel. All the sights could be closed by hinged protective covers.

The fixed barbette armour for the secondary turrets was of 80kg nickel-chrome steel with a uniform thickness of 100mm. The plates were assembled with riveted joints; there was no steel plating to form a backing. The upper band (four plates) had an internal diameter of 7.4 metres, the lower band (four plates) a diameter of 5.7 metres and for the centreline turret, positioned one deck higher than the wing turrets, there was a third, smaller band of 2.3 metres diameter (three plates). The trunk for the hoists was fitted internally with a diaphragm of 80kg nickel-chrome steel 140mm thick at the level of the main armoured deck; the diaphragm was pierced only where strictly necessary to permit the passage of the munitions hoists.

The thickness of the protection for the 152mm turrets and their barbettes was slightly reduced compared with the 130mm quadruple turrets of *Dunkerque* and *Strasbourg*. These reductions in thickness were necessary in order to save weight, which in the original *Richelieu* design exceeded 35,000 tons standard. It should, however, be noted that the three quadruple 130mm turrets of the earlier ships were complemented by two twin mountings amidships, the gunhouses of which received only light plating, whereas all five of the planned 152mm triple turrets of *Richelieu* and *Jean Bart*, had they been fitted, would have received the same level of protection.

UNDERWATER PROTECTION

The underwater protection system of *Richelieu* and *Jean Bart* was modelled on that of *Dunkerque* (*qv*). The compartment outboard of the inclined armour belt, which had a maximum depth of 1.5 metres, had a filling of *ébonite mousse* to absorb the initial impact and to prevent uncontrolled flooding of the side compartments. Inboard of this compartment there was

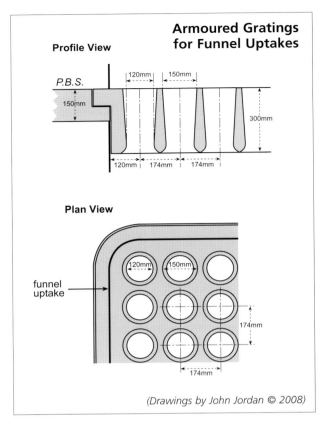

Armoured Gratings for Funnel Uptakes

Profile View

Plan View

funnel uptake

(Drawings by John Jordan © 2008)

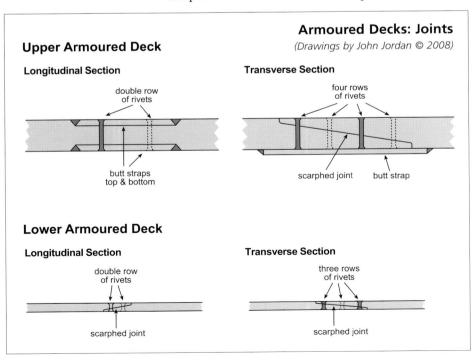

Armoured Decks: Joints

(Drawings by John Jordan © 2008)

Upper Armoured Deck

Longitudinal Section

double row of rivets

butt straps top & bottom

Transverse Section

four rows of rivets

scarphed joint   butt strap

Lower Armoured Deck

Longitudinal Section

double row of rivets

scarphed joint

Transverse Section

three rows of rivets

scarphed joint

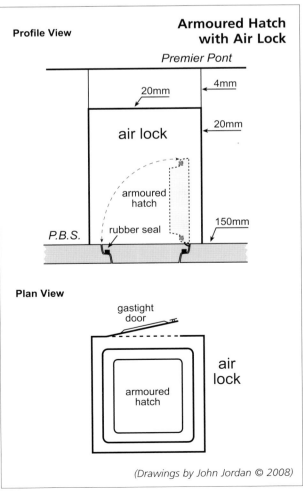

Armoured Hatch with Air Lock

Profile View

Premier Pont

20mm

4mm

20mm

air lock

armoured hatch

rubber seal

150mm

P.B.S.

Plan View

gastight door

armoured hatch

air lock

(Drawings by John Jordan © 2008)

an 18mm bulkhead enclosing a void compartment 0.9 metre deep, which in peacetime could receive oil fuel, followed by an oil fuel bunker 3.4 metres deep, followed by a 10mm bulkhead containing a void compartment 0.67 metre deep, backed by a 30mm torpedo bulkhead of special steel. The compartment between the torpedo bulkhead and the bulkhead enclosing the machinery spaces was used for electrical cabling. The maximum depth of the underwater protection system from the outer skin to the inner face of the torpedo bulkhead was around 7 metres, a reduction from about 7.5 metres in *Dunkerque*, but still an impressive figure.[10]

The underwater protection system covered the same area as the main armoured belt. Abeam the magazines fore and aft the thickness of the torpedo bulkhead was increased to 40/50mm to compensate for the reduction in depth; abeam turret I and the after magazines (frames 51.10 to 72.10 and frames 133.20 to 150.85) the compartment between the fuel bunker and the torpedo bulkhead was filled with *ébonite mousse*, and abeam the diesel compartment and turret I (frames 150.85 to 182.95) the fuel bunker was suppressed altogether in favour of a single broad compartment with an *ébonite mousse* filling.

In a significant departure from the arrangements in *Dunkerque* there was also a substantial filling of *ébonite mousse* forward of the main transverse bulkhead in the compartments above and below the 40mm lower protected deck. The compartments extended from frame 184.20 to frame 195.40, the ceiling being formed by the first platform deck, which was just over one metre above the waterline at this point (see drawing). Outboard of the torpedo bulkheads the filling began at frame 182.95 – it was effectively an extension of the protection system abeam the magazines for turret I – but the compartment inboard was separated from the main transverse bulkhead armour by a void space approximately one metre in depth. Concerns had been expressed regarding the effect that underwater damage might have on the long, virtually unprotected bow section, which, if flooded, would have a major impact on trim and would also create a build-up of pressure on the main transverse bulkhead.[11] It was hoped that filling the broadest compartment of the bow section with the *ébonite mousse* water-excluding compound would resolve this problem – albeit at the cost of a reduction in usable hull volume.

As in *Dunkerque* and *Strasbourg*, the floors of the main and secondary magazines were raised clear of the double bottom to provide protection against mines. These platform decks were of 30mm special steel, the plates being laid longitudinally beneath the magazines for the 152mm guns and for turret II, and transversely beneath the magazine of turret I. The plates were secured to one another by double welded butt straps to provide the same level of watertight protection as for the torpedo bulkhead. In *Richelieu* and *Jean Bart*, the floors of the compartments housing the diesel generators and the forward 152mm magazines, effectively the inner bottom, would also be reinforced to 30mm.

Hull protection in *Richelieu* accounted for 29.1 per cent (11,910 tonnes) of normal displacement, while the protection of the main and secondary armament accounted for a further 10.1 per cent (4135 tonnes). These were impressive figures by any standard; the total weight of protection for her Italian counterparts of the *Littorio* class was 13,600 tonnes – approximately 36 per cent of their standard displacement of approximately 37,750 tonnes.

PROPULSION
The revolutionary new Sural boiler was designed by Ingénieur Général Norguet and built by Indret. Forced circulation and pressure firing resulted in steam production per cubic metre of volume well in excess of conventional boilers (14.4kg/m^3). This enabled overall dimensions to be reduced; the boiler casing had a broadly cylindrical configuration with only a single collector at its base (see drawing). It meant that three boilers could be fitted side by side in a compartment little broader than the boiler rooms aboard *Dunkerque* and *Strasbourg*, which could accommodate only two. Boiler dimensions were: length 6.90 metres (vs 5.33m in *Dunkerque* and *Strasbourg*), height 4.65 metres (vs 5.34 metres) and width – the key dimension for accommodating the boilers side by side – only 4.50 metres (vs 6.50 metres). The reduction from three to two boiler rooms had a major impact on the internal layout of the new ships, and resulted in the more compact topsides arrangement already described. The adoption of a new boiler of revolutionary design for such an important vessel was a considerable gamble on the part of the Marine Nationale.[12] However, the potential benefits were too great to be ignored, and construction of the ships needed to be embarked upon without delay. Fortunately, despite its complexity and the reservations expressed by some, the Sural boiler turned out to be generally successful in operation.

SURAL BOILERS: CHARACTERISTICS

Type	Small-tube pressure-fired with superheating
Pressure rating	27kg/cm^2
Temperature rating	350° C
Dimensions	
Length	6.900m
Width	4.500m
Height	4.650m
Burners	4 Hugé du Temple

---

[10] The machinery compartments in *Richelieu* were broader than those in *Dunkerque*, due not only to the need to accommodate more powerful turbines, but also in particular because of the need to accommodate three Sural boilers alongside in each of the two boiler rooms; this more than compensated for the two metres of additional beam in these ships. The compartment outboard of the machinery which was reduced in depth was the central one containing oil fuel, which was 3.4 metres wide as compared with 3.9 metres in the earlier ships. The outer hull plating was reduced from 10mm to 6mm and the vertical bulkhead inside it was strengthened from 16mm to 18mm.

[11] The British battleship *Nelson*, in which the protection system was based on similar principles, experienced serious problems of this nature when the unarmoured bow struck a mine in December 1939 off Loch Ewe.

[12] The contemporary fleet torpedo boats of *Le Hardi* class would also have the Sural boiler; the model embarked in these ships was rated at 35kg/cm^2 (358° C).

Richelieu: Layout of Machinery

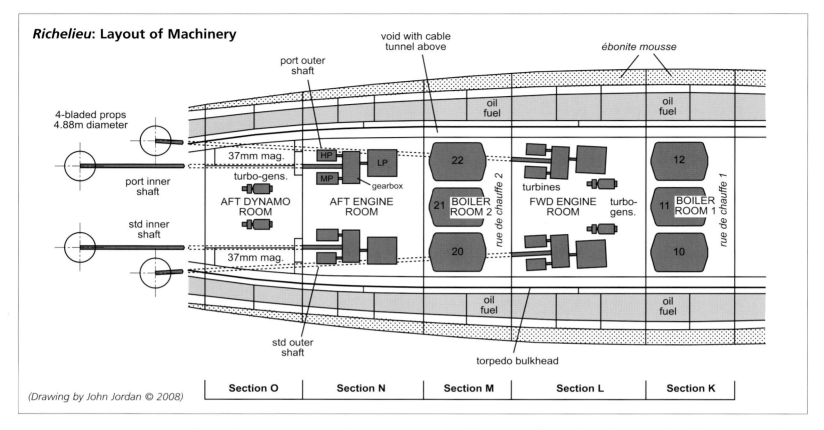

(Drawing by John Jordan © 2008)

Section O	Section N	Section M	Section L	Section K

The reduction to two boiler rooms considerably simplified the layout of the propulsion machinery. Boiler room 1, with three Sural boilers side by side, was followed by the engine room housing the geared turbines for the two wing shafts; boiler room 2, which was directly beneath the funnel, produced steam for the turbines for the two centre shafts (see drawing). The boilers in BR1 were numbered, from starboard to port, 10, 11 and 12; the boilers in BR2 20, 21 and 22. The bulkhead between ER1 and BR2 was reinforced to 18mm and divided the propulsion machinery into two separate, independent units.

The Sural boilers operated at a pressure of 27kg/cm^2 (350°C) and had an automatic feed control system from Rateau. Those for *Richelieu* were built by Indret, while those for *Jean Bart* were manufactured under licence by the shipbuilder: the Penhoët works provided the three boilers for BR1 while those for BR2 were manufactured by Ateliers & Chantiers de la Loire.

There were four sets of Parsons geared turbines, each with its own independent condensers and lubrication pumps, and each driving a four-bladed propeller with a diameter of 4.88 metres. Each set comprised a single HP (27kg/cm^2) turbine, an MP (10kg/cm^2) turbine, and LP forward and reverse turbines (1.25kg/cm^2 and 4kg/cm^2 respectively) which were linked in series to single reduction gearing. The machinery control centre was in the forward engine room (ER1) and communicated directly with the conning tower. Designed horsepower was 155,000shp for 32 knots, 175,000shp with forcing. During trials with *Richelieu*, 179,000shp was attained for a short time, corresponding to a speed of 32.63 knots.

The maximum fuel load for peacetime cruising was 5866 tonnes, but this figure was reduced to 4500 tonnes in wartime in order to maximise the effectiveness of the underwater protection system. Endurance with the maximum fuel load was estimated at 3450nm at 30 knots, 8250nm at 20 knots, and 9850nm at 16 knots.

The single counterbalanced rudder had a useable surface area of 51 square metres and there were two main electric servo-motors, each of which could operate the rudder on its own at any forward speed

MACHINERY TRIALS (*RICHELIEU* 1940)[1]

Date	Nature of trial	Displacement	SHP (Max.)	Speed (max.)
14.04.40(am)	Preliminary trials	40,927t	22,310	18.41kts
			46,300	22.75kts
			90,114	26.80kts
14.04.40(pm)	1H[2] acceptance	40,927t[3]	123,080	30.11kts
13.06.40(am)	3H30 max. power trial	43,800t	155,000	32.00kts
13.06.40(pm)	0H30 with forcing	43,800t[3]	179,000	32.63kts

Notes:
[1] The trials of *Richelieu* were compressed with a view to getting the ship into operational service at the earliest possible date.
[2] H = hour
[3] Only the initial displacement (i.e., prior to the am trials) is recorded.

Sural Boiler: Steam Generator

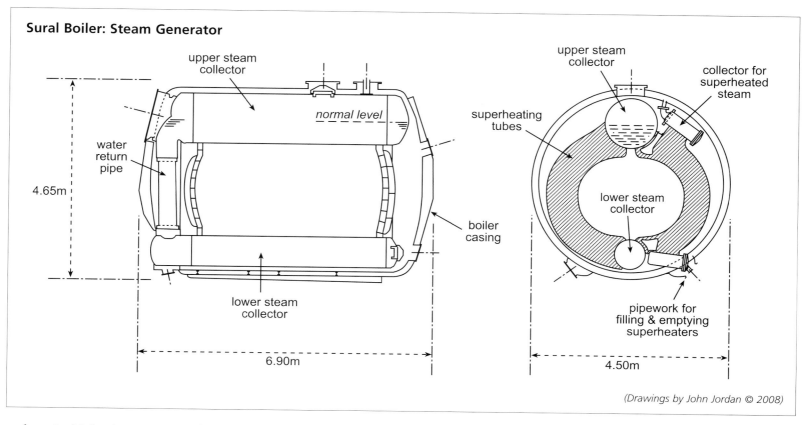

upper steam collector

normal level

water return pipe

4.65m

lower steam collector

6.90m

upper steam collector

collector for superheated steam

superheating tubes

lower steam collector

boiler casing

pipework for filling & emptying superheaters

4.50m

(Drawings by John Jordan © 2008)

and up to 14 knots in reverse. If both motors were engaged there was little additional impact on the speed at which the rudder turned. Each of the motors could be controlled from the conning tower, from the secondary conning position in turret II, or from the steering compartment itself. The rudder could be turned from 0 degrees to a maximum angle of 30 degrees by either of the main motors in fifteen seconds. An emergency motor, which could be controlled from either of the main conning positions, could turn the rudder from 0 degrees to 20 degrees in one minute provided the speed of the ship was below 20 knots. The changeover from main to emergency motor took approximately thirty seconds; the reverse operation took longer (almost one minute). In the event that the rudder was at an angle higher than 20 degrees when the changeover was made the emergency motor could be clutched to the necessary angle in order to return the rudder to 0 degrees.

In the event of a complete power failure the ship could be steered manually from the forward steering compartment; there were six spoked wheels attached to a central shaft crewed by up to twenty-four men, the time taken to turn the rudder 0 degrees to 20 degrees being three minutes (20 knots maximum ship speed). In practice it was found that provided ship speed were reduced to 16 knots manual steering using seventeen men was more effective than steering on the emergency motor.

To provide the ship with the necessary electrical power there were four turbo-generators each of 1500kW. In *Dunkerque* and *Strasbourg*, the turbo-generators (rating: 900kW) had been located in the two engine rooms; in *Richelieu* and *Jean Bart*, which had larger turbo-generators and more powerful turbine machinery, the after pair was located in a separate

compartment directly abaft the main machinery spaces, adjacent to the magazines for the after 152mm guns. To provide power when alongside there were three diesel generators each of 1000kW located low in the ship between the magazines for the main guns; these could produce 1250kW on overload for five

The revolutionary Sural boiler, built by Indret. The unusual configuration of this boiler, which had significantly less width than the one installed in *Dunkerque* and *Strasbourg*, enabled three units to be fitted side by side in each of the two boiler rooms (see drawing), with consequent savings in the length of the machinery compartments and the weight of armour needed to protect them.

ELECTRICAL POWER GENERATION: COMPARISON WITH CONTEMPORARY EUROPEAN BATTLESHIPS

	Dunkerque (France)	Richelieu (France)	Littorio (Italy)	KGV (GB)	Bismarck (Germany)
Turbo-gens	4 x 900kW	4 x 1500kW	8 x 450kW	6 x 350kW	5 x 690kW
					1 x 470kW
Total	3600kW	6000kW	3600kW	2100kW	3920kW
Diesel gens	3 x 400kW	3 x 1000kW	4 x 800kW	2 x 350kW	8 x 500kW
Total	1200kW	3000kW	3200kW	700kW	4000kW
Total	**4800kW**	**9000kW**	**6800kW**	**2800kW**	**7920kW**

minutes. Two emergency diesel generators mounted high in the ship directly beneath the tower were each rated at 140kW (168kW for one hour). Total generator power was 6000kW at sea and 3000kW in harbour; these figures were far in excess of the figures for *Dunkerque* and *Strasbourg* (3600kW and 1200kW respectively), and compared favourably even with contemporary German battleships, which were notoriously heavy consumers of electrical power due to their extensive use of powered auxiliary machinery.

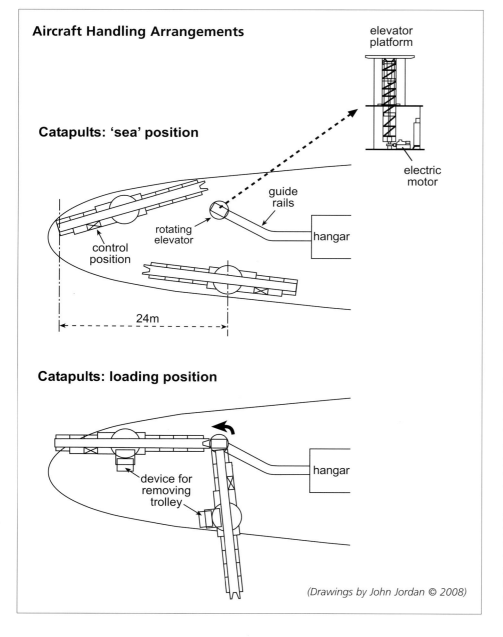

(Drawings by John Jordan © 2008)

AVIATION FACILITIES

The more compact superstructures of *Richelieu* and *Jean Bart* permitted not only a longer forecastle, which would improve sea-keeping, but also a lengthening of the quarterdeck abaft the aviation hangar from 30 metres to around 37.5 metres. This enabled a second catapult to be worked in, the catapults being moved to the deck edge and offset to port and starboard *en echelon* with the elevator between them. The base of the starboard (forward) catapult was centred on frame 24, that of the port-side catapult on frame 9. The catapults were the same model as in *Dunkerque* (for characteristics see p.52).

The long, narrow hangar was located at upper-deck level, between frames 36.50 and 61.50. Dimensions were: length 25 metres, width 7.2 metres (reduced to 5.9 metres abeam the wing 152mm mountings) and height 5 metres. It was designed to accommodate two Loire 130 reconnaissance seaplanes with wings folded one behind the other. The after end of the hangar was closed by a vertically sliding metallic 'curtain'. The aircraft maintenance workshops were directly beneath the hangar, to starboard, and there was a magazine to stow the 75kg bombs as in *Dunkerque* and *Strasbourg*. It was envisaged that the normal air complement would be four Loire 130: two stowed (wings folded) in the hangar and two (wings deployed) readied on the catapults. A fifth aircraft could be accommodated, wings folded, atop the after section of the hangar. In the event, *Richelieu* would be assigned only three Loire 130 (from Flotilla 4E) when her air group was finally formed on 4 July 1941.

The aircraft were moved to and from the hangar on their launching trolleys. Rails set into the hangar floors on the centreline extended onto the quarterdeck and terminated atop the elevator set into the deck, which in *Richelieu* was offset to port to enable it to serve both catapults (see drawing). Each aircraft was manhandled on its launch trolley from the hangar to the elevator, where the wings were deployed. At the end of its mission, the Loire 130 landed on the surface of the sea and then taxied alongside. It was lifted aboard by a recovery crane with a capacity of 4.5 tonnes; wings were then folded and it was again stowed in the hangar. When not in use the articulated crane, which was mounted to port of the hangar, was stowed flat on the quarterdeck.

The authors have been unable to find a precise figure for the quantity of aviation fuel carried. Official plans of *Richelieu* show only three tanks of similar size to those of *Dunkerque*, but offset to port with an unoccupied space to starboard. However, recently released plans of *Clemenceau*, whose aviation arrangements were otherwise identical to those of her near-sister, show a fourth tank in this space. This tank, moreover, is significantly larger with perhaps twice the capacity of each of the other three. This suggests a figure of 18,000-19,000 litres for the maximum complement of five aircraft which could be carried. The plans (ST1469 and ST1470) also show clearly the elaborate safety features, including the inert gas storage system.

APPEARANCE

From her first trials in October 1939 until mid-1940, *Richelieu* was painted medium grey except for:

- rangefinders: painted white to reflect the heat, thereby minimising distortion;
- upper deck and superstructure deck: teak planking except for the forecastle forward of the first breakwater, which was painted steel grey;
- funnel cowling, anchors and chains, waterline: black

During her repairs at Dakar in the second half of 1940, she was repainted light grey with a dark grey vertical band on the stern encompassing the hawse pipe and stern anchor that tapered towards the waterline. After repairs to the after part of the hull were completed in April 1941, the repaired section (section P to starboard) was painted medium grey – presumably the only colour available in quantity to the dockyard at Dakar at that time. Also during 1941, following an instruction originally issued on 7 July 1940, neutrality markings were applied to turret II in the form of tricolore bands.

MODIFICATIONS 28.06.40 TO 30.01.43: *RICHELIEU*[13]

Modifications to close-range AA:
- 12 July 1940: two 13.2mm Hotchkiss CAD from shelter deck forward relocated atop hangar.
- November 1940: two 37mm CAD Mle 1933 (removed from *contre-torpilleur L'Audacieux*) fitted on shelter deck forward, abeam the conning tower.
- 27 December 1940: single 13.2mm Browning CAS (also from *L'Audacieux*) fitted in the starboard after position of the upper platform of the after tower.
- February 1941: a 13.2mm Hotchkiss CAQ was fitted in the port forward position of the upper platform of the after tower, diagonally opposite the Browning CAS.
- 14 June 1941: three new 13.2mm Browning CAS fitted: one on the stern, the remaining two at the forward corners of the shelter deck.
- July 1941: two new 37mm CAD Mle 1933 replaced the 13.2mm CAD atop the hangar, the latter mountings being relocated to their original position abeam turret II.

(The close-range AA armament now comprised: sixteen 37mm (8 X II), twenty-eight 13.2mm (5 X IV, 2 X II, 4 X I).)

Installation of radar (DEM):
A prototype 2-metre DEM (*Détection électro-magnétique*) installation was fitted between February and May 1941. The installation was different to that in *Strasbourg* in that the two rotating antennae for transmission were located at the ends of the after yards of

MISCELLANEOUS EQUIPMENT

Anchors
Forward
Three 10-tonne Guérigny type anchors in hawsepipes: a single anchor to port and to starboard and a third set into the bow.

Aft
A single centre-line stern anchor as above; Guérigny-type 3.15-tonne anchor with 48mm chain. (Also two 1.52-tonne and one 0.32-tonne kedge anchors.)

Boats
Richelieu (as designed)
Three 11-metre motor boats
Three 10.8-metre motor boats
Two 9-metre motor boats
Two 11-metre motor launches
Two 13-metre long boats
One 13-metre motor pinnace
Two 8-metre whalers
Two 5-metre dinghies
Two 3-metre flat-bottom boats

The larger boats were stowed on crutches between the tower and the funnel. The remainder were grouped around the base of the tower on crutches or trolleys; those on trolleys could be moved aft on rails set into the deck to enable them to be handled by the two 22-tonne boat cranes, which were located at the after foot of the tower.

Radio Equipment

Transmitters	Power	Range
One medium-wave transmitter	4/6kW	1000nm
One medium-wave transmitter	2kW	400nm
Two medium-wave transmitters	600W	300nm
One short-wave transmitter	75W	300nm
One short-wave transmitter	2500W	2000nm
One short-wave transmitter	500W	1000nm
One emergency transmitter	2-18kW	100nm

Aerials
- main antenna: six horizontal strands strung between the forward tower and the mainmast.
- 350mm diameter prism between port extremity of mainmast yard and the after side of the upper projector platform.
- two 400mm prisms eight metres long on after tower.

Note: The radio equipment outfit was broadly similar to that fitted in *Dunkerque* and *Strasbourg*; the few changes are of a minor nature.

the forward tower, but the two antennae for reception were at the ends of the yards on the after tower. Results were:

Aerial targets
- Aircraft flying above 1500 metres could be detected at 80 kilomettres.
- At 1000 metres detection range was 50 kilometres.[14]
- Against low-flying aircraft detection range fell to 10 kilometres.

Surface targets
- Surface ships could be detected between 10 kilometres and 20 kilometres, depending on target size and weather conditions, the accuracy in range being of the order of 500 metres.

Removal of catapults and 37mm mountings
In January 1943, prior to the ship's scheduled modernisation in the United States, the aircraft catapults and the 37mm CAD were removed.

---

[13] Details of various AA guns fitted in *Jean Bart* as a temporary measure are given in Chapter 6.

[14] Bearing accuracy was ±3 degrees; range accuracy was to within 300m.

CHAPTER 5

RICHELIEU: 1935-1943

RICHELIEU WAS LAID DOWN IN THE LE SALOU No. 4 dock of the Arsenal de Brest on 22 October 1935, less than three weeks after the incomplete hull of her predecessor, *Dunkerque*, had been floated out. *Richelieu*, which was a significantly larger ship (length oa: 247.85 metres), had to be built in three sections: the 197-metre centre section was built in the dock, the 43-metre bow and 8-metre stern sections elsewhere. The relevant bulkheads of the main body of the hull were shored up and the dock carefully flooded prior to 'launch' to ensure there was no ingress of water; it was then towed to Laninon No. 9 dock (see Chapter 3 p.59) to enable the bow and stern sections to be attached. This took place on 17 January 1939, by which time construction was almost a year behind schedule.

Initially, during 1936, construction had been slowed when the British government expressed its concerns regarding the escalation of new naval construction.

Subsequently, work on the ship had been affected, first, by widespread industrial action in favour of improved pay and working conditions and, second, by improved working conditions.[1] Thirty-nine months from keel laying to launch was by no means an impressive performance.[2]

When war broke out on 3 September 1939, the hull was complete, the bow and stern sections having been

---

[1] Workers in the naval dockyards and the private shipbuilding industry secured reduced contractual working hours and better holiday entitlements, regulations which began to bite during 1937.

[2] It compared with just over thirty-three months for *Dunkerque*, just over two years for *Strasbourg*, a similar figure for the British *King George V* and *Prince of Wales*, and thirty-four and thirty-three months respectively for *Littorio* and *Vittorio Veneto* building for the Italian *Regia Marina*.

Richelieu under construction in the *Forme du Salou* at Brest Naval Dockyard, 8 July 1937. Work has begun on the main armoured deck, or PBS; the 150mm armoured plates are being riveted and welded over the machinery spaces amidships.
(*C Picard collection*)

CONSTRUCTION DATES[1]

Name	Estimates	Builder	Laid down	Launch	Trials	Acc. trials	Commiss'd	Completion	In service
Richelieu	1935	Arsenal de Brest	22.10.35	17.01.39	15.10.39	14.04.40	01.04.40[2]	15.06.40	11.43[3]
Jean Bart	1936	Ateliers et Chantiers de Saint-Nazaire (Penhoët)	12.12.36	06.03.40	07.08.40		[01.08.49]		[01.05.55]

Notes:
[1] For a full account of the different stages of construction of French warships as defined in the *Bulletin Officiel* (BO) see p.59.
[2] Unusually, *Richelieu* was commissioned before she ran her acceptance trials.
[3] *Richelieu*'s entry into service was never officially pronounced. The ship was declared 'available' on 10 October 1943, and the monthly report on Marine Nationale activity of the period states that she entered service during November 1943, but without a specified date.

attached to the main body of the hull during spring 1939. Captain Marzin had taken command of the ship, and fitting out was proceeding at the *Quai d'Armement*. When the French naval construction programme was reviewed during September 1939, it was decided that priority would now be accorded to the rapid completion of *Richelieu* and *Jean Bart* at the expense of other vessels that were less advanced, including *Richelieu*'s successor *Clemenceau*, the keel of which had been laid in the No. 4 dock on the same day the hull of *Richelieu* was floated out.

Ironically, considering the early representations from the British government urging a slowing down of construction, the British were now urging early completion of *Richelieu* due to delays in the construction of the *King George V* class and the imminent entry into service of the new German 15in-gun battleship *Bismarck*. In November, Churchill, at that time First Lord of the Admiralty, secured assurances from Darlan that *Richelieu* would be completed in May 1940 and

ready for service by July of the same year.

Work on the ship proceeded in earnest. Dockyard workers who before the war had benefited from the generous working conditions secured in 1936 were now working an eighty-four-hour week. Once the boilers, generators, turbines and gear-boxes had been lifted aboard the focus turned to the rotating platforms and munitions trunks of the turrets, the guns themselves and the massive armour plates, some of which weighed 30-60 tonnes.[3] The last of the 380mm guns was lifted aboard 21 January 1940. Meanwhile an army of dockyard workers swarmed over the ship, completing the armoured decks over the machinery spaces and installing no fewer than 400 electrically powered motors, 750 kilometres of cabling and 170 kilometres of pipework.

---

[3] Ironically, the floating crane used for this work was a 250-tonne German model which had been a part of the 'reparations' secured following the First World War.

In this later photograph taken on 6 December 1937, the main armoured deck is virtually complete and steel plates for the first deck above are stacked in readiness amidships. Note the large diameter of the aperture needed to accommodate the working chamber of turret II. (*C Picard collection*)

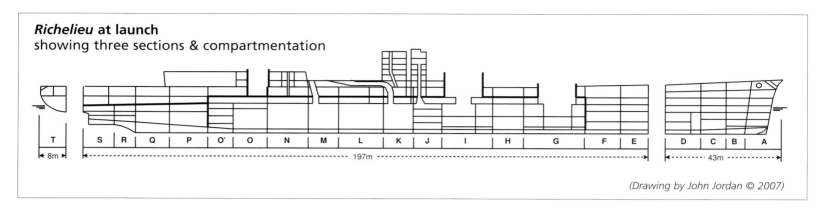

Richelieu at launch
showing three sections & compartmentation

(Drawing by John Jordan © 2007)

The incomplete hull of *Richelieu* is floated out of the Salou building dock. Because of the limited dimensions of the latter the bow and stern sections, which were built separately, would have to be attached in one of the 250-metre Laninon graving docks, located beyond the mouth of the River Penfeld (see map p.59). (*H Landais collection*)

TRIALS AND WORK-UP

The need to get the ship into service at the earliest possible date required some extreme measures, particularly with regard to testing of the new and untried Sural boilers. *Ingénieur 1ère classe du Génie Maritime* Poirier, who was placed in charge of trials, secured permission to run each of the boilers at full pressure on installation, before the turbine machinery was complete and with the ship alongside. Given that each of the six boilers produced in excess of 20 tonnes of steam per hour, this implied a huge consumption of distilled water.

On 14 January 1940, tugs moved *Richelieu* out into the *Rade-Abri* for her first machinery trials, which were conducted the following day with the ship moored to a buoy. She was then docked in Laninon No. 8 dock for checking of the hull and fitting of her propellers. Further machinery trials, together with turning trials, took place between 31 March and 7 April, when power was increased to 100,000shp. In the same month, the first three of the 100mm HA gun mountings were embarked (11 April) and the starboard catapult was installed (13 April). The following day saw *Richelieu's* acceptance trials, which involved three 18.5-knot and three 22.5-knot runs over the fixed course in the Bay of Douarnenez, just to the south of Brest. Because of the risk from U-boats, the ship was escorted to and from the Bay by the *contre-torpilleurs Albatros* and *Vautour.* Firings were conducted with the 100mm and light AA guns. During a one-hour high-speed trial run that afternoon *Richelieu* attained 30 knots with 123,000shp (see table p.118).

By the evening of 15 April, *Richelieu* was back at the *Quai de Laninon* for inspection of her machinery. A six-

degree inclination on 24 April, conducted in heavy rain, revealed problems with the watertightness of the upper platforms of the tower and with the free rotation of the main turrets, and remedial work followed. A further trial on 31 May, when the ship was inclined to 12 degrees, appears to have been successful. The ship was docked during 19-27 May, and following this the remaining three 100mm mountings were embarked, the directors for the main and secondary guns fitted atop the towers (1-4 June), and the 152mm guns installed in the after turrets (5 June onwards).

Full power trials were scheduled for 15 June, but with the Germans approaching, these were advanced by two days. At 0800 on 13 June, *Richelieu* again sailed for the Bay of Douarnenez, where she achieved 32 knots over three and a half hours at full power (155,000shp) during the morning and, during a half-hour 'forcing' trial in the afternoon, she achieved 32.63 knots with 179,000shp – an impressive performance by any standards, and all the more remarkable given that these trials were run at an initial displacement of 43,800 tonnes. On 13 and 14 June, six rounds were fired from each of the 380mm and 152mm guns without incident. Only the replenishment systems for the main guns gave concern, although it was clear that the ship was still some way off full operational status. On her return to Brest, *Richelieu* moored in the outer *Grande Rade* at Brest.

ESCAPE FROM BREST

At 0645 the following day, the ship was moved to the inner harbour, the *Rade-Abri*, where with the German armoured columns fast approaching, she embarked munitions and provisions and a full load (6000t) of oil fuel. For some three weeks the provisional plan had been to sail for the Clyde or for another English port. However, with the decision to explore the possibility of an armistice, the French government immediately became aware of the importance of the French fleet as a bargaining counter in any negotiations with the German authorities, and it quickly became apparent that dispatching major elements of the fleet to British ports to continue the fight would prejudice these negotiations and reduce the chance of securing an honourable outcome for France. During the night of 17-18 June, Admiral of the Fleet Darlan transmitted a new instruction to the C-in-C Brest, Admiral de Laborde, to the effect that a departure for England was less likely, that he should prepare to evacuate to the French colonies, and that no vessel currently in Brest should be left intact. At 0912 the following day, Darlan followed this message with an instruction that *Richelieu* should sail for Dakar.

The new orders posed a problem for Captain Marzin. Although a satisfactory number of 380mm shells (296) had been embarked, there were only 198 quarter-charges aboard, sufficient for only 49 firings.[4] It had been anticipated that in the event of an escape to England, the British naval dockyards could easily furnish the requisite number of charges. However, the only stocks of charges currently at Dakar were for the 330mm guns of *Dunkerque* and *Strasbourg*. This would leave *Richelieu* vulnerable and exposed if subjected to a determined attack by heavy ships either during the transit to North Africa or once deployed to the colonial base.

Moreover, fitting out was by no means complete. Virtually all equipment had now been delivered by the manufacturers, but a substantial quantity of it remained on the dockside in readiness for installation. Everything now had to be rapidly embarked and stowed on the upper decks. Dockyard personnel and constructors were also embarked to supervise installation. During the afternoon of 18 June, the 250 midshipmen of the prestigious officer training school located at Brest, the Ecole Navale, were likewise embarked for the voyage to North Africa, together with heavy cases of gold from the Bank of France.

Sacrifices had to be made in order to accommodate all of these items in the little time available. It was not possible to embark all of the cooking equipment for the galleys, and the white 'tropical' uniforms were left behind. Even so, the ship would have to sail with a reduced complement. At 0400, with the German columns fast approaching the port, *Richelieu*, assisted by four tugs, slowly turned and headed for the pass. As she departed Brest she was subjected to frantic enemy air attacks, to which she responded with her 100mm and light AA guns. Escorted by the torpedo-boats *Fougueux* (flagship of CA Moreau, commander of the Atlantic ASW forces) and *Frondeur*, *Richelieu* increased her speed to 22 knots and headed south for Dakar. The voyage was punctuated by a boiler incident that reduced speed to 18 knots, and by repeated failures of the main rudder servo-motors, which had to be repaired by the crew during transit.

---

[4] No munitions for the 152mm guns were embarked, although there were 1650 fuzed and 120 percussive rounds for the 100mm guns and 2030 rounds for the 37mm guns.

COMMANDING OFFICERS AND FLAG OFFICERS (1939-43)

Commanding Officers

CV Marzin	15.10.39 – 27.02.41
CV Deramond	27.02.41 – 29.04.43
CV Lambert	29.04.43 – 06.05.44

Notes:
CV   *Capitaine de vaisseau*   (RN equivalent rank: captain)

At 1700 on 20 June, when off Casablanca, *Richelieu*'s escorting torpedo-boats, which were by now running short of fuel, were relieved by the brand-new *Fleuret*,[5] which had arrived in Casablanca on 15 June from Toulon. The two ships finally entered Dakar at 1744 on 23 June.

DAKAR

Captain Marzin faced a difficult situation when he arrived at Dakar. The Armistice was currently being negotiated and the captain found a confused political situation at the colonial port. The naval C-in-C of French West Africa, Rear-Admiral Plançon, initially favoured a continuation of the fight alongside the British and communicated an appeal from the British Foreign Secretary, Lord Halifax, to Marzin shortly after his arrival. The Governor General of the West African Federation,[6] Léon Cayla, and much of the population were of a similar persuasion. The British carrier HMS *Hermes*, which had formerly operated alongside *Strasbourg* and French heavy cruisers as part of Force X, was moored in the Inner Harbour, and ships of the British South Atlantic Squadron, including the cruiser *Dorsetshire* and the seaplane carrier *Albatross*, were operating in the vicinity. Marzin's difficulties were compounded by the precarious operational status of his ship; *Richelieu* had consumed half her fuel load in the transit from Brest, and neither her main nor her secondary armament was ready for combat.

During the night of 23-24 June, Marzin received a telegram from Darlan warning of a possible British attack and instructing him to set in motion preparations for sabotage. On the morning of 25 June, Marzin received a further telegram announcing the signature of the Armistice, together with instructions from Darlan that the ship was to remain under the French flag, and that in the event of an attempt against *Richelieu*, he should either sabotage the ship or flee to the (neutral) United States. Marzin determined that in the circumstances the best course was to sail for Casablanca, taking with him *Fleuret*, the armed merchant cruiser *Charles Plumier*, the old sloop *Calais*, and the two fleet submarines *Le Glorieux* and *Le Héros*. Time of departure was fixed at 1430 of the same day, and Marzin requested that one of the two submarines keep an eye on *Hermes* while the other patrolled outside the harbour to intercept the cruiser *Dorsetshire*, which was expected at 1600. The Governor General expressed his concern about the

---

[5] As with *Fougueux* and *Frondeur*, the correct designation of the *Fleuret* and the other ships of her class was *torpilleur d'escadre* (= fleet torpedo-boat). In either of the Anglo-Saxon navies they would have been classified as 'destroyer'.

[6] Known as the AOF (*Afrique Occidentale Française*), the French West African Federation of eight colonial territories was formed in 1904.

effect of this 'desertion' on the local population, but Marzin was set on his course of action.

Richelieu duly weighed anchor at 1430, accompanied by Fleuret. She would be closely followed by Hermes, with torpedo-armed Swordfish on deck. However, the French at Dakar responded by training the 240mm coast defence guns of Cap Manuel and Gorée on the British carrier, and after a pursuit that continued for only ten miles or so, Hermes turned 180 degrees, struck down her aircraft, and returned to Dakar.

This already-fraught episode now rapidly descended into farce. Darlan, learning of Richelieu's departure and assuming that Marzin had sailed to join the British, issued a formal order, transmitted via Admiral Ollive at Toulon and received on board at 0830 on 26 June, instructing Marzin to return to Dakar and await further orders. Totally nonplussed, Marzin obediently turned his ship round and headed back towards Dakar into what was fast becoming a British trap. During the return journey, Richelieu would be shadowed by the cruiser Dorsetshire and by a seaplane from Albatross. However, at 0700 on 26 June, when Richelieu was only 15 kilometres from Dakar, Marzin was ordered by the local naval HQ to proceed with Fleuret to a position 120 miles to the north of the Cape Verde Islands to bring in the 1st Division of Armed Merchant Cruisers, carrying 726 tonnes of gold from the Bank of France, which was headed from Casablanca to Dakar escorted by the contre-torpilleurs Milan and Epervier. Failing to find these ships at the specified rendezvous, and unable to search for them in the absence of embarked seaplanes, Marzin headed back to Dakar, arriving on 28 June. The Flotte d'Or, as it had been christened, arrived six days later on 4 July.

Frantic efforts now began to get the ship fully operational, with a particular focus on the main and secondary guns. The 380mm guns could fire and the main directors were functional. However, the replenishment system needed considerable work; it took fully fifteen minutes to bring up a charge from the magazine to the guns, so the ship was realistically capable of firing only two initial four-gun salvos before her big guns fell silent. The other issue was the small number of SD 21 charges that had been embarked at Brest – sufficient only for forty-nine rounds. Marzin ordered new charges to be manufactured at the local armaments depot from the stock of SD19 charges prepositioned for the deployment of Strasbourg to the port.

The 152mm guns of the secondary armament were ready for combat ten days after the ship's arrival at Dakar, but a further three weeks would be necessary before a simplified fire control system was operational; even so, the guns were incapable of firing against aerial targets, because the upper director of the forward tower (Télépointeur 1) still lacked the means to direct HA fire.

THE ATTACK OF 8 JULY

With the sudden deterioration in Anglo-French relations in late June which followed the Armistice, Churchill was determined that Richelieu should be disabled or sunk to prevent the ship falling into the hands of the enemy. The first step was to ensure that the ship could not return to metropolitan France. The carrier Hermes, currently at Freetown with the cruiser Australia, was ordered to join the cruiser Dorsetshire off Dakar. On 3 July, the day of Operation 'Catapult',

the latter ship received an order from the Admiralty that in the event of an attempted escape by Richelieu to the French West Indies, the ship was to be torpedoed and rammed(!).[7]

Faced with the perceived imminence of a British attack, Rear-Admiral Plançon on 4 July ordered the submarines Le Glorieux and Le Héros to sortie for an attack on the Dorsetshire, and the 240mm batteries of Cap Manuel and Gorée to open fire if the cruiser approached to within 15 kilometres. However, Dorsetshire kept her distance from the port and, aware of the presence of the two submarines, manoeuvred at high speed while catapulting off her Walrus seaplane to attack them. The submarines failed to get closer than 6000 metres and returned to harbour.

Marzin decided to keep Richelieu moored in the anchorage just to the east of the port and north of the island of Gorée with her bows facing roughly south (190 degrees) so that her big guns could engage an approaching force. He surrounded his ship with lines of cargo ships to port and on his starboard quarter (see map). There was a torpedo net to protect the anchorage just north of the island, but to have placed mobile torpedo nets around Richelieu herself would have precluded any possibility of manoeuvre. Marzin also requested that a minefield be laid in the approaches to the harbour, but Plançon did not have the necessary resources at his disposal.

The British planned to despatch Force H to Dakar on 4 July with an ultimatum identical to that presented at Mers el-Kebir, but in the event Somerville was ordered to return to Oran to complete the destruction of Dunkerque. Instead, Captain Onslow of Hermes, temporarily promoted to Rear-Admiral, was put in command of a scratch force assembled specially for this mission, with Hermes and the cruisers Dorsetshire and Australia at its centre.

Following the same procedure as at Mers el-Kebir, the sloop Milford approached the harbour during the afternoon of 7 July flying a white flag from her halyards, and asked for permission to enter Dakar for negotiations with the port authorities. Permission was refused, and at 1805 the ultimatum was transmitted by W/T. In the event of French failure to comply with its terms, Onslow had been ordered to torpedo Richelieu, then to attack the contre-torpilleurs Epervier and Milan.

At Mers el-Kebir on 3 July, many of the French personnel, including some senior officers, had believed the British ultimatum to be a bluff. At Dakar four days later, nobody doubted that the British were deadly serious, and the impact on the crews of the ships moored in the port, and in particular on the many reservists, was immediate. One hundred matelots, bags on shoulders, made their way to the dockyard gates. The commander of the submarine Le Glorieux returned to his boat to find men with bags packed ready to disembark. On Epervier no fewer than 146 out of a crew of 220 crossed the gangway, and it was a similar story on some of the armed merchant cruisers. The authorities mobilised the gendarmes and the colonial troops, and many men were persuaded to return to their ships. However, by the end of the day there

---

[7] There was some irony in this, as passage to the French West Indies was one of the options offered to Admiral Gensoul as part of the ultimatum at Mers el-Kebir.

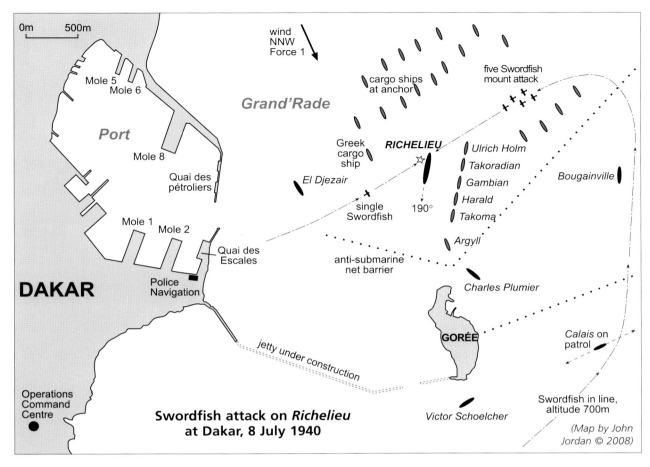

Swordfish attack on *Richelieu*
at Dakar, 8 July 1940

(Map by John
Jordan © 2008)

remained 128 who refused to obey orders and had to be first imprisoned and then escorted to holding camps on the periphery of Dakar.

On board *Richelieu*, Marzin prepared to sortie the following morning, planning to use the eight rounds in his main guns to sink *Hermes*. The coastal batteries were put on alert, the *contre-torpilleur Milan* patrolled outside the harbour entrance and the submarine *Le Héros* sortied and took up a position 11,000 metres to the south of Cap Manuel. The other major naval units were effectively immobilised due to their loss of personnel and remained moored in the port.

Following an abortive attempt by a fast motor boat launched from the sloop *Milford* and manned by British Royal Marines to explode four 420lb (190kg) depth charges under the stern of *Richelieu* during the night, a torpedo strike by Swordfish aircraft was prepared aboard *Hermes* in the early morning. Take-off was at 0415, five minutes before action stations was sounded aboard *Richelieu*, which was preparing to sortie. Five of the torpedoes missed but the sixth struck the battleship on the starboard quarter, lifting the stern and producing a towering column of water that fell onto the quarterdeck. The impact on the ship was magnified by the shallow water in which she was moored – there was less than five metres of water under the keel. Many of *Richelieu*'s electrical and mechanical systems were put out of action, two of the directors atop the forward tower were lifted out of their tracks, and the two starboard shafts were distorted. Flooding quickly spread from the area of impact to the adjacent compartments, including the after part of the armoured citadel via the shaft and cable tunnels, and

the ship began to settle by the stern. Trim was partially restored by pumping the oil from the bunkers in section P into the sea and taking on water ballast forward, and with the aid of the tug *Buffle*, *Richelieu* was moved into the port and moored at the *Quai des Pétroliers* at 1245. She was then surrounded by torpedo nets to protect against further attacks. Flooding was progressive, and by evening there was 2400 tonnes of water in the ship and the stern settled on the harbour bottom at low tide.

THE FLOODING CAUSED BY THE TORPEDO HIT[8]

A breach 9.3 metres long and 8.5 metres high was opened in the hull between the two starboard shafts, and there was rapid flooding of section P, which quickly spread to adjacent compartments via cracks in floors and bulkheads resulting either from the explosion or from defective welding. The armoured citadel, which was immediately forward of this section, should in theory have remained intact, but there was substantial ingress of water into the cable tunnels of section O through the glands where the cables penetrated bulkhead O'P. Two hours after the torpedo struck there were 1566 tonnes of water in the after part of the ship. Countermeasures were then taken to correct trim to enable the ship to be moved into the port: 200 tonnes of fuel oil were pumped from the after bunkers and 200 tonnes of water ballast admitted in sections D and E forward.

It was found that the starboard inner shaft had been

---

[8] This account is based on the official report by Captain Marzin, dated 28 August 1940.

badly buckled by the force of the explosion, and that the outer shaft to starboard was slightly out of true and would not turn freely, so the ship had to be manoeuvred using only the two port turbines. The distortion of the starboard inner shaft had opened up the glands around the shaft where it passed through bulkhead O'P, causing flooding of the tunnels of the central shafts which then spread to the 37mm and 152mm magazines in section O via leaky cable glands, defective welds, and the tubing for the thermometers which measured temperatures in the magazines. By 9 July a further ten compartments in section O were flooded, together with the tank for washing water in section Q. There was now at least 2400 tonnes of water in the stern. On the afternoon of 8 July, tankers started to pump out 2200 tonnes of oil fuel from the after bunkers, but by 0900 on the following day, the ship was drawing 10.87 metres of water aft and the stern was grounding at every low tide.

The water now began to seep through the cable glands of bulkhead O'O into the after turbo-generator compartment, where it could be controlled only by continuous pumping. By the morning of 9 July, the situation was critical and there were fears that the flooding would spread via the cable tunnels to the forward part of the ship. Mobile pumps from Dakar were towed alongside, but in the swell the hoses constantly parted.

The infrastructure problems that had been raised when the construction of 35,000-tonne battleships had first been mooted now became critical. Dakar, despite its strategic importance as a naval base, was capable only of minor maintenance and repair. The only graving docks that could accommodate the 250-metre hull of *Richelieu* were the two Laninon docks at Brest, the Le Homet dock at Cherbourg, the commercial dock at Le Havre, the No. 2 dock at Sidi-Abdallah (Bizerta) and the two Vauban docks at Toulon. The first four were located in Occupied France, more than 4500 miles away; the Vauban and Sidi-Abdallah docks were at an even greater distance, and in order to reach either, *Richelieu* would have had to transit the Strait of Gibraltar. If the ship had been able to be docked, the water inside the hull could have been quickly drained and repairs carried out. As it was, the only option was to apply temporary patches over leaky floors and bulkheads, some of which were completely submerged, and then to pump out sufficient water for more permanent repairs to be carried out. In some cases cabling was ripped out altogether to enable the bulkheads to be patched and made watertight. There was to be a
Continued on p.137

Damage to *Richelieu*, 8 July 1940

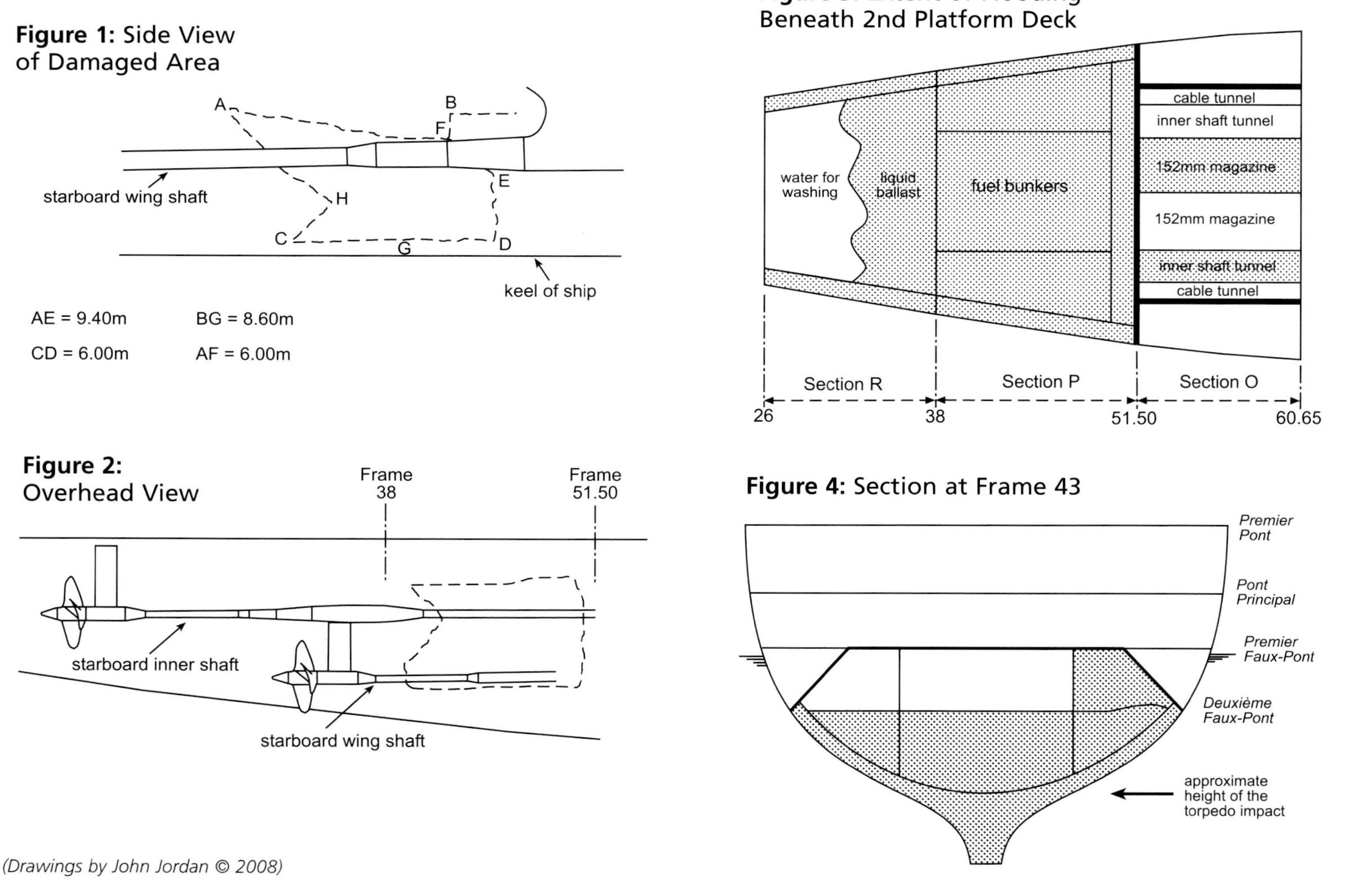

Figure 1: Side View of Damaged Area

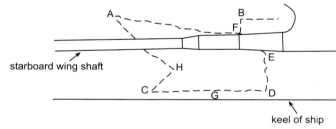

AE = 9.40m   BG = 8.60m

CD = 6.00m   AF = 6.00m

Figure 3: Extent of Flooding Beneath 2nd Platform Deck

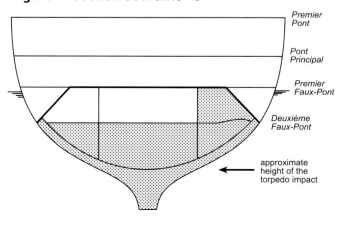

Figure 2: Overhead View

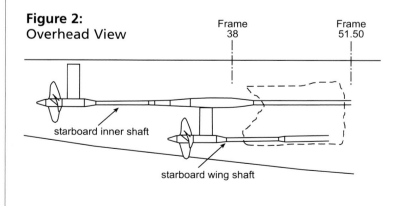

Figure 4: Section at Frame 43

(Drawings by John Jordan © 2008)

Colour Profiles & Plans

The colour artwork in this section has been specially created for the book by the well-known French naval artist Bertrand Magueur in close collaboration with the authors. The following sources have been used: original line drawings by Robert Dumas based on a close study of plans, photographs and, in the case of the number and location of light AA guns, on a personal correspondence with the various COs of the ships; official plans preserved in the archives of the Service Historique de la Marine (SHM) at Vincennes and the Centre d'Archives de l'Armement (CAA) at Châtellerault; and photographs of the ships.

All the paint schemes depicted were symmetrical with the exception of the US Measure 32 camouflage pattern worn between July 1943 and April 1944, when it was replaced with an Admiralty scheme. US Navy photos showing the portside pattern are published on pp. 182-3 and 191-2.

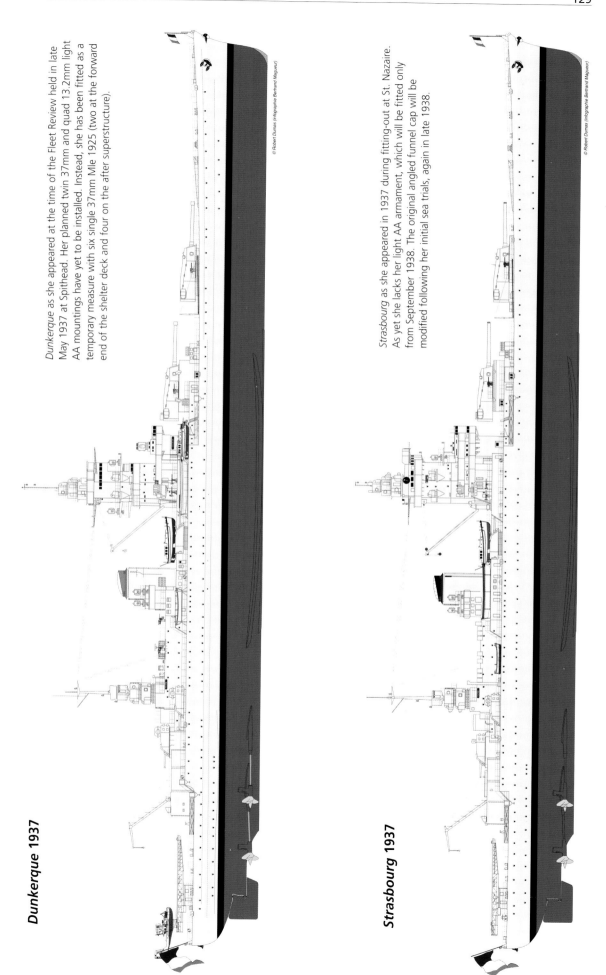

Dunkerque as she appeared at the time of the Fleet Review held in late May 1937 at Spithead. Her planned twin 37mm and quad 13.2mm light AA mountings have yet to be installed. Instead, she has been fitted as a temporary measure with six single 37mm Mle 1925 (two at the forward end of the shelter deck and four on the after superstructure).

© Robert Dumas (infographie Bertrand Magueur)

Dunkerque 1937

Strasbourg as she appeared in 1937 during fitting-out at St. Nazaire. As yet she lacks her light AA armament, which will be fitted only from September 1938. The original angled funnel cap will be modified following her initial sea trials, again in late 1938.

© Robert Dumas (infographie Bertrand Magueur)

Strasbourg 1937

Dunkerque 1939

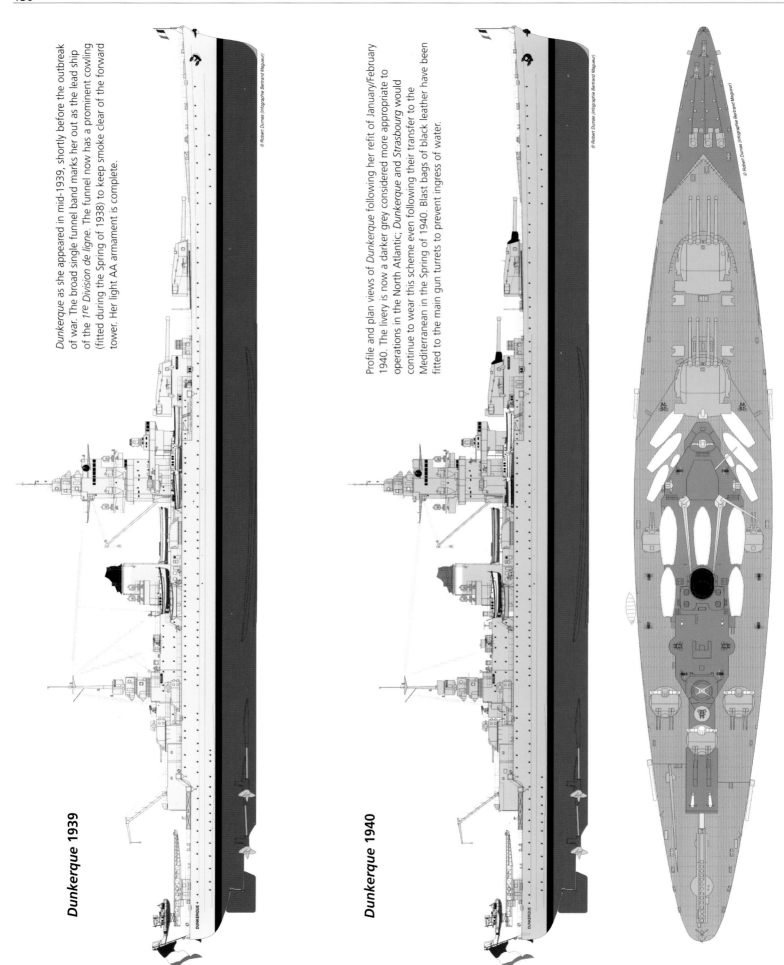

Dunkerque as she appeared in mid-1939, shortly before the outbreak of war. The broad single funnel band marks her out as the lead ship of the *1re Division de ligne*. The funnel now has a prominent cowling (fitted during the Spring of 1938) to keep smoke clear of the forward tower. Her light AA armament is complete.

© Robert Dumas (Infographie Bertrand Magueur)

Dunkerque 1940

Profile and plan views of *Dunkerque* following her refit of January/February 1940. The livery is now a darker grey considered more appropriate to operations in the North Atlantic; *Dunkerque* and *Strasbourg* would continue to wear this scheme even following their transfer to the Mediterranean in the Spring of 1940. Blast bags of black leather have been fitted to the main gun turrets to prevent ingress of water.

© Robert Dumas (Infographie Bertrand Magueur)

© Robert Dumas (Infographie Bertrand Magueur)

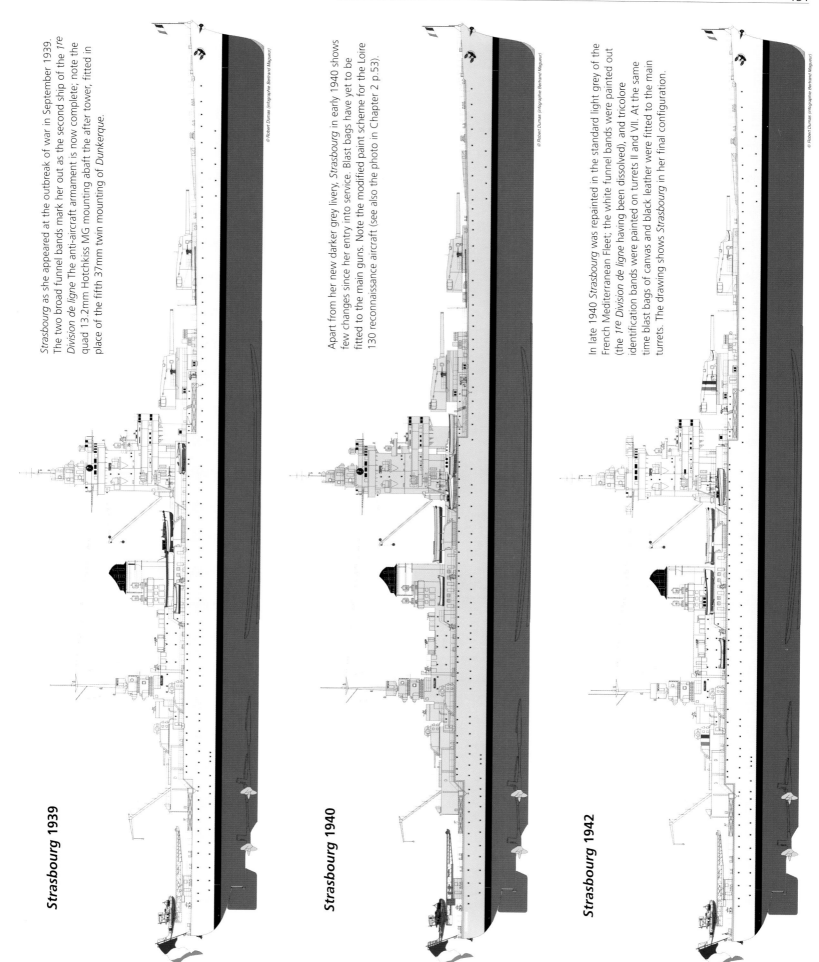

Strasbourg 1939

Strasbourg as she appeared at the outbreak of war in September 1939. The two broad funnel bands mark her out as the second ship of the *1re Division de ligne* The anti-aircraft armament is now complete; note the quad 13.2mm Hotchkiss MG mounting abaft the after tower, fitted in place of the fifth 37mm twin mounting of *Dunkerque*.

© Robert Dumas (infographe Bertrand Magueur)

Strasbourg 1940

Apart from her new darker grey livery, *Strasbourg* in early 1940 shows few changes since her entry into service. Blast bags have yet to be fitted to the main guns. Note the modified paint scheme for the Loire 130 reconnaissance aircraft (see also the photo in Chapter 2 p.53).

© Robert Dumas (infographe Bertrand Magueur)

Strasbourg 1942

In late 1940 *Strasbourg* was repainted in the standard light grey of the French Mediterranean Fleet; the white funnel bands were painted out (the *1re Division de ligne* having been dissolved), and tricolore identification bands were painted on turrets II and VII. At the same time blast bags of canvas and black leather were fitted to the main turrets. The drawing shows *Strasbourg* in her final configuration.

© Robert Dumas (infographe Bertrand Magueur)

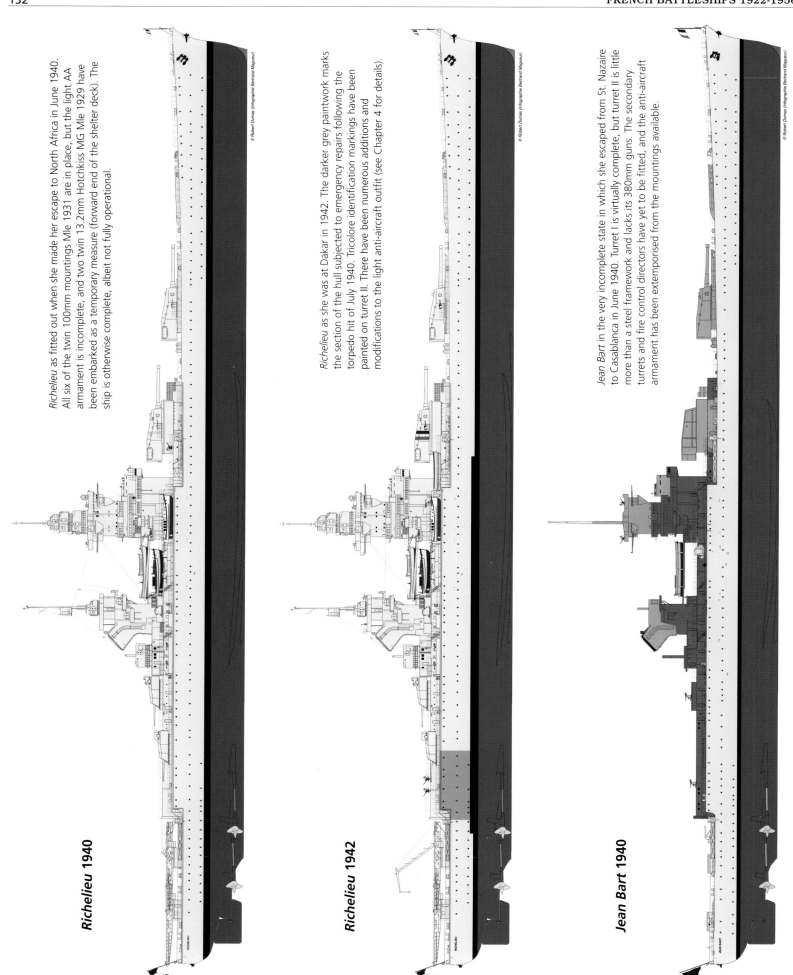

Richelieu 1940

Richelieu as fitted out when she made her escape to North Africa in June 1940. All six of the twin 100mm mountings Mle 1931 are in place, but the light AA armament is incomplete, and two twin 13.2mm Hotchkiss MG Mle 1929 have been embarked as a temporary measure (forward end of the shelter deck). The ship is otherwise complete, albeit not fully operational.

© Robert Dumas (infographie Bertrand Magueur)

Richelieu 1942

Richelieu as she was at Dakar in 1942. The darker grey paintwork marks the section of the hull subjected to emergency repairs following the torpedo hit of July 1940. Tricolore identification markings have been painted on turret II. There have been numerous additions and modifications to the light anti-aircraft outfit (see Chapter 4 for details).

© Robert Dumas (infographie Bertrand Magueur)

Jean Bart 1940

Jean Bart in the very incomplete state in which she escaped from St. Nazaire to Casablanca in June 1940. Turret I is virtually complete, but turret II is little more than a steel framework and lacks its 380mm guns. The secondary turrets and fire control directors have yet to be fitted, and the anti-aircraft armament has been extemporised from the mountings available.

© Robert Dumas (infographie Bertrand Magueur)

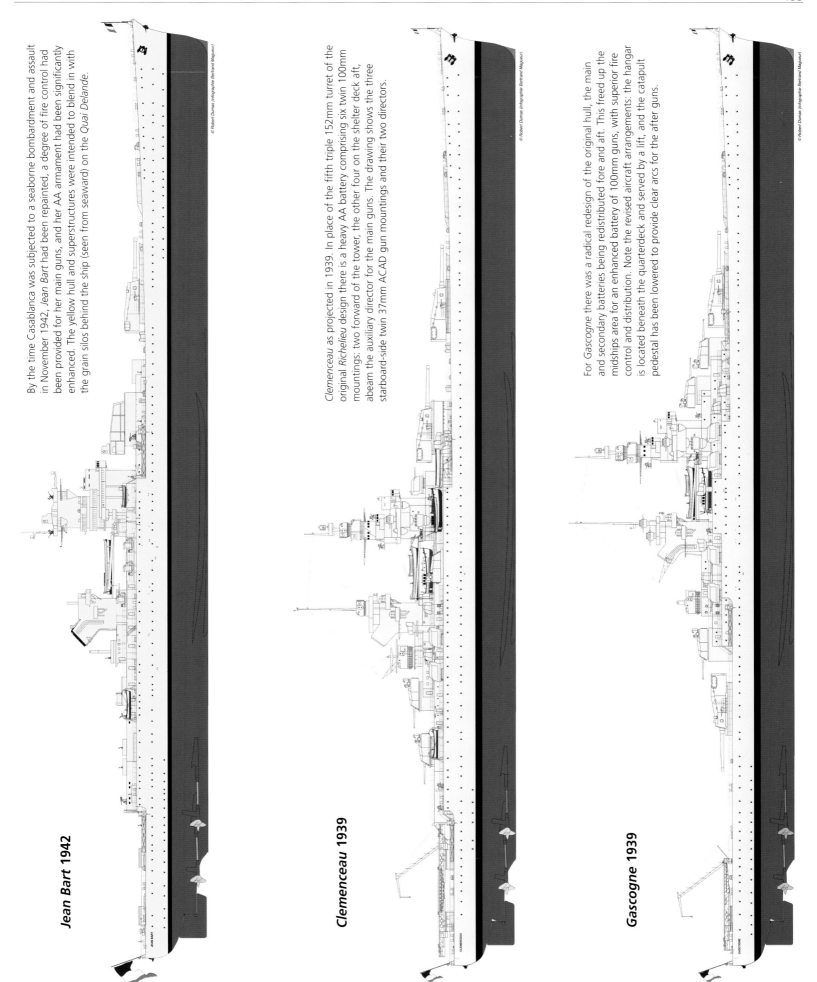

Jean Bart 1942

By the time Casablanca was subjected to a seaborne bombardment and assault in November 1942, *Jean Bart* had been repainted, a degree of fire control had been provided for her main guns, and her AA armament had been significantly enhanced. The yellow hull and superstructures were intended to blend in with the grain silos behind the ship (seen from seaward) on the *Quai Delande*.

© Robert Dumas (infographie Bertrand Magueur)

Clemenceau 1939

Clemenceau as projected in 1939. In place of the fifth triple 152mm turret of the original *Richelieu* design there is a heavy AA battery comprising six twin 100mm mountings: two forward of the tower, the other four on the shelter deck aft, abeam the auxiliary director for the main guns. The drawing shows the three starboard-side twin 37mm ACAD gun mountings and their two directors.

© Robert Dumas (infographie Bertrand Magueur)

Gascogne 1939

For *Gascogne* there was a radical redesign of the original hull, the main and secondary batteries being redistributed fore and aft. This freed up the midships area for an enhanced battery of 100mm guns, with superior fire control and distribution. Note the revised aircraft arrangements: the hangar is located beneath the quarterdeck and served by a lift, and the catapult pedestal has been lowered to provide clear arcs for the after guns.

© Robert Dumas (infographie Bertrand Magueur)

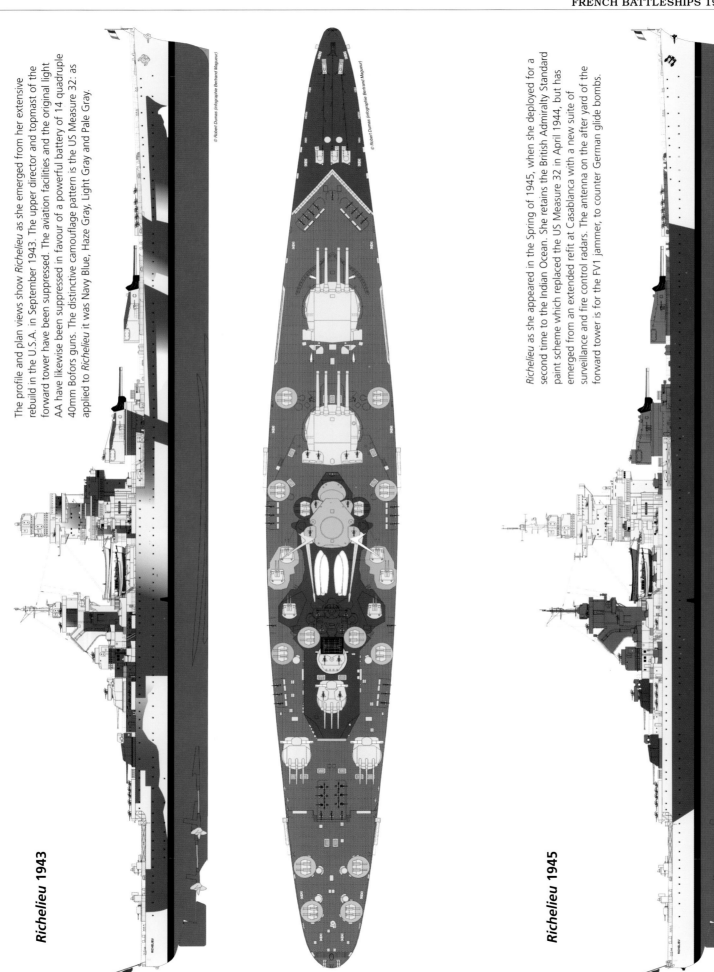

The profile and plan views show *Richelieu* as she emerged from her extensive rebuild in the U.S.A. in September 1943. The upper director and topmast of the forward tower have been suppressed. The aviation facilities and the original light AA have likewise been suppressed in favour of a powerful battery of 14 quadruple 40mm Bofors guns. The distinctive camouflage pattern is the US Measure 32: as applied to *Richelieu* it was Navy Blue, Haze Gray, Light Gray and Pale Gray.

Richelieu 1943

Richelieu as she appeared in the Spring of 1945, when she deployed for a second time to the Indian Ocean. She retains the British Admiralty Standard paint scheme which replaced the US Measure 32 in April 1944, but has emerged from an extended refit at Casablanca with a new suite of surveillance and fire control radars. The antenna on the after yard of the forward tower is for the FV1 jammer, to counter German glide bombs.

Richelieu 1945

© Robert Dumas (infographie Bertrand Magueur)

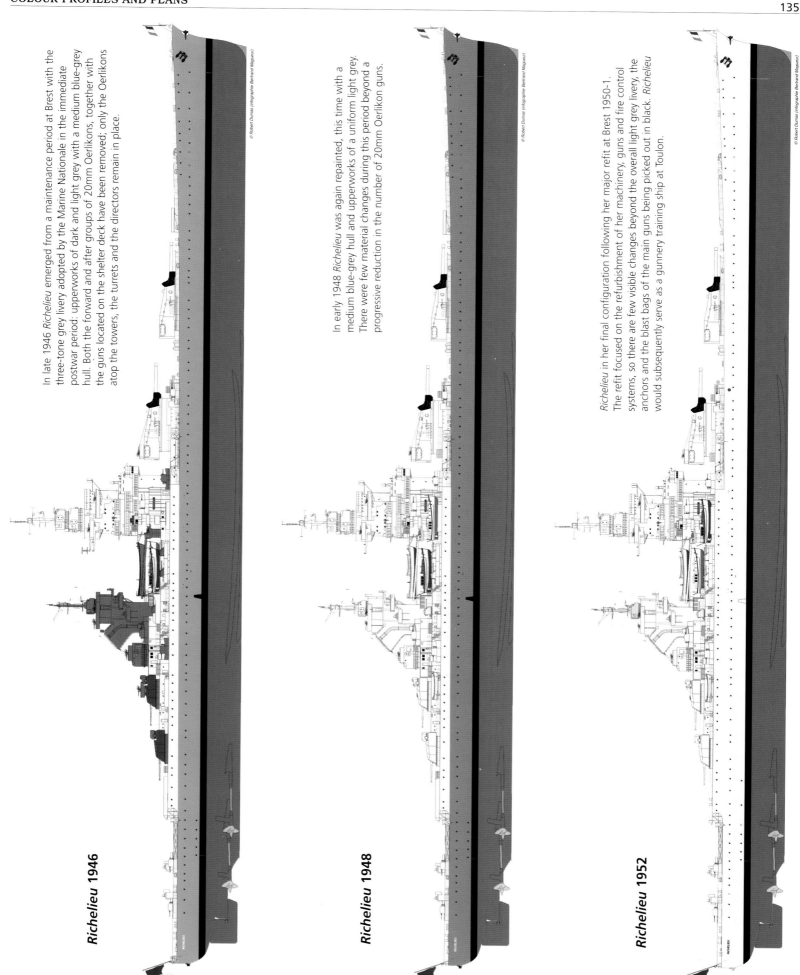

Richelieu 1946

In late 1946 *Richelieu* emerged from a maintenance period at Brest with the three-tone grey livery adopted by the Marine Nationale in the immediate postwar period: upperworks of dark and light grey with a medium blue-grey hull. Both the forward and after groups of 20mm Oerlikons, together with the guns located on the shelter deck have been removed; only the Oerlikons atop the towers, the turrets and the directors remain in place.

© Robert Dumas (infographie Bertrand Magueur)

Richelieu 1948

In early 1948 *Richelieu* was again repainted, this time with a medium blue-grey hull and upperworks of a uniform light grey. There were few material changes during this period beyond a progressive reduction in the number of 20mm Oerlikon guns.

© Robert Dumas (infographie Bertrand Magueur)

Richelieu 1952

Richelieu in her final configuration following her major refit at Brest 1950-1. The refit focused on the refurbishment of her machinery, guns and fire control systems, so there are few visible changes beyond the overall light grey livery, the anchors and the blast bags of the main guns being picked out in black. *Richelieu* would subsequently serve as a gunnery training ship at Toulon.

© Robert Dumas (infographie Bertrand Magueur)

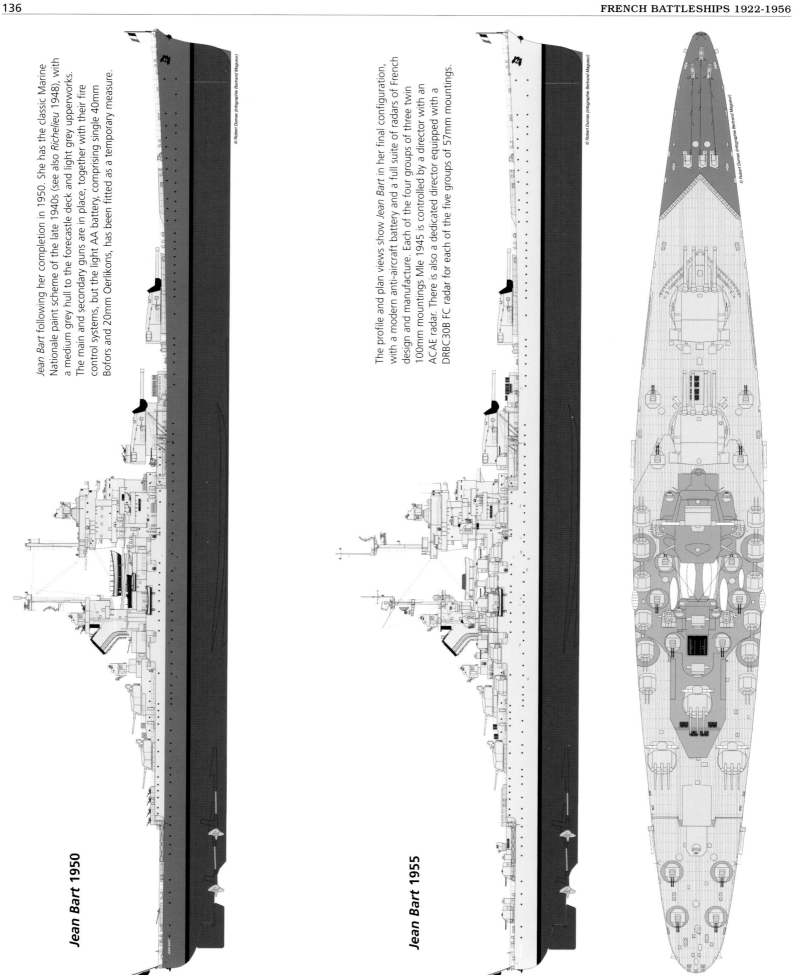

Jean Bart 1950

Jean Bart following her completion in 1950. She has the classic Marine Nationale paint scheme of the late 1940s (see also *Richelieu* 1948), with a medium grey hull to the forecastle deck and light grey upperworks. The main and secondary guns are in place, together with their fire control systems, but the light AA battery, comprising single 40mm Bofors and 20mm Oerlikons, has been fitted as a temporary measure.

© Robert Dumas (infographie Bertrand Magueur)

Jean Bart 1955

The profile and plan views show *Jean Bart* in her final configuration, with a modern anti-aircraft battery and a full suite of radars of French design and manufacture. Each of the four groups of three twin 100mm mountings Mle 1945 is controlled by a director with an ACAE radar. There is also a dedicated director equipped with a DRBC30B FC radar for each of the five groups of 57mm mountings.

© Robert Dumas (infographie Bertrand Magueur)

© Robert Dumas (infographie Bertrand Magueur)

constant battle against rising water levels in compartments O, P and Q over the next two months. By the time Captain Marzin wrote his official report on 28 August, more than seven weeks after the torpedo struck, there remained 1300 tonnes of water in the stern, and seventeen compartments (eight in section O, seven in P and two in Q) were still flooded.

Other factors contributed to these difficulties. Marzin cited the inadequate provision of onboard pumps which, in the absence of pumping facilities located in the port, he considered too few in number and with insufficient capacity. In particular section P, where the torpedo struck, had no pump whatsoever, nor did section R. Moreover some of the fixed pumps were made unserviceable by the shock of the explosion, and had to be repaired before they could begin pumping. The only mobile pumps were two small units capable of pumping 70 tonnes per hour. Marzin proposed: that in future provision should be two 300-tonne, four 70-tonne, four 30-tonne and four 10-tonne mobile pumps, all of which should be submersible; that fixed pumps in the compartments outside the machinery spaces should be 100-tonne (vs 50-tonne) models; and that no section of the ship should be without pumps. In the event the crew had to resort to desperate and time-consuming measures to increase pumping capacity in the damaged compartments. The fixed pump in section D was dismantled and moved aft, and from 11 July mobile 300-tonne and 70-tonne pumps were obtained from the port authorities to drain section P. Because they were in constant use there were to be frequent and regular breakdowns of the pumps themselves over the coming months.

Pumping out was hindered by weaknesses in the ship's design and construction highlighted by Captain Marzin in his report. He recommended that in future careful attention should be paid to securing the water-tightness of bulkheads around the passage of cables, that the welding of floors, angle bars and brackets be closely supervised and monitored, and that the manufacturers of the replenishment trunks of the turrets should ensure that these were watertight before delivery. He also recommended that in future the controls for the drain panels should be located above the waterline, as when the crew attempted to drain the tunnel for the port inner shaft they were unable to access these controls until the water had been pumped out. Marzin was insistent that all these defects were due to poor design, construction and quality control practices, and that they were not in any way the result of the hurried completion of *Richelieu*; the clear implication was that these defects were also present in other contemporary French warships, including *Dunkerque* and *Strasbourg*.

DAMAGE TO OTHER SYSTEMS

Following the torpedo hit, there was a total loss of power of up to two minutes that disabled all of the guns and their control systems. It was subsequently found that the force of the explosion had unseated the directors atop the forward tower. The two aft retaining clips for the main director (*Télépointeur A*) had been broken, the ball race lifted and six ball bearings, freed from the ball race, had caused the director to jam at its current angle of bearing (30 degrees to starboard). Two 50-tonne jacks were subsequently used to raise the director and put the various elements back into place. The director was

back in service on 11 July, but four new retaining clips were still being manufactured by DCN Dakar.

The secondary director above the main director (*Télépointeur 2*) had been trained on the ship's axis when the torpedo struck. The retaining clips had held but three of the bolts securing the ball race to the roof of the main director had been sheared, and the circular ball race had been distorted ('ovalised') by the whiplash of the mast around which it was seated. The director was repaired with difficulty but was again made operational.

The upper director (*Télépointeur 1*) had never been operational and was incapable of training. The after directors, *Télépointeur B* abaft the funnel and *Télépointeur 3* atop the after tower, were undamaged, as were most of the fittings in the directors. The after part of the 14-metre rangefinder in the main director had been slightly dislodged from its guide rails, and the transmission lines of the two after and the upper forward director damaged, but these defects were quickly repaired. On the navigation bridge the binoculars of the port and starboard chiefs of the watch were put out of alignment in elevation and bearing and had to be dismantled or replaced.

There was some damage to the guns themselves. The main 380mm turrets were unaffected, but in the 152mm turrets, which were much closer to the explosion, the counterweights for the elevating floors for the gun crews were lifted and landed on the cabling, breaking the securing clips. The 100mm guns amidships suffered no mechanical failures, but the lighting circuits and the transmission for the Granat system were damaged and had to be repaired.

The director arrangements came in for strong criticism in Captain Marzin's report. He recommended that in future directors should not be superimposed one directly above the other, and that they should not be seated around the mast. He was also of the opinion that the directors were mounted too high in the ship, and that efforts should be made to reduce weight.[9] If the current arrangements were retained, the retaining clips would need to be strengthened to ensure that the directors did not lift from their seating.

When the torpedo struck, all six boilers were on-line, and the force of the explosion triggered the emergency shutdown of the lube oil and cooling pumps for boiler 12 in the forward boiler room and the blowers for boiler 20 in the after room; both boilers had to be shut down temporarily but were successfully fired up shortly afterwards. The point of impact was close to the starboard inner shaft, and the latter was distorted to such an extent that it refused to turn. Damage to the outer shaft was less severe; nevertheless, there was found to be a threefold increase in resistance when the shaft was turned, so it could be used only at low revolutions. The port shafts operated normally, despite some flooding of the shaft tunnels. However, the turbines in the forward engine room were badly shaken, and were found to have shifted slightly both vertically and horizontally.

---

[9] The contrast between the effects of the explosion on the directors of the forward tower, which were mounted high, superimposed and seated around the topmast, and the after directors, which were far closer to the seat of the explosion yet suffered minimal damage, was particularly marked.

Aerial view of *Richelieu* at Dakar in September 1940, prior to the British assault. One of the cruisers of Force Y is in the background.

However, the new fire-resistant cabling known as Pyrotenax,[10] which was employed for some systems, had fared less well and was badly damaged by seawater. Marzin was of the opinion that unless this problem could be resolved the Pyrotenax cable did not justify the additional cost.

A DIFFICULT PERIOD

Although *Richelieu* was considered to be capable of 12 knots on her two and a half shafts, transfer to another port in her current condition was thought undesirable and, given the current aggressive stance of the Royal Navy, fraught with danger. Captain Marzin's two priorities now were: to control the flooding and carry out such repairs to the hull as possible given the limited resources available from DCN Dakar; and to ensure that the main and secondary guns were able to fire so that the ship could be used as a floating battery to defend the port against attack.

Such an attack was now seen as increasingly likely by the French government at Vichy. Admiral de Laborde was despatched to Dakar, arriving by aircraft on 14 July, to conduct a thorough inspection of the port and its defences and to restore order. Within three days, the naval commander and the Governor General, both of whom were suspected of pro-British sympathies, were removed from their posts: CA Plançon was replaced temporarily by CA Platon, and subsequently (17 August) by CA Landriau. Governor General Cayla was moved to Madagascar and replaced by Pierre Boisson.

Work to repair *Richelieu* and to restore her to fighting condition was accelerated. To patch the breach in the hull, a mattress 11.5 metres square was fabricated by the sail makers of the local dockyard using materials scavenged from other ships in the port. Reinforced by ten vertical and three horizontal steel strands, it was due to be completed by early September and put in place on 10 September. If successful, this measure would enable at least the after 152mm and 37mm magazines to be drained and a further 500 cubic metres of water pumped out of the ship. From 15 August, the dockyard also began construction of a steel cofferdam, the side walls of which followed the lines of *Richelieu*'s hull. Once this was in place at the end of October the remaining water could be pumped out, enabling permanent repairs to the outer hull to take place from January 1941.

Captain Marzin had the ship cleaned and repainted, and work continued apace to ensure that the main and secondary guns could fire. In this latter task the ship's crew were assisted by twenty dockyard workers from Brest who had sailed with the ship to North Africa. The

When the torpedo struck it caused the circuit-breakers on the main and secondary switchboards to trip, resulting in a complete power failure throughout the ship which lasted between thirty seconds and two minutes according to the sector of the ship. The circuit-breakers were closed manually by the duty personnel. During the power outage, the emergency lighting system cut in and functioned as anticipated.

The diesel generators, which were located in section H in the forward part of the ship, suffered no ill-effects from the explosion of the torpedo warhead. However, turbo-dynamos Nos 3 and 4, which were in section O, immediately forward of the section where the torpedo struck, were severely shaken. There was damage to the lube oil pipework for turbo-dynamo No. 4, which took one hour and forty-five minutes to repair before the unit was again on-line. Turbo-dynamo No. 3 also had to be shut down temporarily. Throughout the ship many pumps and motors were put out of action, some permanently. The main rudder servo-motors were completely unserviceable, the brush housings being cracked in several places, and similar damage was sustained to one of the converter groups for the searchlight projectors and another for the Granat transmission system. All of these pumps and motors were rigidly mounted, although it is only fair to note that this would generally have been the case in other contemporary foreign battleships, and that the forces to which they were subjected were exaggerated by the shallow waters in which the ship was moored, which caused the shock wave of the explosion to rebound from the sea floor 4-5 metres beneath the ship.

In his report, Captain Marzin was generally critical of the ship's electrical systems, which he described as fragile and prone to failure even in the course of normal service. The standard type of steel-sheathed electrical cable, termed *câble armé*, coped reasonably well when the after part of the ship was flooded; the cable retained its insulation except where the terminals had been soaked in oil in sections P and Q.

---

[10] The first patent for MI (mineral insulated) cable was issued to the Swiss inventor Arnold François Borel in 1896. Much development ensued by the French company Société Alsacienne de Constructions Mécaniques. In 1937, a British company, Pyrotenax, having purchased patent rights to the product from the French company, began production. During the Second World War, much of the company's product was used in military equipment. The insulator in Pyrotenax cable was magnesium oxide (MgO) with copper sheathing. Magnesium oxide is hygroscopic in nature and care needs to be taken to protect it from moisture, otherwise it forms magnesium hydroxide and loses its insulating properties.

ship's official war complement was fifty-nine officers and 1542 men; *Richelieu* had arrived at Dakar with forty-one officers and 1348 men. One hundred and thirty-two reservists were demobilised. A further 106 men were assigned to replace the reservists aboard the AMCs during July, and the sixty-four men who crewed turret I were put ashore to man the 240mm coast defence battery at Cap Manuel. There were now only 1039 men left aboard the ship.

Only turrets II (380mm) and VII (centreline 152mm) were manned, although work continued on the two 152mm wing turrets. As stated previously, there were 269 380mm shells aboard but only forty-nine complete charges, so 600 new quarter-charges (i.e., 150 complete charges) were manufactured using the stock of SD19 charges intended for the 330mm guns of *Strasbourg*; the new silk bags were run up by the nuns at the local convent. There were 600 152mm shells plus a further 195 ashore, and 1010 charges. The six twin 100mm mountings were all fully operational and were manned at all times, as were the 37mm and 13.2mm close-range AA. Stocks of ammunition for the anti-aircraft weapons were more than adequate: 2035 fixed rounds for the 100mm, 5352 for the 37mm.

PREPARATIONS FOR 'MENACE'

Meanwhile, the British were preparing to take advantage of the uncertain political situation at Dakar. From late July, Churchill envisaged an intervention led by the exiled General de Gaulle and the 'Free French' forces loyal to him. De Gaulle was initially sceptical, feeling that the British actions first at Mers el-Kebir and then against *Richelieu* at Dakar had turned the local colonial populations against them. However, at a meeting with Churchill on 6 August, de Gaulle was persuaded to see this as an opportunity to impose his own authority and to re-establish a new Free France in a corner of Africa.

A large force of warships and transports was assembled for this new adventure, appropriately christened Operation 'Menace'. On 26 August, a slow convoy of five ships carrying vehicles, cased aircraft and supplies, and escorted by the FNFL sloop *Savorgnan de Brazza* and a converted trawler, *Président Houduce*, left Liverpool. Five days later, six troopships and a cargo ship carrying food for the population of Dakar,[11] escorted by the cruiser *Fiji* and seven destroyers, departed Liverpool and Scapa Flow. The two halves of the convoy met up off Ireland, where they were joined by the cruiser *Devonshire*, with the force commanders aboard, and by two small FNFL minesweeping sloops. The military operation was to be spearheaded by 2400 Free French troops in the Dutch liners *Westernland* and *Pennland*, the former being the HQ ship of de Gaulle and Major-General Spears, Churchill's personal representative to the Free French general. Major-General Irwin, commanding the British troop contingent (4270 men, including four battalions of Royal Marines), was with the naval commander, Admiral John Cunningham, initially aboard *Devonshire* and later aboard the battleship *Barham*.

---

[11] British Intelligence thought that there was a food shortage at Dakar; this was not the case. Intelligence was likewise in error in believing that Dakar was being infiltrated by German and Italian officers, who were said to be arriving under various official pretexts or even as 'tourists'!

OPERATION 'MENACE': DAKAR

Force M (V-Ad J. Cunningham)

RN Ships

Battleships:	Aircraft-carrier:	Cruisers:
Barham (fl)	*Ark Royal*	*Devonshire*
Resolution	(30 Swordfish, 21 Skua)	*Australia*
		Cumberland
		Dragon

8th Destr. Flot.	12th Destr. Flot.	Sloops:
Faulknor (L)	*Inglefield* (L)	*Bridgwater*
Foresight	*Echo*	*Milford*
Forester	*Escapade*	
Fortune		
Fury		
Greyhound		

FNFL Ships

Colonial Sloop:	M/S Sloops:	Armed trawler:
Savorgnan de Brazza	*Commandant Duboc*	*Président Houduce*
	Commandant Dominé	

Troopships:	Mechanical Transport Ships:	Supply Ships:
Westernland ⎫ (2400 FF)	*Anadyr*	*Belgravian* (food)
Pennland ⎭	*Casamonce*	*Ocean Coast* (oil)
Ettrick ⎫	*Fort Lamy*	
Karanja ⎬ (4270 Brit)	*Nevada*	
Kenya ⎪		
Sobieski ⎭		

Vichy French Forces Dakar (CA Landriau)

Battleship:	1ère DCX	6e DSM
Richelieu (CV Marzin)	*El Djezaïr*	*Ajax*
	El Kantara	*Bévéziers*
Destroyer:	*El Mansour*	*Persée*
Le Hardi	*Victor Schoelcher*	
	Ville D'Oran	Sloops:
		D'Entrecasteaux

Force 'Y' (CA Lacroix)

4e DC	10e DCT	*D'Iberville*
Georges Leygues (fl)	*Le Fantasque*	*Calais*
Montcalm	*L'Audacieux*	*Commandant Rivière*
	Le Malin	*Gazelle*
		La Surprise

The divided command structure was essential to the plan. De Gaulle was to attempt to rally Dakar to the cause using only Free French units and personnel, the British 'support' forces remaining out of sight over the horizon. In the event of formal resistance by the Vichy authorities and sporadic resistance from their colonial troops, de Gaulle would make opposed landings supported by FNFL ships, calling on the British support forces only if he encountered difficulty. If there was organised and determined resistance the British squadron would close; the fortifications would be reduced, and British troops would be landed to put an end to enemy resistance ashore and occupy Dakar.[12] When the worst-case scenario materialised early on

---

[12] The code words for these three situations were: 'Happy', 'Sticky' and 'Nasty'.

240mm Coast Defence Battery, Dakar

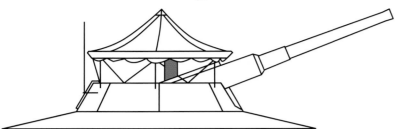

240/50 Mle 1902-6 in Schneider Turret

240/50 Mle 1902-06 in the modified Schneider twin turret. The guns, which fired the 220kg 240mm OPf Mle 1909 shell, had a range of 19,100 metres at their maximum elevation of 23°55 and a firing cycle of one round per minute. The plates of the eight-sided turret were of 200mm cemented armour but the mounting was unprotected from above, the framed canvas canopy providing protection for the gun crew only from the hot sun. Replenishment was from magazines buried deep within the fortifications; the shell and charges were brought up to the guns by hoists.

The 240mm guns of the Gorée Battery, manned by naval personnel brought from Toulon by Force Y. These guns kept up an effective fire against the British ships throughout the three days, scoring several damaging hits in the process.

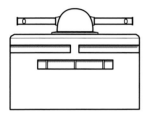

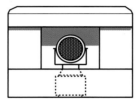

Poste de Direction de Tir (PDT)

When the turrets were rebuilt in 1934, a modern PDT (*Poste de Direction de Tir* = battery command post) was provided in a concrete emplacement. It was equipped with an SOM armoured rangefinder with a 5-metre base and a *Colonies*-model fire control table.

150cm GP Bréguet Searchlight Projector & Sound Mirror

For night firing there was a 150cm GP Bréguet searchlight projector in a concrete emplacement. The installation was completed by an acoustic target location system called a *mur d'écoute* (= sound mirror, lit. 'listening wall') to cue the searchlight; the wall was vertical and had a concave parabolic face.

(Drawings by John Jordan © 2008)

---

the first day, this divided command structure was to become a major liability, with communications difficulties between *Barham* and *Westernland* compounded by the prevailing poor visibility.

The naval support force allocated to 'Force M' was substantial, given the known presence of *Richelieu* plus the powerful 240mm shore batteries located at Cap Manuel, Bel-Air and Gorée Island, which dominated the approaches to the harbour. Cunningham would have the battleship *Barham*, the cruisers *Devonshire* (flag) and *Fiji* – torpedoed en route and subsequently replaced by HMAS *Australia* – and four destroyers from the Home Fleet. They would be joined at Gibraltar by the battleship *Resolution*, the carrier *Ark Royal* (thirty Swordfish, twenty-one Skua) and six destroyers. At Freetown, which Force M would use as the springboard for the operation, he would be joined by the cruiser *Cumberland* and two sloops of the South Atlantic Command.[13]

FORCE Y

Meanwhile, although as yet unaware of a specific threat to Dakar, the Vichy government was becoming very concerned about the stability of the French

colonies in West and Equatorial Africa. Already on 18 June, the Governor General of Tchad (AEF[14]), Félix Éboué, had declared his personal support for de Gaulle, and on 26 August he issued an official proclamation rallying Tchad to the Free French cause and encouraging the entire French Empire to rise up against the government at Vichy; all the equatorial African colonies except Gabon would follow suit in the next few days. Thus, on 27 August, when the forces for Operation 'Menace' were assembling in British ports, Darlan made a formal request to the Germans to reinforce the French naval presence in the AEF region. Agreement was obtained on 3 September, and the *Amirauté* readied a powerful force of modern ships, to be designated 'Force Y', which would sail from Toulon on 9 September. The ships selected were all from the former *Force de Raid*: the cruisers *Georges Leygues*, *Montcalm* and *Gloire* (4th DC) and the *contre-torpilleurs* *Le Fantasque*, *L'Audacieux* and *Le Malin* (10th DCT),[15] under the command of Rear-Admiral Bourragué in the *Georges Leygues*.

---

[13] The cruisers *Cornwall* and *Delhi* would be diverted to escort the cruiser *Primauguet* and the oiler *Tarn* to Casablanca (see below). The Home Fleet destroyer *Eclipse* would suffer machinery problems en route and would be replaced by the cruiser *Dragon*.

[14] Known as the AEF (*Afrique Équatoriale Française*), this federation comprised four territories: the Republic of the Congo, Tchad, Oubangui-Chari and Gabon.

[15] *Le Malin* was strictly a member of the 8th DCT (she carried the pennant number X82 throughout the operation), but was assigned to the 10th DCT as a replacement for *Le Terrible*, currently undergoing a major refit.

Following the agreed procedures Bourragué notified the British admiral commanding at Gibraltar, Dudley North, of his intention to pass the straits. North, whom the Admiralty had not seen fit to inform of the imminent Operation 'Menace' despite the fact that the troop convoys were now at almost the same latitude as Gibraltar, saw no objection to the passage of the French ships, which were left to proceed without obstruction. Unfortunately North's message to the Admiralty informing them of events was delayed. Churchill was furious and North's 'failings', together with his pro-French sympathies, were to cost him his job.

The battlecruiser *Renown* was promptly despatched from Gibraltar in pursuit of the French squadron, and Admiral Pound (First Sea Lord) ordered Cunningham to turn some of his ships about. However, Bourragué, fearing a British aggression, decided to leave his short-legged *contre-torpilleurs* at Casablanca and to proceed at speed with the cruisers to Dakar, where he arrived at midday on 14 September. The cruisers were loaded with welcome supplies, together with gunners despatched from Toulon to help man the coastal batteries.

The arrival of Force Y at Dakar caused the British to surmise that Operation 'Menace' was compromised and that the Vichy French had received prior warning of an assault;[16] they had no inkling that the true destination of the cruisers was Gabon, many miles to the south. However, de Gaulle was now set on his course and on 18 September it was decided to continue with the Dakar operation as originally planned.

On that same day, Force Y left Dakar for Gabon with 250 infantry embarked,[17] preceded by the cruiser *Primauguet* and the tanker *Tarn*. The latter two ships were intercepted by the British cruisers *Cornwall* and *Delhi*, and shortly afterwards the cruisers *Cumberland* and *Australia* compelled Bourragué to reverse course. He was advised not to return to Dakar, but again entered that port at 0730 on 20 June with *Georges Leygues* and *Montcalm*. *Gloire*, which had suffered a catastrophic machinery breakdown off Conakry, had been left behind, and was subsequently escorted by *Australia* to Casablanca, where she was docked for repairs.

Although the three *contre-torpilleurs* of the 10th DCT had duly arrived in Dakar on 19-20 September, Darlan had been less than impressed with Bourragué's performance thus far, and on 21 September Vice-Admiral Lacroix was flown into Dakar to replace him as commander of Force Y, which now comprised two cruisers plus the three modern *contre-torpilleurs* of the 10th DCT.

DAKAR 23 SEPTEMBER 1940

The following day, 22 September, French early morning reconnaissance flights from Dakar were concentrated to the north in order to provide air cover for the liner *Banfora*, which was bringing additional 380mm shells for *Richelieu*. At the same time the Anglo-FNFL Force M was approaching from the south. Thus despite the French forces in West Africa being alerted to a possible British aggression, the arrival of Force M off Dakar at dawn on 23 September was a complete surprise; the ships of Force Y were caught alongside in the port with awnings spread.

Just before 0600, two French Luciole biplanes flown from *Ark Royal* landed at Ouakam, and four Free French airmen attempted to rally the air base to the Gaullist cause. British Swordfish aircraft dropped leaflets on Dakar. At the same time, de Gaulle broadcast an appeal to the local population, and the FNFL sloop *Savorgnan de Brazza* lowered two motor boats three miles from the 'gate' in the western net barrier of the harbour. The first boat carried a thirteen-man delegation which, after disembarking in the inner harbour, was to meet up with the airmen from Ouakam and proceed to the Governor General's Residence; the second boat had a twelve-man 'security detachment'. Both flew a French tricolore with a Croix de Lorraine at the stern and a white flag of truce at the bow. They passed under the stern of *Richelieu* and the first boat came alongside at Mole No. 2 at 0655.

The response was not the one de Gaulle had hoped for. The airmen at Ouakam were taken prisoner and Landriau ordered the arrest of d'Argenlieu, the head of the harbour delegation. The motor boats departed in haste, seen on their way by machine gun fire from the post at the head of the jetty which wounded d'Argenlieu. At 0700, Admiral Landriau sounded the alert, the warships in the harbour raised steam and prepared to cast off moorings, and the approach of *Savorgnan de Brazza* was greeted by warning shots from the 100mm guns of *Richelieu*. De Gaulle responded by threatening to call on support from the British fleet offshore if his Free French forces were not permitted to land. The FNFL sloops *Commandant Dominé* and *Commandant Duboc*, with 120 French *fusiliers marins* on board, attempted to enter the port at 0810 but were forced to leave under a smoke screen when again *Richelieu* fired warning shots from her 100mm guns.

This initial setback resulted in a hurried conference between de Gaulle and Spears aboard the *Westernland*. At 0958, de Gaulle asked Admiral Cunningham to ensure that no French ships left the port. The British fleet approached to within visual range of the shore, to be greeted by fire from the powerful 240mm batteries at Cap Manuel and Gorée. When Cunningham protested, he was informed by General Barrau that his ships would be fired upon if they encroached within a twenty-mile radius of Dakar.

It was now clear to Cunningham that he needed to force the issue if Operation 'Menace' was to meet with success and the battleships and cruisers, accompanied by destroyers, duly approached Dakar from the southwest. The submarine *Persée*, one of two 1500-tonnes boats patrolling in the approaches to the harbour, attempted to intercept the British force but was hindered by the shallow waters and was sunk by the cruiser *Dragon* and the destroyers *Inglefield* and *Foresight*, which were heavily engaged at short range by the shore batteries.

At 1105, the British battleships opened fire on *Richelieu* and the port, causing panic among the local popu-

---

[16] Security for this operation had been lax, particularly if compared with the later preparations for D-Day: Free French forces had talked openly of Dakar prior to their departure from Liverpool, and had purchased colonial uniforms; celebratory banquets had been organised at prestigious hotels in London and Liverpool; and propaganda leaflets addressed to the population of Dakar had spilled from a broken crate at one of the London stations to be read and trampled on by the general public.

[17] They were to retake Pointe Noire from the Gaullists.

lation when the first shells overshot their mark. The bombardment lasted twenty minutes, and was hindered by the poor visibility prevailing. There was splinter damage to the cruiser *Montcalm*, and *Le Malin* suffered a near miss as she sortied from the port. *Richelieu* was surrounded by shell splashes but was not hit. A furious response from the shore batteries damaged the destroyers *Foresight* and *Inglefield* and the cruisers *Dragon* and *Cumberland*, the latter sustaining serious damage from a 240mm shell which destroyed her main switchboard and reduced her speed to 10 knots; she limped away to Gambia for repairs.

The available French ships were by this time ready for action. At 1212, *Montcalm*, her departure delayed by splinter damage, sortied to join the flagship *Georges Leygues* in the Baie de Hann, while *L'Audacieux* and *Le Malin* were stationed northeast of Gorée Island to monitor the movements of the British fleet.[18] *Richelieu* had been moored bows north against the jetty and had been unable to take part in the earlier engagement. Marzin now had the tugs move her stern at an angle of 30 degrees to the jetty to enable the battleship to fire her main guns at an approaching force.

During the afternoon, a French reconnaissance aircraft spotted a small convoy of ships six miles to the south of Gorée apparently making for Rufisque, some twenty kilometres to the east of Dakar. Lacroix despatched *L'Audacieux* to patrol there. However, despite the poor visibility she was spotted by a Walrus aircraft and was set upon just outside the eastern gate of the outer harbour by the cruiser *Australia* and two destroyers. *Australia*'s second salvo struck the bridge and the forward bank of torpedo tubes and there was a massive explosion. *Australia* continued to fire rapid three-gun salvos into the ship at a range of little more than 3000 metres, and *L'Audacieux* was beached by her captain west of Rufisque with the loss of eighty-one dead and seventy wounded.

Having abandoned the idea of a direct assault on Dakar, the Anglo-FNFL force had decided on an alternative landing site at Rufisque and at 1725 the FNFL sloops, with the *fusiliers marins* assembled on deck, approached the wharf, to be greeted by fire from machine guns backed by two elderly 95mm 'mobilisation' coast defence guns. The landings were abandoned.

Governor General Boisson now set about rallying the population of Dakar and reorganising the town's defences; Force M withdrew to regroup. De Gaulle was despondent and proposed to Cunningham the abandonment of the operation. However, Churchill would have none of it, and a telegram from London received aboard *Barham* shortly afterwards advised Cunningham: 'Having begun we must go on to the end. Stop at nothing.' A new ultimatum was therefore broadcast to Boisson with an expiry time of 0600 the following day.

Boisson prepared to defend Dakar to the last shell, and conferred with Landriau regarding the best deployment of the naval forces available. The cruisers and *contre-torpilleurs* of Force Y were to be assembled in the Baie de Hann and were to manoeuvre within the *Rade-Abri* under the cover of smoke screens and the coastal batteries. At 0445, the destroyer *Le Hardi*, with only two of her four Sural boilers available, sortied

from the port to join Force Y, to be followed at 0500 by *Le Fantasque*, with only one set of turbines operational; at 0530, the submarine *Bévéziers*, with only a single motor in service, prepared to dive south of Gorée Island. Every available warship was now fully mobilised for the defence of Dakar.

THE SECOND DAY

Visibility on the second day was marginally better: 6000 metres at the outset, improving to 13,000-18,000 metres at times, but with a thick haze clinging to the surface. At about 0645 the first Swordfish reconnaissance aircraft appeared above Dakar, to be greeted by heavy AA fire from the ships manoeuvring in the harbour. Three successive air strikes, each of six aircraft, were launched from *Ark Royal* between 0625 and 0800. The first, comprising Skuas armed with 500lb SAP bombs, was directed at the ships in the harbour. *Richelieu* was near-missed by two bombs, but there were no direct hits. The second, mounted by Swordfish against the 240mm battery at Cap Manuel, was equally unsuccessful. Finally, at 0910, there was a glide-bombing attack on *Richelieu* by six Swordfish armed with four 250lb SAP bombs, which it was hoped would at least disable her fire control systems and put some of her increasingly effective AA guns out of action. There were several near-misses, but by now the AA crews were fully roused and the Curtiss fighter patrols from Ouakam were in the air. Three Swordfish and three Skuas were shot down or had to make forced landings as a result of these attacks, which achieved nothing. The AA gunners of *Richelieu* claimed three aircraft shot down and one damaged.

Fifteen minutes after the first air attack, at 0730 a Loire 130 reconnaissance aircraft reported that the British battle squadron was approaching the harbour, preceded by a flotilla of destroyers. Three 240mm rounds from the battery at Gorée were fired at the destroyers at 6000 metres, the limit of visibility. As the British battle squadron was approaching Dakar on a heading of NNE the captain of the submarine *Ajax*, which had been badly shaken by depth charging the previous day, prepared to fire his four forward tubes at two battleships and a cruiser, now only 1000 metres distant. His periscope was spotted, and *Ajax* was pounced on by the destroyers *Fortune* and *Fury*. With depth charges bursting around him Captain Guimont attempted to take his boat deeper, but in these relatively shallow waters it struck the bottom at 52 metres, causing serious damage to the control surfaces and the batteries, which with the influx of seawater began to spread poisonous fumes throughout the submarine. The submarine was forced to the surface, and with the British destroyers close by Guimont was compelled to order 'Abandon ship', the crew being rescued by the destroyer *Fortune*. *Ajax* sank at 1015, 23,000 metres SSE of Cap Manuel.

At 0930, the British squadron, comprising the battleships *Barham* and *Resolution* accompanied by the cruisers *Devonshire* and *Australia*, was sighted from Cap Manuel, and five minutes later opened a steady and deliberate fire on Dakar. The 15in guns of the battleships targeted *Richelieu*, the 8in guns of the cruisers Force Y, manoeuvring in the Baie de Hann, and the secondary 6in guns of the battleships the coastal batteries on Gorée.

Richelieu attempted to reply with her main guns at

---

[18] The lead ship of the 10th DCT, *Le Fantasque*, was immobilised at Dakar with machinery problems.

The port of Dakar during the British bombardment on 24 September. *Richelieu* can be seen on the far right of the picture, with huge 15in shell splashes rising around her.

0940, but gun No. 7 was shattered when a shell exploded in the barrel. Gun No. 8 fired two more rounds before a jet of flame shot out from the breech and it was found that serious damage had been caused to the barrel, which had been stripped of its rifling over a length of 8 metres. Guns Nos 5 and 6 continued to fire following a close inspection, but without effect. The British were experiencing their own problems, and a director failure aboard *Resolution* caused her to shift fire to the coast defence battery at Cap Manuel.

At 0957, *Richelieu* secured a hit on *Barham* with her 152mm secondary guns, producing a 7-metre gash in the bulge abeam the bridge. Despite the multitude of 15in shells raining down on the port *Richelieu* suffered only minor damage from a shell splinter which pierced the unarmoured hull just above the waterline in section R.

Meanwhile the cruisers and *contre-torpilleurs* of Force Y were manoeuvring furiously at 25 knots in what was christened the 'ratodrome', a stretch of water 4 kilometres by 2 kilometers in the Baie de Hann (see map). *Georges Leygues* and *Montcalm* kept up a steady fire on the British cruisers, which were accompanied by the destroyers *Inglefield*, *Foresight* and *Forester*. As the British cruisers closed a thick smoke screen was laid by *Le Malin* and *Le Fantasque*. At 1007, the British ships ceased fire and moved off to the south to regroup. General de Gaulle would now broadcast a second appeal to the population of Dakar.

Captain Marzin took advantage of this respite to request from VA Lacroix the allocation of one of his destroyers to lay a smokescreen to the southeast of *Richelieu* when the British returned; he was duly allocated *Le Hardi*, which took up position between the jetty and Gorée Island in readiness.

At 1200, *Le Hardi* was ordered to a position 7000 metres to the south of Cap Manuel to pick up a downed British pilot. She was engaged on this task when *Barham* and *Resolution*, accompanied by two destroyers, emerged from the mist and at 1253 opened fire on her at a range of 11,000 metres. CF Tannenberg quickly raised speed to 25 knots, opened fire on the second destroyer with his main 130mm guns, and beat a hasty retreat, which was covered by a thick smoke screen and a lively fire from the coastal batteries.

The British battleships then shifted fire to the port at a range of 15,500 metres. They fired 160 15in rounds in four-gun salvos before ceasing fire at 1320; hits were obtained and fires started on several of the merchant ships in the port, but *Richelieu* herself remained miraculously unscathed. At 1256, *Richelieu* opened fire with her remaining main guns (Nos. 5 and 6) on one of the British cruisers, which was straddled by towering yellow splashes and promptly retired into the mist; turret VII was unable to fire due to a breakdown in the replenishment system. A further two-gun 380mm salvo was fired at *Barham* at 1311, and another two minutes later. No hits were obtained, but *Barham* was struck by no fewer than four 240mm shells from the coastal batteries. *Resolution* suffered less serious damage, and on the French side *Le Malin* was near-missed by an 8in cruiser shell; she lost steering and had her speed reduced to 14 knots.

During the temporary ceasefire de Gaulle made a further appeal at 1400, but this fell largely on deaf ears; many locals had fled the town, leaving an increasingly determined administration to carry on the fight. A final attack on the French cruisers by nine Swordfish armed with torpedoes and escorted by three Skua fighter-bombers came in at 1534, but was thwarted by desperate manoeuvres and concentrated AA fire that downed two of the attackers.

De Gaulle and Spears now boarded *Barham* for a final conference with Admiral Cunningham. All accepted that an opposed landing was now out of the question, given that the French cruisers and coastal batteries remained fully operational. De Gaulle subsequently announced to his staff aboard *Westernland* that the operation was over. However, Cunningham and Irwin, their resolve stiffened by the constant promptings of Churchill, decided to make one last attempt the following day.

Meanwhile, the French at Dakar were reviewing their situation, which was precarious. Although relatively undamaged, *Richelieu* had lost the use of two of her four main guns and Marzin decided to transfer the gunnery personnel from turret II to turret I, which had all four guns operational but had not been used since early

RICHELIEU: EXTRACT FROM *JOURNAL D'OPÉRATIONS* 23-5 SEPTEMBER 1940

23 September 1940

Time (local)   Events in chronological order

Time	Event
0610	*Richelieu* sounds the alert over the anchorage and opens fire with all her AA guns on several British biplanes dropping leaflets in the name of ex-General de Gaulle.
0640	End of the air alert. A sloop of the *Savorgnan de Brazza* class approaches from the south of Gorée. Visibility poor: 4000/5000 metres.
0644	Two motor boats, apparently British, flying the French flag at the stern and a white flag at the bow, crewed by sailors in French uniforms, enter the inner harbour (*Rade-abri*) without warning shots being fired either by the sloop on duty, or from the head of the jetty. At 0650 they come alongside Mole 2, depart at 0710, and receive a few machine gun bursts from the head of the jetty (Admiral Landriau telephones beforehand with an instruction to allow them to leave).
0722	The sloop on patrol close to the net barrier, enters the anchorage without having noticed the sloop of the *Savorgnan de Brazza* class.
0745	Fire several 100mm warning shots across the bows of the sloop of the *Savorgnan de Brazza* class, which makes its appearance 6000m to the east, and which aroused our suspicions by persistently manoeuvring with the sun behind her to the east of the anchorage.
0750	The colonial sloop disappears to the south.
0810	Two sloops of the *Commandant Rivière* class enter the outer harbour (*Grand'rade*), passing through the net barrier. They hoist recognition flags identifying them as *Commandant Duboc* and *Commandant Dominé*. The head of the South jetty hoists the signal for them to stop.
0815	On the orders of Navy HQ (AOF), which had been informed by telephone, fire three warning salvoes across the bows of the sloops, the crews of which, in French uniforms, are lining the decks; the sloops are flying French manoeuvring pennants.
0820	The sloops turn about and make for the open sea. One of them emits a plume of smoke.
0844	*Calais* [sloop on patrol outside harbour] in sight outside the net barrier in the mist.
0859	*Calais* on course to enter the outer harbour.
0916	Plane no.2 of Squadron 4.E takes off on a patrol mission (not armed with bombs).
0940	The [cruiser] *Montcalm* changes her moorings within the inner harbour and comes alongside the fuelling station on the main jetty.
0950	The [sloop] *Gazelle* leaves the inner harbour.
1000	The [sloop] *La Surprise* leaves the inner harbour.
1005	The [cruiser] *Georges Leygues* leaves the inner harbour and anchors in the outer harbour inside the net barrier.
1020	The [submarine] *Persée* casts off and makes for the open sea.
1040	The [submarine] *Ajax* leaves the inner harbour and makes for the open sea.
1101	The cruisers open fire on a plane (not seen by *Richelieu*).
1111	The [*contre-torpilleur*] *Le Malin* leaves the inner harbour.
1113	The British open fire on the anchorage: several shell splashes of medium-calibre guns straddle the *Richelieu*. Continue to pass lines from the stern of [the tug] *Buffle* in order to move the stern away from the jetty and open up the arcs of the main battery towards the south.
1117	The *Ajax* passes through the net barrier into the outer harbour from the open sea.
1121	Light cruiser in view to the southeast is signalling by projector to a nearby sloop of the *Gazelle* class.
1126	The Gorée battery opens fire, probably on the same cruiser, which is not recognised by *Richelieu*'s 152mm fire control officer in time to engage.
1127	The British cruiser disappears into the mist. Visibility of the order of 4000m.
1135	The British cruiser reappears at 135°.
1140	Open fire (with 152mm turret VII and 100mm) on two British light cruisers. The [sloop] *D'Entrecasteaux* leaves the inner harbour.
1150	Glimpse at 165° shadowy shapes around a submarine (*Persée*) outside the net barrier.
1200	In answer to our query *La Surprise* signals: '*Persée* sinking'.
1210	*Georges Leygues* firing at aircraft. *La Surprise* enters the inner harbour to disembark the crew of the *Persée*, which she has picked up. Curtiss fighter patrol flies overhead. *Calais* enters the inner harbour.
1230	Manoeuvre with tug completed (30° angle from jetty).
1342	Enemy plane spotted at a bearing of 120°, angle of elevation 80°. Open fire.
1344	Cease fire. End of alert.
1352	Two Curtiss fighters taking off.
1415	Torpedo nets again in place around *Richelieu*. Visibility scarcely 2500m.
1440	Hear gunfire to west. Air alert sounded by the watch.
1630	Enemy firing at the [*contre-torpilleur*] *L'Audacieux* as she leaves the outer harbour to the northeast of Gorée. Large-calibre shell splashes surrounding this ship, which has been hit and is in flames. *La Surprise* and [colonial sloop] *Commandant Rivière* sortie from the inner harbour.
1728	Hear gunfire in the direction of Rufisque.
1749	Two battleships, one cruiser, three destroyers at 202° twelve nautical miles from Cap de Naze (signalled by aircraft). Gunfire to the east. *Calais* leaves the inner harbour.
2015	*L'Audacieux* burning at 110° 7700m away. Moon rises and appears from behind the clouds.

24 September 1940

Time	Event
0210	Searchlight projector at Gorée sweeps the horizon.
0415	Action stations on *Richelieu*.
0500	The [submarine] *Bévéziers* leaves the inner harbour and heads out to sea.
0515	*Le Fantasque*, *Le Hardi* and *La Surprise* leave the inner harbour.
0544	Curtiss fighter patrol takes off from Ouakam Airfield. A Loire 130 takes off from the outer harbour.
0550	A second Loire 130 takes off from the outer harbour.
0644	*Georges Leygues* opens fire on a plane.
0713	Three enemy planes (fast monoplanes [Skua]) approaching from the port beam make a glide-bombing attack on *Richelieu*; some of the bombs fall about 500m to port, the others about 200m to starboard. Open fire.
0724	Three Curtiss fighters take off from Ouakam.
0730	The *Montcalm*'s aircraft signals two battleships and a cruiser 10nm to the south of Gorée. The battery at Gorée opens fire.
0805	Low-flying aircraft spotted at 135°. Open fire on this aircraft when at 170°.
0815	Open fire on several enemy aircraft passing from starboard to port; one dives on the residence of the Governor General. A few seconds later a Curtiss patrol flies over the harbour.

July; this required the wholesale transfer of shells and charges between the respective magazines overnight. The cruisers and the shore batteries had expended large quantities of ammunition. *Le Fantasque* and *Le Hardi* were running on only half their machinery, and it had been found that the Sural high-pressure boilers of *Le Hardi* were poorly suited to laying smokescreens; for the following day's action she would be equipped with smoke floats and tasked with screening *Richelieu* from the enemy guns. In the early morning the last remaining submarine *Bévéziers*, still with only a single motor in service, was ordered to patrol the area where the British battleships had appeared the previous day.

THE FINAL DAY

British reconnaissance flights over Dakar began at

0910	Second attack on *Richelieu* by biplane bombers [Swordfish]. Our AA opens fire on five British planes whose bombs fall on the jetty, severing the fuel lines. A plane taken down by our AA comes down close to Bel Air; another, also shot down by our AA, comes down outside the jetty under construction; a third, probably shot down by our AA, appears to come down in the direction of the cathedral. A few seconds later a Curtiss patrol flies over the harbour.
0937	Alert. The British battleships open fire on us. Visibility is poor. Gorée opens fire as well as the two French cruisers manoeuvring between Bel Air and Rufisque, under cover of a smoke screen laid by the *contre-torpilleurs*.
0940	Open fire with 380mm (Turret II which breaks down after the first salvo; later found that gun no.7 had shattered, in no.8 outer sleeve bulged and rifling stripped over 8m – unusable). *Richelieu* is straddled by 15in shells.
0954	The 152mm (Turret VII) open fire on *Barham*; bearing 118°. 15in shells falling to the east of us and to the north of Gorée following a turn about by the enemy battleships.
0959	The *Barham* (2nd in line) is hit between mast and funnel by at least two of our 152mm shells. [Battery on] Gorée fires.
1002	Again straddled by 15in shell splashes. Machinery room ordered to make smoke.
1003	Breakdown in replenishment of Turret VII; not repairable in short term.
1007	Cease making smoke – Turret II repaired – Wind NNW Force 2-3.
1010	Request to *Georges Leygues* for smoke screen to be laid to SE of *Richelieu*.
1015	Enemy masked by Cap Manuel. The 4th DC is continuing to fire.
1020	Cease fire.
1032	The cruisers (4th DC) are firing with their AA. Signal to the *Le Hardi*, placed under our orders by the Admiral in *Georges Leygues*, to be ready to lay a smoke screen between Gorée and the head of the jetty. Enemy disappears behind Cap Manuel. First assessment made of damage resulting from explosion in no.7 gun of Turret II. Hole made by a shell splinter above the waterline in Section R sealed with a Colomès patch.
1253	Observe large-calibre shell splashes around *Le Hardi*, which had sortied from the anchorage at our request to pick up British airmen from the plane downed by our AA. *Le Hardi* signals that she is being pursued by the main enemy force.
1256	Turret II (left half-turret) opens fire on a cruiser which replies. Breakdown in the loading mechanism of Turret VII, which had been ordered to fire on the cruisers.
1301	Our 380mm straddle the cruiser. The 4th DC is firing from the Bay of Rufisque.
1304	Cease firing. The enemy cruiser breaks off the action. At that moment two battleships are seen 5° to the right of the cruiser.
1305	Change of target for 380mm: battleship to right. *Le Hardi* lays a thick smoke screen between Gorée and the jetty.
1311	Our 380mm fire a [two-gun] salvo.
1313	We are closely straddled by 15in shell splashes.
1320	Several enemy shells fall on the town. Enemy ceases fire and disappears behind Cap Manuel (1330). Each of the enemy battleships has fired approximately 20 [four-gun] salvoes (about 160 rounds). Freighters *Porthos* and *Tacoma* (Swedish) on fire in the port.
1430	Air alert.
1510	Low-flying enemy aircraft between 150° and 160°.
1540	Air alert. Attack on cruisers (4th DC) by enemy torpedo planes. *Tacoma*, still on fire, towed out of inner harbour by *Buffle*. The freighter burns all night in the north of the anchorage, drifts and beaches herself on the northern point of Gorée.

25 September 1940

0450	Action stations.
0540	[Submarine] *Bévéziers* casts off. Curtiss fighter patrol airborne.
0615	Open fire on enemy reconnaissance plane at extreme range to the SE.
0652	Enemy reconnaissance floatplane downed over the sea, to the south, by a Curtiss fighter.
0750	Spot two battleships and a cruiser. Our guns trained 120°.
0815	Enemy firing (probably on submarine contact). Enemy at 33,000m. The two battleships are approaching ready to attack.
0820	Turret I ordered to target the battleship to the right and not to open fire beyond 20,000m
0825	Enemy turns away without having fired a shot. Distance: 34,400m.
0830	Distance to enemy ships: 35,000m.
0833	Plane takes off from one of the enemy ships.
0840	Distance to enemy ships: 37,000m.
0841	Enemy ships returning on a course of 30°. Curtiss patrol takes off.
0847	Distance to enemy ships: 30,000m. 380mm guns ordered to target battleship on the left and 152mm battleship on the right (most favourable angles of bearing for guns).
0900	*Le Hardi* lays very effective smoke screen to east of *Richelieu*. *Richelieu*'s motor boat prepares to lay smoke floats to the east of the jetty. The 4th DC, manoeuvring in the Bay of Rufisque, is protected by a smoke screen laid by the two *contre-torpilleurs*. The battleship to the left (probably *Barham*) fires, almost certainly in response to a submarine alert. Distance to enemy ships: 22,000m.
0904	*Richelieu* is first to open fire: two-gun salvo from Turret I. Gorée fires at the same time. Order to the 380mm to continue firing; to the 152mm to open fire when in range.
0905	Observe huge column of water alongside battleship on right (*Resolution*, torpedoed by *Bévéziers*), which takes on a list of 15°. Order to 152mm to engage battleship on left, *Barham*. *Barham* opens fire.
0910	Turret VII breaks down. Order for Turret V to take over and to target listing battleship.
0915	*Richelieu* struck by 15in shell (Section L). Other salvoes fall close, straddling the ship. *Barham* turns away. Cease fire with 380mm.
0917	Order to 152mm to open fire on *Resolution*. *Barham* resumes firing.
0920	Enemy spotter plane downed by Curtiss fighters. Cease fire with 152mm; target no longer in range.
0925	380mm ordered to engage *Barham*. Latter hit aft, turns hard about and significant reduction in speed.
0930	Action broken off; *Resulution* limps off to the south, still with a heavy list. Signal to *Georges Leygues* and to Naval HQ AOF: 'The two enemy battleships are clearly in difficulty.'
1100	Enemy aircraft carrier *Ark Royal* signalled to be at 35,000m on a bearing of 215° from the water tower, heading west, surrounded by flotilla craft. This information transmitted to *Georges Leygues*.
1125	Five planes taking off from *Ark Royal*.
1135	Signal *Bévéziers*: 'Warning: danger of magnetic mines in eastern pass'.
1140	AA alert.
1200	End of AA alert.

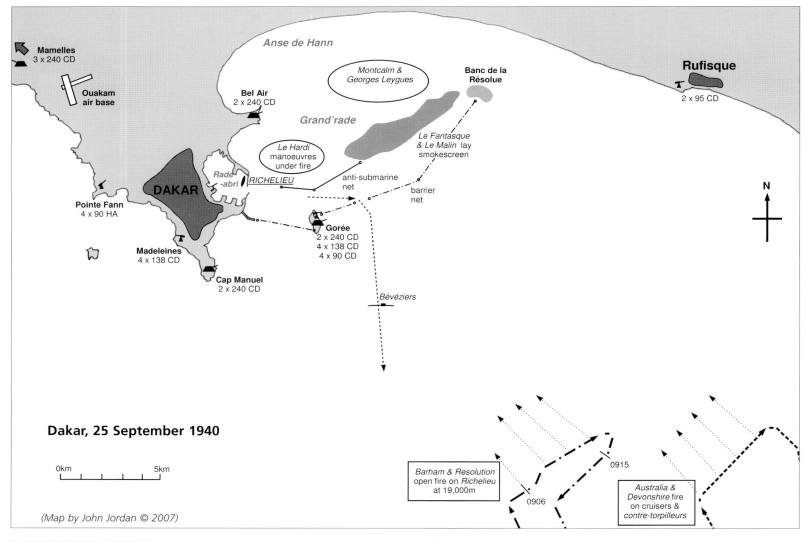

Mamelles
3 x 240 CD

Ouakam air base

Anse de Hann

Bel Air
2 x 240 CD

Montcalm & Georges Leygues

Banc de la Résolue

Rufisque
2 x 95 CD

Grand'rade

Le Hardi manoeuvres under fire

Le Fantasque & Le Malin lay smokescreen

Rade -abri | RICHELIEU

anti-submarine net

barrier net

Pointe Fann
4 x 90 HA

DAKAR

N

Gorée
2 x 240 CD
4 x 138 CD
4 x 90 CD

Madeleines
4 x 138 CD

Cap Manuel
2 x 240 CD

Bévéziers

Dakar, 25 September 1940

0km   5km

(Map by John Jordan © 2007)

Barham & Resolution open fire on *Richelieu* at 19,000m

0906

0915

Australia & Devonshire fire on cruisers & contre-torpilleurs

Looking aft onto the triple 152mm turrets of *Richelieu*. Despite occasional breakdowns these turrets gave good service during the British attack of 23-5 September 1940. (*H Landais collection*)

0600 on 25 September. In contrast to the conditions of the previous day, visibility was excellent; a difficult day for the Vichy French forces was in prospect. The masts of *Barham* and *Resolution* were spotted at 40,000 metres at 0750. *Richelieu*'s turret I was trained to 120 degrees ready to open fire once the range closed to 20,000 metres; only 24 full charges remained for the 380mm guns. Turret I was to take *Barham* as its target, while *Resolution* would be engaged by 152mm turrets V (starboard side) and VII (centreline). *Barham* catapulted her Walrus spotter aircraft at about 0830, and shortly afterwards French Curtiss fighters took off from the air base at Ouakam.

As a result of damage to *Barham* the previous day, Cunningham had transferred his flag to the cruiser *Devonshire*, which followed in the wake of the battleships with *Australia* closing the line. At 0900, with the range at 22,000 metres, *Le Hardi* began to lay her smoke screen; a motor boat prepared to lay further smoke floats. *Richelieu* opened fire on the British battleships at 0904 with a half-salvo that fell short. Shortly afterwards the battery at Gorée opened fire, and the cruisers of Force Y engaged the British cruisers.

As the British battleships made a 70 degrees turn together ready to resume their bombardment, the submarine *Bévéziers*, pre-positioned in the area for that precise purpose, fired four torpedoes from a position 2500 metres off the port beam of the battleships. The tracks of the torpedoes were spotted by a Swordfish from *Ark Royal*; *Barham* managed to avoid them by turning hard to starboard but *Resolution*, which was following in her wake, was struck amidships by a single torpedo. She quickly took on a list of 12.5 degrees and pulled out of line. *Barham* opened fire on *Richelieu* at a range of 19,000 metres, quickly straddling her with her four-gun salvos; *Richelieu* responded but her fire control system had difficulty adjusting to the remanufactured SD19 charges.[19] At 0910, turret VII broke down. Five minutes later, *Richelieu* was shaken by the impact of a 15in shell, which struck amidships above the armoured belt and penetrated section L. There were no casualties, but a mess deck was devastated and the main armoured deck was

pushed in to a depth of 20cm. A Walrus from the cruiser *Australia* was providing spotting, and this was promptly shot down by a Curtiss fighter.

The engagement continued until 0925, when the British withdrew behind a smokescreen laid by the destroyers *Forester* and *Inglefield*. The cruiser engagement continued at a range of 20,000 metres for three more minutes until 0928, by which time *Devonshire* had expended 200 rounds without securing a single hit on the French cruisers, which as on the previous day had manoeuvred at speed behind a thick smoke screen. Cunningham had been reluctant to close the range in the face of the powerful coast defence batteries of Gorée Island.

Informed of the increasingly parlous situation, and fearing further losses and a possible declaration of war by the Vichy government, Churchill and the War Cabinet finally bowed to the inevitable and ordered the suspension of the operation. Although the British press had rallied behind Churchill following his 'decisive action' at Mer el-Kebir, the Prime Minister was heavily criticised for his poor judgement in launching Operation 'Menace'. The Royal Navy had suffered serious material losses, and the loss of British prestige was keenly felt; Vichy France had been pushed into the arms of Britain's enemies.

The French suffered heavy casualties at Dakar and material losses included the *contre-torpilleur L'Audacieux* and two submarines. However, most of the damage to *Richelieu*, a key target of the Anglo-FNFL operation, had been self-inflicted. Guns Nos 7 and 8 were effectively out of action, and they would soon be joined by No. 5, which following the attempted discharge of the shell remaining in the barrel suffered similar damage to No. 8 three days previously and jammed in the recoil position at an angle of 15 degrees. As a precaution gun No. 6 was discharged via the breech after the charges had been hosed down; this was now the only gun in service in turret II.

Rounds fired by *Richelieu* during the three-day action were as follows: 24 x 380mm, 102 x 152mm, 501 x 100mm, 456 x 37mm, 3060 x 13.2mm.

LENGTHY REPAIRS

Although the damage sustained during Operation 'Menace' would have been regarded as relatively minor had circumstances been otherwise, even the most rudimentary repairs proved difficult given the relatively small skilled workforce available at DCN Dakar and the shortage of materials and spare parts. The damage caused by the 15in shell hit barely affected the fighting capability of the ship, but the devastation to fittings and bulkheads above the level of the main armoured deck was extensive: the armoured deck had been forced downward some 20cm where the shell impacted on it. There was also damage to the uptakes for the forward boiler room, which were protected only by a box of 20mm plating; boilers 10 and 11 were temporarily out of service, and boiler 12 (port side) could be used only with care. Much of the electrical cabling which served this section had been severed and needed to be replaced. The hole in the outer plating of section L where the shell had entered needed to be patched, as did the hole in section R caused by a shell splinter.

The major impediment to the ship's operational capability, however, continued to be the lack of water-

19 There was a loss of muzzle velocity estimated at 50m/s with these charges.

Richelieu moored at Dakar during 1941. Employed by this time as a floating battery, she is protected by anti-submarine nets. Note the irregular black 'boot-topping' which was a feature after the completion of hull repairs.

Cofferdam Structure

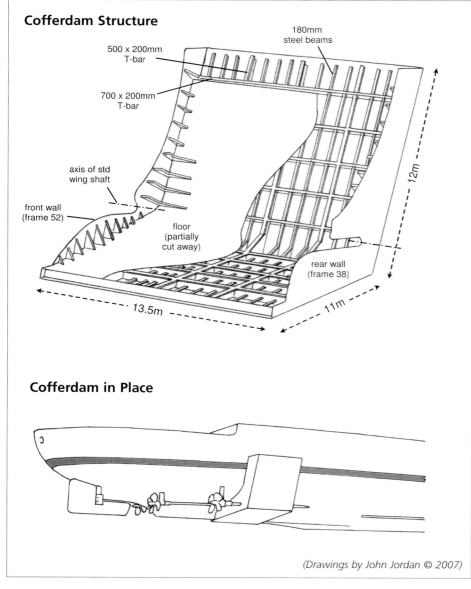

500 x 200mm T-bar

700 x 200mm T-bar

180mm steel beams

axis of std wing shaft

front wall (frame 52)

floor (partially cut away)

rear wall (frame 38)

12m

11m

13.5m

Cofferdam in Place

(Drawings by John Jordan © 2007)

tight integrity aft as a result of the torpedo hit on 8 July. On 10 October, an attempt was made to place the canvas and steel mattress under construction in the dockyard since mid-July over the damaged area. It failed; the patch proved difficult to position and secure to the hull, and was insufficiently watertight to enable the large quantity of water remaining in the hull to be pumped out. However, work was now proceeding on the design and construction of the steel cofferdam, which it was hoped would be far more effective in making the hull watertight.

In order to match the curves of the outer hull to the sides of the cofferdam, two divers were aided by two draughtsmen flown in from DCN Toulon, both of whom were specialists in descriptive geometry. Frame 38, immediately forward of the support for the outer shaft, was taken as the seat of the after end of the cofferdam, and the forward end was to be secured to the hull just forward of the armoured bulkhead. The cofferdam itself was 13.5 metres wide, 11 metres wide at its base and 12 metres high. The outer face was angled out from the base, while the two side walls followed the contours of the hull. The outer shell was of 10mm steel plating over a framework of 500mm x 200mm T-bars reinforced by 180mm steel beams (see drawing). The watertight seal where the cofferdam joined the hull comprised a wooden frame with a canvas 'sausage' filled with sisal. This ingenious structure had an inner 'floor' of steel plating over the framing, the volume between the floor and the outer wall of the cofferdam being utilised to create ballast tanks, as in a submarine, enabling the cofferdam to be partially submerged while being manoeuvred to the correct position over the hull, then pumped out once in place.

The cofferdam was 'launched' in early December, and following trials with the ballast system was towed to the ship a few days later. It was successfully secured to the underside of the hull, the ballast tanks were emptied and leaks eliminated. Large-capacity pumps were put in place, but they constantly broke down. Fortunately, the dockyard found a pump of English manufacture – it dated from 1873! – with an AC motor, and once a suitable electrical supply was rigged this began to pump the water out of the after part of the ship. Work could now begin on sealing the breach in the hull with welded plates reinforced with quick-setting cement. The breach was finally sealed on 28 February, and the focus now turned to the internal bulkheads and frames. The damaged shaft was finally lifted out by floating crane on 18 March.

Although the German authorities were quite happy to facilitate temporary repairs to the hull to enable *Richelieu* to serve as a floating battery, all attempts by Marzin and Darlan to make the ship fully operational were obstructed, as it was feared that this might make the ship a more attractive proposition to the British. A request in January for more welders to be sent from Toulon was sanctioned only in April. The Armistice Commission allowed 316 380mm shells to be delivered on 28 November 1940, with a further consignment in May of the following year, but refused to allow the replacement of the damaged guns or the damaged shaft. Desperately needed spare parts such as cables and motor parts arrived only in a trickle.

Nevertheless, there were grounds for optimism. Work on the hull was completed on 27 March, and on 24 April the cofferdam was filled with water to check that the hull was now completely watertight. The cofferdam was removed, and the boilers repaired. Darlan authorised sea trials to begin on 28 May, but there was concern about a possible British response; should the ship be intercepted while at sea only half the main guns were serviceable. On 5 July, the ship was moved to the *Quai des Escales*, with her guns facing the sea, and tricolore identification bands were applied to turret II. The following day, two Loire 130 seaplanes arrived from Brest, to be designated HDR 1 and 2 – a third, provisionally numbered HDR 3, was not assigned.[20] Because the hangar was cluttered with spares and stores the aircraft were based at Bel-Air. The catapults, however, could now be tested and the first catapult launch took place on 7 October.

THE OFFICIAL ENQUIRY

Following the serious incidents involving the 380mm guns of turret II on 24 and 28 September an official enquiry was set up on 8 October 1940 under VAE de Penfentenyo de Kervéréguen. The investigations of the damage to guns Nos 5, 7 and 8 revealed similar damage to all three. In the gunhouse jets of flame shot from the rear end of the breech, electrical connections were torn away, and the breech was jammed or manoeuvrable only with difficulty. The jacket of the gun was bulged, the steel masks pushed back, and fretted joints opened up 4-12mm; inside the barrel there was an egg-shaped deformation, and the rifling was intact between the bulge and the breech but torn away or flattened between the bulge and the muzzle. It was clear that the damage resulted from a premature explosion of the shell in the barrel. A careful study of the barrels, the shells and the charges led to the conclusion that the fault lay in the interaction between the base of the shells and the powder of the charge.

A number of tests were carried out ashore, and the old battleship *Condorcet*, moored in Toulon harbour, conducted test firings using charges made up of SD19 and SD21 sample powders from *Richelieu*. The 380mm shells of the latter ship had been designed to resist a

A 1942 view of *Richelieu* moored quay-side at Dakar. (*R Dumas collection*)

pressure of 3200kg/cm^2; however, it was estimated that on 24 September, when temperatures in the turrets reached 40° C, the combustion gases of the SD21 powder had attained 3700kg/cm^2. This alone could not have caused the shell to explode in the barrel, given that there was a safety margin in the shells as designed. Attention therefore turned to the construction of the base of the shell.

The 380mm shells of *Richelieu* had four cavities intended to accommodate cartridges of toxic gas in their base. These cavities were sealed by screw caps 10mm thick at the centre and 5mm where they overlapped the cavity (see drawing). Bomb tests revealed that when these caps were removed the roof of the cavity could withstand a pressure of 4200kg/cm^2. However, it was found that when the caps were fitted they shattered at a pressure of only 2800kg/cm^2, and that the fragments then went on to penetrate (or at least to seriously deform) the roof of the cavity. If the latter was penetrated the combustion gases of the charge came into direct contact with the explosive charge of the shell, causing the shell to explode in the barrel.

Contrary to speculation in some sources, the use of SD19 propellant in the newly manufactured charges was found to be in no way responsible for the explosion of the shells. The charges in turret II employed on

---

Richelieu at Dakar, September 1940: the premature explosion of the shells

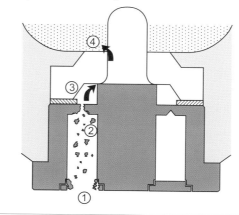

The Root of the Problem

1 The overpressure resulting from the high temperature of the SD21 propellant (3700kg/cm^2) causes the screw cap over the cavity to shatter.

2 Fragments of the cap bombard the roof of the cavity, which cracks at its weakest point where it has been machined.

3 The combustion gases from the propellant are forced through the roof of the cavity under pressure.

4 The hot combustion gases make contact with the explosive, causing the shell to explode in the barrel.

24 September had the standard SD21 propellant, whereas those used for turret I the following day were the remanufactured charges with SD19. The only problem experienced with the latter was that they proved to be seriously underpowered, the resulting decline in muzzle velocity making fire control difficult – rounds generally fell short of the target. Tests by the commission established that muzzle velocity for the SD21 charge was 830m/s and pressure on the day 3700kg/cm^2, whereas the comparable figures for the SD19 (remanufactured) charge were 785m/s – significantly less than the 805m/s originally estimated – and 3200kg/cm^2. The guns of turret I narrowly avoided the catastrophic failure of those in Turret II by using the underpowered SD19 charge.

The problem with the bases of the shells was resolved by filling the cavities with cement and sealing them with more robust caps. Tests established that they could now withstand an overpressure of 6000kg/cm^2. The SD21 propellant would again be made standard, but in order to avoid problems at higher temperatures muzzle velocity was to be reduced from 830m/s to 785m/s.

The investigations and trials conducted by the Commission of Enquiry were so time-consuming that its official report was submitted only on 10 April 1942. It recommended that in order to dispel any apprehension among *Richelieu*'s gunners a test-firing of six of the modified shells with charges of SD21 propellant should take place using gun No. 6. The test firing could also be used to confirm the nominal initial velocity with the new charge.

FROM 'MENACE' TO 'TORCH'

For Dakar, the period October 1940 to November 1942 was relatively uneventful. On 28 July and 29 September 1941, and again on 26 February and 12 May 1942, *Richelieu* opened fire with her AA guns on unidentified aircraft that overflew the port. The Allied landings of Operation 'Torch' of 8 November 1942 took place farther to the north at Casablanca, leaving *Richelieu* and the ever-present cruisers and *contre-torpilleurs* of Force Y unscathed. However, with the German occupation of southern France on 11 November, all French naval forces in North Africa and West Africa, on the orders of Admiral Darlan, rallied to the Allied cause.

A US naval mission now met representatives of the French Navy to determine which ships should undergo refurbishment and modernisation in the United States. *Richelieu* was naturally the first ship on the list and between 25 and 29 January 1943 ran sea trials to check that her machinery, virtually unused since 8 July 1940, was in working order. During the same period the aviation installations and the light AA were removed. *Richelieu* sailed for the United States on 30 January, accompanied by the cruiser *Montcalm*, which was likewise to undergo modernisation. A speed of 14 knots was maintained, the rudder having to be set to 7 degrees to compensate for the deformation of the hull aft. *Richelieu* arrived in the Hudson River, New York, on 11 February, and a week later entered Dock No. 5 of the Brooklyn Navy Yard. She was able to pass under the suspension bridge of the East River only after the removal of the upper director from the forward tower.

Richelieu arrives in New York ready for her reconstruction at the Brooklyn Navy Yard. Note the early DEM radar antennae at the ends of the yards projecting from the forward and after towers. The prototype installation had arrived in Dakar aboard the *contre-torpilleur Le Terrible* on 26 February 1940. It comprised transmitting and receiving antennae, which were fitted to starboard. Following trials which took place during April and May, the installation was modified and extended to cover the port side. There was a blind sector of 60 degrees forward. (*H Landais collection*)

Richelieu is towed upriver to the Brooklyn Navy Yard in this well-known photo dated 28 February 1943. The upper director has been removed to enable her to pass beneath the Brooklyn Bridge. Note the shattered barrel of No. 7 gun in turret II.

CHAPTER 6

JEAN BART: 1936-1943

*J*EAN BART WAS LAID DOWN AT THE A.C. LOIRE Shipyard of St. Nazaire on 12 December 1936. The keel was laid in a newly completed construction facility designed specifically for the new generation of battleships which the local populace and the shipyard workers christened the *'Forme Jean Bart'* but which was officially referred to as the *'Ouvrage Caquot'* after its designer, the distinguished civil engineer Albert Caquot. The Caquot construction facility was a revolutionary structure which in certain aspects anticipated postwar developments in shipbuilding. Built throughout of the reinforced concrete of which Caquot had been one of the most prominent pioneers, the facility comprised two parallel docks: one for construction of the hull, the other for fitting out (see drawing).

The construction of *Jean Bart* proceeded relatively slowly during the first two years, and despite a renewed urgency from the Spring of 1939 the ship would be 'launched' only on 6 March 1940, six months

after the war in Europe had begun. Completion was now scheduled for early 1941, but when the German offensive in the west began in May 1940 and quickly began to roll up the French and British armies in Belgium and Northern France it became clear that normal work on the ship would have to be suspended in favour of readying her for a hasty departure.

It was estimated that the most favourable date for departure would be 19 June, when the tides were at their highest. The ship was currently confined within the building facility, as the channel linking the latter to the river Loire had yet to be dredged. Originally it had been estimated that a channel 70 metres wide and more than five metres in depth would be required in order to provide sufficient clearance for the ship at a projected draught of 9m. This was simply not feasible in so short a period of time. However, if the ship were incomplete and the minimum of fuel oil and water embarked, displacement could be kept to an estimated 8.10m, and it was agreed that a channel 50m wide and 3.50m deep could be achieved by 19 June. Even this proved too ambitious, and when the time came to move the ship the channel was barely 45m wide (for a beam of 33m!), and clearance beneath the hull only 30cm at full tide.

Between 28 May and 15 June the number of shipyard workers increased from 2500 to 3050, almost the entire labour force of Penhoët and A.C. Loire, and

12-hour shifts were the norm. Work on *Jean Bart* had been prioritised, and in little more than a month the three after boilers and the forward two sets of turbines (half the propulsion plant), two turbo-dynamos, two pumps, and the key internal communications systems were in place and ready. On 6-7 June the propellers were fitted to the outer shafts, and on 12-14 June the three after boilers were lit for the first time. The rudder, anchor chains and capstans were fitted, and the double bottom sealed. There were ongoing problems with the electrical circuits, and up to the time of departure systems dependent on electrical supply such as lube oil and water pumps, ventilation and cooling machinery could be kept running only by inserting wooden wedges into the main circuit-breakers to prevent them from jumping – a dangerous practice on a ship with only rudimentary damage control.

The ship's armament had an altogether lower priority, in part because of delivery problems but also because a full outfit of main and secondary guns in armoured turrets would have increased draught – a quadruple 380mm turret weighed 2500 tonnes. The four 380mm guns and the heavy armour plates of the forward turret were in place; however, the replenishment hoists and loading mechanisms remained incomplete, and the fire control system and searchlight projectors had yet to be fitted. Turret II was little more than a steel framework, lacking not only its guns but also its armour plating.[1] Not one of the three 152mm turrets was in place. The aviation facilities also remained incomplete: only the bases of the catapults,

---

[1] The four 380mm guns for Turret II were in the process of being delivered to the shipyard. One of the two already at the dockside was loaded into a freighter, but the crane then failed and the remaining gun was sabotaged; this gun, together with a third en route to St. Nazaire and a fourth at Ruelle, was captured by the Germans [see table Chapter 4 for subsequent fate]. The freighter, the *Mécanicien Principal Lestin*, was subsequently sunk by German air attack off the Gironde Estuary en route to Casablanca.

The Caquot Construction Facility

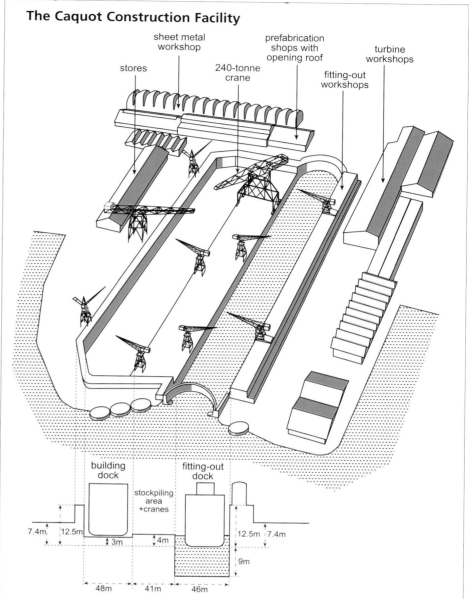

(Drawing by John Jordan © 2009)

The *Ouvrage Caquot* was one of the most remarkable shipbuilding facilities of the prewar era. Conceived by the distinguished civil engineer Albert Caquot, it featured parallel construction and fitting-out docks of reinforced concrete served by specially designed workshops optimised for prefabrication and ease of assembly. It was built on the site of the Loire shipyard, St. Nazaire, from 1935, and marked a departure from traditional slipway construction. The battleship *Jean Bart* was the first ship to be built there.

The central construction enclosure was 325 metres long and 135 metres wide. It comprised a construction dock 48 metres across, the floor of which was at the half-tide level of +3 metres, and a fitting-out dock 46 metres wide, the floor of which was 9 metres below the low-tide level. A low platform between the two docks was used for stockpiling materials to be used in the construction of the ship, and was the base for five wheeled cranes, the largest of which was capable of lifting 250 tonnes. Once the hull was complete, the whole enclosure was flooded to a sufficient depth at high tide to enable the ship to be moved sideways over the central platform and into the fitting-out dock. The latter was connected to a specially dredged channel of the same depth by a 45-metre lock gate of hemispherical configuration, which was capable of withstanding a load of 15 metres of water (i.e., maximum high tide) when the dock was empty. It was from this fitting-out dock that *Jean Bart* made her escape a matter of hours before German troops occupied St. Nazaire on 19 June 1940.

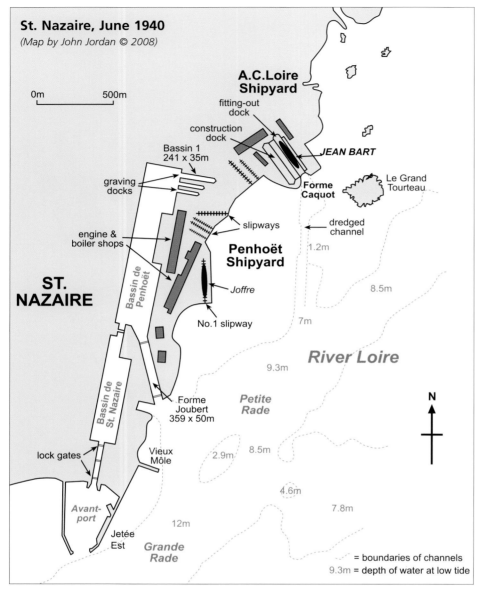

St. Nazaire, June 1940

(Map by John Jordan © 2008)

0m   500m

A.C.Loire Shipyard

fitting-out dock

construction dock

Bassin 1 241 x 35m

graving docks

JEAN BART

Forme Caquot

Le Grand Tourteau

engine & boiler shops

ST. NAZAIRE

slipways

dredged channel

1.2m

Penhoët Shipyard

Joffre

8.5m

No.1 slipway

7m

River Loire

9.3m

Bassin de Penhoët

Forme Joubert 359 x 50m

Petite Rade

Bassin de St. Nazaire

lock gates

Vieux Môle

2.9m   8.5m

Avant-port

Jetée Est

12m

4.6m

7.8m

Grande Rade

N

- - - = boundaries of channels
9.3m = depth of water at low tide

the elevator and the base of the crane had been installed when the ship departed St. Nazaire on 19 June. No boats were aboard; in their place there were 46 Brest life rafts.

Because of delays in the manufacture of the 100mm CAD guns which *Jean Bart* was to receive in lieu of her midships 152mm turrets, it had been decided to mount 90mm CAD Mle 1930 mountings in their place. Two of these were to come from the AA defences of Brest Naval Dockyard and two from the netlayer

RANGEFINDERS (AS FITTED IN *JEAN BART* 1941)

Main armament

1 x OPL 14-metre S (triplex)	Improvised director atop fwd tower
1 x OPL 8-metre S (duplex)	Housing atop Turret II

General use

3 x SOM 3-metre S	Atop conning tower (navigation)
	Two bridge wings (October from *Dunkerque*)

Notes:

OPL	*Optique de Précision Levallois-Perret*
SOM	*Société d'Optique et de Mécanique de Haute Précision*
S	Stereoscopic RF

Gladiateur, while the remaining pair were refurbished mountings from the naval armaments establishment at Ruelle which had been used for trials and testing. Only the latter arrived in time, and they were duly bolted on in the two forward positions on 18 June, the day before the ship's departure; there were as yet, however, no munitions for these guns, and no HA fire control. Three 37mm CAD Mle 1933 were obtained at the last minute, and these were fitted aft atop the hangar and the barbette for the centre-line 152mm mountings, and forward to port abeam the conning tower. There were also two 13.2mm CAQ mountings, installed port and starboard on the shelter deck aft, and four 13.2mm CAD, installed at the four corners atop the forward tower. All of these weapons fired through open sights, so they were usable against hostile aircraft, but there was as yet no target designation or unified control system.

Initially it was envisaged that *Jean Bart* would make for the Clyde, but on 11 June the captain of the ship, CV Ronarc'h, received the order to sail for Casablanca. At 0330 on 19 June, when it was still dark, the tugs *Minotaure*, *Ursus* and *Titan* of the Compagnie Générale Transatlantique moved *Jean Bart* out of the fitting-out dock and into the hastily-dredged channel.[2] In the pitch darkness the marker buoys were barely visible, and the bow of *Jean Bart* soon grounded, the stern swinging to settle on the opposite side of the channel. She was eventually hauled off by the tugs (at the cost of a bent propeller blade), and at 0445 the engines were started for the first time. At about the same time three German Heinkel bombers appeared, flying at 1000m, and one dropped a 100kg bomb between the two turrets, but there was little damage beyond a hole 20cm in diameter and some distortion to internal bulkheads. *Jean Bart* now increased her speed to 12 knots and headed for the open sea.

At 0630 she was met by her escort: the brand-new *torpilleur d'escadre Le Hardi*, flying the flag of Admiral de Laborde (*Amiral Ouest*), and her sister *Mameluk*, which had been working up at Lorient. She was also met by the British destroyer *Vanquisher*, despatched with two tugs to take her to Britain. The offer was declined, and once at sea *Jean Bart* took on fuel oil, diesel oil and water from the tankers *Odet* and *Tarn*.[3] At 1800 she headed for Casablanca, escorted by the two destroyers. On 20 June, when off Lorient, the *Le Hardi* was replaced by the *Epée*, which had been running sea trials from that port, and the three ships continued on their way to Casablanca at 24 knots. There were numerous machinery breakdowns, including problems with the ventilation of the single operational engine room (which meant that personnel were working in temperatures of 40-70°C), and a major problem with a condenser, which could be remedied only by changing over the vacuum pumps between the forward and after (incomplete) engine rooms, work which took the onboard shipyard personnel and the ship's own mechanicians half a day to complete, during which time the ship was virtually immobilised in seas patrolled by German U-boats.

---

[2] The draught of the ship when she exited the dock was just under 8.2m, leaving a very slim margin for error.

[3] She had to be replenished at sea because draught had to be kept to a minimum during the passage from the dock to the Loire Estuary.

Following these repairs *Jean Bart* worked up to 18 knots, experiencing some vibration in her port turbine in the process She finally entered Casablanca at 1700 on 22 June, and dropped anchor in the outer harbour.

CASABLANCA

While the priority of Captain Ronarc'h was to give the ship the means to defend herself, the authorities at Casablanca were inclined to regard her as a resource, and their first action was to remove most of the AA guns which had been hastily fitted at St. Nazaire to boost the port's anti-aircraft defences. On 24 June they ordered the 90mm CAD mountings to be disembarked and relocated on the *Jetée des Phosphates*, and the 37mm CAD to be relocated on the *Grande Jetée* (see map p.157). On 6 September the two 13.2mm Hotchkiss CAQ were removed and mounted on lorries. This left only the four 13.2mm CAD mounted atop the forward tower.

Following the British attacks on Oran and Dakar on 3-8 July there were not unreasonable fears that Casablanca and *Jean Bart* might be subjected to similar treatment. Ronarc'h responded by ordering a number of safety measures. The circular emplacements for turrets II (380mm) and V, VI and VII (152mm) were concreted over, and three quarters of the empty compartments were sealed off with access forbidden. On 11 August authorisation was obtained to moor the ship in shallow water at the northern end of the *Quai Delande*.

On 7 September the Direction des Armes Navales (DAN) Casablanca allocated sixteen of the new Browning 13.2mm CAS guns, together with seventeen of the older – and comparatively useless – 8mm MG to the ship. Only one of the latter was mounted (just forward of the barbette for the centreline 152mm mounting), but the Brownings were fitted as three sections: one group of four forward, and two groups of six amidships and atop/abeam the aircraft hangar. A lead gun in each section was responsible for target designation.

Further work on the ship proved difficult due to the non-delivery of material, most of which was being manufactured in factories within the Occupied Zone. It became clear that the directors essential for effective fire by the main guns would not arrive, so during 1941 considerable ingenuity was employed to provide a temporary solution. A torpedo tube platform scavenged from the old destroyer *Enseigne Gabolde* was used as the base of an improvised director incorporating a triplex 14-metre base OPL rangefinder which was mounted atop the forward tower; the director was capable of providing only rudimentary bearing data to the guns. A duplex 8-metre OPL rangefinder was housed in a small turret located atop turret II, but the vibration of the diesels below made it virtually impossible to use while the ship was alongside. A 3-metre SOM rangefinder was fitted atop the conning tower for navigation, and in October 1941 two further units of this type removed from the *Dunkerque* were fitted in the bridge wings. Work began around this time on the transmitting station, but it would comprise just an incomplete ballistics panel and a graphical calculator which could average the range 'takes' from the various rangefinders.

By this time CV Ronarc'h, promoted rear-admiral in

March 1941, had been replaced as CO by CV Barthes, who took command on 22 August. A note from the latter dated January 1942 expressed the hope that six new 37mm CAD mountings Mle 1933 would be delivered from France in the near future: two in January, two in February/March, and two after March. In the event these delivery dates could not be met, and they were constantly deferred. In April four of the older 37mm CAS mountings Mle 1925 were fitted as a temporary measure: two abeam the conning tower forward and two on the shelter deck aft, abeam the barbette for the centre-line 152mm. At the same time the first two newly-manufactured 90mm CAD mountings were delivered and mounted in the forward (shelter deck) position port and starboard. The new AA weapons effectively displaced six of the 13.2mm Browning MG, which were relocated to the forward end of the shelter deck (four), the lower platform of the after tower (one), and the port side of the quarterdeck (one). The 90mm *'tubes*

Jean Bart shortly after her arrival at Casablanca in June 1940. It is readily apparent that the ship is a long way from completion. Only turret I is fully fitted out and the secondary armament has yet to be installed. The superstructures are almost complete but still have their red and yellow ochre priming paint (see artwork p.132). The ship had made the passage from St. Nazaire on half her propulsion machinery.

ANTI-AIRCRAFT GUNS (*JEAN BART* 1940-43)

Gun Data	90/50 Mle 1926	13.2mm Browning MG
Construction	Monobloc autofretted barrel	
Breech mechanism	SA concentric ring	
Weight of gun	1570kg	N/A
Type of munitions	Fixed	Fixed
Projectiles	OEA Mle 1925 (9.5kg) tracer	OEA Mle??
Propellant	3.1kg BM5	??kg
Complete round		
weight	18.1kg	N/A
dimensions	1.00m x 0.13m	N/A
Muzzle velocity	850m/s	825m/s
Max. range	15,440m	2000m theoretical
Ceiling	10,600m	
Mounting Data		
Mounting designation	CAD Mle 1930	CAS Mle??
Weight of mounting	13.7t	N/A
Elevation of guns	-10° / +80°	N/A
Firing cycle (per gun)	10-15rpm theoretical	1000rpm theoretical
6-8rpm practical		

Notes:
CAD *Contre-Avions Double*   AA twin mounting
CAS *Contre-Avions Simple*   AA single mounting
Mle *Modèle*   Model

An aerial view of *Jean Bart* being manoeuvred by tugs onto the *Quai Delande* (see map of Casablanca) on 11 August 1940. She has been repainted yellow overall so that she blends in with the grain silos farther down the quay.

Jean Bart at Casablanca during 1941. Most of the AA weaponry hastily installed prior to the ship's departure from St. Nazaire had by this time been commandeered to bolster the defences of the port. The photo was taken from the grain silos on the *Quai Delande*.

canons' for sub-calibre firing were installed on the glacis plate of turret I at about this time.

May 1942 was a landmark in that turret I was now fully operational. On 19 May *Jean Bart* was moved to the *Jetée Delure* and a standard test-firing of the 380mm guns was conducted without incident; the first four rounds were fired using the E3[4] charge, followed by 24 with the E1 charge. The ship was then moved back to the *Quai Delande*. As fire control for the main guns remained problematical and the ship was little more than a floating battery firing from a fixed station in the harbour, a fire control system using triangulation was conceived which used observation from three points:

– the forward tower of *Jean Bart*, which was moored with her bows facing the sea;
– Sidi-Abderhamane to the west;
– Dar Bou Azza to the east.

---

[4] Charges designated 'E' (*exercice*) were for practice; those designated 'C' (*combat*) were for use in action.

In June 1942 two of the promised 37mm CAD mountings finally arrived, and were installed atop the hangar roof and the forward end of the shelter deck, to starboard of turret II. Of the four 37mm CAS only one was retained, to port of the conning tower. The second pair of 90mm CAD mountings was now in place. June also saw the installation of a DEM (radar) installation similar to that of *Jean Bart*'s sister-ship *Richelieu*, the two rotating antennae being located atop the forward tower. Results from trials were generally satisfactory against aircraft, which were detected at 55-70km, but it was difficult to assess capabilities against surface ships because of the electromagnetic 'clutter' of the port. The DEM installation was passed for operational service 6 October 1942, a month before Operation 'Torch'.

During early November a fifth 90mm CAD was installed to starboard; installation of the sixth was precluded by the events of 8 November. On this date the AA armament of the ship was as follows:

– five 90mm CAD Mle 1930
– two 37mm CAD Mle 1933
– one 37mm CAS Mle 1925
– four 13.2mm Hotchkiss CAD
– fourteen 13.2mm Browning CAS
– one 8mm Hotchkiss CAS

OPERATION 'TORCH'

The Allied assault on French North Africa known as Operation 'Torch' began on 8 November. The 'Center Attack Group' (TG 34-9) under the overall command of the Task Force Commander, Rear-Admiral Hewitt in the cruiser *Augusta*, was to lead the attack on Casablanca. Built around the carriers *Ranger* (54 Wildcat fighters, 18 Dauntless dive-bombers) and the escort carrier *Suwanee* (29 Wildcat, 9 Avenger torpedo-bombers), TG 34-9 included one heavy and two light cruisers, fifteen destroyers and an oiler; there were fifteen transports with 19,000 men aboard, together with minesweepers to clear their way to the beaches.

Although it was hoped that the French authorities would put up only a token resistance to the Americans, who following the events at Mers el-Kebir and Dakar were more favourably regarded than their British allies, the port of Casablanca was known to be well-defended. Besides the 380mm guns of *Jean Bart* and the powerful 194mm coast defence battery at El

COS AND FLAG OFFICERS (1940-43)

Commanding Officers

CV Ronarc'h[1]	09.06.40 – 22.08.41	
CV Barthes[2]	22.08.41 – 17.03.43	
CV de La Fournère	17.03.43 – 15.03.43	
CV Ansaldi	15.03.43 – 18.04.47	

Notes:
[1] Promoted Rear-Admiral 26.03.41, Ronarc'h retained command of the ship.
[2] Promoted Rear-Admiral 18.11.42, Barthes retained command of the ship.

Flag Officers

CA Ronarc'h	26.03.41 – 22.08.41	[see note 1 above]
CA Barthes	18.11.42 – 17.03.43	[see note 2 above]

Notes:

CV	*Capitaine de vaisseau*	(RN equivalent rank: Captain)
CA	*Contre-amiral*	(RN equivalent rank: Rear-Admiral

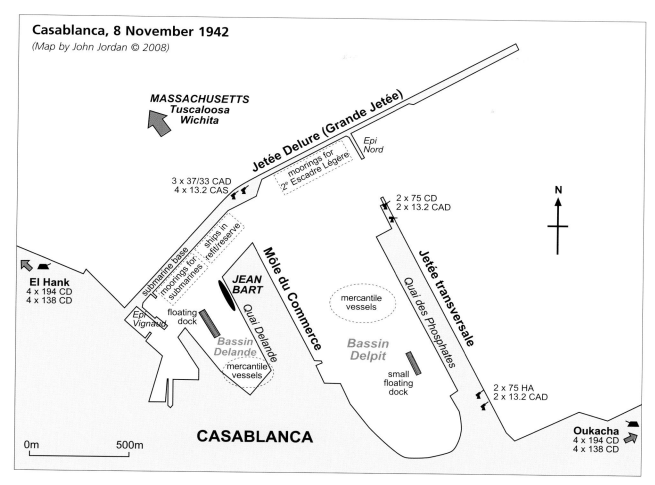

Casablanca, 8 November 1942
(Map by John Jordan © 2008)

Hank to the west of the port, the *2e Escadre Légère*, comprising the light cruiser *Primauguet*, two *contre-torpilleurs* and seven of the older *torpilleurs d'escadre*, was currently based there, together with three divisions of submarines (one fleet, two coastal). A direct frontal assault was out of the question, so the landings would take place at Fedala, some fifteen miles north of Casablanca. In order to subdue the fixed defences and to prevent interference with the landings by the ships of the 2nd EL there was a powerful covering force under Rear-Admiral Giffen (TG 34-1), comprising the brand-new 16-inch gun battleship *Massachusetts* and the heavy cruisers *Wichita* and *Tuscaloosa* (each nine 8in guns), escorted by four destroyers.

Despite warnings about the possibility of Anglo-American operations against French North Africa there was no specific intelligence about an assault on Casablanca, and the huge American armada was discovered only at 0700 on 8 November, when a Glenn Martin bomber of *Escadrille 2B* from Port-Lyautey was despatched on a reconnaissance mission.

Four of the coastal submarines had left the port in the early morning to patrol sectors from El Hank in the west to Fedala in the north, and a fifth boat, *La Sibylle*, was despatched to reinforce the northern sector just after 0700. The ships of the *2e Escadre Légère* had kept boilers lit throughout the night in order to be at 90 minutes notice to sail from 0630. At 0633 they were ordered to get underway to oppose the American landings taking place at Fedala. However, the first of the destroyers did not cast off until 0737, more than 30 minutes after the bombardment of Casablanca had

ANTI-AIRCRAFT ARMAMENT (*JEAN BART 1940-42*)

18 June 1940	2 x 90mm CAD Mle 1930	Amidships (fwd position p&s)
	3 x 37mm CAD Mle 1933	2 atop hangar (centreline)
		1 to port of CT
	2 x 13.2mm CAQ Mle 1929	Abeam centre-line 152mm (02 deck)
	4 x 13.2mm CAD Mle 1929	Atop fwd tower
16 Sept 1940	4 x 13.2mm CAD Mle 1929	Atop fwd tower
	16 x 13.2mm CAS Browning	4 p&s forward (02 deck)
		6 p&s amidships (02/03 decks)
		6 aft (2 abeam/2 atop hangar,
		2 after director platform)
	1 x 8mm Hotchkiss MG	Aft
Jan 1942	2 x 90mm CAD Mle 1930	Amidships (02 deck)
	16 x 13.2mm CAS Browning	8 fwd
		8 aft
	1 x 8mm Hotchkiss MG	Aft
April 1942	4 x 90mm CAD Mle 1930	Amidships (02 deck)
	4 x 37mm CAS Mle 1925	2 fwd, 2 aft (03 deck)
	14 x 13.2mm CAS Browning	6 fwd
		8 aft
	1 x 8mm Hotchkiss MG	Aft
June 1942	4 x 90mm CAD Mle 1930	Amidships (02 deck)
	2 x 37mm CAD Mle 1933	Std turret II (02 deck)
		atop hangar
	1 x 37mm CAS Mle 1925	Port of CT
	14 x 13.2mm CAS Browning	6 fwd
		8 aft
	1 x 8mm Hotchkiss MG	Aft

The bare steel framework of turret II. The open barbette was sealed with concrete. (*H Landais collection*)

Towering orange splashes from the 380mm shells of *Jean Bart* fall close to Admiral Hewitt's cruiser flagship USS *Augusta* on the morning of 10 November 1942. (*USNHC*)

begun, and the departure of the flagship *Primauguet* was delayed until 0900. By the end of the day, despite skilful handling and a display of considerable courage and determination, all of these ships would be sunk or disabled. The fleet submarines *Sidi-Ferruch* and *Le Tonnant* had managed to get underway under a hail of shells some minutes earlier; the third, *Le Conquérant*, exited the floating dock off *Jean Bart*'s port beam just before the latter was sunk by a 16in shell.

The American assault on the harbour was devastating. An attack by SBD Dauntless aircraft armed with 500lb bombs from the carrier *Ranger* was accompanied by a bombardment of the inner harbour by *Massachusetts* and *Tuscaloosa* using spotting aircraft; the cruiser *Wichita* engaged the coastal battery at El Hank. Bombs from *Ranger*'s Dauntlesses quickly

accounted for three of the coastal submarines and two destroyers. At 0718 *Jean Bart* herself was damaged by two bombs: one which struck the catapult mounting to port causing a small fire and flooding of the manual steering compartment, and another which struck the quay to starboard, causing a large breech in the outer hull plating in section M.

Jean Bart managed to get away four two-gun salvoes between 0708 and 0719, when the US cruisers approached to 22,000m, but the fall of shot could not be observed and from 0721 the cruisers were hidden by the smokescreen laid by the 2nd EL to cover its departure. *Massachusetts* now began to focus her fire on the French battleship. At 0725 a 16in shell struck the shelter deck in section O, passing through both armoured decks before exploding in the 152mm magazines, which fortunately were empty. The two parts of the nose cone, which had split longitudinally, were subsequently found in the lower magazine lying close to the after transverse armoured bulkhead (see drawings).

At 0735 a 16in gun salvo fell close to the bow, passing through the forefoot and causing deformation of the hull plating to starboard. One minute later a shell hit the quay, projecting large chunks of masonry which wounded some of the gunners of the 90mm guns and breached the hull in sections B and C, causing the flooding of a number of compartments. At 0737 a 16in shell passed through the funnel, clipping the edge of the armoured deck as it exited the side of the ship to port.

A fourth 16in shell hit the edge of the quay, passed through the hull plating and struck the main armour belt, being deflected downwards and out through the hull plating beneath the waterline. This shell failed to explode – probably because of the oblique angle (60-70°) at which it struck the armour plate – and no trace of it was subsequently found.

There were no further hits until 0806, when turret I was struck to port by a 16in shell which carried away the 90mm gun fitted for sub-calibre firings and pushed the glacis plate downwards, jamming the turret. Workers from a private company would set to work with cutters later in the day to free the turret, which was available again only from 1724. A second shell from the same salvo struck the barbette armour of turret II to starboard; it broke up, and the base of the shell ricocheted through several compartments, pushing in the armoured deck in section J and ending up close to the munitions trunk for turret V (starboard after 152mm). The First Officer, CC Quéré, was a casualty of this hit.

At 0810 the final 16in shell struck the quarterdeck just forward of the starboard catapult and went on to penetrate the 100mm inclined deck over the propeller shafts. It exploded in the liquid ballast compartment beneath the steering gear, and the nose cone and several fragments exited the hull, causing some flooding in the steering compartment.

Although *Jean Bart* had been severely battered by this bombardment, which lasted for some 35 minutes, the damage to the ship's fighting capabilities was not as great as the Americans thought. Only the first of the 16in shells had managed to penetrate the heavily-armoured citadel. Had the 152mm magazines been in use there would surely have been a magazine explosion which would have destroyed the after end of the ship, but in the event the magazines were empty and damage was limited to the holes in the armoured decks and bent and burnt-out bulkheads in the lower magazine.

Turret I, its four 380mm guns intact, was again service-able by late afternoon, and the 90mm HA battery had suffered only minor damage from masonry fragments from the jetty. The 90mm guns would be used against advancing enemy columns on the coastal roads the following day; with 16in and 8in ammunition severely depleted in the American ships[5] and fears that *Richelieu* might attempt to intervene, the port of Casablanca remained free from seaborne assault on 9 November.

It therefore came as something of a shock to the Americans when at 1141 on 10 November *Jean Bart* opened fire with her main guns at Admiral Hewitt's flagship *Augusta* when the latter approached to 16,000m. The second two-gun salvo fell close to the bow, the great orange shell splashes drenching the bridge and the upper decks. Between 1141 and 1151 *Jean Bart* fired no fewer than nine two-gun salvoes, with the last three straddling *Augusta*. The cruiser sped seaward to open the range, and Hewitt ordered the carrier *Ranger* to mount a dive-bombing attack on the French battleship. Nine SBD Dauntless armed with 1000lb bombs were to lead the attack, with eight Wildcats in support to strafe the AA batteries on the jetties. They arrived over the ship shortly before 1500.

Only two bombs from this attack struck the *Jean Bart*, but the devastation caused was of a different order to that of the smaller 500lb bombs of the first day. The first hit the forecastle near the capstan; it

---

[5] When *Massachusetts* ceased fire at 1103 on 8 November she had expended 60 per cent of her 16in shells. The situation was even worse for the two cruisers, which had been detached to engage the *2e Escadre Légère*; by early afternoon *Wichita* and *Tuscaloosa* had only 20 per cent of the their 8in ammunition remaining.

obliterated the capstan itself, lifted the forecastle deck and started a fire. There were large breaches in the hull above the main deck between frames 195 and 226 to starboard, and frames 217 and 224 to port.

The other bomb hit the quarterdeck just forward of the starboard catapult pivot and caused damage so extensive that the official enquiry was convinced that two bombs had hit in the same area. Although the 100mm inclined deck over the shafts was not breached, a large section of the hull plating above this level was completely destroyed (frames 25-55) and the upper deck was lifted and bent back over the quarterdeck; it looked to all intents and purposes as if the

The devastated quarterdeck of *Jean Bart* following the Dauntless attack. The bomb which struck close to the hangar ripped up the hull like a can-opener, the upper deck ending up draped over the base of the starboard catapult. (*USNHC*)

The damage caused to the bow of *Jean Bart* by the 1000lb bombs of US Navy Dauntless aircraft on the afternoon of 10 November 1942. Note the aerials for the DEM radar installation atop the tower. (*H Landais collection*)

Casablanca 8/9 November 1942
16in shell no.1

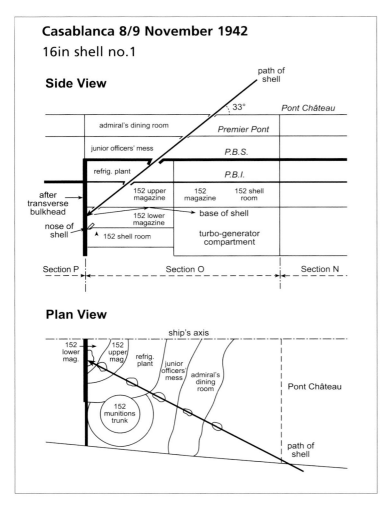

Side View

Plan View

Section Through Port Side of Turret I

Profile View

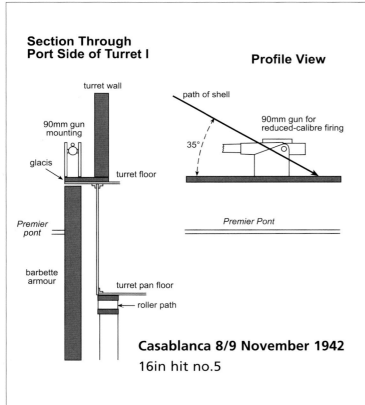

Casablanca 8/9 November 1942
16in hit no.5

Casablanca 8/9 November 1942
16in shell no.2

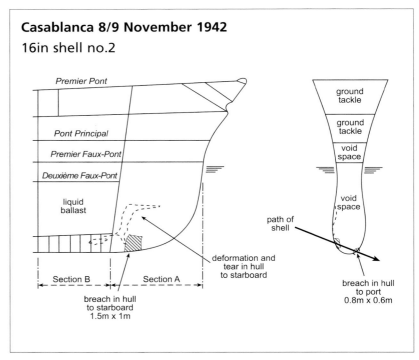

Casablanca 8/9 November 1942
16in hit no.6

Profile View of Path of Shell

Plan View of Path of Shell

Deformation of Armoured Deck (Section J)

From Side

From Above

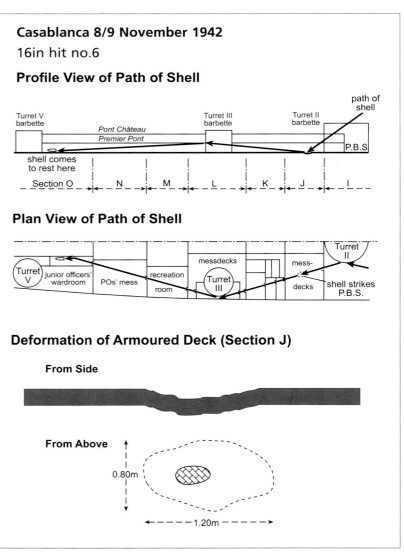

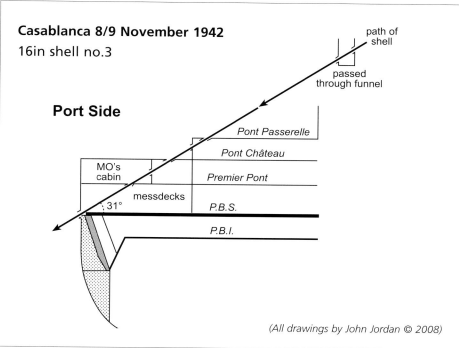

Casablanca 8/9 November 1942

16in shell no.3

Port Side

path of shell

passed through funnel

Pont Passerelle

Pont Château

MO's cabin

Premier Pont

messdecks

31°

P.B.S.

P.B.I.

(All drawings by John Jordan © 2008)

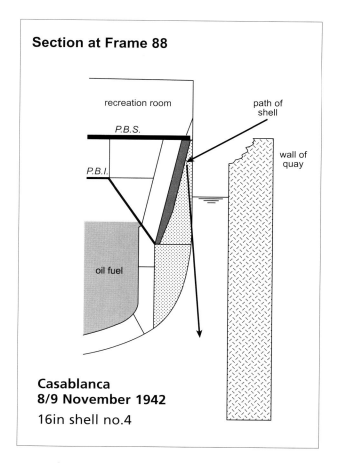

Section at Frame 88

recreation room

P.B.S.

path of shell

P.B.I.

wall of quay

oil fuel

**Casablanca
8/9 November 1942**

16in shell no.4

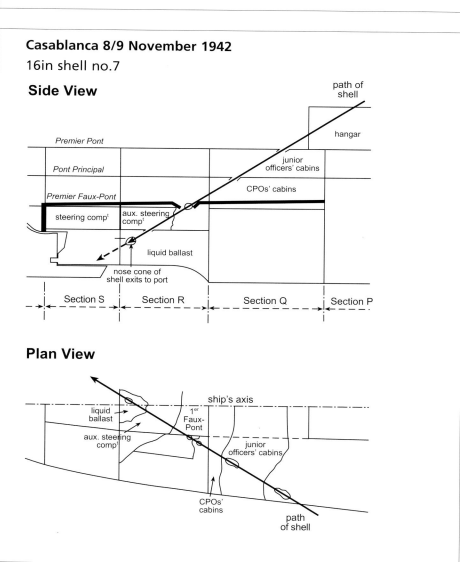

Casablanca 8/9 November 1942

16in shell no.7

Side View

path of shell

Premier Pont

hangar

Pont Principal

junior officers' cabins

Premier Faux-Pont

CPOs' cabins

steering comp[t]

aux. steering comp[t]

liquid ballast

nose cone of shell exits to port

Section S | Section R | Section Q | Section P

Plan View

ship's axis

liquid ballast

1[er] Faux-Pont

aux. steering comp[t]

junior officers' cabins

CPOs' cabins

path of shell

stern of the ship had been opened up with a giant can-opener. There were also deformations in the after part of the shelter deck abeam the hangar. Fires broke out, the after turbo-generator room was flooded, and smoke filled the after engine room which had to be evacuated.

The fires were eventually put out at 2000 with the aid of three tugs and firemen from the town, but extensive flooding meant that the ship's stern was now resting on the bottom. Two compartments in section B, and most of the compartments in sections O, P, Q, R, S and T were full of water. As with the *Richelieu* following the aerial torpedo hit at Dakar on 8 July 1940, water leaked into the cable tunnels, and from there into both engine rooms and the after boiler room. The turbo-generator room was flooded and the diesel generators forward had been badly damaged by the force of the bomb explosion, so power was available only from the emergency diesels.

By the end of 10 November 22 of *Jean Bart*'s crew had died, and a further 22 had been wounded. The ship had fired off twenty-five 380mm rounds over the three days. Damage to the hull outside the citadel was extensive and there was flooding fore and aft. However, the main guns and the 90mm HA guns were still operational, and could be worked provided the electrical supply could be restored.

THE QUESTION OF REFIT IN THE USA

Repairs on the ship began in earnest from 11 November with a focus on making her seaworthy. By 15 February the wing turbines were operational and manual steering had been restored. It was at about this time that the Naval General Staff envisaged sending the ship to the USA for repair and completion,

Jean Bart 1943: Project 1

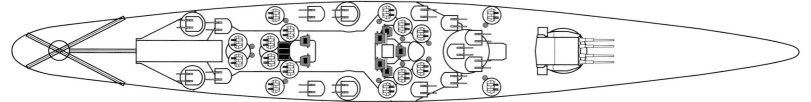

Jean Bart 1943: Project 2

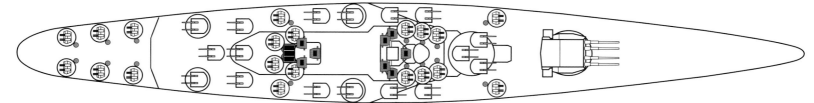

Key

   US Mk 37 director
with Mk 4 radar

●   US Mk 51 director

(Drawings by John Jordan © 2008)

and it fell to the head of the French naval mission, Admiral Fénard, to convince the Americans of the importance the Navy accorded to this. On 15 April Fénard gave a detailed report to the American Admiral Horne on the state of the ship. However, in a reply dated 1 May the US Navy stated that it was unable to complete the ship to the original plans, so a compromise was sought.

On 6 May the US Navy agreed to repair the steering motors to enable the ship to sail for the USA, and on 5 August the date of departure for the USA was provisionally fixed for September. Plans were drawn up by the Service Central des Constructions et Armes Navales (SCCAN) for completion of the ship to a simplified design which would make minimal technical demands on the American shipyards while securing a major increase in capabilities. There were two variants. Both involved the replacement of the 380mm guns in turret I – required to refit *Richelieu* – with 340mm guns from the old battleship *Lorraine* using cradles from the Métline Battery at Tunisia; maximum elevation was to be 35°.

The first variant (see drawings) envisaged modification of the aviation facilities to enable six aircraft (a mix of US Avenger or British Barracuda torpedo bombers, and US Hellcat or British Seafire fighters) to be embarked. There was to be a two-tier hangar for four aircraft with a lift, together with two British-style fixed catapults 35m long and capable of launching a fully-loaded aircraft at a speed of 140km/h. The incomplete turret II, the three triple 152mm turrets – which had never been fitted – and the twin 90mm mountings were to be replaced by no fewer than fifteen 5in/38 (127mm) Mk 32 twin mountings of US manufacture and sixteen 40mm Bofors quad mountings, backed up by some fifty single 20mm Oerlikons. Optical fire control for the main guns was to be provided by a 12-metre triplex OPL stereoscopic rangefinder in the main director on the forward tower, and by a 14-metre duplex OPL stereo RF in turret I.

Seven US Mk 37 directors each with Mk 4 fire control radar were to be provided for the new secondary battery: three atop the forward tower, two in the bridge wings, and two side-by-side atop the after tower.

In the second variant the aviation facilities disappeared altogether in favour of an even more substantial anti-aircraft battery. There were now to be seventeen 5in twin mountings in eight groups, with an additional Mk 37 director superimposed on the after tower, and twenty 40mm quads, of which six would be mounted on the quarterdeck. The rangefinder in the main director was to be an 8-metre base duplex OPL stereo model, but fire control arrangements were otherwise unchanged.

It was felt that the second variant had two advantages over the first: it required fewer structural modifications, and was therefore likely to be more acceptable to the Americans; and after AA arcs were considerably improved by removing the aviation facilities. However, on 18 August Horne informed Fénard that the French request had been refused. A proposal by Fénard that the ship be completed as a carrier was also subsequently rejected. The French NGS finally made a direct approach to Admiral King on 8 December, but in March 1944 it was informed that the US Navy was unwilling to divert resources to the ship.

While these talks were proceeding the French did everything possible to get *Jean Bart* in a fit condition to sail. On 15 September she ran sea trials off Casablanca escorted by the French fleet torpedo boats *Basque* and *Le Fortuné* and three US Navy destroyers, and achieved 22.5 knots despite a dirty and deformed hull. The French also explored the possibility of a docking at Gibraltar, but the workload of the latter was such that this did not prove possible. From the end of 1943 the battleship was used for training; *Jean Bart* would have to wait until the end of the war before a return to Brest offered the chance of permanent repairs and completion.

CHAPTER 7

CLEMENCEAU AND GASCOGNE:
Design, Characteristics and Fate

THE YEAR 1937 SAW A RAPIDLY DETERIORATING political situation in Europe. France was faced with the possibility of conflict with both Germany and Italy and was compelled to respond accordingly. *Dunkerque* and *Strasbourg* had been laid down to counter the German *Panzerschiffe*, and *Richelieu* and *Jean Bart* as a response to the new Italian battleships of the *Littorio* class. Since that time, German naval expansion had seen the redesign of the fourth and fifth *Panzerschiffe*, *Scharnhorst* and *Gneisenau*, with a view to matching *Dunkerque* and *Strasbourg*, followed by the laying down in late 1936 of two new battleships, *Bismarck* and *Tirpitz*, to match *Richelieu* and *Jean Bart*. As a result of the division of the French fleet between the Atlantic and the Mediterranean, the Marine Nationale had to respond to these new developments, and it was provisionally agreed that two new 380mm battleships of the *Richelieu* type would be needed to counter the new German ships. These ships, to be named *Clemenceau* and *Gascogne*, would be authorised on 2 May 1938 as part of *Tranche* 1938 *bis*.

Infrastructure remained a major issue. The Salou No. 4 building dock at Brest and the new Forme Caquot at St. Nazaire were the only facilities available. The Penhoët slipway at St. Nazaire, from which *Strasbourg* had been launched in December 1936 would be required for France's first modern aircraft carrier, *Joffre*, to be laid down on 26 November 1938. The Salou No. 4 dock at Brest would be vacated only when the hull of *Richelieu* was floated out – scheduled for late 1938 but in the event delayed until January 1939. *Jean Bart*, which had been laid down at St. Nazaire only in December 1936, was at least a year behind *Richelieu*, so it was unlikely that the second of the new ships could be laid down until the winter of 1939-40.

Given these inevitable delays in executing the programme, the Naval General Staff (NGS) wanted

further studies undertaken to determine whether the existing design could be improved upon. All of the latest foreign battleships, including the British *King George V* class, had main batteries distributed fore and aft. Moreover, the new German and Italian ships combined separate low-angle secondary batteries with a dedicated heavy AA battery: the *Scharnhorst* and *Bismarck* classes had 15cm LA guns in armoured turrets for the engagement of surface targets such as destroyers and light cruisers, with 10.5cm HA guns in open 'rapid-response' mountings above them; the *Littorio*s had 152mm LA guns in armoured triple turrets at the outer 'corners' of the ship, with single 90mm HA guns in light automatic mountings amidships abeam the funnels (see table). The French, together with the British and the Americans, had opted for dual-purpose secondary batteries in order to save weight, but trials with *Dunkerque* during late 1937 had revealed problems with the twin and quad 130mm DP mountings, and the NGS naturally wanted this arrangement reviewed.

On 2 December 1937, the Chief of Naval Staff (CEMG), Vice-Admiral Darlan, formally requested studies from the STCN for new battleships to be based on the *Richelieu* design but having the following characteristics:

– eight 380mm guns distributed as in *Richelieu* or in quadruple turrets fore and aft; or nine 380mm guns in three triple turrets, two forward and one aft;
– secondary armament to comprise: 152mm DP as in *Richelieu*; 130mm DP as in *Dunkerque*; or a mix of 152mm LA and 100mm DP (the latter being the new enclosed mounting *type aviso-dragueur* with 30mm plating on the gunhouse);
– aviation facilities to comprise a single catapult and two aircraft (no hangar);
– protection as *Richelieu*.

SECONDARY AND TERTIARY BATTERIES IN EUROPEAN BATTLESHIPS OF THE LATE 1930S

Dunkerque (France)	Littorio (Italy)	Scharnhorst (Germany)	Richelieu (France)	Bismarck (Germany)	King George V (UK)
16 x 130mm DP (3 x IV, 2 x II)	12 x 152mm LA (4 x III)	12 x 15cm LA (4 x II, 4 x I)	15 x 152mm DP (5 x III)	12 x 15cm LA (6 x II)	16 x 5.25in[1] DP (8 x II)
	12 x 90mm HA (12 x I)	14 x 10.5cm HA (7 x II)		16 x 10.5cm HA (8 x II)	

Note: [1] Equivalent to 134mm.

STCN STUDIES FOR 1938 *BIS* PROGRAMME

Study	Main Guns	Secondary Guns	Tertiary Guns	Aviation	Weight Gain/Loss	Change in ρ_a	Protected Length
Richelieu	2 x IV 380mm (2 fwd)	5 x III 152mm DP	None	2 catapults	None	None	131.45m
Project A1	"	5 x III 152mm DP (as *Richelieu*)	2 x II 100mm DP (forward)	(as *Richelieu*)	+140T	-0.04m	"
Project A2	"	4 x III 152mm DP (2 fwd, 2 aft)	6 x II 100mm DP (2 fwd, 4 aft)	"	+50T	-0.09m	"
Project A3	"	4 x III 152mm DP (2 fwd, 2 aft)	3 x IV 100mm DP (1 fwd, 2 aft)	"	None	-0.02m	"
Project A3 bis	"	4 x III 152mm DP (2 fwd, 2 aft)	6 x II 100mm DP (2 fwd, 4 aft)	"	None	-0.01m	"
Project B1	2 x IV 380mm (1 fwd, 1 aft)	5 x III 152mm DP (2 fwd, 3 aft)	None	2 catapults (amidships)	-115T	+0.34m	135.10m
Project B2	"	5 x IV 130mm DP (2 fwd, 3 aft)	None	2 catapults (amidships)	-325T	+0.36m	"
Project B3	"	3 x III 152mm DP (2 fwd, 1 aft)	8 x II 100mm DP (8 fwd)	2 catapults (aft)	-360T	+0.34m	"
Project B3 bis	"	3 x III 152mm DP (2 fwd, 1 aft)	8 x II 100mm DP (4 fwd, 4 aft)	1 catapult (amidships)	-385T	+0.34m	"
Project B3 ter	"	3 x III 152mm DP (2 fwd, 1 aft)	8 x II 100mm DP (4 fwd, 4 aft)	2 catapults (amidships)	-360T	+0.34m	"
Project C1	3 x III 380mm (2 fwd, 1 aft)	4 x III 152mm DP (1 fwd, 3 aft)		2 catapults (amidships)	+2265T	Not given	143.50m
Project C2	"	4 x IV 130mm DP (1 fwd, 3 aft)		2 catapults (amidships)	+2085T	Not given	"
Project C3	"	3 x III 152mm DP (1 fwd, 2 aft)	6 x II 100mm DP (6 aft)	2 catapults (amidships)	+2245T	+0.08	"

Note: T = long tons.
Source: STCN documents *Avant-Projets de 35 000TW*: S.T.1017 *Solutions A*, S.T.1019 *Solutions B*, S.T.1020 *Solutions C*.

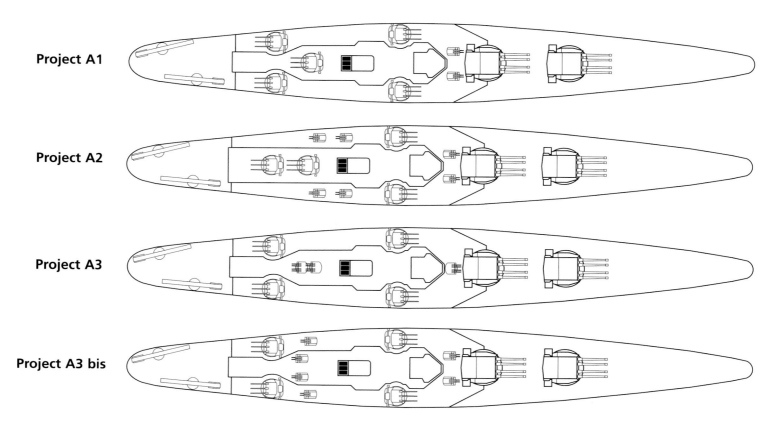

Project A1

Project A2

Project A3

Project A3 bis

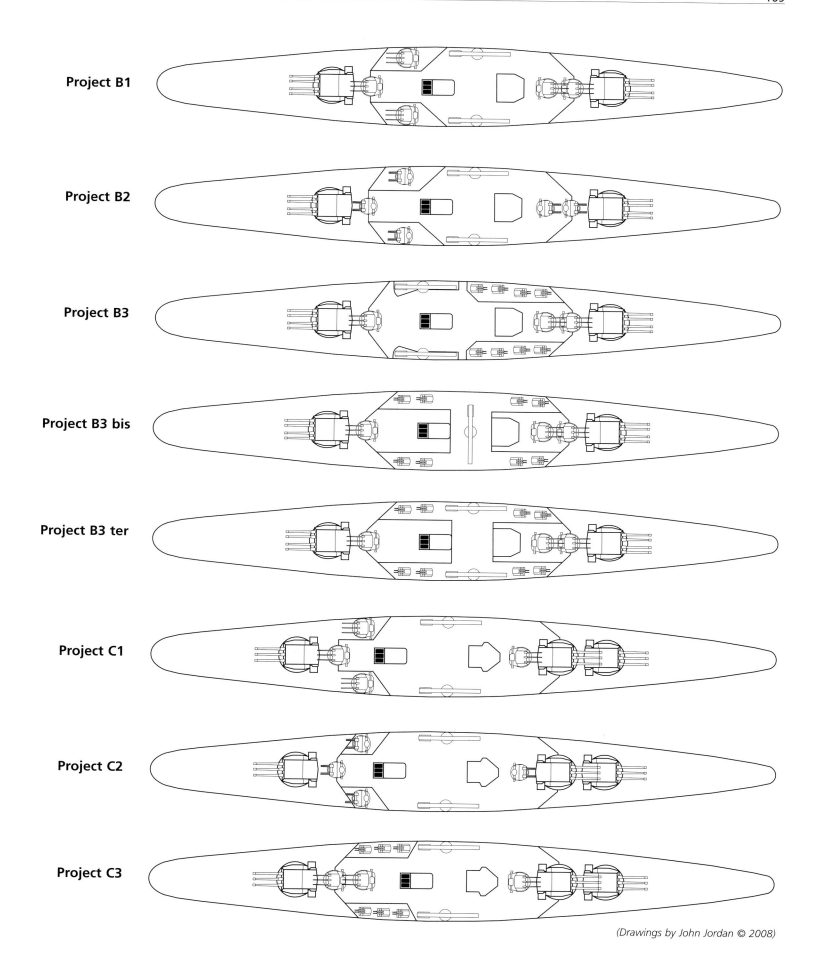

Project B1

Project B2

Project B3

Project B3 bis

Project B3 ter

Project C1

Project C2

Project C3

(Drawings by John Jordan © 2008)

The STCN responded with a series of studies designated 'A', 'B' and 'C', which corresponded to the three possible variations in the layout of the main armament. The numbered variants (A1, A2, etc.) reflected the possible arrangement of the secondary – and in some variants tertiary – batteries and the various options for aviation facilities. The key elements of these proposals are outlined in the accompanying table.

As with the early studies for *Richelieu*, the three-turret option approached 40,000 tons standard, and was therefore not submitted for consideration. The inability of the STCN to come up with a satisfactory three-turret design on 35,000 tons must have been a constant source of puzzlement to the French Naval Staff, who saw the new battleships as a natural response first to the three-turret Italian *Littorio*, and subsequently to the four-turret German *Bismarck*, both of which had a nominal standard displacement of 35,000 tons. What the EMG was not aware of at the time was that, even as designed, both the latter designs exceeded Washington Treaty limits by a large margin: the *Littorio* by 2500 tons, *Bismarck* by 4000 tons.[1]

Projects A and B were submitted to Admiral Darlan on 19 March 1938. He opted for A2 (*qv*) as the basis of the design for *Clemenceau*, and B3 *ter* as the basis for *Gascogne*.[2] The former would retain the all-forward main armament layout of *Richelieu*. She would also retain the two 152mm triple secondary guns amid-

---

[1] Moreover, both types emerged from the shipyards significantly overweight: the standard displacement of *Littorio* on completion was 40,500 tons, that of *Bismarck* around 41,000 tons.

[2] Note the extent to which Darlan had increased his powers as Chief of the Naval General Staff; in earlier years these schemes would have been presented to the NGS and the CSM for discussion of their merits before any decision was taken.

ships, but the wing turrets aft would be replaced by a second centreline mounting atop the hangar. This would release the necessary space and weight for four of the new 100mm DP automatic mountings abeam the after tower and the auxiliary director for the main guns. A further two 100mm mountings of the same type would be fitted forward, between turret II and the tower (as in Project A1); in order to accommodate the latter a reduction of 10 degrees in the after arcs of turret II had to be accepted. The 100mm DP mountings were to be complemented by six of the 37mm ACAD twin mountings. In order to compensate for the reduction in the length of the hangar resulting from fitting in a second centreline 152mm turret together with its ammunition trunk, the hangar was broadened to accommodate two aircraft side by side; there would therefore be no reduction in aviation capabilities, which remained as in *Richelieu* (two quarterdeck catapults, four aircraft).

Gascogne, however, represented a much more radical redesign. Relocating the second of the two quadruple 380mm turrets aft necessitated moving the catapults to the deck edge amidships, with a hangar for two aircraft at the base of the after tower divided by the funnel uptakes. Only three triple 152mm secondary turrets were retained – two forward, one aft – but these could now be located on the centreline, so there was no reduction in the number of 152mm guns which could fire on the broadside as compared with the five-turret *Richelieu*. The broadly symmetrical arrangement of the main and secondary guns resulted in a much-improved distribution for the eight 100mm DP mountings, with four groups of two at the 'corners' of the ship each with its own fire control director. Again these were to be complemented by six 37mm ACAD mountings.

When these proposals were presented for approval to the CSM the *Gascogne* redesign was particularly well received, and there was puzzlement regarding the retention of the *Richelieu* arrangement of the main and

Clemenceau (July 1939)

(Drawings by John Jordan © 2008)

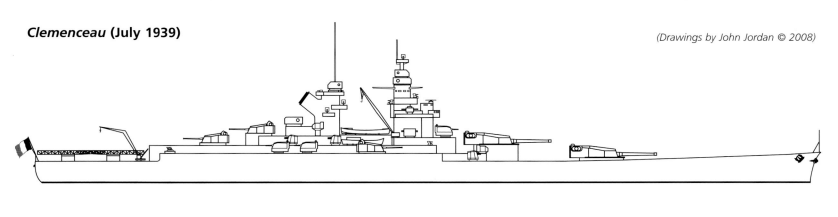

Gascogne (July 1939)

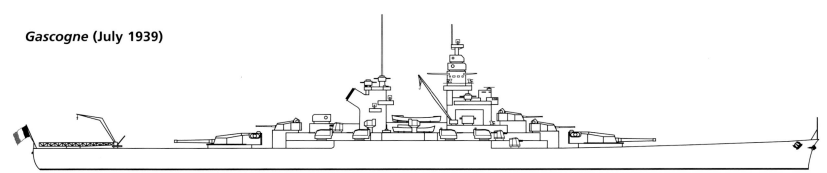

secondary batteries for *Clemenceau*. However, it was explained that the radical redesign of the internal spaces of the hull implicit in the division of the main battery in *Gascogne* would require a minimum of twelve months, and that it was still hoped to lay down the third battleship of the series before the end of the year following the floating out of *Richelieu*. Following the authorisation of *Tranche 1938 bis*, the order for *Clemenceau* was duly placed with Brest Naval Dockyard on 24 August. However, work on the *Gascogne* redesign, which had to compete with a number of other new projects, was to prove even more long drawn-out than anticipated. The first developed plan for the ship, showing two midships catapults and an aircraft hangar behind the forward tower, was presented to Darlan only on 22 December, and there followed a series of discussions on the siting of the aviation facilities and the AA guns. There was particular concern that the proposed central location of the catapults would inevitably push the 100mm and 37mm mountings closer to one another, thereby interfering with arcs, and closer to the main and secondary guns, from which they would inevitably suffer from blast effects. This led to a proposal to relocate the catapults to the quarterdeck (as on the *Littorios*), thereby freeing up the midships section for the anti-aircraft guns.

It had originally been envisaged that *Gascogne* would be laid down in August 1939.[3] In the event, the first materials for *Gascogne* would not be ordered until 16 June of that year, and the start date for construction was put back to June 1940.

CLEMENCEAU: DESIGN AND CHARACTERISTICS

The Project A series of STCN studies, of which *Clemenceau* was the second variant, was drawn up with a view to minimising the structural alterations that would need to be made to the hull, while at the same time maximising anti-aircraft capabilities by introducing an intermediate 100mm calibre between the 152mm dual-purpose guns and the 37mm ACAD light AA weapons.

The major structural modification as compared with *Richelieu* as originally conceived was the elimination of the two wing 152mm turrets aft in favour of a single

---

[3] This was presumably the date on which *Jean Bart* was scheduled to be moved from her construction dock to the fitting-out dock; due to slippage the latter event did not take place until March 1940.

GENERAL CHARACTERISTICS: *CLEMENCEAU* AS DESIGNED

Displacement

Standard	35,000 tons
Normal	40,750 tonnes
Full load	44,800 tonnes

Dimensions

Length pp	242.00m
Length oa	247.80m
Beam	33.08m
Draught (normal)	9.18m max.
Draught (full load)	9.92m max.

Machinery   As *Richelieu*

Armament

Main guns	Eight 380/45 Mle 1935 in two quadruple mountings Mle 1935
Secondary	Twelve 152/55 Mle 1930 in four triple DP mountings Mle 1936
HA guns	Twelve 100/45 Mle 1933 in six twin mountings Mle 1937
Light AA	Twelve 37/70 Mle 1935 ACAD in six twin mountings
	Thirty-six 13.2/76 Mle 1929 Hotchkiss MG in nine quad mountings[1]
Aircraft	Four Loire 130 seaplanes

Protection

Belt	320mm
Deck	150/170mm + 40mm
CT	340-160mm
380mm turrets	430mm-170mm
152mm turrets	116mm-60mm

Complement   1670

Note:
[1] There were also to have been two 37mm CAQ *zénithaux* abeam the hangar. This mounting was designed by Hotchkiss to counter dive-bombers; its development was suspended following the outbreak of war.

centreline mounting in the same longitudinal position (frame 54.45) but raised above the level of the hangar. There were considerable advantages in this arrangement: all six of the 152mm guns aft could fire on the broadside, for a total broadside of nine guns – the same figure as for *Richelieu* as designed, and three more guns than the latter could deploy on the broadside as completed; the upper deck abeam the after auxiliary director for the main guns was freed up for the mounting of four of the new 100mm DP enclosed mountings; and there was a weight saving of 230 tonnes on the fifth turret. However, there were also costs: the existing centreline 152mm mounting would have to be raised in order to superfire above the

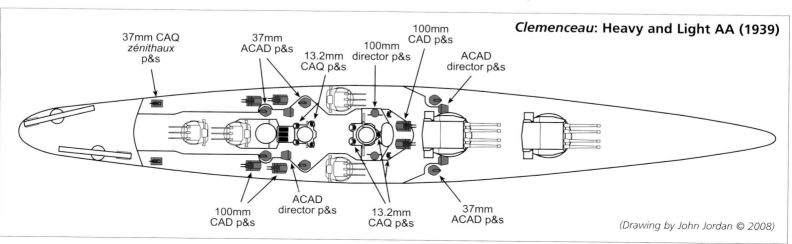

Clemenceau: Heavy and Light AA (1939)

37mm CAQ zénithaux p&s

37mm ACAD p&s

13.2mm CAQ p&s

100mm director p&s

100mm CAD p&s

ACAD director p&s

100mm CAD p&s

ACAD director p&s

13.2mm CAQ p&s

37mm ACAD p&s

(Drawing by John Jordan © 2008)

100mm/45 CAD Mle 1937

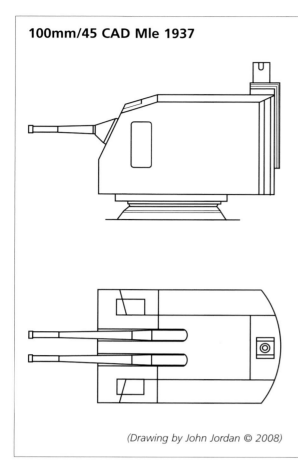

(Drawing by John Jordan © 2008)

The CAD Mle 1937 dual-purpose employed the 100mm Mle 1933 gun, developed from the Mle 1930 gun which, in the open Mle 1931 twin mounting, equipped the cruiser *Algérie* and was belatedly adopted for *Richelieu* (qv) in 1940. The Mle 1937 was a base-ring mounting and was fully enclosed in order to protect the guncrew from the elements and from the blast of other weapons. It was originally designed for the series of small minesweeping sloops of the *Elan* and *Chamois* classes (first ships: 1934 and 1935 Estimates respectively), and was generally referred to as *type aviso-dragueur*. It was also subsequently chosen as the main armament of the 1010-ton torpedo boats of the *Le Fier* class and as the secondary armament of the light cruisers of the *De Grasse* class (both 1937 Estimates).

The guns, which were in individual cradles, could elevate to 90 degrees. There were two pusher hoists per gun which turned with the mounting, one for anti-surface rounds, the other for time-fuzed AA rounds; loading was mechanical. The twin mounting in *Le Fier* would have weighed 29.8 tonnes and would have had a ball track diameter of 1.9 metres. In the modified Mle 1937 mounting planned for *Clemenceau* and *Gascogne* the power of the servo-motors was increased to cope with the greater weight of the gunhouse, which was to be have been protected by 30mm plating (the *Le Fier* model had 4mm plating only). Like *Richelieu*, these ships would probably have been provided with a handful of anti-surface rounds (perhaps ten per gun), but ammunition would have comprised predominantly time-fuzed anti-aircraft rounds and starshell.

CHARACTERISTICS

	100/45 Mle 1933
Gun Data	
Construction barrel	Monobloc autofretted
Breech mechanism	Horizontal sliding breech
Weight of gun	1500kg
Type of munitions	Fixed
Projectiles	OPf Mle 1928 (14.9kg)
	OEA Mle 1928 (13.5kg)
	OEcl. Mle 1928
Propellant	BM7 4kg
Complete round	
Weight	24.8kg
Dimensions	1.02m x 0.15m
Muzzle velocity	765m/s
Max. range	15,800m
Ceiling	10,000m
Mounting Data	
Mounting designation	CAD Mle 1937
Weight of mounting	N/A
Elevation of guns	-10°/+90°
Firing cycle (per gun)	16rpm per gun theoretical 10rpm practical

second, and both the after main director and the after tower structure (which incorporated the funnel uptakes) would have to be raised accordingly, for a substantial increase in topweight. Raising the height of the two after 152mm mountings by two to three metres[4] meant that the weight saving of fixed (barbette) armour by reducing the number of 152mm turrets from five to four was in part compensated by the additional hoops of 100mm armour required for the barbettes of the after turrets in *Clemenceau*; and the ammunition trunk for the new centreline mounting eliminated the forward part of the original hangar, which now had to be broadened at its after end in order to accommodate two aircraft side by side.

There were to be six of the new twin 100mm CAD enclosed mountings, disposed as in Project A2: two on a raised deckhouse between turret II and the forward tower, which was 'slimmed down' in order to accommodate them, giving the ship's superstructures an altogether lighter appearance; the remaining four on the shelter deck aft, abeam the auxiliary director for the main guns. The gunhouses were protected by 30mm plating to keep out shell splinters and to prevent blast damage from the firing of the main guns on after bearings and the secondary guns on forward bearings. Even so, the after arcs of turret II were to be restricted from 143 degrees on either beam to 139 degrees when the 100mm guns were firing.

For similar reasons the four after 37mm ACAD enclosed mountings were raised one deck level, and were now located on the superstructure deck above the 100mm guns, while the two forward mountings were located on the forecastle deck abeam the after end of the barbette for turret II. There was a proposal to supplement them with a new quad high-angle mounting under development by Hotchkiss to counter the dive-bomber and known as the 37mm *zénithaux*. Unfortunately little documentation concerning this unusual mounting has survived. The four barrels would have been aligned with the vertical axis and the mounting, which had a rectangular base, would have

The prototype 37mm ACAD mounting, designated Mle 1936, was trialled aboard the sloop *Amiens* from 1939 and was used, apparently successfully, during the evacuation of Dunkirk. The photo dates from 1942.

---

[4] The height of the mountings above the waterline was 11.88 metres and 13.68 metres respectively in *Richelieu*, and 14 metres and 16.68 metres in *Clemenceau*.

37mm Mle 1935 ACAD Air Defence System

The French 37mm ACAD mounting was one of the most advanced light AA guns in the world at the time of its conception in 1935. The earlier semi-automatic 37mm Mle 1925 CAS had proved to be a reliable weapon, but with a comparatively slow rate of fire (c.30rpm). Its successor, the Mle 1933 CAD, was essentially a twin-barrelled development of the Mle 1925, and its improved rate of fire was simply a function of having two barrels vs one barrel on the same mounting. Neither the Mle 1925 nor the Mle 1933 was judged to be an effective weapon against the modern high-performance aircraft which would enter service in the late 1930s, hence the development of the fully automatic Mle 1935 ACAD.

Requirements for the new gun were for a rapid rate of fire, a high-speed projectile to minimise 'dead time' (implying a high muzzle velocity), and a highly sensitive contact fuze for instant detonation with as powerful a burster as possible to ensure maximum damage to the aircraft. These demanding – and partially conflicting – requirements proved extremely difficult to meet.

Initial tests involved a 40mm gun from Bofors, 37mm weapons from Hotchkiss and Schneider, and a 37mm 'in-house' design from the *Artillerie Navale* at Ruelle. The latter appeared the most promising and was adopted by the Naval General Staff.

For a high sustained rate of fire it was important that the rapid fire possible with a single cartridge box (six rounds) be matched by a fast, reliable continuous replenishment system. This was realised in the Mle 1935 gun by inserting the cartridge box into the breech horizontally via the trunnion axis (see drawing) – a technique also used in the Schneider gun. Continuity was achieved by using a continuous-belt hoist capable of rapid replenishment located beneath the rotating mounting and emerging on either side of the guns. Loaders in the ammunition lobby transferred cartridge boxes from a ready-use rack to a feed which replenished the hoist. Loaders in the gunhouse then transferred the boxes to the horizontal feed for the breech.

A problem experienced with the older-model 37mm guns was that the flash and vibration of rapid firing made aiming using the on-mount sights difficult. For continuous fire against a fast-moving target the mounting ideally needed to be controlled remotely from a separate position in which the personnel were isolated from the effects of firing. This was achieved by locating a director equipped with a two-metre rangefinder close to the mounting and linking the two by a remote power control (RPC) system driven by Sautter-Harlé electric servo-motors. The director had a five-man crew: the control officer, a director layer, a director trainer, a cross-levelling operator and a rangetaker. The gun mounting itself was power-controlled in training but not in elevation. A complete 37mm ACAD installation, as exemplified in the accompanying drawing, comprised the twin mounting, its ammunition lobby and the director. In some shipboard installations, notably in the *Richelieu* class and its later half-sisters, a single director controlled two gun mountings.

The 37mm ACAD mounting was built at Ruelle. Very high rates of fire were achieved with the prototype single gun. In early trials at Sevran several bursts of 100 rounds were fired in under thirty-six seconds at zero elevation, and bursts of 150-170 were subsequently successfully fired at angles varying between zero elevation and 70 degrees at Gâvres during the late 1930s, including one continuous burst of 142 rounds. A prototype ACAD mounting, designated Mle 1936, was trialled aboard the sloop *Amiens* from 1939 and was used, apparently successfully, during the evacuation of Dunkirk.

However, the high muzzle velocity and the comparatively

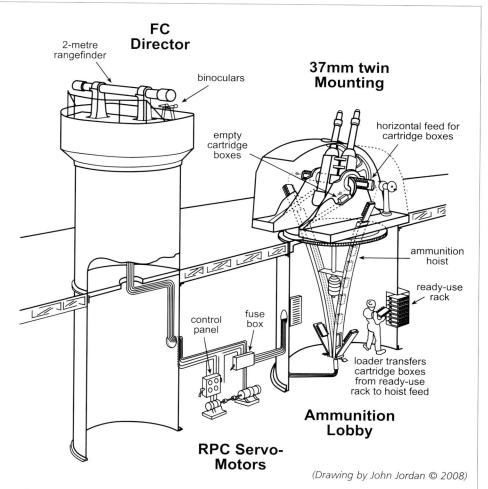

(Drawing by John Jordan © 2008)

heavy projectile combined to create a firing pressure of around 3000kg/cm^2, and this resulted in rapid barrel wear. The delay in the 37mm ACAD's entry into service was largely attributable to continuing efforts to resolve this problem. Even after extensive testing to find the metal with the best resistance, barrels still needed replacing after only 600 rounds – equivalent to three-four minutes of continuous fire. When development was halted experiments were underway with water-cooling of the barrel.

CHARACTERISTICS

	37/70 Mle 1935
Gun Data	
Weight of gun	1450kg
Ammunition type	Fixed
Projectiles	OEA Mle?? (0.816kg)
tracer	
Bursting charge	50g HMn
Complete round	
Weight	0.816kg
Dimensions	N/A
Muzzle velocity	825m/s
Max. range	8000m theoretical
Ceiling	–
Mounting Data	
Mounting designation	ACAD Mle 1936 (prototype)
Weight of mounting	8070kg
Elevation of guns	-10°/+85°
Firing cycle (per gun)	165-172rpm theoretical

Clemenceau: Protection

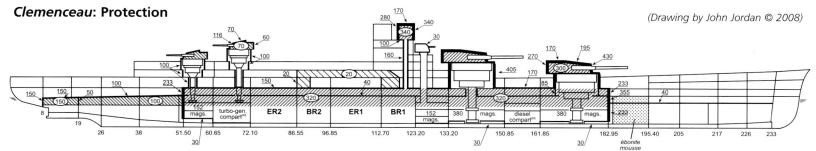

(Drawing by John Jordan © 2008)

Clemenceau: Directors on Fwd & After Towers

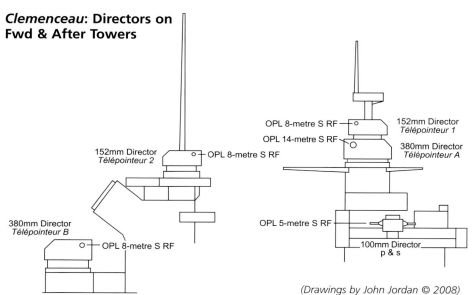

(Drawings by John Jordan © 2008)

Clemenceau: 152mm Turret Armour

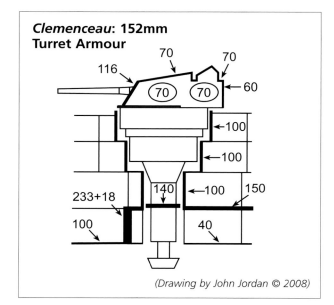

(Drawing by John Jordan © 2008)

been countersunk in the deck and loaded from beneath. The guns, which were normally pointed skywards, could be angled in both the horizontal and vertical planes to a maximum of 45 degrees to give arcs in the shape of an inverted pyramid. In *Clemenceau*, the 37mm *zénithaux* would have been mounted abeam the hangar to take advantage of the suppression of the 152mm wing turrets.

For close-range air defence the 13.2mm Hotchkiss quad MG was retained. Five were grouped around the

forward tower, and four were located atop the funnel structure as in *Richelieu*.

There were some modifications to the original director outfit to match the new armament. The 100mm guns were controlled by two new directors mounted in the bridge wings; each of these was fitted with a 5-metre OPL stereoscopic rangefinder. There were four directors for the 37mm guns: those for the forward group were mounted at the forward end of the shelter deck immediately above the corresponding mountings, while the

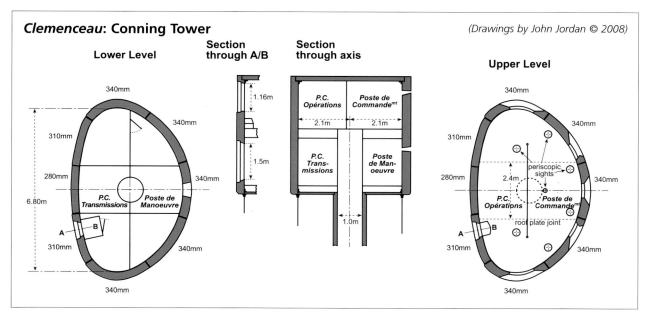

directors for the after group were mounted atop pedestals abeam the after tower. The largest of the three original directors for the 152mm guns (the centre director atop the forward tower) was suppressed as weight compensation. The remaining secondary directors were fitted with 8-metre OPL stereo rangefinders in place of the original 6-metre base models.

Modifications to the hull and its fittings were kept to a minimum; space in the existing magazines was simply reallocated to provide ammunition stowage for the new 100mm guns. The propulsion and electrical generating systems were identical in power and layout. The protection system was likewise identical to that of *Richelieu*, although there was some minor trimming in the thickness of the vertical armour. The original STCN studies had highlighted an overweight figure of 50 tons for the A2 design; a comparable saving was achieved by reducing the thickness of the main armour belt from 327mm to 320mm; the thickness of the rear plates on the main turrets was reduced from 270/260mm to 250mm, and that of the inclined face plates of the 152mm turrets from 130mm to 116mm. This would undoubtedly have proved insufficient; *Richelieu* as completed was several hundred tonnes overweight, and this would undoubtedly have been true of *Clemenceau*.

CONSTRUCTION AND FATE

Named after one of France's great political figures, *Clemenceau* was laid down in the Salou No. 4 dock at Brest on 17 January 1939, the same day that the hull of *Richelieu* was floated out and towed to the Laninon No. 9 dock for completion. With the situation in Europe fast deteriorating and a new sense of urgency in the dockyards, she was due to be launched in 1941 and to enter service before the end of 1943. Even this ambitious schedule would put her some three years behind the German *Bismarck*, which would complete during autumn 1940.

Work was suspended on 28 September 1939 due to the large-scale mobilisation of the industrial workforce, including many dockyard workers; priority was now to be given to the completion of *Richelieu*. Work on *Clemenceau* restarted on 6 December 1939, as workers drifted back during the 'phoney war', but slowly. When work was again halted on 10 June only 10 per cent of the hull (3600 tonnes) had been completed. With the *Wehrmacht* at the gates of Brest the building dock was flooded.

The Germans initially considered completing *Clemenceau* – she was designated *Schlachtschiff R* – but this was never a realistic possibility given the shortage of materials and an uncooperative French workforce. The incomplete hull was floated out to clear the dock during 1941 and moored in front of the submarine base. On 27 August 1944, it was sunk by Allied bombers. Put up for sale on 23 February 1948, it attracted no buyers. The hull was then refloated to clear the anchorage and towed to Poullic Al Lor during September 1948; however, it foundered and broke into two while under tow. The remains of *Clemenceau* were finally sold for scrap on 1 August 1951.

GASCOGNE: DESIGN AND CHARACTERISTICS

Gascogne was derived from STCN study B3 *ter*, and like the other variants of the 'B' series had a radically different layout of the main and secondary guns.

RANGEFINDERS: *CLEMENCEAU* AND *GASCOGNE*

Main armament

One OPL 14-metre S (triplex)	Lower director fwd tower
One OPL 8-metre S (duplex)	Director abaft after tower
Two OPL 14-metre S (duplex)	Turrets I and II

Secondary armament

Two/one OPL 8-metre S	Upper director fwd tower (both ships)
	Director after tower (*Clemenceau* only)
Four/three OPL 8-metre S	Turrets III, IV, V (both); VI (*Clemenceau* only)

100mm guns

Two/four OPL 5-metre S	Two sided directors fwd tower (both ships)
	Two directors atop after tower (*Gascogne* only)

Light AA

Four OPL 1-metre	Two atop fwd tower (Platform 8)
	Two after superstructure

General use

One SOM 3-metre	Atop conning tower (navigation/tactical)
Two SOM 4-metre S	Sides of lower bridge (night vision)

Notes:

OPL	*Optique de Précision Levallois-Perret*
SOM	*Société d'Optique et de Méchanique de Haute Précision*
S	Stereoscopic RF
C	Coincidence RF

Variants B1 and B2, which had a homogeneous secondary armament of 152mm and 130mm DP guns respectively, retained wing turrets, but the three B3 variants had all the main and secondary guns on the centreline. The division of the main armament fore and aft resulted in a more symmetrical layout which had two principal benefits: both the main and the secondary guns could fire on forward and after bearings, and locating all secondary guns fore and aft on the centreline freed up the sides of the ship for the heavy and light AA guns and their directors. There were costs to the new arrangement, however: the arrangement of the aviation facilities adopted successfully in *Dunkerque* and *Richelieu* was no longer possible due to the location of one of the two 380mm quad mountings on the quarterdeck; if the catapults and hangar were relocated amidships the AA gun mountings would inevitably be pushed into closer proximity to the main and secondary guns, where they would be subject to blast damage; and the more symmetrical layout could be achieved only by shifting the superstructures and machinery spaces farther forward, which meant that all internal spaces had to be redesigned and weights recalculated to maintain trim.

This heavy workload for the constructors of the STCN was further increased by the ongoing debate regarding the best way of accommodating the aviation facilities. The arrangement initially proposed, with trainable deck-edge catapults amidships and a hangar at the base of after tower, resulted in an extremely cramped layout which not only pushed the AA mountings in close proximity to one another and to the main and secondary guns, but made it difficult to accommodate the ship's boats. The *Littorio* solution of leaving both aircraft and catapults exposed to the elements on a cut-down quarterdeck did not appeal, and would have resulted in a halving of the air complement.

The solution eventually adopted was similar to that evolved for the latest generation of US battleships and cruisers – that of an internal hangar aft served by a lift which raised the aircraft to the quarterdeck for launch.

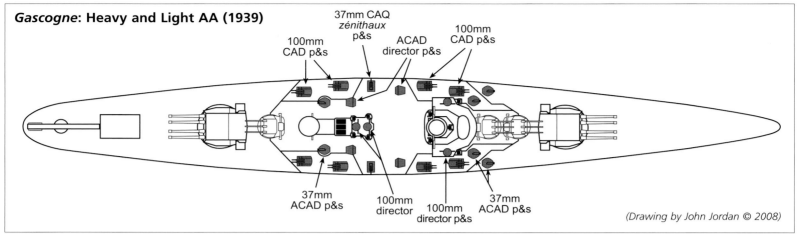

Gascogne: Heavy and Light AA (1939)

37mm CAQ *zénithaux* p&s

100mm CAD p&s

ACAD director p&s

100mm CAD p&s

37mm ACAD p&s

100mm director

100mm director p&s

37mm ACAD p&s

(Drawing by John Jordan © 2008)

Gascogne: Directors on Fwd & After Towers

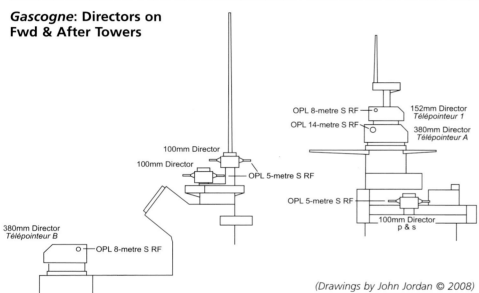

100mm Director

100mm Director

OPL 5-metre S RF

380mm Director *Télépointeur B*

OPL 8-metre S RF

OPL 8-metre S RF

OPL 14-metre S RF

152mm Director *Télépointeur 1*

380mm Director *Télépointeur A*

OPL 5-metre S RF

100mm Director p & s

(Drawings by John Jordan © 2008)

Gascogne: 152mm Turret Armour

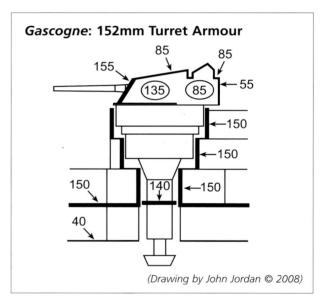

(Drawing by John Jordan © 2008)

The single catapult would have had its pedestal countersunk into the quarterdeck to reduce its profile – it was seated on the main deck – and alongside it to starboard was mounted a crane for aircraft recovery which could be stowed flat on the deck. Two reconnaissance aircraft with wings folded could be accommodated in line in the hangar, and a third could be stowed on rails on the port side of the quarterdeck (see drawing). Although the STCN note of 20 February 1939, which outlined the new arrangements, specified an elevator to raise the aircraft to the level of the catapult beam, as in earlier French battleships, the official plans make it clear that the lift itself could be raised above the level of the upper deck so that the aircraft could be winched directly onto the catapult.

The aircraft to be embarked was the SNCAC[5]/Farman NC 420 (see drawing). Adopted following a competition to replace the Loire 130 which was initiated in March 1937, the aircraft was to have had an endurance of six hours (later reduced to five in an effort to increase payload), and was to be capable of glide-bombing and of taking off in a 0.75 metre swell. Missions were to include reconnaissance, spotting, and the laying of smokescreens, although the latter capability was dropped from the specifications, again

---

[5] SNCAC = Société Nationale des Constructions Aéronautiques du Centre, a company created in 1937 by the nationalisation of Farman and Hanriot; there were factories at Billancourt, Bourges and Fourchambault.

Gascogne: Protection (July 1939)

(Drawing by John Jordan © 2008)

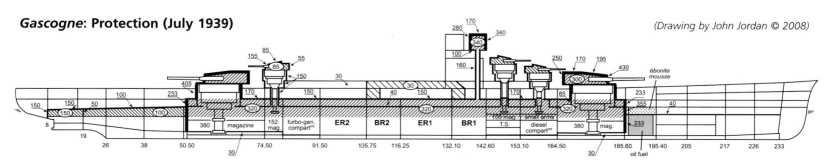

to save weight. Despite its unusual twin-engine config-uration the NC 420 had a width of only 4.75 metres with wings folded – the wings were hinged immediately outboard of the engines and folded back against the tail-plane. Overall dimensions and weight were compa-rable to the Loire 130.

The first prototype was almost complete in June 1940 but the Armistice then intervened, and although fifteen aircraft were to have been ordered as replace-ments for 'natural wastage' with the approval of the German Armistice Commission under the 1943-4 naval estimates, this ill-fated aircraft never flew. When finally completed in mid-1943 the single prototype had its controls disabled by the Italians to prevent it being flown to North Africa.

Relocating the aviation facilities to the stern enabled the AA guns to be moved closer to the centre of the ship and away from the main and secondary guns. The STCN note of 20 February specified the following changes:

– the forward group of 100mm CAD to be moved aft by 10 metres;
– the after pair of 100mm CAD to be moved forward by 2 metres, the remaining pair by 4 metres;
– the forward group of 37mm ACAD mountings, together with their directors, to be moved slightly aft, and the after group slightly forward, away from the heavy guns;
– the two 37mm CAQ *zénithaux* to be moved from their original quarterdeck location and to be relocated as far outboard as possible amidships in order to maximise overhead arcs – in this position they were nevertheless restricted to an inboard angle of 60

GENERAL CHARACTERISTICS: *GASCOGNE* AS DESIGNED

Displacement	
Standard	35,000 tons
Normal	40,567 tonnes
Full load	44,438 tonnes

Dimensions	
Length pp	As *Clemenceau*
Length oa	As *Clemenceau*
Beam	As *Clemenceau*
Draught (normal)	9.14m max.
Draught (full load)	9.82m max.

Machinery	As *Clemenceau*

Armament	
Main guns	Eight 380/45 Mle 1935 in two quadruple mountings Mle 1935
Secondary	Nine 152/55 Mle 1930 DP in three triple mountings Mle 1936
HA guns	Sixteen 100/45 Mle 1933 in eight twin mountings Mle 1937
Light AA	Twelve 37/70 Mle 1935 ACAD in six twin mountings
	Thirty-six 13.2/76 Mle 1929 Hotchkiss MG in nine quad mountings[1]
Aircraft	Three NC 420 seaplanes

Protection	
Belt	320mm
Deck	150/170mm + 40mm
CT	340-160mm
380mm turrets	430mm-170mm
152mm turrets	135mm-60mm

Complement	1670

Note:
[1] There were also to have been two 37mm CAQ *zénithaux*. In the original design, these were to have been mounted on the quarterdeck. When the aviation facilities were relocated to the stern they were moved to the superstructure deck amidships.

Gascogne: Superstructure

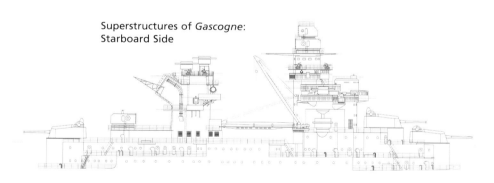

Superstructures of *Gascogne*: Starboard Side

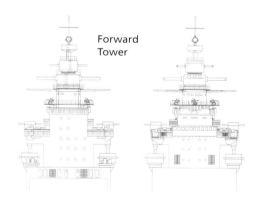

Forward Tower

Decks & Platforms: Forward Tower

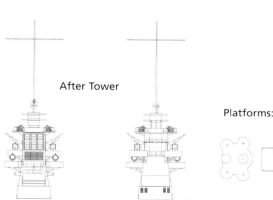

After Tower

Platforms: After Tower

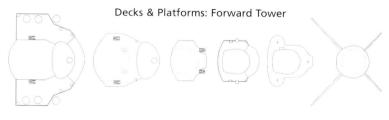

In 2007, the Austrian illustrator Harold Winkel presented to the Centre d'Archives de l'Armement, Châtellerault, a set of plans of *Gascogne* in her final form based on the surviving official documentation. These have now been accommodated in the archives. Harold's drawings of the superstructures of the ship are reproduced here.

(Drawings by Harold Winkel)

PROTECTION: COMPARISON BETWEEN *RICHELIEU*, *CLEMENCEAU* AND *GASCOGNE*

	Richelieu	Clemenceau	Gascogne (1939)
Vertical protection			
Main belt	330mm	320mm	320mm
Horizontal protection			
PBS over magazines	170mm	170mm	170mm
PBS over machinery	150mm	150mm	150mm
Conning tower			
Rear wall	280mm	310-280mm	310-280mm
Main turrets			
Turret rear	270mm (I)	250mm (I)	250mm (I)
	260mm (II)	250mm (II)	250mm (II)
Secondary turrets			
Turret face	130mm	116mm	155mm
Turret sides	70mm	70mm	135/85mm
Turret roof	70mm	70mm	85mm
Turret rear	60mm	60mm	55mm
Barbette	100mm	100mm	150mm
100mm mountings			
Gunhouses	–	30mm	30mm
Seatings	–	30mm	30mm

Note: The protection of *Clemenceau* and *Gascogne* was otherwise as *Richelieu*. The authors have been unable to confirm reports in some secondary sources that the thickness of the main armoured deck in *Gascogne* was subsequently reduced from 170mm to 150mm over the magazines and from 150mm to 140mm over the machinery spaces in order to save weight. An early STCN note, dated 5 March 1938, stated that preliminary weight calculations suggested that there would be a weight saving of about 350 tonnes over the *Richelieu* design, and recommended that this be used to strengthen the protection of the secondary turrets and the funnel uptakes.

degrees (compared with the designed 45 degrees) by the superstructures;

– the five 13.2mm CAQ around the forward tower to remain as in the original project, but the three mountings atop the tower now to be at the same level, on the roof of the Admiral's bridge.

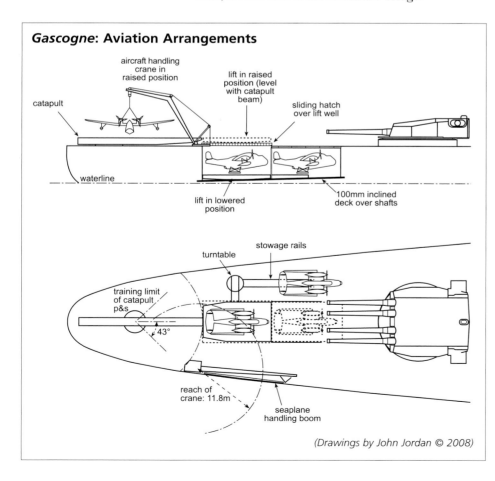

Gascogne: Aviation Arrangements

aircraft handling crane in raised position

lift in raised position (level with catapult beam)

catapult

sliding hatch over lift well

waterline

100mm inclined deck over shafts

lift in lowered position

stowage rails

turntable

training limit of catapult p&s

43°

reach of crane: 11.8m

seaplane handling boom

(Drawings by John Jordan © 2008)

The funnel was moved forward 3.7 metres, resulting in an increase of 7 degrees in training arcs on forward bearing for the auxiliary director for the main guns. The arcs of the two inner 152mm turrets were likewise increased, this time by 5 degrees. It was decided to suppress the auxiliary director for the 152mm guns, and to replace it with the two after directors for the 100mm guns, which would now be superimposed atop the tower to maximise all-round arcs in anti-aircraft fire. Whereas *Clemenceau* had only two side-mounted directors for the 100mm guns located in the bridge wings, *Gascogne* had one for each group of guns. Each of the four 100mm directors could provide fire control with RPC for its own group of two mountings, and fire control without RPC for the four mountings on that side of the ship.

The 152mm turrets were to be directed in the surface fire mode by the single director (equipped with an 8-metre rangefinder) atop the forward tower, but firing solutions for anti-aircraft fire were presumably to be provided by the directors for the 100mm guns. Night firing against surface targets was to be controlled, as in *Clemenceau*, by two directors equipped with OPL 4-metre rangefinders mounted port and starboard on the lower sides of the forward tower.

CHANGES TO PROTECTION

The need to accommodate all five of the main gun mountings on the centreline resulted in an increase in the length of the armoured citadel from 131.45 metres in *Richelieu* and her half-sister *Clemenceau* to 135.10 metres in *Gascogne*. The after transverse bulkhead was at frame 50.50 (compared with frame 51.50 in *Richelieu*) and the forward transverse bulkhead at frame 185.60 (frame 182.95 in *Richelieu*). This had the effect of shortening the relatively long and unprotected bow section by almost three metres. The 'filler' compartment immediately forward of the transverse bulkhead was compressed, and the broad central compartment below the level of the second platform

Gascogne: Deck Plans

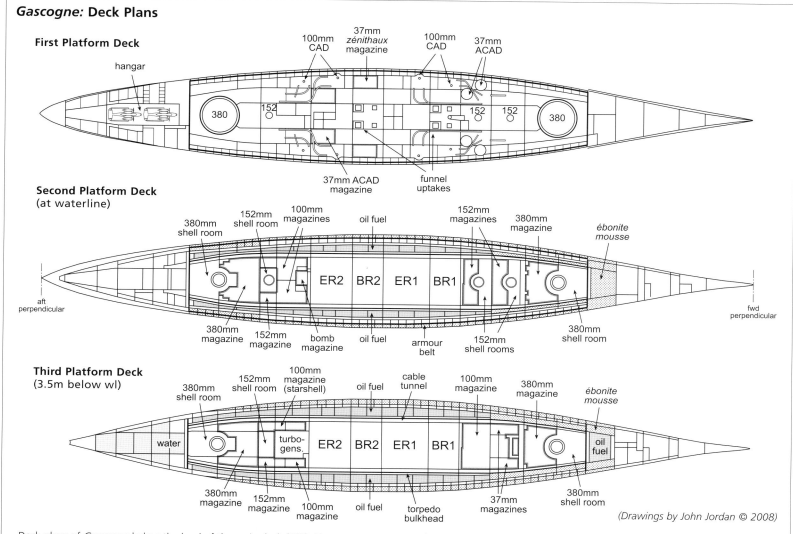

(Drawings by John Jordan © 2008)

Deck plans of *Gascogne* below the level of the main deck (PBS). The upper plan, based on S.T.1448 and dated 3 July 1939, shows the new hangar aft. The magazines for the after 37mm ACAD mountings and for the proposed 37mm *zénithaux* (both mounted at the level of the superstructure deck) are located on this level, immediately beneath the mountings themselves – in the original design the mountings would have been countersunk into the quarterdeck, with the magazine located centrally beneath the 100mm deck over the shafts. The pivots for the 100mm CAD mountings are marked, as are the cylindrical ammunition lobbies for the four forward 37mm ACAD guns. Note the conveyors used to transfer the 100mm fixed rounds and the 37mm ammunition boxes horizontally at this level from the hoists serving their respective magazines (third platform deck).

The other two deck plans, which are based on S.T.1358, show the layout of the machinery and the main magazines. The forward generator room is directly beneath the forward 37mm/small arms magazines on the third platform deck (shown here at 3.5 metres beneath the waterline), and the transmitting station directly beneath the 100mm magazine. The forward generator room is labelled 'turbo-dynamos' on some plans, suggesting the forward turbo-generators were relocated from the forward engine room, and that the diesel generators were distributed between the forward and after generator rooms – a logical arrangement given the 'symmetrical' layout of the main armament. Note that the space immediately forward of the forward transverse bulkhead is filled with *ébonite mousse* between the first and second platform decks, but is used for additional oil fuel bunkerage beneath this level (see also Protection plan).

deck became a fuel bunker (see protection and decks drawings). The *ébonite mousse* water-excluding compound continued to be used outboard of this compartment and in the central compartment above it, between the first and second platform decks at the level of the ship's waterline.

The reduction from four 152mm turrets in *Clemenceau* to three in *Gascogne* offered the opportunity of strengthening the protection of the secondary battery and the long, exposed funnel uptakes above the level of the main armoured deck. The initial protection plan, dated 18 July 1938, shows 190mm plating on the turret faces, 120mm on the roofs and 100mm on the sides; the plating on the barbettes, however,

which were now particularly exposed above the level of the upper deck by the superimposition of the turrets above the main battery, remained at 100mm. This was a clear weakness, and the modifications of February 1939 specified a reduced thickness of the plating on the turrets in favour of an increase to 150mm on the barbettes (see table). This was described in the STCN note as a 'rebalancing' exercise, but it was also pointed out that the revised thickness of the plating on the turrets – still an increase of 20 per cent over *Richelieu* – was the maximum possible without increasing the power of the converters and servo-motors. The plating on the funnel uptakes was also increased, from 20mm to 30mm.

FARMAN/SNCAC NC 420 SEAPLANE

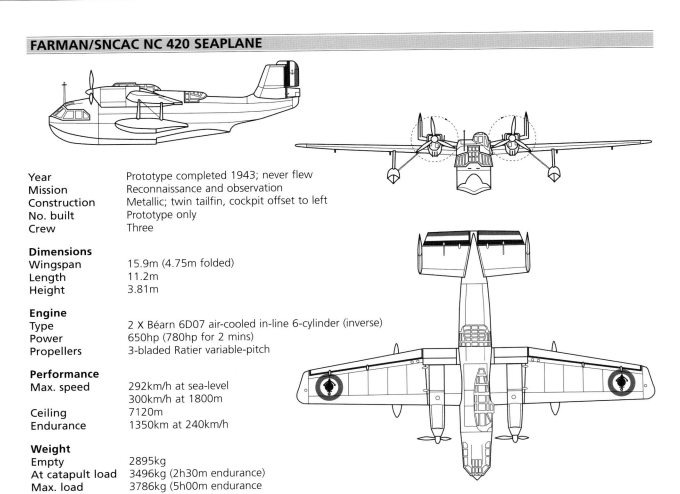

Year	Prototype completed 1943; never flew
Mission	Reconnaissance and observation
Construction	Metallic; twin tailfin, cockpit offset to left
No. built	Prototype only
Crew	Three

Dimensions

Wingspan	15.9m (4.75m folded)
Length	11.2m
Height	3.81m

Engine

Type	2 X Béarn 6D07 air-cooled in-line 6-cylinder (inverse)
Power	650hp (780hp for 2 mins)
Propellers	3-bladed Ratier variable-pitch

Performance

Max. speed	292km/h at sea-level
	300km/h at 1800m
Ceiling	7120m
Endurance	1350km at 240km/h

Weight

Empty	2895kg
At catapult load	3496kg (2h30m endurance)
Max. load	3786kg (5h00m endurance

Armament

Machine guns	Two Darne 7.5mm (one in nose, one dorsal aft-facing)
Bombs	Two 75kg G2 type

(Drawings by John Jordan © 2008)

CONSTRUCTION AND FATE

As a result of the protracted design process for *Gascogne*, which could not in any event be laid down until the transfer of the completed hull of *Jean Bart* to the fitting-out dock of the *Forme Caquot*, the orders for the armour plating and the main guns were not placed until June 1939. Production was then suspended, together with the construction of *Clemenceau*, on 28

September 1939. Work restarted only on 12 April of the following year, and by 1 June 1940 some 6 per cent of the construction materials had been supplied and it was envisaged that the ship would be laid down during the summer months. The ship was scheduled to be launched during spring 1942 with entry into service projected for June 1944. However, on 10 June 1940 work was halted and never resumed.

The name selected for the ship indicated that she was regarded by the Marine Nationale as the first of a new class, to be named not after famous Frenchmen but after the major provinces of France. The hand of Darlan can be seen in the naming of the first ship *Gascogne* after the province of Gascony where he was born. The previous *Gascogne*, one of five 'super-dreadnought' battleships of the *Normandie* class laid down 1913-14, was equally ill-fated; she was launched but never completed, and the hull was broken up in 1923-4.

BIGGER AND BETTER

The 1936 Treaty of London had retained the Washington displacement limit of 35,000 tons for capital ships while at the same time reducing maximum gun calibre to 14in (356mm). However, the US Navy had insisted on an 'escalator' clause that permitted a reversion to the original 16in gun calibre

BOATS

	Clemenceau	Gascogne
11-metre motor boats	three	two
10.8-metre motor boats	three	three
9-metre motor boats	two	two
11-metre motor launches	one	–
13-metre long boats	one	–
13-metre motor pinnace	two	two
7-metre whalers	two	–
5-metre dinghies	one	one
3-metre flat-bottom boats	two	two

Note: *Clemenceau* was to have an outfit of boats similar to that of *Richelieu* as designed (see p.121). The larger boats were stowed on crutches between the tower and the funnel. The remainder were grouped around the base of the tower on crutches or trolleys; those on trolleys could be moved aft on rails set into the deck to enable them to be handled by the two 22-tonne boat cranes, which were located at the after foot of the tower. *Gascogne* had a much-reduced complement of boats as compared with the earlier ships. The positioning of the forward 100mm and 37mm mountings around the base of the tower meant that all boats had to be carried between the towers.

in the event of failure of the Japanese to sign up to the new agreement, and this was duly invoked on 31 March 1937. Following a further exchange of notes during spring 1938, an Anglo-US-French protocol of 30 June 1938 declared that battleships up to 45,000 tons could now be built.

France was initially reluctant to take advantage of this new possibility given the limitations of existing infrastructure; construction of even the 250-metre, 35,000-ton *Richelieu* class had proved problematic. The French therefore declared that they would respect the 35,000-ton limit as long as the other European powers observed it. However, France's assumption that only the Pacific powers would really be interested in building 45,000-ton leviathans was upset by the German 'Z'-Plan, which was presented to Hitler by Admiral Raeder on 27 January 1939. The

centrepiece of the plan was the construction of six new battleships of 56,000 tons armed with 406mm (16in) guns, and the keels for the first two ships, allocated the temporary designations 'H' and 'J', were laid on 15 July at the Blohm & Voss shipyard in Hamburg and on 15 August at AG Weser, Bremen, respectively. Despite the secrecy with which the Germans attempted to enshroud the programme, news of the construction of 'H' and 'J' did not escape the French intelligence services, which estimated displacement (incorrectly) as 40,000 tons and gun calibre (correctly) as 406mm. Thus, on 20 July 1939, Darlan made a formal request for studies by the STCN of battleships with a displacement greater than 35,000 tons, and for studies by the Direction des Armes Navales (DAN) of guns of 400mm (15.75in), 406mm and 420mm (16.5in) calibre.

STCN STUDIES 1939-40

(USS *Iowa* included for comparison)

	Type 1	Type 2	Type 3	*Iowa* (USS)[1]
Displacement (standard)	40,000 tons	42,500 tons	45,000 tons	45,000 tons
Displacement (normal)	45,500 tonnes	47,800 tonnes	51,500 tonnes	–
Length (oa)	252m	256m	265m	270m
Beam	35m	35.5m	35.5m	33m
Armament				
Main	9 – 380mm (3 x III)	9 – 406mm (3 x III)	12 – 380mm (3 x IV)	9 – 406mm (3 x III)
Secondary	9 – 152mm DP (3 x III)	9 – 152mm DP (3 x III)	9 – 152mm DP (3 x III)	20 – 127mm DP (10 x II)
Tertiary	16 – 100mm DP (8 x II)	16 – 100mm DP (8 x II)	24 – 100mm DP (12 x II)	
Light AA	? – 37mm (? x II)	?? – 37mm (? x II)	?? – 37mm (? x II)	16 – 28mm (4 x IV)
	?? – 25mm (??x IV)[2]	?? – 25mm (??x IV)	?? – 25mm (??x IV)	
SHP	170,000	190,000	220,000	212,000
Speed	31 knots	31 knots	32 knots	32.5 knots
Protection				
Belt	330mm	330mm	350mm	305mm
PBS	170/180mm	170/180mm	170/180mm	150mm
PBI	40mm	40mm	40mm	20mm[3]

Notes:
[1] Characteristics as designed.
[2] There was to be a new quad 25mm MG from Hotchkiss to replace the lightweight 13.2mm mounting.
[3] The US ships also had 40mm plating on the upper deck to detonate bombs. Note also that armour in the US ship was distributed over a significantly larger area due to different design practices, hence the reduced thickness of the belt and main armoured deck.

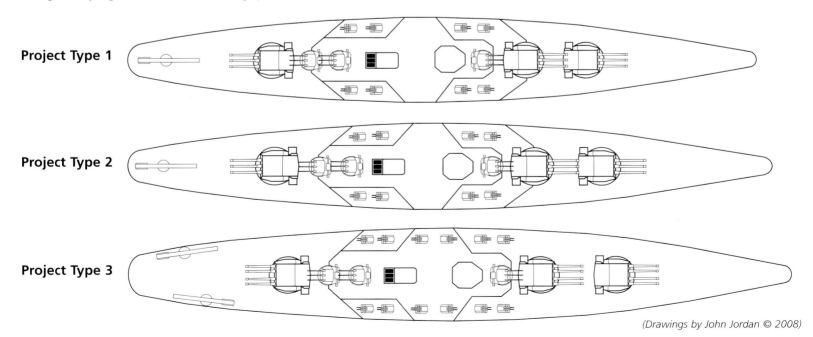

Project Type 1

Project Type 2

Project Type 3

(Drawings by John Jordan © 2008)

Project for the Development of the Laninon Docks

The decision to build a new generation of battleships of even greater size than the *Richelieu* class would have required a major programme of works to provide the necessary infrastructure for construction and maintenance. Fundamental to this programme was the development of the existing Laninon Docks at Brest. The plan, redrawn from recently discovered documents, shows the new building dock (to be designated Dock No. 10) to the north of the existing Dock No. 8, and the new graving dock between Dock No. 9 and the *Quai d'Armement*. The first stage in the construction of the building dock, which continued after the Armistice and which was well advanced by July 1941 (see accompanying photo), envisaged a dock 275 metres long and 58 metres wide capable of accommodating the new 40,000-ton battleships of the *Alsace* class, which had a designed length overall of 252 metres and a maximum beam of 35 metres. It would have been supported by a large metal-working shop. A second stage would have involved enlarging the dock to a maximum length of 360 metres. Labour, plant and funding implications meant that work on the graving dock would only commence after the completion of the building dock, which was scheduled for 1942. The graving dock had identical dimensions to the latter, and would need to be ready when the first of the new battleships completed, probably in 1946. The plan suggests that the existing Dock No. 9 would also have been lengthened to 300 metres – no easy task given that all the Laninon docks had to be hacked out of granite. Further expansion of the complex would see the redevelopment of The Point (La Pointe), at the mouth of the River Penfeld, which would accommodate two new slipways: one of c.220 metres capable of cruiser construction, and one of c.175 metres capable of building *contre-torpilleurs*.

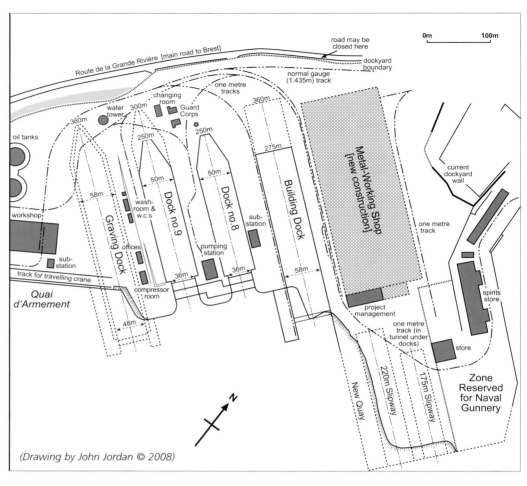

(Drawing by John Jordan © 2008)

Other infrastructure issues

A note dated 6 May 1940 by CA Michelier of the *Service Central des Travaux Maritimes* outlines some of the infrastructure issues facing the Navy in providing for the new generation of battleships, and reviews the progress made so far.

Michelier stated that the provision of suitably equipped berths and moorings was proceeding well. Berths for between two and four ships of 35,000 tons would shortly be available at Cherbourg, Brest, Casablanca and Toulon, while numerous moorings would be equipped at Brest (*Rade-Abri*, *Grande Rade*), Toulon (*Petite Rade* and the Milhaud finger piers), Bizerta (the Narrows and ultimately the lake), Mers el-Kebir (North Jetty), and eventually Dakar (Dakar-Gorée Jetty). Work was also planned or proceeding on berths capable of undertaking repairs: the *Quai de Laninon* and *Quai Richelieu* at Brest, the West Quay of the Vauban *Grands Bassins* at Toulon, and the Sidi-Abdallah Dockyard Basin at Bizerta. Some of the current moorings (particularly those at Brest and Cherbourg) had a depth of only 11 metres, and there were legitimate concerns that a 35,000-ton battleship of the *Richelieu* class with torpedo or mine damage could prove difficult to dock given that draught at deep load in the undamaged condition was estimated at 10.75 metres (for the 40,000-ton ships this would rise to more than 11 metres). Berths and moorings would therefore have to be dredged to a new standard depth of 12 metres.

The main requirement, and one which would be costly in terms of investment and labour, was for graving docks. At present there were only six naval (plus one commercial) docks capable of accommodating a 35,000-ton battleship (see accompanying table), and the projected 40,000-ton ships would require larger docks sufficiently wide for a beam of 35 metres – ideally with at least two metres clearance on either side at the entrance. Of the naval docks, only the Vauban *Grands Bassins* at Toulon and the new graving dock planned for Brest would have the necessary dimensions. The enlargement of some of the existing docks would need to be considered – the *Forme du Homet* at Cherbourg, the two Laninon docks at Brest, and No. 2 Dock at Bizerta were the primary candidates – but it was not yet clear whether this was technically feasible. In particular there were concerns as to whether No. 2 Dock at Bizerta had the necessary structural strength to accommodate a ship of the *Richelieu* class.

Other concerns focused on the provision of tugs and heavy lift machinery. A large number of sea-going and harbour tugs of 2000hp, 1000hp and 600hp were to have been ordered under the 1937-41 Estimates, but completion of the first two batches was being delayed because of bottlenecks in the production of machinery, and because of these delays the 1940 orders had proved impossible to place with French shipyards. Serious consideration had even been given to ordering tugs from Italian yards. Shipyards in the Netherlands were also considered, but the Dutch government had placed restrictions on sales to combatants.

The only heavy-lift floating crane currently in service was the 250-tonne model at Brest which had been acquired from Germany as reparations after the First World War. A similar crane was to have been ordered for Toulon under the 1940 Estimates, but again it proved impossible to order in France. Talks were currently proceeding on the purchase of a 200-tonne crane from the Port of Le Havre, to be based initially at Toulon and subsequently at Mers el-Kebir. Toulon Dockyard had also received instructions to refurbish the 'Atlas' floating crane belonging to Forges & Chantiers de la Méditerranée, La Seyne, to restore its original 170-tonne capacity – necessary to lift the 380mm gun installed in the new 35,000-ton battleships. Finally, a floating crane with a capacity of 150 tonnes had been ordered for Cherbourg under the 1938 Estimates and was due for delivery at the end of 1941.

Rear-Admiral Michelier's pessimistic conclusion to this note was that the current programme to provide the necessary infrastructure for the new battleships was inadequate, and that it would be extremely difficult to remedy this within the foreseeable future.

CHARACTERISTICS OF EXISTING GRAVING DOCKS

		Length		Breadth		Depth
		Upper	Lower	Upper	Lower	
Le Havre	No. 7 Dock	319m	313m	38m		-8m
Cherbourg	Le Homet	249m	235m	36m		-8m
Brest	Laninon Nos 8 and 9	250m		36m		-8m
Toulon	Vauban 1-2, 3-4	408m[1]		40.6m	36m	-12m
Bizerta	No. 2 Dock	254m	250m	40.6m	36m	-12m

Note:
[1] The Vauban docks were double-ended, with a movable watertight central caisson which divided each dock into two. The maximum length permitted by the 'stops' was currently 250 metres, but this could have been modified to allow a longer ship to be accommodated.

Overall dimensions of *Richelieu*
Length oa: 247.5m
Beam: 33.1m
Draught: 10.2m (normal)
10.75m (deep load)

Source: Note 838 EMG4, dated 6 May 1940.

The Laninon Docks at Brest in July 1941, under the German occupation. The ship in Dock No. 9 is the fast battleship *Gneisenau*; her sister *Scharnhorst* is moored at the *Quai d'Armement* at the top of the picture. At lower right the new 360-metre building dock (No. 10) has been partially excavated.

If the Marine Nationale were to embark on the construction of such ships, serious infrastructure problems would have to be addressed. At present the only facilities available for capital ship construction were:

- the Salou No. 4 building dock at Brest:
  200 metres x 40 metres
- the *Forme Caquot* at St. Nazaire:
  300 metres x 40 metres
- the Penhoët No .1 slipway at St. Nazaire

The Salou No. 4 dock at Brest was incapable of building a battleship larger than the current 35,000-ton series. Even the relatively small *Dunkerque* had to be built minus 17 metres of bow, while the hulls of *Richelieu* and *Clemenceau* were built minus both bow and stern; these had to be attached in the Laninon No. 9 graving dock before fitting out. The Penhoët No. 1 slipway had previously launched both *Strasbourg* and the liner *Normandie*. The latter had an overall length of 313.6 metres and a beam of 36 metres. However, the slipway was currently occupied by the keel of the new carrier *Joffre* (18,000 tons, length 236 metres oa, beam 24.6 metres), and was earmarked for the building of the second ship of the class, *Painlevé*, following the launch of *Joffre* in early 1941.

The situation with regard to graving docks, required for the maintenance of the new battleships, was little better despite the major works undertaken in the naval dockyards since 1911. Naval docks currently capable of accommodating the hull of a modern battleship were as follows: Le Homet, Cherbourg; Laninon docks Nos 8 and 9, Brest; the Vauban *Grands Bassins*, Toulon; and Dock No. 2 at Sidi-Abdallah, Bizerta. Dock No. 7 at the commercial port of Le Havre could also be used in an emergency (see table for dimensions).

The length overall of *Richelieu* and her near-sisters was 248 metres, just below the 250-metre figure which was regarded as the maximum for the six existing naval graving docks. However, a fast battle-ship in excess of 35,000 tons standard would have a larger hull, and given that the existing graving docks were barely sufficient to maintain the current fleet this implied a further massive investment in infra-structure. Of the existing building ways and docks only the Penhoët No. 1 slipway and the *Forme Caquot* at St. Nazaire would be capable of building the larger ship; the former would be available only following the launch of *Joffre* in 1941, the latter with the move of *Gascogne* to the fitting-out dock in 1942. In July 1939, Darlan therefore took the decision to proceed with the construction of a new building dock 310 metres x 42 metres[6] at Brest Naval Dockyard, close to the existing Laninon graving docks, to be completed during 1942. A second dock of similar dimensions was to be built to serve as a graving dock, with work beginning following the completion of the building dock (see plan).

During late 1939, the STCN drew up studies for ships of 40,000 tons, 42,500 tons and 45,000 tons standard displacement. All were essentially develop-ments of the 'C' series of 1937-8, with two main

---

[6] The length of both the new docks would subsequently be increased to 360 metres (see plan and caption).

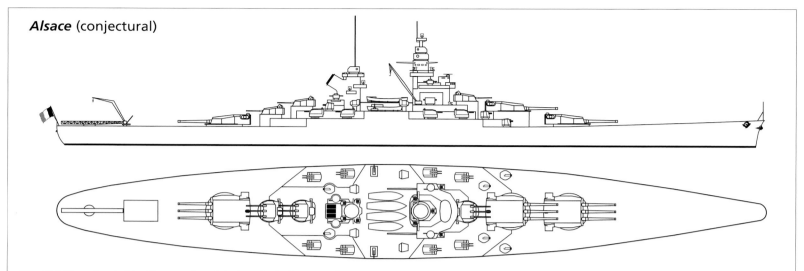

Alsace (conjectural)

The 40,000-ton battleship *Alsace* as she might have looked on completion. Essentially an enlarged *Gascogne* with three triple 380mm turrets, she would have had two of the three triple 152mm secondary turrets superfiring above the after main turret and the third firing above the two main turrets forward. The tertiary battery of sixteen 100mm DP guns in twin mountings would have been disposed as in *Gascogne*, and the aviation arrangements would undoubtedly have been similar, with a hangar beneath the quarterdeck and a single catapult.

The relatively short space between the funnel and the after 152mm turrets would probably have led to the auxiliary director (serving both the main and secondary guns) being relocated atop the tower, with the directors for the after 100mm guns being sided immediately abaft the funnel. The light AA weapons would have been located on the superstructure deck (37mm) and the towers (25mm).

(Drawing by John Jordan © 2008)

turrets forward and one aft and nine 152mm secondary guns in triple centreline turrets. However, following experience with the detailed design of *Gascogne*, the aviation facilities were moved to the quarterdeck to permit a satisfactory arrangement of the 100mm DP tertiary battery amidships (see drawings and table for details).

Type No. 1 was a slightly enlarged C3 (the original C3 had a standard displacement of 37,425 tons), with four metres additional length and two metres extra beam. There were nine 380mm in triple turrets, with one triple 152mm turret forward and two aft. The 100mm were disposed symmetrically as in *Gascogne*, and as in the latter there was a single centreline catapult on the quarterdeck. Protection was slightly increased over the *Richelieu* class, the most notable difference being a main armoured deck of 170mm over the machinery and 180mm over the magazines. There was a cost of an extra 15,000shp and a loss of one knot in maximum speed for the larger hull.

The second project was essentially Type No. 1 scaled up to accommodate 406mm guns. The cost of the larger hull was a further 20,000shp to provide a maximum speed of 31 knots.

Type No. 3, which can be considered the French attempt at a 'super-battleship', reverted to the 380mm gun but in three quadruple turrets, with a corresponding increase in the heavy AA battery to twenty-four guns. A marked increase in length to 265m permitted the fitting of two catapults, but the design was characterised by 'quantitative' rather than qualitative improvements.

The choice of the Naval General Staff was relatively straightforward. The 406mm calibre had a number of disadvantages: it introduced a fourth gun calibre to the battle fleet – the other major fleets all had only

two;[7] and the prolonged development of the new gun would inevitably create delays in the programme. Type No. 3, although attractive because it outclassed almost all (known) current foreign construction, was regarded as a step too far in terms of its size and impact on current French infrastructure. Type No. 1, on the other hand, was a well-balanced design which used existing weaponry and which could be accommodated with relatively minor adjustments to current infrastructure.

Two battleships of 40,000 tons were duly authorised on 1 April 1940. The first was to be laid down on the Penhoët No. 1 slipway following the launch of the carrier *Joffre* in 1941;[8] the second in the new building dock at Brest Naval Dockyard before the end of 1942. All materials for their construction were to have been ordered in mid-1940, and an EMG note of 15 May 1940 proposed two names from *Alsace, Normandie, Flandre* and *Bourgogne*, to be chosen by the Navy Minister. These plans were to come to nothing when the French Army collapsed in June 1940, and the latter month effectively marked the end of the French battleship programme, which had begun with the laying down of *Dunkerque* in December 1932.

---

[7] The US Navy and the IJN 14in and 16in – though the Japanese would shortly add the 46cm (18.1in) calibre; the Italians the 320mm (12.6in) and 381mm (15in); and the Germans the 28cm (11in) and 38cm (15in) calibres. The Royal Navy had the 15in and 16in, but had been compelled to move to 14in in the *King George V* class for political reasons.

[8] This, however, raises the question of where the second carrier, *Painlevé*, would have been built. For the Marine Nationale, the battleship clearly had priority over the carrier.

CHAPTER 8

RICHELIEU: 1943-1956

THE PERIOD 1943-5 WAS ONE OF INTENSIVE activity for *Richelieu* following the relatively quiet two years at Dakar that preceded it. It would see the complete refurbishment and modernisation of the ship in the United States, followed by service with the Royal Navy, first in the North Atlantic, and then in two campaigns in the Indian Ocean. The latter part of 1945 would see *Richelieu* at Saigon as part of an operation to re-establish control in the former French colony of Indochina.

The US Navy had agreed to the modernisation of *Richelieu* in the Brooklyn Navy Yard, largely in response to intensive pressure both from the Free French authorities and from the British. For the Free French, the repair and modernisation of *Richelieu* was a matter of prestige. *Dunkerque* and *Strasbourg* had been scuttled at Toulon and the completion of *Jean Bart* would present problems because of the technical difficulties involved; *Richelieu* was France's only surviving modern battleship, and was to become the dominant symbol of the new French Navy.

Churchill had long desired to see this powerful French unit either as a part of, or fighting alongside the Royal Navy. In early 1943, the Royal Navy continued to be stretched in the various theatres. Despite Hitler's fury following the inconclusive attack by *Lützow* and *Admiral Hipper* against Convoy JW51B in December 1942 and the subsequent repercussions for the German surface fleet, the *Kriegsmarine* maintained a substantial force of major units in Norway, including the modern battleships *Tirpitz* and *Scharnhorst*. In the Mediterranean, the *Regia Marina* had recently completely a third modern battleship, *Roma*, to complement *Littorio*, *Vittorio Veneto* and its three older but reconstructed battleships. Following the loss of *Prince of Wales* to Japanese aircraft off Malaya in December 1941, the Royal Navy had only four modern battleships with which to oppose the German and Italian ships. The construction of the *Lion* class had been abandoned and there was no immediate prospect of reinforcements from British shipyards. A modernised *Richelieu* would therefore be a valuable addition to the British battle fleet, and it was planned to deploy her initially to the Mediterranean, where she would join *King George V* and *Howe*, despatched there in May 1943 to support the landings in Sicily.

The US Navy was less enthusiastic. Reconstruction of a ship of this size was costly in terms of resources and shipyard labour. Meanwhile, a new generation of US Navy battleships was rolling off the production line:

the two *North Carolina*s in 1941, the four *South Dakota*s in 1942, and the first two units of the *Iowa* class in early 1943. The course taken by the Pacific War had effectively relegated the new battleships to the role of AA platforms, and the new priority was aircraft carriers and their cruiser/destroyer escorts. In the circumstances, the US Navy had been happy to loan one or more of its most modern battleships to the British Home Fleet during 1942-3.[1]

There were also 'political' issues. The US Navy, which had been happy to share its latest technology with the Royal Navy because of the generosity of the latter in this respect during the period 1940-1, was less happy about according this concession to the French. As a result, *Richelieu* would be fitted with the latest AA weaponry, but the models of surveillance radar fitted were those standard on small surface escorts of destroyer size and below, and the US Navy refused point blank to release gunnery fire control radars as 'too sensitive'. Thus, when she finally emerged from refit in late August 1943, *Richelieu* could steam and fight, and could defend herself against hostile air attacks. However, she could detect aerial attacks at only relatively short ranges and was dependent on her British consorts for long-range air warning. If battle were engaged with hostile surface units she would continue to rely on traditional optical fire control methods, which would be a particular problem in the conditions of poor visibility prevailing in northern waters. These limitations would have to be remedied over time by the British, who despite their more limited manufacturing capacity were anxious to bring *Richelieu* up to the level of their own modern units.

As the war proceeded, other, more fundamental political issues would come into play. The Americans had never been particularly enamoured of de Gaulle and his Free French associates, preferring to deal with a 'legitimate' France liberated from the German yoke rather than this group of rebels and mavericks, many of whom had been condemned to death as traitors in their absence. However, there were also broader issues that reflected traditional American interests and beliefs. By mid-late 1944, the outcome of the twin-track wars in Europe and the Pacific was no longer in

---

[1] USS *Washington* served with the British Home Fleet from March to July 1942; *South Dakota* and *Alabama* would be attached to the Home Fleet from April to August 1943.

doubt and the three major world powers, Britain, the Soviet Union and the United States, were already turning their attention to the postwar world. There were many Americans who wanted the European imperialists out of the Pacific altogether, seeing the Japanese conquests as an opportunity to liberate the peoples of Malaya, Indochina and the East Indies from all foreign control, and in the process to realise the American dream of the Pacific rim as one vast free-trade zone open to US manufactured goods. Hence the fierce opposition from the US Admiral King and others to the formation of a British Pacific Fleet, and Churchill's equally fierce determination that Britain should again become a Pacific power with legitimate economic and political interests in the region. The United States would be equally obstructive towards French attempts to regain a foothold in the Pacific by reasserting control over their key colony of Indochina. This embryonic power struggle between the Allied nations would have an impact on the deployment of *Richelieu* during 1944-5.

MODERNISATION IN THE UNITED STATES

Work on *Richelieu* at the Brooklyn Navy Yard began on 24 February 1943. Workers swarmed over her hull, decks and superstructures; three teams of 2000 workers would be operating in three shifts, twenty-four hours a day, seven days a week, for the next five months. The level of activity was such that virtually the entire ship's company was disembarked for the duration and housed in nearby barracks.

The hull was scraped and sanded. It was found to be in remarkably good condition considering that the ship had gone more than two and a half years in tropical waters without docking. Only a few of the thinner 10mm hull plates were found to be pitted and eroded, and were reinforced by welding new plates over them. The lower row of scuttles, which following the ship's modernisation would be even closer to the water due to an increase in displacement, was blanked off.

Sections O, P and Q, which had suffered the worst effects of the torpedo hit in July 1940, were completely stripped out. The concrete was broken up and the plates deformed by the explosion cut away over a length of 34 metres. The starboard shaft brackets were straightened, but it was found that the badly buckled inner shaft was irreparable, and a replacement had to be ordered from the Bethlehem Steel Corporation; it was delivered and fitted in June.

All equipment now considered obsolete was removed

Main photo:
Aerial view of *Richelieu* during her post-refit trials. The former aviation facilities and the quarterdeck aft have been used to good effect to bolster the AA armament. (*US National Archives*)

Inset:
A profile view of *Richelieu* during her post-refit trials. Note the distinctive US Measure 32 disruptive camouflage pattern with its blocks of Navy Blue, Haze Gray, Light Gray and Pale Gray (*US National Archives*)

Left:
The quarterdeck of the *Richelieu* following reconstruction viewed from the roof of the centreline 152mm turret, on which single 20mm Oerlikon guns in tubs have been located. In the centre of the picture, atop what was formerly the aircraft hangar, is the 'cemetery' with its nine single 20mm Oerlikons; beyond, on the quarterdeck, are four quad 40mm Bofors mountings. (*US National Archives*)

Right:
View forward taken during *Richelieu*'s major reconstruction at the Brooklyn Navy Yard. Two of the new 40mm quad Bofors AA mountings are in the foreground. Behind them can be seen the original French 100mm Mle 1931 twin DP mountings. (*US National Archives*)

Original USN key – above:
1 New 20mm guns atop of 152mm turret C (#16 & #17).
2 New 20mm battery nos. 1-9 incl.
3 New 40mm mount no.3 (S), no.4 (P).
4 New 40mm mount no.1 (S), no.2 (P).
5 New rungs on shield.
6 H.W.T. hatch with 18" dia. scuttle to former hanger space.
7 New lifelines.
8 Support for wake light.
9 Buoyant life net stowage baskets.
10 Fair leaders.

Original USN key – right:
1 New 20mm battery nos. 11, 13 & 15 (S).
2 New 40mm director no.5.
3 New 40mm director no.7.
4 New 40mm mount no.7
5 New 40mm mount no.5.
6 New 100mm splinter shield.
7 New 20mm guns – nos. 18 & 19.
8 New 20mm guns – nos. 22 & 23 (P/S).
9 New 20mm guns – nos. 21 & 25 (S).
10 New 20mm guns – nos. 29 & 37 (S).
11 New antennae lead-in trunk.
12 New vertical ladder on shield.

13 Deadlights & vent. covers in pantry, laundry, galley & vegetable lockers.
14 Yard stay modified for signal halyard blocks, P & S.
15 Outrigger for yard stay P & S.
16 Support for T.B.S. antenna.
17 Support for anemometer.
18 Padeyes for flat top antennas, P & S.
19 Foremast foundation for 'SF' radar.
20 Support for middle group of fighting lights, P & S.
21 Support for lower group of fighting lights, P & S.
22 Buoyant life net stowage.
23 Life float stowage.
(Both photographs dated 14 August 1943)

PATRIE

to make room for the new light AA battery. Both catapults and the aircraft crane had been disembarked at Dakar prior to the ship's Atlantic passage. The upper section of the hangar was now reduced in height and the lower section used to stow AA ammunition and to provide a rest room for the after AA gun crews. The boats which had previously been stowed on rails around the forward tower were disembarked; in their place twenty-eight frames for life rafts were installed at upper deck and shelter deck levels. The remaining service boats were stowed on the former boat deck between the towers.

There were modifications to the towers and masts. The upper (HA) director of the forward tower, which had never become operational and was removed to enable the ship to pass beneath the Brooklyn Bridge, was suppressed, as was the short topmast around which the directors were originally seated. The tiny thimble radome of the SF surface surveillance radar was located atop the remaining 152mm director on the forward tower, and the small rectangular mattress antenna for the SA-2 air surveillance radar atop the mainmast on the after tower. Virtually all of the command spaces in the forward tower were reallocated and fitted with new equipment.

Propulsion and auxiliary machinery
The propulsion and auxiliary machinery was completed refurbished. The boilers were retubed and the turbines overhauled and repaired; much of the

existing electrical cabling was removed and replaced, and new switchboards fitted. There was a new, invisible degaussing cable, and the original Anschutz gyrocompasses were replaced by Sperry models.

In machinery trials conducted on 26 September 1943, *Richelieu* comfortably sustained 26.5 knots for six hours at her new 'normal' displacement of 43,600 tonnes, followed by two hours at 28.9 knots and a fifty-minute burst at 30.2 knots. The previous day she had attained a top speed of 31.5 knots for thirty minutes. These were impressive figures given an increase of almost 3000 tonnes in displacement and a hull which was found to be slightly bowed amidships – there was a settling of the keel of around 10cm by comparison with the bow and the stern, possibly as a result of the torpedo damage sustained in July 1940.

Armament modifications
During May the armour plates which formed the roof of turret II were lifted off by crane and the three damaged guns – Nos 5, 7 and 8 – removed. The cradles were found to be undamaged, so the guns were simply replaced by three of the four removed from *Jean Bart*.[2] Munitions posed a problem. Stocks of the French 380mm Mle 1936 APC shell were limited, and once fired these could not be replaced as

---

[2] The fourth was used for trials with the newly developed munitions at the Naval Surface Weapons Center Dahlgren.

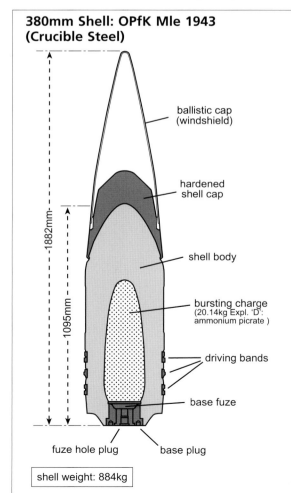

380mm Shell: OPfK Mle 1943 (Crucible Steel)

- ballistic cap (windshield)
- hardened shell cap
- shell body
- bursting charge (20.14kg Expl. 'D': ammonium picrate)
- driving bands
- base fuze
- fuze hole plug
- base plug

1882mm
1095mm

shell weight: 884kg

The external dimensions and configuration of the 380mm shell ordered from the American company Crucible Steel were modelled on the French Mle 1936 shell (see Chapter 4). However, internally it resembled contemporary US Navy 14in shell, with a heavy AP cap, a simpler base plug and a single-action Mark 21 BDF fuze. The base plug was screwed flush with the base of the shell, so the projectile was 8.5mm shorter than the Mle 1936.

The hardened armour-piercing cap, which accounted for 14 per cent of total projectile weight, was configured as a very blunt cone with the tip rounded off in the centre. It had the characteristic US Navy 'sheath-hardening' pattern, with the maximum nose hardness carried down the outside of the projectile middle body to quite near the base. The softening was very gradual on the outer surface of the side and much more rapid near the centreline. The AP cap of the French Mle 1936 (*qv*) was thinner and more pointed and probably had a greater degree of hardening at the tip; it may have performed less well at oblique angles than the American cap. Note that the nose of the US-manufactured shell was likewise more rounded, thereby increasing the depth of the AP cap.

The long, thin windshield of the Crucible Steel shell had two rings of pop-out plugs to allow a 0.68kg (1.5lb) dye bag to be inserted. Unlike the French-developed *Dispositif* 'K' the US Navy water-ram-through splash dye method, developed during the 1920s, did not use an explosive to disperse the colorant, and was used only to colour shell splashes; hits on an adversary by more than one vessel could not be identified.

The base plug with its distinctive funnel-shaped inner face, the fuze adapted ring and the Mark 21 base detonating fuze (0.033-second delay) with a Mark 5 tracer (for following the projectile in flight) were all US Navy standard, as was the explosive 'D' burster. However, filler weight (2.27 per cent of projectile weight) was greater than in US Navy AP shells of the period (1.5 per cent approx.), the cavity size being closer to that of British, Japanese and German shells.

Sources: Crucible Shell manufacturers' plans; data and analysis from Bill Jurens and Nathan Okun.

AMMUNITION ABOARD *RICHELIEU*, APRIL 1943

Gun calibre	380mm	152mm				100mm			37mm
Shell Type	OPfK Mle 36	OPfK Mle 37	OPfK Mle 31	OEA Mle 37	OEA Mle 36	OEA Mle 28	OPf Mle 28	OEcl Mle 28	
No. of shells	407	713 D	1191 D	501	215	3046 D	174 D	474	36,456
		175 N	39 N			1682 N	5 N		
No. of charges	373		2498			(fixed ammunition)			

Notes:
OPfK = <u>O</u>bus de <u>P</u>er<u>f</u>oration (APC/SAPC) with yellow 'K' colorant
OEA = <u>O</u>bus <u>E</u>xplosif en <u>A</u>cier (HE: contact or time-fuzed AA)
OEcl = <u>O</u>bus <u>Ecl</u>airant (starshell)
D = day rounds; N = night rounds

Source: Inventory from *Devis de Campagne* of CV Deramond (27.02.41–29.04.43)

the whole of metropolitan France was now occupied. Exercise rounds were also an issue, as using combat rounds with full charges for gunnery trials and practice would have resulted in rapid barrel wear and would have further depleted stocks of APC shell. New rounds would have to be manufactured in the United States on the basis of plans traced at Dakar; these were ordered from the US Crucible Steel Company (see drawing and caption). An initial order for 930 combat rounds was placed on 6 May 1943, to be delivered in two lots: the first of 500, and second of 430. A further order for 600 shells was mooted.

The exercise rounds were delivered ready for the firing trials which began in late August; shipments of the combat rounds followed at intervals; the first batch was delivered to Scapa Flow in early March 1944. Charges of US manufacture were also supplied.

The secondary armament posed fewer problems in this respect, as the 152mm calibre corresponded to the 6-inch calibre standard on US light cruisers. One of the guns from the centreline triple turret (VII) was removed for test firings ashore, and new shells and charges were manufactured concurrently. The shells were based on the munitions for the US 6in/47 Mark 16 gun. There was an APC shell weighing 58.8kg and a shell adapted from the HC and AA Common shells weighing 47kg; the latter would be known as the OEA Mle 1943 in French service and would still be in use postwar.

Repairs were carried out to the run-out cylinders of the guns and the converters for training and elevation, the defective cabling was replaced, and the replenishment systems modified for barrage fire. Considerable work was necessary on the replenishment systems of both the main and the secondary guns, which were unfinished when *Richelieu* arrived at Dakar and which, despite the best efforts of the crew and DCN Dakar, had never worked satisfactorily

LIGHT ANTI-AIRCRAFT GUNS: CHARACTERISTICS

	40/56 Bofors	20mm Oerlikon
Gun data		
Weight of gun	508kg	68kg
Type of munitions	Fixed	Fixed
Projectiles	HE (0.89kg)	HE (0.12kg)
Propellant	0.07kg Cast TNT	0.01kg tetryl
Complete round		
Weight	2.15kg	0.24kg
Dimensions	45cm x 4cm	18cm x 2cm
Muzzle velocity	853m/s	845m/s
Range		
Max.	10,200m	4390m
Practical	3600m	900m
Ceiling	6800m	3050m
Mounting data		
Mounting designation	(US) Mark 2	(US) Mark 4
Weight of mounting	10.5t	0.77t
Elevation of guns	-6°/+90°	-5°/+90°
Training rate	26°/sec	N/A
Elevation rate	24°/sec	N/A
Firing cycle (per gun)	120rpm	450rpm max.

Notes:
CAQ   <u>C</u>ontre-<u>A</u>vions <u>Q</u>uadruple   AA quad mounting
CAS   <u>C</u>ontre-<u>A</u>vions <u>S</u>imple   AA single mounting

The major modifications to the armament of *Richelieu* concerned anti-aircraft capabilities. The twin 100mm mountings, which had proven robust and reliable, were retained. They were to be complemented by no fewer than fourteen quadruple 40mm Bofors guns in tubs, each mounting having its own associated Mk 51 director. There were two quad mountings on the forecastle deck on either side of turret II, four superimposed mountings abeam the forward tower, four similarly arranged abeam the after tower, and four on the quarterdeck in place of the former aircraft catapults. The new mountings were numbered in a non-standard fashion which reflected neither established French nor US Navy practice: mounting No. 1 was the starboard after mounting, the sequence proceeding from aft to forward in pairs (i.e., odd numbers to starboard,

Richelieu late 1943: Numbering of Turrets & Gun Mountings

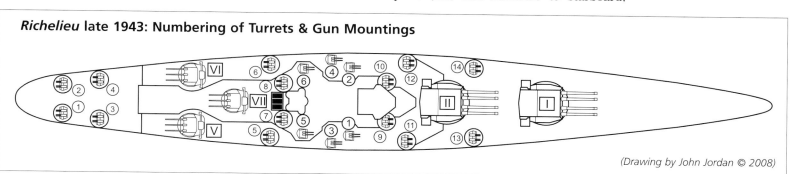

(Drawing by John Jordan © 2008)

evens to port), so that No. 14 was the port-side mounting abeam turret II (see drawing).

For close-range AA defence, multiple single 20mm Oerlikon guns, intended for independent fire using on-mount gunsights, were provided. These were grouped behind screens on deck or located on platforms on the superstructures, centreline turrets and the after director: a group of nine behind the breakwater on the forecastle, a group of nine in an enclosure atop the former hangar aft,[3] four groups of three and two singles at the edge of the shelter deck arranged symmetrically fore and aft of amidships, four atop each of the towers plus two on the lower platform of the after tower (in place of the searchlights), four atop turret II, and four (in pairs) atop the centreline 152mm turret and director B abaft the after tower, for a total of fifty guns.

Firing trials took place in Chesapeake Bay from 29 August 1943 and continued until mid-September. In his official report the new CO, CV Lambert, was complimentary about the new 40mm Bofors, which he considered to be an excellent weapon with good director control and RPC, but which was nevertheless complex and needed careful maintenance by highly trained personnel – which were in short supply in the Free French Navy of the period. The main concern expressed concerned the precarious replenishment of

the guns in combat; Lambert was concerned about the small number and slow speed of the hoists, which were capable of delivering only one/two cases every forty seconds. As a result stocks of ready-use munitions were stowed above the armoured deck during intensive aerial combat operations. Lambert was unconvinced of the value of the 20mm weapons against fast modern aircraft. The 20mm guns located behind the breakwater on the forecastle proved particularly vulnerable when the 380mm main armament was fired on forward bearings, and following an incident which involved the complete destruction of two of the mountings and their associated ready-use lockers on 29 August a blast screen was fitted behind this group of guns.

Fire control

Following modernisation the 380mm guns could no longer be controlled from the 100mm directors. The two remaining 152mm directors were refurbished: new cabling and telephones were installed, and three windows cut out of each director to facilitate target designation in the AA mode.

The 100mm mountings and their associated directors were fitted with a Vickers hydraulic system which provided RPC in elevation and bearing for the mountings, and elevation only for the directors. A barrage fire system was installed which allowed the guns to be fired by the rangetaker. A tannoy system now linked the directors and the mountings with the AA control centre, and new telephones were provided.

The RPC system for the 40mm quad mountings was an electric/hydraulic system from York and Safe, each of the mountings being controlled by a Mk 51 director with the latest Mk 14 gunsight, which used a crude but simple and effective relative-bearing system to

---

[3] The latter grouping was known as *le cimetière* because when the guns were at maximum elevation, their shields forming the arms of a cross, this enclosure reminded the crew of a country cemetery; in similar vein, the forecastle grouping was known as *la tranchée*, as the breakwater forward combined with the blast shield abaft the mountings to form a 'trench', thereby recalling ground combat during the First World War.

A bow quarter aerial view of the ship. Turret II has been trained aft as far as its stops allow; turret VII (centre-line 152mm) has its guns almost fully elevated. (*US National Archives*)

the guns. Back-up systems included on-mount elec-trical or, in the case of power failure, manual training and elevation. The 20mm single Oerlikons were fitted with the same Mk 14 Sperry gyroscopic gunsight.

Target designation

Data acquired by radar or optical means were centralised in an 'open control centre' (*P.C. Découverte*) located on platform 7 of the forward tower, which also handled data received from off-board sources – ships, aircraft, shore stations – by W/T transmission. The open control centre was tasked with filtering this data and transmitting it to the senior officers of the ship in the conning tower, on the bridge and on platform 8 (*Chef de la Défense*). Fighter direction was also coordi-nated from the open control centre using radar and optical inputs.

Target designation for the guns was as follows: from the conning tower for the 380mm; from the conning tower (surface mode), or the *Chef de la Défense* or the *Chefs de Veille*[4] (platform 8 – AA mode) for the 152mm; from the *Chefs de Veille* for the 100mm; and from the *Chef de la Défense CA* for the 40mm and 20mm guns – who would in practice often give autonomy to the gun commanders.

The American SF surface surveillance and SA-2 air surveillance radars proved robust and reliable, but were criticised in Lambert's report as having a very limited range. This is hardly surprising given that they were 'small-ship' radars – the SF radar had originally been intended to be mounted on the topmast of PT boats! Lambert pointed out that the SA-2 was markedly inferior in performance to the (Type 281) radar installed in the British battleships of the *King George V* class, and the French authorities would soon be making representations to the British to secure the latest surveillance and fire control radars for the ship. In this they were pushing at an open door, as succes-sive British C-in-Cs who subsequently took the *Riche-lieu* under their wing pressed to have the ship brought up to a similar standard to their own first-line units.

With the fitting of radar the number of searchlight projectors could be reduced from five to two. The projector located on platform 8 and the two lower projectors on the after tower (replaced by two single 20mm Oerlikon) were disembarked; only the two upper projectors on the after tower remained. The four searchlight control positions on the forward tower were suppressed; the remaining two projectors were now controlled (via RPC) from the 100mm directors.

Boats

The much-reduced outfit of boats, stowed on crutches between the two towers, was as follows:

two 11-metre motor boats
one 10.8-metre motor boat
one 13-metre motor pinnace
one 5-metre dinghy

In part-compensation ninety-three life rafts were provided.

---

4 'Chief of the Watch': on French battleships there was one to port, one to starboard to co-ordinate the information coming from the lookouts on their respective sides of the ship.

RADARS INSTALLED USA AND UK, 1943-4					
Model	Function	Frequency	Range	Accuracy	Resolution
SA-2	Air surveillance	1.36m (P-band)	68,000m	30m/1°	150m/25°
SF	Surface surveillance	10cm (S-band)	22,000m	70m/2°	50m/6°
Type 284P	Main gunnery	50cm (L-Band)	22,000m	25m/0.2°	150m/1°

Source: Norman Friedman, *Naval Radar* (Conway, 1981).

Richelieu: Radars as Fitted Jan 1944

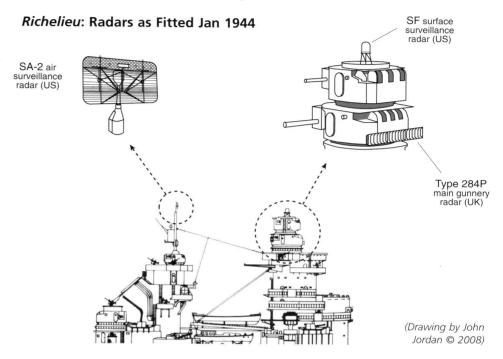

(Drawing by John Jordan © 2008)

Changes in displacement, draught and complement

Richelieu emerged from the Brooklyn Navy Yard with a significantly increased displacement and draught. Displacement was now 43,957 tonnes normal, 47,728 tonnes fully loaded. Draught had increased from 9.22 metres to 9.78 metres at normal displacement, and from 9.9 metres to 10.68 metres at deep load.

The ship's complement was now eighty-six officers, 287 petty officers and 1557 men, for a total of 1930. This compared with a designed wartime complement of 1569, and illustrates the demands of the new AA armament and sensors on manning and accommoda-tion. Many of the new crew members were brought by ship from North Africa.

Camouflage

Before she left the Brooklyn Navy Yard *Richelieu* received a USN Measure 32 disruptive camouflage of Navy Blue, Haze Gray, Light Gray and Pale Gray. The decks were painted Deck Blue and the roofs of the turrets Light Gray. Some modifications were made to this camouflage scheme at the end of September before the ship left for European waters.

EUROPEAN WATERS

Following an intensive period of trials and work-up which lasted some four weeks, *Richelieu* finally left Boston on 14 October 1943 for Gibraltar. Escort was initially provided by the US destroyers *Tarbell* (DD142) and *Ellet* (DD398); the battleship then proceeded unaccompanied at a sustained speed of 24 knots, despite the stormy weather conditions. When she reached the Azores she was met by the former *contre-torpilleurs* – now redesignated 'light cruisers' to conform to Allied ship classification – *Le Fantasque* and *Le Terrible*,[5] in company with the British destroyer *Active*. The latter was limited to a speed of 20 knots, and soon departed, leaving *Richelieu* and her two French consorts to proceed not to Gibraltar, as had been first announced, but to Mers el-Kebir..

It had initially been envisaged that *Richelieu* would be assigned to the British Mediterranean Fleet under Admiral John Cunningham. However, the surrender of the Italian fleet in early September left the latter with a surplus of heavy units. After storing at Mers el-Kebir, *Richelieu* departed on 14 November to join the Home Fleet at Scapa Flow with a strong recommendation from Cunningham that something be done about providing the ship with gunnery radars. She was escorted in by the destroyers *Musketeer* and *Scourge*. Riding at anchor on her arrival at Scapa Flow were the British battleships *King George V*, *Duke of York* and *Howe*; these would shortly be joined by *Anson* and the older battleships *Nelson*, *Rodney* and *Valiant*.

Following an inspection on 24 November by Admiral Bruce Fraser, C-in-C Home Fleet, *Richelieu* was subjected to an intensive work-up with units of the Home Fleet. Work also began on installing British Type 284 fire control radar for the main battery – a task which took some six weeks and was performed by the personnel on board with British technical supervision. The model fitted was the latest P4 variant, which featured single-aerial working, increased power over earlier models and beam-switching. In favourable weather conditions the radar could detect a hostile battleship at a range in excess of 30,000m.[6] The 21-foot (6.4-metre) dual-function aerial was installed on the face of the main director (A) atop the forward tower (see drawing).

Richelieu was short of spares for her machinery and her main and secondary guns, and it was decided that *Jean Bart* would be 'cannibalised' to keep her sister in service. The first consignment of 380mm shells and charges ordered from the United States was not expected until the end of February, and this placed constraints on gunnery practice. However, the impressive performance in practice of the gun crews manning the light AA weapons persuaded the British that the ship could be treated as a fully operational unit once the gunnery radar was installed.

OPERATION 'POSTHORN'

The winter of 1943-4 was a frustrating time for the captain and crew of *Richelieu*. The ship was swinging at anchor in Scapa Flow when the German battleship *Scharnhorst* was engaged and sunk by *Duke of York*. The bitter weather conditions and the spartan recreational facilities available in this remote anchorage did little to raise French morale.

The only operation of note in which *Richelieu* was actively involved during this period was Operation

'Posthorn', which took place during 10-12 February 1944. *Richelieu* followed the battleship *Anson*, flying the flag of the force commander, Vice-Admiral Henry Moore (Second in Command, Home Fleet), and the carrier *Furious* out of Scapa Flow and, with the Orkney and Shetland Islands to starboard, headed NNE into increasingly heavy seas. The objective was to attack German shipping in the Stadlandet area of northern Norway, hopefully provoking a reaction on the part of the German heavy cruisers known to be in the area. Ten Barracuda bombers, escorted by ten Seafire fighters, duly took off from *Furious* at dawn on 11 February, returning in the late morning. Once the aircraft were safely on board, the Allied force withdrew to the south-west at 18 knots. The results of the operation were frankly disappointing: a cargo ship of 3000 tonnes sunk by three bombs, a repair ship damaged and a single Me109 fighter shot down at a cost of one Seafire.

Richelieu moored at the *Quai des Charbons* in the port of Algiers 23 March 1944 en route to the Indian Ocean. Currently the provisional capital of France, the port is crowded with shipping of all nationalities. (*ECPAD*)

5 These two ships had also modernised in the United States during February to June 1943.

6 The slightly older Type 284M model on the *Duke of York*, operating in markedly less favourable conditions, is reported to have held *Scharnhorst* in bearing at 23,600 metres during the engagement of December 1943.

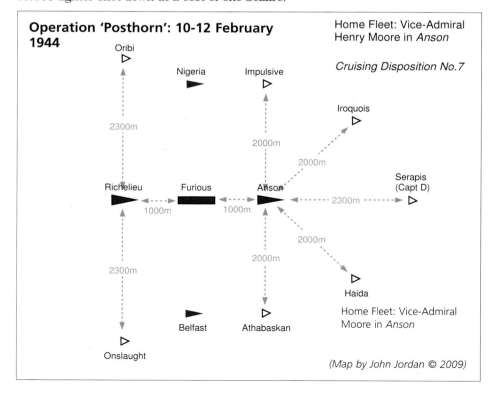

Operation 'Posthorn': 10-12 February 1944

Home Fleet: Vice-Admiral Henry Moore in *Anson*

Cruising Disposition No.7

Home Fleet: Vice-Admiral Moore in *Anson*

(*Map by John Jordan © 2009*)

Following a ten-day rest period at Rosyth, *Richelieu* was to have taken part in a similar operation scheduled for late February, but as the ships sortied from Scapa Flow two of the destroyers collided, and postponement of the operation was followed by four days of appalling weather, leading to its cancellation.

TO THE EASTERN FLEET

Early March 1944 saw an Allied review of capital ship requirements in the light of the ever-changing military situation. Although *Tirpitz* was under repair following the 'X'-craft attack of September 1943 and would soon run sea trials, the retention of five modern capital ships in northern waters could no longer be justified. In the event, three of the *King George V* class were retained at Scapa, so that there would always be two to oppose *Tirpitz* even with the third in refit or maintenance. *King George V* was undergoing a much-needed refit at Liverpool, and her sister *Howe* was in refit at Devonport. The ageing but still-powerful *Nelson* and *Rodney* were allocated to the preparations for the Normandy landings. *Richelieu* was also considered for the fire support mission but was rejected because she was equipped with only APC shell.

At the same time it was decided to bolster the British Eastern Fleet based on Trincomalee with modern ships. Rumours of IJN heavy units east of Bali led the Americans to believe that the bulk of the Japanese fleet was retreating on Singapore, leading to a request from Admiral Ernest King that *Richelieu* be redeployed to the Indian Ocean to join the embryonic fleet of Admiral Somerville. The British *Howe* would follow in June. In order to boost British carrier air power in the region, King agreed to loan Somerville the US fleet carrier *Saratoga*, which with the latest ships of the *Essex* class rolling off the production line could easily be spared.

An impressive shot of *Richelieu* in heavy weather off Egypt during her passage to the Indian Ocean to join the British Eastern Fleet. Note the 21-foot aerial for the British Type 284 P4 main gunnery radar on the face of the lower director. The photo is dated 27 March 1944. (*USNHC*)

On 15 March, *Richelieu* duly called into Greenock, where she took on fuel and munitions: 1500 152mm charges were embarked in six hours. She then made her way south escorted by three British destroyers, passing via the Strait of Gibraltar and arriving in Algiers – now the French 'capital in exile' – on 26 March. There she took on stores, and following official visits by General Giraud and Admiral Lemonnier, headed for the Suez Canal at 25 knots. At this point, *Richelieu* began to experience serious problems with her boilers which would plague her for the next few months. The blowers were proving inadequate and this resulted in poor fuel combustion, the inevitable consequences of which were the emission of thick black smoke from the funnel and the rapid sooting-up of the boiler tubes. Some tube repairs were undertaken at Aden, but there was still serious overheating above 26 knots (half power) – a problem that

was to be exacerbated by the very high temperatures experienced east of Aden.

Richelieu was escorted across the Indian Ocean by the British destroyers *Rotherham*, *Racehorse* and *Quadrant*, and arrived at Trincomalee on 10 April. She entered this magnificent anchorage to find the British battlecruiser *Renown*, the battleships *Valiant* and *Queen Elizabeth*,[7] the carrier *Illustrious* and the USS *Saratoga* already at anchor, together with a host of modern cruisers and destroyers.

OPERATION 'COCKPIT'

Within six days of *Richelieu*'s arrival, Somerville embarked on his first offensive mission against Japanese shipping and island installations. Operation 'Cockpit' was intended primarily as a diversionary raid to distract the Japanese from the American assault on New Guinea, and envisaged an aerial assault on Sabang, the port city of the island of Pulau Weh,[8] strategically placed off the northwest corner of Sumatra, where it served as a guard post for the Malacca Strait. Sabang was 2000nm from Trincomalee and therefore comfortably within the range of the big ships, but the latter would have to refuel the accompanying destroyers en route.

Somerville divided his ships into two forces: a carrier force (Force 70) with the battlecruiser *Renown* (Vice-

Richelieu at Trincomalee in mid-1944. In the background is Admiral Somerville's flagship, the battleship *Queen Elizabeth*. (*USNHC*)

---

[7] All three of these vessels had been rebuilt during the late 1930s and they were the most capable of the older British capital ships.

[8] There are various spellings for the name of this island.

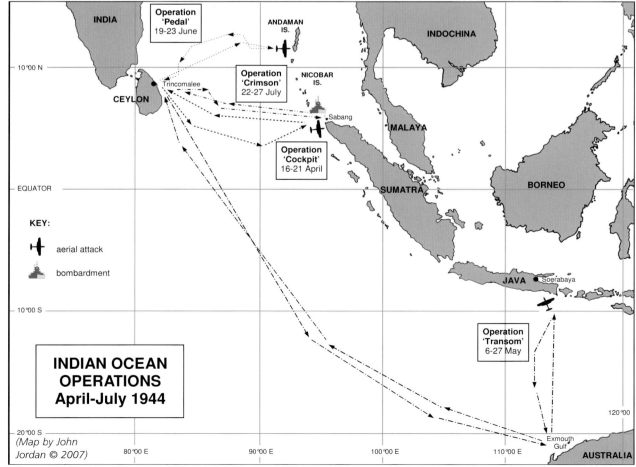

Admiral Power, Second in Command Eastern Fleet) and the carriers *Illustrious* and *Saratoga*; and a main force (Force 69) with the battleships *Queen Elizabeth* (Somerville himself), *Valiant* and *Richelieu*. (For composition and cruising formation of the two groups, see illustration.)

At dawn on 19 April, the air strike was duly launched from the two carriers: seventeen Barracuda bombers and thirteen Corsair fighters from *Illustrious*; eleven Avenger bombers, eighteen Dauntless dive-bombers and twenty-four Hellcat fighters from *Saratoga*. The strike returned at 0900. Somerville's force then headed back towards Trincomalee; there was no response by IJN surface units, and air attacks were sporadic and poorly coordinated, and were easily dealt with by the carrier air patrols. Estimates of damage were: two merchant ships bombed, two escorts on fire, a fuel storage dump on fire, twenty-four planes destroyed on the ground and damage to aviation facilities.

This was a relatively comfortable debut for *Richelieu*. Only during the evening attack did she get to open fire with her 100mm and 40mm guns on Japanese bombers. However, the ship's captain was complimented by Somerville on his station-keeping. On her return to Trincomalee, *Richelieu* would be repainted, the US Measure 32 replaced by an Admiralty Standard scheme: light grey hull with a large blue trapezium over the midships section. The turrets and the after tower were painted medium grey and the forward tower light grey; the decks remained blue.

OPERATION 'TRANSOM'

May 1944 saw the most ambitious operation yet by the Eastern Fleet against the Japanese in southeast Asia. With MacArthur now moving against the Carolines, it was proposed that Somerville make a diversionary attack on the former Dutch naval port of Soerabaya on the island of Java with a view to distracting the main Japanese fleet currently based on Singapore. Besides its role as a major base, Soerabaya was a key oil refinery centre; it was, however, much farther from Trincomalee than Sabang. Whereas the raid on Sabang had been a five-day round trip, the raid on Soerabaya would take three weeks, and it would be necessary to refuel all ships at the half-way point.

The carrier strike and battleship support task forces (Force 66 and Force 65 respectively), were generally similar in their composition to those for the previous raid on Sabang; they left Trincomalee on 7 May. The replenishment force (Force 67), comprising six oilers and a water tanker escorted by two cruisers and three destroyers, had already left for Exmouth Bay on the northwest corner of Australia. After refuelling on 15 May, Force 66 and Force 65 headed north, and at dawn on 17 May *Illustrious* launched twenty-one Avengers[9] and fifteen Corsairs, and *Saratoga* twenty-nine Dauntless dive-bombers and twenty-five Hellcats. At 1050, the strike aircraft returned and Somerville's fleet again headed for Exmouth Bay to refuel. On 18 May, *Saratoga* and her three escorting destroyers departed to rejoin their US counterparts in the central

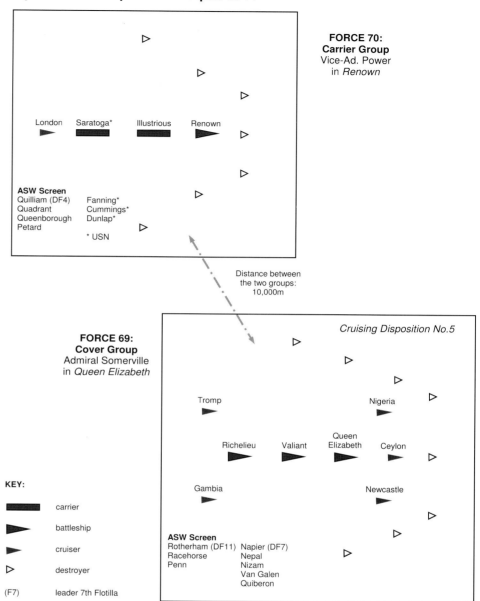

Operation 'Cockpit': 16-21 April 1944

FORCE 70:
Carrier Group
Vice-Ad. Power
in *Renown*

London   Saratoga*   Illustrious   Renown

ASW Screen
Quilliam (DF4)   Fanning*
Quadrant   Cummings*
Queenborough   Dunlap*
Petard
                 * USN

Distance between
the two groups:
10,000m

FORCE 69:
Cover Group
Admiral Somerville
in *Queen Elizabeth*

Cruising Disposition No.5

Tromp   Nigeria

Queen
Richelieu   Valiant   Elizabeth   Ceylon

Gambia   Newcastle

ASW Screen
Rotherham (DF11)   Napier (DF7)
Racehorse   Nepal
Penn   Nizam
                   Van Galen
                   Quiberon

KEY:

▬▬▬   carrier

◣   battleship

▸   cruiser

▷   destroyer

(F7)   leader 7th Flotilla

Pacific. For the remainder of the force the return journey was uneventful, and the British and French ships were again anchored at Trincomalee on 27 May.

The performance of *Richelieu* during this sortie was particularly impressive in one respect. Despite refuelling two destroyers at the halfway point of the outward passage and a third during the return, she entered Trincomalee with half her fuel remaining, whereas the British *Queen Elizabeth* and *Valiant* were reduced to 20 per cent of their capacity. The British were also impressed with *Richelieu*'s ability to conduct alongside replenishment, American-style, which was significantly faster than the traditional over-the-stern method employed by the British ships.

Two days after the return of Somerville's fleet, *Richelieu*, *Queen Elizabeth* and six of the destroyers left for Colombo for a ten-day recreation period. While in that port, the ship received an official visit from Vice-Admiral Mountbatten, the Allied Supreme Commander in South-East Asia.

---

[9] *Illustrious*' Barracuda torpedo bombers had to be replaced by Avengers for this operation because the former had insufficient range – Soerabaya was on the north side of Java.

OPERATION 'PEDAL'

News of the Allied landings in Normandy served to reinforce the feelings of frustration among the crew of *Richelieu*. However, there would soon be another operation, this time against the Japanese base of Port Blair, capital of the Andaman Islands in the Bay of Bengal. This time only the fast ships were involved: *Renown* (Vice-Admiral Power), *Richelieu* and *Illustrious*, together with the light cruisers *Nigeria*, *Kenya* and *Ceylon* (4th Cruiser Squadron); the light cruiser *Phoebe* was to provide close escort for *Illustrious*, and eight destroyers of the 4th and the 11th Destroyer Flotillas were deployed in advance as an antisubmarine screen.

Force 60 departed Trincomalee on 19 June. Fifteen Barracuda bombers escorted by fourteen Corsairs were launched at dawn on 21 June; they returned just over two hours later, having caused extensive damage to shore installations at the cost of one Barracuda shot down. The ships returned to Trincomalee on 23 June without incident.

OPERATION 'CRIMSON'

The absence of any co-ordinated Japanese reaction to these three raids emboldened Somerville, who now envisaged a close bombardment of the next objective, with the carrier aircraft providing aerial cover and spotting for the battleships. On 7 July and again on 14-15 July and 17 July, intensive gunnery practice was carried out against shore targets.

With the Americans moving against Guam and Tinian, the British strike was again to be against Sabang, at the mouth of the Malacca Strait, through which all Japanese cargo vessels supplying their army in Burma had to pass. The battle line comprised the battleships *Queen Elizabeth* (Admiral Somerville), *Valiant*, *Renown* (Vice-Admiral Power) and *Richelieu*. It was to be supported by five ships of the 4th Cruiser Squadron. A sixth light cruiser, the Dutch *Tromp*, was to lead the destroyers into the anchorage, conducting a close bombardment of the ships in the port and the port installations and launching torpedoes against targets of opportunity. Air cover and spotting was to be provided by the carriers *Illustrious* and *Victorious*, the latter having arrived on 7 July to replace *Saratoga*, with the AA cruiser *Phoebe* again allocated as close escort.

The force weighed anchor on 22 July and arrived off Pulau Weh at dawn on 25 July, when eighty Corsairs and eighteen Barracudas were launched to dominate the air space over the ships and the island. The battle line headed south towards the northwest point of the island, leaving Rondo Island to starboard, while the cruisers broke off to conduct a close bombardment of Sabang from east to west, focusing their fire on the radio station and the coastal batteries. Meanwhile, *Tromp* led the destroyers close to the northwest tip of Pulau Weh ready for the high-speed run into the anchorage (see map). At 0654, *Queen Elizabeth* opened fire at a range of 6000 metres on Sabang, followed by the other ships of the line. The lighthouse was used as the reference point for the ranging salvos, with Corsairs overhead to spot for each of the battleships. The bombardment continued until 0715 when, with the target shrouded in smoke, *Queen Elizabeth* broke off and turned onto a heading slightly north of west, followed by her consorts.

Firing in four-gun salvos (two guns from each turret), *Richelieu* hit the target from the second salvo, demolishing several workshops and warehouses in the area of the port and scoring three hits on the power station. The blast from the main guns proved too much for the AA crews of the forward guns, who were compelled to take shelter. In just over twenty minutes, *Richelieu* fired eighty-one 380mm projectiles in twenty-one salvos at a rate averaging one salvo every fifty seconds – almost twice the rate of fire of the other battleships.

The port-side and centreline 152mm turrets (VI and VII), despite a lack of practice because of the late delivery of shells and charges, fired at a Japanese 120mm coastal battery with which *Tromp* and the destroyers were heavily engaged, silencing it from the second salvo. The destroyers then turned away under a smokescreen.

Three-quarters of the 380mm charges in *Richelieu's* magazines at this time were of the SD19 (re-bagged 330mm) type or US-manufactured charges filled with 420 CI powder. The experience of Dakar revealed that the SD19 charges were slightly underpowered, and the projectile therefore tended to fall short. The US-manufactured charges, on the other hand, proved poorly

Richelieu fires her main guns against Sabang on 25 July 1944 during Operation 'Crimson'. The photograph was taken from HMS *Renown*. (IWM)

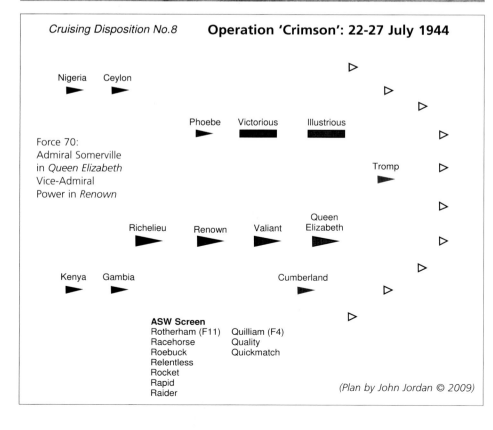

Operation 'Crimson': 22-27 July 1944

Cruising Disposition No.8

Nigeria   Ceylon

Force 70:
Admiral Somerville
in *Queen Elizabeth*
Vice-Admiral
Power in *Renown*

Phoebe   Victorious   Illustrious

Tromp

Richelieu   Renown   Valiant   Queen Elizabeth

Kenya   Gambia   Cumberland

ASW Screen
Rotherham (F11)   Quilliam (F4)
Racehorse   Quality
Roebuck   Quickmatch
Relentless
Rocket
Rapid
Raider

(Plan by John Jordan © 2009)

suited to the French replenishment systems. The 420 CI powder was packed in the canvas bags as small sticks; the cartridges lacked rigidity and were said to behave like 'sacks of coal'; this resulted in tears and jams en route to the guns. During firing practices bags frequently snagged, spilling powder onto the spanning trays; powder then spread into the firing chamber, so that the turret had to be taken out of service for half an hour to be swept clean. Because of these problems, the French-manufactured SD21 charges were kept back for combat, and CV du Vignaux, the new CO, decided to use them in combination with the standard APC shell at Sabang. The shells proved effective against concrete installations but those that hit the ground tended to bury themselves without exploding. After the landings at Sabang the following year, several of *Richelieu*'s 380mm shells were found buried but intact. The lack of an HE shell for shore bombardment led the French to order a consignment of specially designed shells from the British, which subsequently became the OEA Mle 1945; these shells featured in the inventories of both *Richelieu* and *Jean Bart* during the postwar era.

As the force withdrew, the Japanese mounted several desperate air attacks against it, but these were all successfully beaten off by the Corsairs and the

ships' AA weapons. On 27 July, *Richelieu* was again swinging at No. 2 Buoy in China Bay, Trincomalee.

RETURN TO FRANCE AND REFIT AT CASABLANCA

After a short rest period at Colombo, *Richelieu* again sailed for Trincomalee, this time accompanied by the recently arrived *Howe*. Admiral Power, who had succeeded Somerville as C-in-C Eastern Fleet, was anxious that *Richelieu* should undergo a docking and refit, as her speed was by now reduced as a result of marine growth on her hull and ongoing problems with her boilers which resulted in a trail of easily detected black smoke at higher speeds. The new floating dock AFD 28, recently arrived from Australia, was offered, but *Richelieu*'s captain declined, fearful – rightly, as it turned out – that the dock would have trouble coping with a ship displacing 48,500 tonnes. The battleship *Valiant* took her place, and on the evening of 8 August was severely damaged when the dock almost capsized.

On 6 September, *Richelieu* received the order to sail for Algiers. She left the following day and was escorted by the destroyers *Quickmatch*, *Pathfinder* and the Dutch *Tjerk Hiddes* as far as Aden. Following her transit of the Suez Canal the escort was taken up by *Le Terrible* and *Le Fantasque*, and she arrived in Algiers on 23 September.

From there she went to Toulon, arriving on 1 October to find the rest of the French fleet gathered in a *Grande Rade* which was littered with the wrecks of sunken ships. A 52-metre war pennant flew from her mainmast to mark the fifty-two months she had spent away from France. With the dockyard in ruins from the sabotage and the Allied bombing, it was decided to send *Richelieu* to refit at Casablanca. Again escorted by *Le Terrible* and *Le Fantasque*, she moored at the *Jetée Delure* on 10 October. The twin tower masts of her incomplete sister *Jean Bart* could be seen rising above the *Quai Delande*; by this time the latter ship had not only given up her four main guns to *Richelieu*, but also her boilers.

For the British Admiralty and for the ship's CO, the priority was the installation of new surveillance and fire control radars. Once this material had been brought in by ship,[10] installation was supervised by a British liaison officer, Lt-Cdr Stanford. The work was to be completed by 1 February so that *Richelieu* could relieve *Renown* in the Eastern Fleet.

The latest Type 281B air surveillance radar, with single aerial working, four PPI range plots and a Type 243Q IFF interrogator, was to be installed atop a new foretopmast around which were seated the two directors of the forward tower (see drawing). Surface surveillance would now be provided by American SG-1 radar, with three PPIs and an IFF interrogator; the small, solid parabolic antenna would be fitted on a platform projecting from the new mast. It effectively displaced the SF radar, which was relocated to the roof of the conning tower and would henceforth be used, in principle, for navigation – it was usable only on forward bearings as it now had an 80-degree blind arc aft.

Type 285P fire control radars were to be fitted atop the two secondary directors, together with two auto barrage units (ABU) for anti-aircraft barrage fire. The

The Bombardment of Sabang
25 July 1944

RONDO IS.

95°10

BA 0646

BB 0650

CA

6°00N

BC 0657

firing at shore installations

CB

firing at shore batteries

DA

CD

BD
0715

DB

Ponimpum Hill Battery

DD

firing at shipping

Iboih

SABANG

DC

airstrip

5°50N

PULAU WEH

Kulam

- - - ►○ battleships
······ ►• cruisers
········ ►• *Tromp* + destroyers
       ⊤ coastal batteries

0nm 1nm 2nm 3nm 4nm 5nm

(Map by John Jordan © 2007)

---

[10] The cruiser *Duquesne* made the first delivery of 84 tonnes on 1 November 1944.

RADARS INSTALLED UK AND CASABLANCA, 1944-5

Model	Function	Frequency	Range	Accuracy	Resolution
Type 281B	Air surveillance	3.5m	120nm	N/A	N/A
SG-1	Surface surveillance	10cm (S-band)	40,000m	180m/2°	360m/3°
Type 285P	Secondary gunnery	50cm (L-Band)	15,000m	45m/0.25°	150m/1.5°

Source: Norman Friedman, *Naval Radar* (Conway Maritime Press, 1981).

Below: The forward tower of *Richelieu* with No.13 (forecastle, starboard side) 40mm Bofors quad in the foreground. The paint scheme suggests that the photo was taken in mid-1944, following repainting with the Admiralty Standard scheme.

latter were designed to calculate the range to target, with fire being opened automatically with the guns; fuzed 152mm projectiles set for a range of 3000m were put up in the path of enemy torpedo- and level/glide-bombers. *Richelieu* was also to be fitted with an FV1 jammer (to counter the German Fritz X and Hs 293 glide bombs) and the latest British HF/DF gear.

Work on installing the radars was delayed by the late delivery of special cabling ordered from the UK. Teams of electricians worked day and night to get the ship ready for an anticipated deployment to the Far East. For the second time since *Richelieu*'s completion, some 60 per cent of the ship's crew was renewed. Of the new personnel many had served for less than a year, and it would take many weeks to train them to the required level.

SECOND INDIAN OCEAN DEPLOYMENT

Richelieu left Casablanca on 24 January 1945. The French authorities had been pressing for the ship to be deployed, together with the four remaining modern 152mm cruisers and the four *Le Fantasques*, to the Pacific, with a view to reasserting French influence in that ocean. This proposal, however, was resolutely opposed by Admiral King and the US Navy. King demanded that any French surface force deployed to the Pacific should be completely self-sufficient – a condition also imposed on the embryonic British Pacific Fleet (BPF), but a condition that the Americans were well aware could not be met by the French because of their inability to furnish the carriers, escorts and auxiliary support ships required. It was agreed that *Richelieu* could deploy as part of the British forces east of Suez, but not the smaller ships.

Prior to deployment, *Richelieu* was docked at Gibraltar on 25 January; the hull was scraped and repainted, and munitions embarked. She was floated out on 10 February and refuelled, and subsequently ran machinery trials. These were successful, and the ship now made noticeably less smoke at higher speeds. *Richelieu* then left for Mers el-Kebir and an intensive work-up for her largely untried crew. She again passed through the Suez Canal and arrived at Trincomalee on 20 March.

By this time, the British Pacific Fleet, with four of the modern carriers and the battleships *Howe* and *King George V*, had been formed at Sydney under Admiral Bruce Fraser. The former Eastern Fleet (now rechristened the East Indies Fleet), built around the old battleship *Queen Elizabeth* and the battlecruiser *Renown*, remained at Trincomalee under Admiral Power. To support these ships, Power had nine cruisers, ten escort carriers, twenty destroyers and thirty submarines. The IJN forces opposing them had declined, the battleships *Ise* and *Hyuga* having returned to Japan in February. At Singapore, there remained only the four heavy cruisers *Haguro*, *Ashigara*, *Myoko* and *Takao*, plus a handful of destroyers.

OPERATION 'SUNFISH'

For the first three weeks following the arrival of *Richelieu* at Trincomalee there was little activity beyond exercises: two gunnery shoots, in which the 380mm and 152mm were fired against shore and towed targets, and simulated air attacks to test radar operators and command systems and the gun crews of the AA weapons.

On 8 April, *Richelieu* weighed anchor and joined her consorts of Force 63 ready to unleash Operation 'Sunfish'. The overt objective of this operation was bombardment of Sabang and an aerial assault on Padang, on the southern coast of Sumatra; in reality the operation was cover for aerial reconnaissance of the south Malayan coast as a preparatory step to landings scheduled by the South-East Asia Command for the autumn.

Force 63 comprised Power's flagship *Queen Elizabeth* and *Richelieu*, accompanied by the two 8in cruisers *London* and *Cumberland* (Rear-Admiral Patterson), the escort carriers *Emperor* and *Khedive*, and five destroyers of the 26th Destroyer Flotilla. A specialist Hellcat strategic photographic unit of 888 Squadron was embarked in *Emperor*.

At dawn on 11 April, as the force was approaching the island of Pulau Weh, it divided into two groups: a bombardment group with the two battleships, *London* and three destroyers, and an air support group with the two escort carriers, *Cumberland* and two destroyers. At 0755, *Queen Elizabeth* opened fire on Sabang at a range of 17,000 metres and *Richelieu*, following 900 metres in her wake, opened fire ten minutes later. The main guns fired seven salvos at the auxiliary control position and the coal dump, hitting the targets with twelve out of twenty-four shells; the 152mm guns engaged the coastal battery at Ponim Poi, silencing it with rapid salvos within four minutes. The bombardment group then turned away to the north-west, rejoining the carrier group and fending off poorly co-ordinated attacks by Japanese land-based aircraft.

Under the cover of night Force 63 turned onto a southwesterly course, heading for a rendezvous the following day with the oiler *Easedale* and her escorting destroyer (Force 70). The five destroyers of the 26th DF

Richelieu: Radars as Fitted Jan 1945

Type 285P
AA gunnery
radar (UK)

Type 281B
air surveillance
radar (UK)

SG-1 surface
surveillance
radar (US)

(Drawing by John Jordan © 2008)

took turns to refuel – *Richelieu* still had her bunkers 78 per cent full – and Force 63 headed east for the Sumatra coast, where diversionary aerial attacks were made on Padang, under cover of which the Hellcat photographic aircraft were launched for their scheduled reconnaissance of Port Swettenham and Port Dickson on the south coast of Malaya. Again enemy retaliation was spasmodic and ineffectual.

The Allied force then turned away to the south ready for a second 'fuel stop' on 17 April. It returned to Trincomalee at dawn on 20 April.

Richelieu undergoing repairs at Casablanca in October 1944. Note the Admiralty Standard paint scheme (see artwork p.134), which replaced the US Navy Measure 32 from May 1944.

OPERATION 'BISHOP'

With the availability of landing craft released from the European Theatre, the next six weeks would see an increase in the tempo of operations. Mountbatten envisaged amphibious landings in the Bay of Bengal with the aim of clearing the Japanese out of Burma and the Andaman Islands. These were to be followed by landings on the south coast of Malaya, for which the photo reconnaissance missions of Operation 'Sunfish' had been a preparatory step. With the operations of the British 14th Army against Rangoon stalled, Mountbatten wanted amphibious landings against the capital (Operation 'Dracula') to be mounted before the June monsoon. These landings were to be protected against Japanese intervention by a naval operation, 'Bishop', against the airfields of the Andaman and Car Nicobar Islands.

Fighter cover for the landings was to be provided by the escort carriers *Khedive*, *Emperor*, *Hunter* and *Stalker* escorted by the AA cruisers *Phoebe* and *Royalist* and four destroyers of the 26th Destroyer Flotilla (Force 63). The surface forces were divided into two groups: Force 64 comprised the battleship *Queen Elizabeth* (Vice-Admiral Walker), the cruisers *Suffolk* and *Tromp* and three destroyers of the 10th Destroyer Flotilla; and *Richelieu* with the cruisers *Cumberland* (Rear-Admiral Patterson) and *Ceylon* escorted by two destroyers. Two further escort carriers, *Empress* and *Shah*, with Avenger torpedo aircraft as well as fighters, were detached from Force 63 to provide cover for the surface groups, and there was a picket line of five submarines to intercept IJN cruisers attempting to interfere with the landings emerging from the Malacca Strait. Replenishment was to be provided by Force 69, comprising the oilers *Olwen* and *Easedale* with the destroyer *Paladin*.

The ships departed Trincomalee on 27 April and arrived off Car Nicobar two days later. A dawn bombardment of the two airfields was particularly successful. *Richelieu* opened fire at 23,600 metres, and her first salvo was within 100 metres of the target; the second struck the airfield. Eighty 380mm shells and forty-five 152mm shells from turrets V and VII landed within a 100-metre radius. The only downside was that several members of the gun crews for the 20mm Oerlikons received severe burns from the blast of the 380mm guns when the turrets trained close to the ship's axis during a turn. There was also damage to the 20mm guns themselves, despite the protective bulwark that now separated them from the main guns.

Force 64 then headed north towards the Andaman Islands. *Richelieu* and *Cumberland* opened fire at 1730, and fired twenty-one two-gun salvos at the airfield of Port Blair. The weather then deteriorated, making spotting difficult, and the ships ceased fire at 1807. *Queen Elizabeth*, with *Cumberland* and *Ceylon*, returned to finish the job on 1 May. By this time, *Richelieu* had used up her entire 380mm allocation for the mission. However, on 2 May she closed Port Blair and bombarded the dockyard using her 152mm secondary guns, spotting being provided by a Hellcat. After a three-gun ranging salvo, *Richelieu* fired four salvos, spaced at six seconds, from each turret. One hundred and twenty rounds were despatched in only a

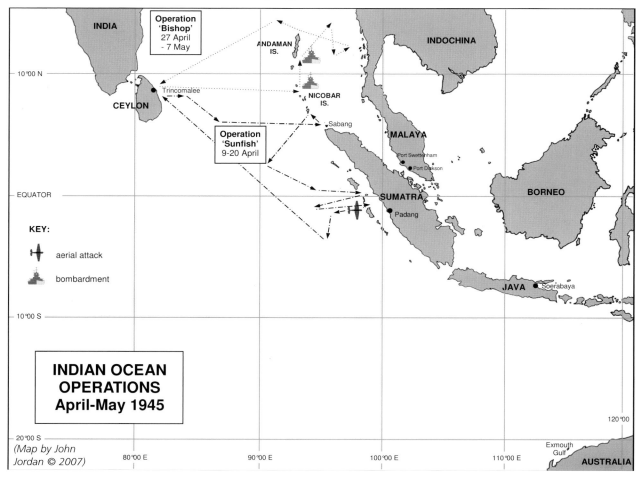

INDIAN OCEAN OPERATIONS April-May 1945

KEY:

aerial attack

bombardment

(Map by John Jordan © 2007)

few minutes, with full salvos striking the dockyard installations. Port Blair would never again be used as a naval base by the Japanese.

Having neutralised the Andaman Islands, the Allied surface forces headed north to provide cover for the landings at Rangoon. Two Indian brigades were duly landed in eighty LCAs, but it was found that the Japanese troops had already withdrawn, sabotaging the port installations. Planned to be a five-week operation, 'Dracula' lasted only two days. *Richelieu* and her consorts were back in Trincomalee on 8 May.

OPERATION 'DUKEDOM'

At Colombo, a decryption of a Japanese signal alerted the British to a sortie by the cruiser *Haguro* and the destroyer *Kamikaze* from Singapore. *Haguro* was tasked with evacuating the Japanese garrison at Port Blair during the night of 12-13 May; at the same time an escorted transport would evacuate the garrison at Car Nicobar (Operation 'Sho'). On 9 May, the submarines *Subtle* and *Statesman*, patrolling in the Malacca Strait, confirmed that a cruiser of the *Nachi* class was on course for the Andaman Islands.

The Allied response was Operation 'Dukedom'. Vice-Admiral Walker was again in command in *Queen Elizabeth* (Force 61 Group 1), with *Richelieu* and *Cumberland* under Rear-Admiral Patterson (Group 3) in the van. Forewarned of the Allied operation, the Japanese cruiser turned back, but after the transport reached Car Nicobar without interception on 14 May, *Haguro* again sortied from Singapore. This time she was located by Avengers flying from the accompanying escort carriers. The 26th Destroyer Flotilla, which was well advanced, launched a pursuit, while *Richelieu* and *Cumberland* headed for a point 75nm off the northernmost tip of Sumatra to bar the cruiser's path. *Haguro* then attempted to flee, with the British ships in full chase. She was 200nm ahead of *Richelieu* but was limited to 25 knots, and *Richelieu* and *Cumberland* charged along at a sustained 27 knots. They were 50nm northwest of the cruiser when news reached them that *Haguro* had been sunk by ships of the 26th Destroyer Flotilla.

Having previously missed out on the sinking of *Scharnhorst*, it must have seemed to Captain du Vignaux and his crew that they were fated not to have the opportunity of a surface action against the enemy.[11] The return passage was marked by furious but poorly executed Japanese aerial attacks, and *Richelieu* finally dropped anchor at Trincomalee on 18 May.

No sooner had she anchored than she was replenished from an oiler to port and an ammunition ship to starboard. More than 4000 tonnes of fuel were embarked, together with 122 US-manufactured 380mm shells and their corresponding charges, and more than 20,000 40mm cartridges. On 29 May, *Richelieu* hosted Vice-Admiral Walker for two days at sea during which the ship demonstrated her US Navy-style alongside refuelling capability; fuel oil was embarked from an oiler at a rate of 350 tonnes per hour – as compared with the 150t/h maximum the Royal Navy could sustain using the astern refuelling method. These lessons were then passed on to Admiral Fraser

COMMANDING OFFICERS AND FLAG OFFICERS (1943-56)

Commanding Officers

CV Lambert	29.04.43 – 06.05.44
CV Merveilleux du Vignaux	06.05.44 – 31.10.45
CV Géli	31.10.45 – 10.05.47
CV Rosset	10.05.47 – 10.05.49
CV Antras	10.05.49 – 23.12.50
CV Castelli	23.12.50 – 03.05.52
CV Allain	03.05.52 – 21.09.53
CV Reynaud	21.09.53 – 26.03.56
CV Duthu	26.03.56 – 06.09.57

Flag Officers

CA Merveilleux du Vignaux	02.11.46 – 11.11.46
VA Jaujard	20.04.47 – 20.10.48
CA Champion	14.05.52 – 23.09.54
CA Cirier	23.09.54 – 20.10.55

Notes:

CV	*Capitaine de vaisseau*	(RN equivalent rank: captain)
CA	*Contre-amiral*	(RN equivalent rank: rear-admiral)
VA	*Vice-amiral*	(RN equivalent rank: vice-admiral)

and the BPF, which had been experiencing problems in maintaining the tempo demanded by the US Navy for task force operations in the Pacific.

Advantage was taken of this pause in operations to conduct boiler repairs and also to pursue the issue of the over-large dispersion of the main guns. Gunnery practices and aerial observations of the recent shore bombardment operations had revealed that when 'half-turret' salvos were fired,[12] if the first shell struck the target the other was over or short, dispersion being measured at around 450 metres at ranges of 16,000-25,000 metres. Admiral Walker pointed out that the comparable figure for *Queen Elizabeth* was 250 metres. Firing trials were subsequently conducted using a single gun. Eight combat rounds were fired using SD19 charges and dispersion measured at 270 metres – close to British values. The deterioration in accuracy when firing both guns in the half-turret together was a puzzle, and would remain so until the problem was investigated and resolved by the *Service Technique* postwar (see p.204).

REFIT AND REPAIR AT DURBAN

On 3 June, the French light cruiser *Le Triomphant* arrived from France with spares for *Richelieu*. The French saw in these two ships the embryo of a future French Far East Fleet which would reassert French sovereignty over the colonies currently occupied by the Japanese. However, the Americans resolutely opposed the formation of such a force and the British, although more sympathetic to the French imperial cause, were concerned that a French fleet should not prove a drain on their own limited resources, particularly as the Japanese naval presence at Singapore had all but evaporated. Although *Le Triomphant* was the nominal replacement for the Dutch *Tromp*, Admiral Power was concerned about the poor endurance of the former *contre-torpilleur*, and because she had lost her sonar dome en route to Trincomalee it was decided that she should be sent to Diego Suarez for repairs. Power

---

[11] They were in good company, their consort *Cumberland* having narrowly missed the Battle of the River Plate in December 1939.

[12] Normal practice was to fire half-salvos on the British pattern, but firing the guns of two of the four 'half-turrets' together (as opposed to one gun from each half-turret).

The forward turrets of *Richelieu* in September 1945. The forward group of nine 20mm Oerlikons behind the breakwater has been replaced by four single 40mm Bofors Mk III. These guns were fitted during an overhaul at Durban during July-August of the same year. Note the screen abaft the 40mm Bofors to protect the guns and their crews from the blast of the main 380mm guns. (*ECPAD*)

decided to take advantage of the lull in fleet activity by sending *Richelieu* to refit in Durban. Having spent two out of every three days at sea since her last docking in Gibraltar, her hull was in serious need of scraping,[13] and her troublesome boilers – which were still emitting thick black smoke at higher speeds – needed partial re-tubing. Repairs to the starboard bilge keel, damaged by a trailing buoy cable, were also needed.

Richelieu arrived at Durban, having first put in to Diego Suarez to disembark non-white personnel,[14] on 18 July, and remained there until 10 August. The ship was docked on 31 July; the hull was scraped and repainted and the rust on the forecastle deck was chipped away. Boilers 10 and 11 were repaired by the onboard personnel using spare tubes delivered to Diego Suarez by the cruiser *Suffren*. It had for some time been apparent that the 20mm Oerlikons were of little value against modern aircraft and particularly against *kamikaze* attacks, and they were to be replaced where possible by single 40mm Bofors guns. The dockyard personnel removed thirteen of the 20mm mountings from the foredeck and the after tower; these were stowed on board. In their place four single Bofors were fitted, all on the foredeck; mounting plates for

---

[13] During the *Haguro* chase, 28 knots was the maximum that could be attained with shaft revolutions that would normally have secured 30 knots.

[14] This request from the South African authorities caused considerable shock and resentment aboard *Richelieu*; a petty officer from Martinique and a seaman from French Indochina were disembarked at Diego Suarez for the duration of the refit.

seven more were installed, and two 1.5-metre OPL rangefinders were fitted atop the bridge to provide fire control. The quad 40mm Bofors mountings at the after end of the shelter deck, which had previously suffered from the blast of the 152mm guns, had their protective screens raised, and their Mk 51 directors were relocated on the lower platforms of the after tower vacated by the 20mm mountings.

Richelieu left Durban on 10 August for gunnery and machinery trials, and then took on stores and ammunition at Diego Suarez. By the time she returned to Trincomalee on 18 August Japan had surrendered.

CLEARING UP

The period following the Japanese surrender was marked by somewhat messy clearing-up operations that aimed to re-establish British and French authority in Malaya and Indochina respectively and to receive the formal surrender of the various Japanese garrisons. The French military operation in particular was obstructed by the Americans. Alarmed by French plans to despatch 55,000 troops under General Leclerc to the region, they responded by dividing responsibility for Southeast Asia between the Chinese in the north and the British in the south,[15] in an attempt to squeeze out the French altogether.

On 7 September, *Richelieu* left Trincomalee and joined up with the British *Nelson*, which had arrived in July to take the place of *Queen Elizabeth*. The battleships were to provide cover for Operation 'Zipper', the long-awaited amphibious landings at Port Swettenham on the southern coast of Malaya. On 9 September, *Richelieu* set off a mine that exploded 17 metres to starboard abeam turret I. Damage was fortunately of a minor nature: a number of plates below the waterline were pushed in 10-12cm, there was shock damage to lighting systems and some shells in the forward shell room were displaced. For the crew the worst loss was that of 3000 litres of wine, which set off the flood warning sensors. A subsequent British report suggested it was a magnetic mine with a 200kg payload laid by aircraft. *Richelieu* continued to support the operation, and the hull was not repaired until she was docked at Cherbourg in April the following year. There was some vibration at high speeds but the ship was otherwise fully seaworthy.

The landings at Port Swettenham met with no Japanese resistance, and on 12 September *Richelieu* was at Singapore for the formal surrender. On 16 September she was back in Trincomalee, leaving for Indochina on 27 September in company with the light cruiser *Le Triomphant*. The two ships were to provide escort for the transports *Queen Emma* and *Princess Beatrix*, carrying the troops destined to restore the French administration in Saigon. This was a mission fraught with difficulty: not only did the occupying Japanese forces prove uncooperative but the restoration of French colonial control was bitterly opposed by the nationalist Viet-Minh forces, which had the tacit support of the United States. With the hinterland largely under the control of the Viet-Minh, *Richelieu* was used initially as a support base and hospital for the newly arrived French troops, and subsequently as a troop transport and fire support ship. During Operation 'Mapor' at Nha-Trang between 20 and 26

---

[15] The dividing line was the 16th Parallel.

November, 391 rounds of 152mm and 1622 rounds of 100mm were fired in support of the forces ashore, *Richelieu* being joined on this occasion by the light cruisers *Le Fantasque* and *Le Triomphant*.

With the arrival of the cruisers *Gloire*, *Suffren* and *Emile Bertin*, the carrier *Béarn* and the *Le Fantasque*, the presence of *Richelieu* was no longer required, and after re-embarking her landing party, she left Indochina on 29 December for France, finally arriving at Toulon on 11 February 1946. She was then used for the repatriation of French troops to North Africa prior to docking and repairs at Cherbourg during 16 March to 20 July.

POSTWAR DEPLOYMENT AND MODIFICATIONS

The France to which *Richelieu* returned was not the France of 1939. The great harbours of Brest, Cherbourg and Toulon were littered with wrecks, the graving docks cluttered with debris. Those dockyard installations that had not been sabotaged by the French in June 1940 had been flattened by the Allied bombing. The French economy was bankrupt; reconstruction of her battered infrastructure and industries would have to take priority over expenditure on military hardware. Attempts to restore French authority in the former colonies now encountered opposition from indigenous populations that scented a new mood of self-determination, leading to fresh and unwanted military commitments and widespread 'policing' operations. Trained naval personnel, many of whom had spent the past five years away from France, wanted nothing more than to get ashore, find a new job and rebuild their lives. This led to severe manning shortages, which in turn exacerbated the deterioration in the ship's military capabilities due to lack of maintenance. This is the context in which *Richelieu*'s postwar career needs to be considered.

Richelieu had disembarked her four single 40mm guns, most of her 20mm Oerlikons, and a large quantity of 152mm, 40mm and 20mm ammunition at Saigon. Only sixteen single 20mm remained: four on the roof of turret II, four atop the forward tower, four on the after tower, two on the after director and two atop turret VII. The repairs made at Cherbourg focused on the rudder shaft and one of the blades of the outer portside propeller; the outer starboard propeller, which had struck a submerged wreck when the ship attempted to berth at Cherbourg, had to be replaced. The hull plating damaged by the mine explosion was cut away and renewed. The boilers and auxiliary machinery, which until now had been maintained by the crew, were inspected and repaired by engineers from the naval propulsion establishment at Indret.

In early August, *Richelieu* visited Portsmouth, serving as a transport for personnel and stores destined for the light fleet carrier *Colossus*, which was to be loaned to the Marine Nationale for five years as *Arromanches*. She then embarked on an autumn cruise that took in Casablanca, Arzew, Mers el-Kebir and Dakar. At the latter port she was repainted, the hull up to the level of the upper deck receiving a uniform mid-grey livery in place of the former blue lozenge with light grey ends of the Admiralty standard scheme. *Richelieu* was still using exercise charges of US manufacture; these were continuing to give problems, as was the poor quality of the US-manufactured 100mm munitions. There was a general concern that the main and secondary guns were deteriorating. Modifications aimed at simplifying the local training and elevation of the 152mm turrets were carried out at Brest during February and March 1947.

In early 1947, the French surface and submarine forces were reorganised as four battle groups:

- the *Richelieu* group (based at Cherbourg) comprising the battleship plus the ex-German destroyers *Hoche*, *Desaix* and *Marceau* (1st DCT)
- the cruiser group (Toulon) comprising the 152mm cruisers *Montcalm* and *Gloire* (1st DC) and the light cruisers *Le Fantasque* and *Le Terrible* (10th DCL)
- the carrier group (Toulon) centred on *Arromanches*
- the 1st Submarine Flotilla, comprising the French submarines (Brest) and the ex-German boats (Lorient)

In response to a UN directive of May 1946, the first three groups were to be combined as the *Force d'Intervention* (FI) under Vice-Admiral Jaujard in *Richelieu*. The FI was first activated for a summer cruise to North

Richelieu in Portsmouth (UK) in August 1946. She brought personnel and stores destined for the light fleet carrier *Colossus*, which was to be loaned to the Marine Nationale for five years as *Arromanches*. She retains her Admiralty Standard colour scheme. Note the aerials for the British Type 285P gunnery radar atop the upper director, and the 1.5-metre OPL rangefinders atop the bridge for the single 40mm Bofors installed on the forecastle at Durban in August 1945. (*ECPAD*)

Right:
Richelieu on a visit to Algiers in the Spring of 1948. She now has the standard French postwar paint scheme known informally as *trois tons de gris* (Eng: 'three shades of grey'), which was applied in the fourth quarter of 1946 (see artwork on p.135). The hull up to the First Deck is painted medium blue-grey; all the upperworks above this level are light grey except for the funnel, the secondary turrets and the 100mm mountings, which are painted dark grey.

Far right:
Richelieu in the anchorage at Salins d'Hyères in 1952. (*H Landais collection*)

Below:
This 1947 close-up of the after tower gives an excellent detail view of the director for the secondary battery, with its 6-metre main RF and the shorter-base duplex RF at its front end for scartometry (the measurement of the distance between the shell splash and the target). Atop the director are the six distinctive Yagi aerials of the British Type 285 gunnery radar. (*ECPAD*)

Close-up of the superstructures taken in 1948. The radar outfit remains essentially unchanged from wartime. The after tower and turrets have by this time been repainted light grey. (*C Picard collection*)

to Cherbourg on 13 June for her annual docking. A shortage of spares for her British and US radars – especially the gunnery radars – was now beginning to tell. Large numbers of trained personnel left the ship, which spent three months from July tied to the jetty conducting basic training for new recruits. Numbers were now down from an official peacetime complement of 1375 to 1100. Morale among the remaining trained personnel was low.

During an autumn cruise to North Africa, *Richelieu* conducted firing tests with her main guns in an attempt to shed light on the dispersion problem. At a subsequent docking at Cherbourg in March of the following year, delay coils with a delay of sixty milliseconds were fitted to the firing circuits of the outer guns. Further firings off Mers el-Kebir with APC shell and combat charges confirmed that these made a significant improvement: a maximum dispersion of 577 metres and an average of 300 metres at a range of 25,000 metres as compared with 1710 metres and 950 metres respectively with the delay coils disabled. This was considered satisfactory considering the level of wear of the guns, each of which had fired an average of 150 rounds.

The spring cruise during which the latter tests took place saw the reactivation of the *Force d'Intervention*, which following assembly at Toulon conducted exercises off the French North African ports, then in the Atlantic off Casablanca. Budgetary cuts meant that *Richelieu* continued to lack basic equipment such as canvas awnings and towed targets for AA practice. A berthing incident at Mers el-Kebir resulted in minor damage to the stern. It was at the latter anchorage that the firing trials of the main guns took place, *Richelieu* being tied to the jetty to enable the fall of shot to be calculated precisely; sixty-eight rounds were fired.

Africa during May and June 1947, the ships gathering at Casablanca on 8 May. Jaujard assembled a flag staff but found that the antiquated command spaces of *Richelieu* were in no way up to the task. Platform 5 of the forward tower was employed for the purpose, but this was cramped and communications were totally inadequate for command of such a large and diverse force. Jaujard would continue to insist on the need for a new transmissions centre (*PC Transmissions*) and combat information centre (*Central Informations*), but the funding was simply not available; expenditure on the ship was reduced to the minimum necessary to keep her in service.

Following the dispersal of the FI, *Richelieu* returned

At the conclusion of the spring cruise the FI was disbanded and *Richelieu* returned to Brest 29 May. In

Richelieu in 1952, following a major refit at Cherbourg Naval Dockyard during 1950-1. She is wearing her new (and final) paint scheme of light grey overall, with only the anchors and the blast bags for the main turrets picked out in black.

August and September, she was docked at Cherbourg to assess the extent of the work which needed to be done at a major refit scheduled to take place at Brest, and in October Vice-Admiral Jaujard hauled down his flag. At the same time the ship's complement was reduced to 750 men, and following the postponement of the refit *Richelieu* was placed in reserve (*Disponibilité Armée*) from 1 April 1949. With the defence budget under severe pressure it was decided that priority should be given to the completion of *Jean Bart*, which would be the test-bed for a new generation of weapons and sensors of French design and manufacture (see Chapter 9).

REFIT CHERBOURG 1950-1

The major refit at Brest finally began on 1 January 1950 and the ship was in dockyard hands until 24 October 1951. It was the first major refit the ship had undergone since her reconstruction in the United States in 1943.

Machinery

The propulsion and auxiliary machinery was subjected to a complete overhaul, and some of the electrical cabling replaced. The boilers were completely re-tubed by Indret. Following her refit, *Richelieu* comfortably sustained speeds of 29-30 knots during machinery trials, and on 15 February 1952 attained 31.5 knots for two hours. Smoke emissions were noticeably reduced.

Main armament

During the earlier inspection the barrels of the 380mm guns had been found to be much worn. Those in turret I were replaced: the left-side guns by one new and one relined gun from Meppen in Germany, the right-side guns by one from Norway and one from Octeville (near Cherbourg) (see table in Chapter 4 for the history of these guns); the latter had been employed as coast artillery and had fired only forty rounds. The guns removed from turret I were then relined and reinstalled in turret II. The delay coils were removed but the firing mechanism of the outer guns was modified to give the same sixty-millisecond delay. The replenishment and reloading mechanisms were modified to enable the guns to fire every thirty-two seconds – the previous figure was forty-five seconds – and the converters for the hoists removed and refurbished. Finally, the 14-metre base duplex rangefinders originally installed in the two main turrets were replaced by quadruplex models.

Secondary armament

The 152mm guns in turrets V and VI were relined at Ruelle, and those in turret VII replaced by new guns of monobloc construction manufactured in Canada. Welding was used to reinforce the turret armour. Changes were made to the stops for bearing and elevation, and the replenishment and reloading systems modified as in *Jean Bart* (see Chapter 9). New regulators to permit the use of German fuzes were installed.

Heavy AA guns

The 100/45 Mle 1930 guns had been installed as a 'stop-gap' in early 1940. They had seen good service, but the barrels were now worn (average: 625 rounds)

and neither the guns nor their fire control systems were capable of tracking modern high-performance aircraft. In July 1949, there had been a proposal to replace the 100mm Mle 1930 with a combination of the German twin 10.5cm SKC 33, which had a significantly higher rate of fire (see table), and the new tri-stabilised director to be fitted in *Jean Bart*.[16] A number of sketch plans were drawn up with provision for between six and ten 10.5cm mountings – the additional mountings replacing the 40mm quads on the shelter deck – with those featuring eight/ten mountings having two directors per side. However, a final decision had to await trials aboard the former *contre-torpilleur Albatros*. The German mounting was twice the weight of the original CAD Mle 1931. Consideration was also given to the 100/55 Mle 1945 developed for *Jean Bart*, which was nearly as heavy. Both solutions would have required the ship to be bulged in order to maintain buoyancy. This was out of the question in the current financial climate, so a decision was postponed, and during mid-1950 the original mountings were

Richelieu at anchor during a visit to Villefranche-sur-mer in 1952.

---

16 The director was derived from the German *Wackeltopf*, which equipped the battleships and cruisers of the *Kriegsmarine*. The mountings and directors slated for *Richelieu* would be fitted in the two ex-Italian cruisers *Châteaurenault* and *Guichen* when they were rebuilt as AA escorts during 1951-4.

100/45 MLE 1930: REPLACEMENT OPTIONS

Gun data	100/45 Mle 1930	10.5cm/65 SKC/33	100/55 Mle 1945
Projectile weight	13.45kg	15.1kg	13.3kg
Muzzle velocity	785m/s	900m/s	855m/s
Range	15,800m	17,700m	17,260m
Ceiling	10,000m	12,500m	11,300m
Mounting Data			
Weight of mounting	13.5t	27.0t	26.6t
Max. elevation	80°	80°	80°
Firing cycle (per gun)	10rpm	15-18rpm	20-25rpm

refurbished by the crew. The port-side director was repaired, but repairs to the starboard director had to be left until later due to a shortage of skilled personnel.

Light AA

The 40mm quad mountings were completely refurbished, as was the associated RPC system, which had been prone to breakdown. The Mk 51 directors for mountings 5 and 6 were disembarked and sent to Toulon for training purposes, and the two 20mm Oerlikons on Turret VII were also disembarked.

Boats

The new boat outfit comprised:

two 8.3m motor boats
three 11m motor launches
one 10m motor launch
two 7m whalers
one 5m dinghy

Radar

The existing radars received new designations as follows:

Type 281B – GBVA (*Grand Bâtiment Veille Air* = air surveillance, large ship)
SA-2 – PBVA (*Petit Bâtiment Veille Air* = air surveillance, small ship)
SG-1 – GBVS (*Grand Bâtiment Veille Surface* = surface surveillance, large ship)
SF – PBVS (*Petit Bâtiment Veille Surface* = surface surveillance, small ship)

The British Type 281B was assessed as having good range performance but poor directivity; replacement by the Type 281Q, which had a power-rotated aerial, was envisaged but did not materialise. Of the American radars the SG-1 was highly regarded; however, the SF was sited too low to be useful, and the aerial of the SA-2 was found to be badly corroded. Consideration was given to replacement of the SA-2 by the British Type 277, but this was never implemented. Finally, the FV1 jammer was disembarked.

When she emerged from refit in October 1951, *Richelieu* had been restored to the state she was in at the end of her reconstruction in the United States. Some limited improvements had been made to the main and secondary guns, but it was recognised that further modifications would need to be made to the secondary fire control system and the heavy HA armament if the ship were to operate effectively in a modern air-intensive environment. The latter would also require a new electronics suite allied to improved command spaces and internal communications.

The financial outlay that would have been required to bring *Richelieu* fully up to date proved prohibitive, and it was decided in February 1951, when the ship was still undergoing refit, that she should be assigned to the *Ecoles Navales* as a gunnery training ship. Accommodation arrangements now had to be reviewed to incorporate the necessary berthing, classrooms, dining and other facilities required by a school ship.

From May 1952, *Richelieu* would be based at Toulon as flagship of Rear-Admiral Champion (*Groupe des Ecoles de la Méditerranée*). As a gunnery training ship, *Richelieu* would conduct training sorties to the range at

Richelieu, now used as a barracks, moored at the *Quai des Flotilles* at Brest in 1956. (*H Landais collection*)

Richelieu at anchor late in her career.

Salins d'Hyères on perhaps four days of every month, with only an annual summer visit to Algeria to break the monotony. The ship's livery by this time was light grey overall, with the 380mm blast bags and the anchors picked out in black.

In a refit from October 1953 to February 1954, the 100mm mountings were again refurbished and the British Type 284P main gunnery radar was replaced by a DRBC10A of French design and manufacture. It was used only for training, however, because the last firings of the 380mm guns had taken place in November 1951, when the statutory nine rounds per

gun had been fired during trials following the ship's major refit at Brest.

Richelieu was laid up at Brest in February 1956; dehumidifying equipment was installed in the main and secondary turrets, and the 100mm twin mountings and the 40mm quads cocooned; all the remaining single 40/20mm mountings were removed. *Richelieu* would serve as a school for reserve officer training until 30 September 1967, when she was stricken, becoming hull Q432. She was sold to an Italian firm of shipbreakers, Cantieri Navali Santa Maria, of Genoa, and broken up at La Spezia during 1968-9.

Richelieu has just arrived at La Spezia ready to be broken up in 1968. The 380mm guns of turret I had been removed at Brest prior to *Richelieu*'s departure under tow for Italy. One would subsequently be preserved at Brest and another at Ruelle. (*Courtesy Erminio Bagnasco*)

CHAPTER 9

JEAN BART: 1945-1956

THE DECISION TO COMPLETE *JEAN BART* WAS taken on 22 February 1945, but not without a debate between those who believed that the war that was still in progress had demonstrated the dominance of air power and those who believed that the battleship still had a major role to play at sea. During two meetings of the Conseil Superieur de la Marine (CSM) in July 1945, Admirals Barjot and Fénard emerged as fervent supporters of completing the *Jean Bart* as an aircraft carrier.

In the absence of any consensus among the admirals, the Navy Minister insisted on a definitive decision on one of three courses:

(1) to stop work on the ship altogether;
(2) to complete *Jean Bart* as a battleship;
(3) to complete her as an aircraft carrier.

While these deliberations were taking place, *Jean Bart* sailed from Casablanca on 25 August accompanied by the elderly *contre-torpilleur Tigre*. Following an uneventful passage that was conducted at a speed of 14 knots, she arrived at Cherbourg on 29 August and was moored at the *Jetée du Homet*.

On 21 September 1945, the CSM reconvened, and its members were unanimous in rejecting the first alternative. Kahn, the Ingénieur-Général and head of the DCCAN[1] then presented a scheme for the conversion of the ship into a carrier, at an estimated cost of

---

[1] *Direction Centrale des Constructions et Armes Navales.*

5000 million Francs and a delay of five years in completion. The design, drawn up in July 1945, included a 90mm thick armoured flight deck, which accounted for a significant proportion of the cost. According to this scheme the *Jean Bart* would have carried forty aircraft with fourteen additional planes slung from the hangar deckhead, and was to have a defensive armament of sixteen 130mm AA guns in eight twin mountings – a modified variant of the twin mounting fitted in the *Dunkerque*s.

The CSM was decidedly unimpressed. Concern was expressed regarding the relatively small number of aircraft that could be embarked – only half the number embarked by contemporary American and British fleet carriers. There were corresponding concerns about the reduction in hangar volume associated with the arrangement of the boiler uptakes. When certain members of the council expressed astonishment at the projected costs and delays Kahn was forced to admit that these were on the high side, and that his own personal estimate was 3500 million Francs and three years. This statement only served to reinforce the impression that the *Services Techniques* were opposed to the carrier conversion project and had decided to present it in the most unattractive light possible.

The CSM now focused its discussion on the plans for the completion of *Jean Bart* as a battleship. An exhaustive list of existing material was drawn up, and from this a projected schedule of works was calculated as follows:

(1) manufacturing the 380mm guns: three years

Jean Bart leaves Casablanca on 25 August 1945 for metropolitan France. The guns in turret I had previously been removed and used as replacements for the three guns of *Richelieu* damaged during Operation 'Menace' in September 1940. (*ECPAD*)

Jean Bart arrives in Cherbourg on 29 August 1949. Note the battered state of the hull, which had been patched up following the damage sustained during Operation 'Torch' in November 1942. (*ECPAD*)

Below:
Jean Bart in Laninon Dock No. 9, where she would undergo repairs to her hull prior to being refitted. Note the ruined buildings at the dock side; it would take some considerable time before the support infrastructure of the Marine Nationale was fully restored. (*H Landais collection*)

(2) finishing turret II (380mm): four years
(3) stockpiling the associated munitions: five years

Whichever course was taken, *Jean Bart* would clearly not be available for some time, the alternatives being: three and a half years to five years if completed as an aircraft carrier; four years for a battleship without munitions; or five years for a battleship with munitions. The CSM finally decided to opt for a battleship (a second *Richelieu* but with much improved AA defence). This decision was subsequently much criticised, particularly by officers of the naval air arm, who responded in the following terms:

> It was surprising in 1945 to see the Naval General Staff supporting the cause of the battleship against that of the aircraft carrier. This attitude, which dominated the discussions of 21 September 1945, clearly reveals that despite the experience of the war the mythology surrounding the big gun continues to rule our naval thinking.[2]

There can be no doubt that the decision against a carrier conversion was correct in that it would have resulted in a ship which was poor value for the effort and expenditure involved. Moreover, the last years of the Second World War had demonstrated that the battleship still had value as a fire support ship, as a carrier escort, and as a command ship. However, this was an argument for the retention of existing assets rather than new construction, and for the postwar Marine Nationale the major issues were funding, rebuilding infrastructure and a limited pool of skilled personnel. The reconstruction of *Jean Bart* was attractive in a number of respects, but it would have a major impact on other programmes which would become

[2] Rear-Admiral Barjot, minutes of meeting of 24 September 1945, No. 858/EMG/DN.

increasingly fundamental to the rebuilding of the Marine Nationale

WORK BEGINS

The work of completing *Jean Bart* began at Brest on 11 March 1946. The first stage of reconstruction involved repairing the damage done to the hull during the bombardment of Casablanca, completing the propulsion machinery, mounting the main and secondary armaments, and modifying the superstructures to accommodate new radar and fire control equipment. The big guns had already been ordered from Ruelle, and a new series of nine would be manufactured beginning in 1945 (see table for details). The reconstruction aimed to provide a ship that could perform three roles: task force flagship, heavy AA vessel, and fire support ship for shore bombardment.

On 26 November 1947, her hull repairs complete, *Jean Bart* was moved out of the Laninon No. 8 dock and moored at the new fitting-out quay (the *Quai d'Armement*) currently under construction – only 50 metres of this was usable! Work then continued on the superstructures, and the main and secondary guns were embarked. She was then docked again from 20 March to 9 October 1948, this time in Laninon No. 9, where a new external bulge was fitted to the lower hull and repairs to the shafts were carried out. Work continued on the completion of the main and secondary armaments. *Jean Bart* then returned to the new *Quai d'Armement*, some 200 metres of which were now complete. She conducted preliminary trials of her machinery 4 December, again returning to the fitting-out quay. Full machinery trials were run in January 1949, followed by turning and gunnery trials.

In May 1949 the *Groupe des bâtiments de ligne* was formed with *Jean Bart* and *Richelieu* under Rear-Admiral Branellec. The group would be disbanded the following year to enable *Jean Bart* to show what she could do as the command ship of a large surface formation. She took part in various exercises off the coast of North Africa in May and June 1950 before returning to Brest. In spring 1951, she continued her

380MM GUNS BUILT POSTWAR

Number of Gun	Destination
R 1945-1	Ruelle/Gâvres?
R 1945-2	*Jean Bart* TI
R 1946-1	*Jean Bart* TI
R 1946-2	*Jean Bart* TI
R 1946-3	*Jean Bart* TII
R 1947-1	*Jean Bart* TII
R 1947-2	*Richelieu* TI
R 1947-3	*Jean Bart* TII
R 1947-4	*Jean Bart* TII

Notes:
Nine guns were built at Ruelle over three years, primarily to arm *Jean Bart*. One was installed in turret I of *Richelieu*, and another retained at Ruelle and Gâvres (testing ground).
All of these guns were scrapped with the ships.

Jean Bart 1949

Turret I	Turret II
R 1937-4	R 1946-3
R 1945-2	R 1947-1
R 1946-1	R 1947-3
R 1946-2	R 1947-4

Richelieu 1950

Turret I	Turret II
R 1947-2	R 1936-2
R 1938-5	R 1936-4
R 1938-6	R 1937-2
R 1937-8	R 1937-5

work-up, and in May was docked at Le Havre to be fitted with a degaussing system. After further work-up sorties and fuel consumption trials in June she was back at the *Quai d'Armement* at Brest on 7 July.

At the end of this first phase of her reconstruction, *Jean Bart*'s machinery was complete and the main and secondary guns in place. However, the projected AA battery and the fire control equipment remained to be fitted. Early in November 1951, she was again moved to the fitting-out quay in order to carry out the following programme of work:

– improvements to the main armament fire control;
– modification of the 152mm mountings for AA fire, and recalibration of the fire control system;
– removal of the interim light AA armament of 40mm and 20mm single mountings;
– installation of twelve twin 100/55 Mle 1945 heavy AA mountings, disposed in four groups of three each controlled by its own director;
– installation of fourteen twin 57mm AA mountings, disposed in five groupings;
– installation of a combat information centre (*Centre d'Informations* or CI); and
– installation of two master gyroscopes for fire control.

Jean Bart moored in the *Rade-Abri* at Brest. The photo probably dates from 1949, following her first sea trials. Note the postwar colour scheme of medium blue-grey hull and light grey superstructures.

The emphasis during this second phase was principally on gunnery and fire control. Both of the superstructure towers and their masts were radically altered to allow the fitting of new radar antennae and fire control equipment.

COMPLETION OF THE MAIN AND SECONDARY ARMAMENTS

From the end of 1951, turret I was mothballed and turret II partially so. The latter could in theory be reactivated in two weeks, and when *Jean Bart* was being prepared to take part in the Suez Campaign (see p.221) this was effectively achieved; work on the turret began in early August and the first practice firings took place on the 22nd. (When the ship was deployed with the French Naval Intervention Force during the campaign only turret II was operational.)

Work on the main armament was confined to that necessary to make it operational. The main armament was controlled from a director tower incorporating a 14-metre triplex OPL stereoscopic rangefinder and located on the uppermost platform of the bridge structure. An early problem with vibration was remedied by increasing the height of the pedestal by 1.70 metres and the fitting of additional supporting struts. The director utilized a fast-reacting electrically powered RPC system similar to that used by the 100mm directors, and was regarded as very flexible in service. The DRBC 10A radar allowed surface targets to be engaged at 25,000 metres, and trials at the end of 1955 demonstrated that its performance was satisfactory. For optical back-up there were 14.2-metre quadruplex OPL stereoscopic rangefinders in each of the two main turrets, and binocular sights in the main director and the conning tower.

There was a single main transmitting station equipped with a Mle 1937 (analogue) fire control table, and auxiliary fire control stations equipped with a mechanical FC table in each of the main turrets.

JEAN BART: GENERAL CHARACTERISTICS AS REBUILT 1950

Displacement

Light	42,806 tonnes
Normal	46,500 tonnes
Full load	48,950 tonnes

Dimensions

Length wl	(As built)
Length oa	(As built)
Beam (over bulges)	35.542m
Draught (normal)	10.04m max.
Draught (full load)	10.69m max.

Machinery

Boilers	(As built)
Turbines	(As built)
Power	155,000shp for 31 knots
Oil fuel	6031 tonnes (5600t usable)
Endurance	8,832nm at 16 knots, 3,181nm at 30 knots
Generators	(As built)

Armament

Main guns	Eight 380/45 Mle 1936 in two quadruple mountings Mle 1935 (368 AP/386 HE rounds)
Secondary	Nine 152/55 Mle 1930 in three triple mountings Mle 1936 (750 SAP rounds + 2250 HE rounds)
HA guns	(not fitted)
Light AA	Eight 40mm Bofors Mk III in single mountings
	Twenty 20mm Oerlikon Mk 4 in single mountings

Radar[1]

Surface surveillance	DRBV 10 (ex-GBVS)
Air surveillance	DRBV 20 (ex-GBVA)
Navigation	DRBV 30
FC (380mm)	ABM (main director)
FC (152mm)	ACAE (secondary directors)

Protection   (As built)

Complement   911 as schools ship (May 1950)

Note: [1] see separate table for details.

152mm guns

A Ward Léonard RPC system was fitted for the secondary 152mm turrets. The main converter for each turret had been modified in anticipation of the future fitting of RPC for anti-aircraft fire, so surface fire was possible only by using the auxiliary converter. The firing circuits were electro-mechanical, with a split-second delay for the centre barrel to minimise dispersion. Both secondary directors were intended for surface firing, but the upper director was difficult to use in certain wind conditions when it was affected by funnel gases, and the latter often hindered optical rangefinding in both directors. In case of damage to the directors, the 152mm guns would be controlled from the centreline turret, or fired independently using the 8-metre duplex OPL stereo rangefinders mounted on each turret top.

Each of the two secondary directors was fitted from the outset with an 8-metre rangefinder of the same model as in the 152mm turrets. From the early 1950s, there was also a fire control radar designated ACAE, characterised by its twin dish antennae, which proved less than successful (see below).

There was a single main fire control station with a Mle 1940 (analogue) FC table for surface fire, and auxiliary FC stations equipped with the FC table Mle 1936 in each of the turrets for autonomous fire. In June 1954 it was decided to install an anti-aircraft fire control system for the 152mm guns. In AA fire the secondary armament would be controlled by the two after 100mm directors, using two 100mm Mle 1947 fire control tables suitably adapted for the 152mm guns. This installation was never completed.

COMPLETION OF THE AA ARMAMENT
100mm guns

The first magazines and mountings for the 100mm guns were fitted in July 1952; the twelve mountings were formally accepted after extensive trials of the rate and reliability of their firing during May to July 1953. The four directors were in place by May 1953, and the port forward group carried out its first firings against a towed target in July 1953. Major modifications followed as a result of these firing trials, and by October 1954 the starboard forward group was essentially complete and was fitted for fire against surface targets.

The twelve 100mm mountings were controlled by four gyro-stabilised directors modelled on German types.[3] Training angle and elevation could be transmitted automatically using a Ward Léonard RPC system, and there were also semi-automatic and emergency manual alternatives. Each director and its corresponding fire control station could control the three mountings of its designated group or all six mountings on that side of the ship. The changeover could be made instantly by automatic switches operated from the main AA fire control station or the target designation position.

Each of the directors was fitted with a 4-metre OPL stereoscopic rangefinder. For each director there was a corresponding fire control station; each of the two forward FC stations was equipped with separate FC tables for surface and AA fire, while the two after stations had FC tables for both 100mm and 152mm AA fire – although the latter, embarked in 1955, were never operational.

The weak link in the system was the ACAE radar sets. Performance was poor: the ACAE could neither follow the target automatically in range nor automatically generate height and bearing information. The sets on the forward directors were never operational and were removed in April 1956; those on the after directors did work after a fashion and were retained. They would have been replaced by the DRBC 30 in the projected third phase of modernisation.

57mm guns

The guns were manufactured under a licensing arrangement agreed with Bofors in 1947, but this did not include the mounting. The twin mounting, together with the loading arrangements, remote power control, munitions and the associated radar, were developed by the *Services Techniques*. The fire control gear was designed by the Swiss Contraves company to French specifications, and later the manufacturing rights were acquired by France.

The fourteen twin enclosed mountings, designated ACAD Mle 1948, were controlled by five self-contained fire control systems. Each of these comprised a radar director triaxially stabilised for roll, pitch and yaw, and a Contraves fully automated fire control system. This allowed for:

– fire against targets outside visual range (range and aiming data provided by the DRBC 30 radar mounted on the director);
– fire against visible targets (optical aiming by the director officer, range data from the radar); and
– fire against visible targets in the event of radar failure (range data from the director's rangefinder).

---

[3] The director was also fitted in the two reconstructed Italian cruisers *Châteaurenault* and *Guichen*, in which it was paired with the German 10.5cm SKC/33 twin mounting.

100mm Mle 1945 on CAD Mle 1946 mounting

Side Elevation

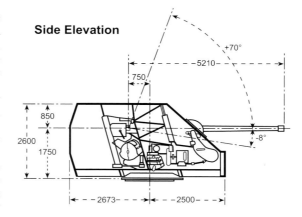

Rear Elevation

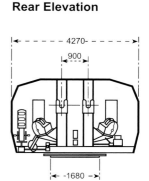

Cartridge

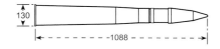

Cartridge Case (light alloy)

(Drawings by John Jordan © 2008)

ANTI-AIRCRAFT GUNS: CHARACTERISTICS

	100/55 Mle 1945	57/60 Mle 1947
Gun data		
Construction barrel	Monobloc autofretted	
Breech mechanism	SA sliding wedge	
Weight of gun	1840kg	N/A
Type of munitions	Fixed	Fixed
Projectiles	OEA Mle 1945 (13.3kg) OEA Mle 1951 (night)	OEA Mle 1950 (2.96kg)
Propellant	4.01kg BM7	0.94kg BM4
Complete round		
Weight	22.9kg	6.4kg
Dimensions	1.09m x 0.13m	0.62m x 0.057m
Muzzle velocity	855m/s	850m/s
Max. range	17,000m	14,500m
Ceiling	11,500m approx.	5500m
Mounting data		
Mounting designation	CAD Mle 1946	ACAD Mle 1948
Weight of mounting	26.55t	18t
Elevation of guns	-8°/+70°	-8°/+90°
Firing cycle (per gun)	20-25rpm	120rpm

Notes:
ACAD   *Automatique Contre-Avions Double*   AA twin mounting (automatic)
CAD   *Contre-Avions Double*   AA twin mounting
Mle   *Modèle*   Model

In all cases, the aiming data (bearing and elevation) were calculated and sent to the guns by the fire control table. After acquisition the DRBC 30 radar followed the target automatically; fire could then be opened and sustained until the ready-use ammunition on the mounting (160 rounds) was expended, with no more human intervention than the pressing of a button in the central fire control station. The 57mm mountings could also use a back-up system of nine Mk XIV gyroscopic optical fire control sights. In the event of damage to the fire control system or RPC system, each mounting could fire under local control using a Bronzavia gunsight.

Left:
Jean Bart fitting out at the *Quai d'Armement* at Brest in 1950.

Below:
The rebuilt forward tower in 1950. On the face of the director for the main battery is the French-built ABM fire control radar. Note the single 40mm Bofors and 20mm Oerlikon mounts fitted as a temporary measure before the embarkation of the new purpose-designed AA armament. (*H. Landais collection*)

Opposite, top:
Jean Bart revisits Casablanca in June 1950. She is moored at the *Grande Jetée*; behind her is her former mooring at the *Quai Delande*, to the right of the grain silos.

Opposite, below:
Jean Bart at Brest in 1950 following the first stage of her reconstruction.

CHANGES IN CHARACTERISTICS AS COMPLETED 1955

Displacement

Light	43,052 tonnes
Normal	46,809 tonnes
Full load	49,196 tonnes

Dimensions

Draught (normal)	10.23m max.
Draught (full load)	10.90m max.

Armament

HA guns	Twelve 100/55 Mle 1945 in six twin mountings Mle 1946 (900 day, 3000 night rounds + 680 starshell; 12,000 proximity-fuzed rounds)
Light AA	Twenty-eight 57/60 Bofors Mle 1947 in fourteen twin mountings Mle 1948 (28,000 HE day, 14,000 HE night rounds)

Radar[1]

Air/surface surv.	DRBV 11 (mainmast)
Air surveillance	DRBV 20 (foremast)
Navigation	DRBV 30 (foremast)
Height-finder	SP (US model – mainmast)
FC (380mm)	DRBC 10A
FC (152mm)	ACAE (x 2)
FC (100mm)	ACAE (x 4)
FC (57mm)	DRBC 30B (x 5)

Complement

Schools ship	757
Overseas missions	1149
Suez Operation	1280
Full wartime	2220

Note: [1] See separate table for details.

Designated 'standard batteries' of two, three or four mountings, could be controlled by a single radar director. Many different combinations of mountings and directors were possible: batteries could be reinforced by other groups on the same side of the ship; alternatively, control could be completely decentralised, giving each mounting its own optical or radar director (there were nine and five respectively).

Firing trials using standard and reinforced batteries were completed by September 1955. The optical positions were only fitted out in August 1956 and trials were carried out shortly afterwards.

The eight 40mm Bofors single mountings fitted as a temporary measure on the ship's completion were landed in 1952, and the twenty remaining 20mm Oerlikons were disembarked at the beginning of 1954.

RANGEFINDERS 1946-56

Main armament

1 x OPL 14-metre S (triplex)	Director fwd tower
2 x OPL 14.2-metre S (quadruplex)	Turrets I and II

Secondary armament

2 x OPL 8-metre S (duplex)	Directors atop/abaft after tower
3 x OPL 8-metre S (duplex)	Turrets V, VI and VII

100mm guns

4 x OPL 4-metre S	Each of four directors

Notes:
OPL   *Optique de Précision Levallois-Perret*
S   Stereoscopic RF

Jean Bart moored in the *Rade-Abri* at Brest in 1951. Although structurally complete she still has her interim AA armament of single 40mm Bofors and 20mm Oerlikon guns (see colour artwork: *Jean Bart* 1950 p.136). The main gunnery director, fitted with its ABM fire control radar, is trained to port. Note that the upper of the two secondary directors, located atop the after tower, has received the two dish reflectors for its ACAE fire control radar, but the lower director has yet to be so fitted.

Target designation

Optical target designation was exercised either from platform 7 (two 380mm positions, two 152mm, and four 100/57mm – one per sector), or from the conning tower (two 380mm, two 152mm – surface combat only). Transmission to the main and secondary directors was via a traditional Granat Follow the Pointer (FtP) system. The 100mm directors and the optical directors for the 57mm guns received target designation information via a similar system, but the 57mm directors were guided to the target by remote power control.

Target designation using radar was in principle effected from the CIC (*Centre d'Informations*). However, for the main and secondary guns it could also be exercised from platform 6.

IN SERVICE AT LAST

The second phase of *Jean Bart*'s reconstruction was punctuated by sea trials of the various items of equipment installed. The ship was not ready to join the active fleet until 1 May 1955, and she then embarked on a prestigious series of visits in which she represented the new and rebuilt Marine Nationale. During that same month, escorted by the brand-new *escorteur d'escadre* (EE) *Surcouf*, she transported the President of the Republic to Denmark for a state visit, and in July she represented French arms at the 175th Anniversary of the landing of Rochambeau's troops at Newport during the American War of Independence, arriving at Hampton Roads on 8 July and returning to Brest on 26 July. Following various sorties off the coast of Brittany during August and September she left Brest for the last time to become flagship of the Training Squadron in the Mediterranean. She arrived at Toulon on 17 October and immediately joined the *Groupe Ecole Sud* (GES), under Rear-Admiral Cirier; the latter would transfer his flag to her on 21 October.

Jean Bart on sea trials during 1951. All the emplacements for the new anti-aircraft armament are ready.

Except for a single training exercise with the fleet ('Ajax II'), *Jean Bart*'s activities during winter 1955-6 were restricted to regular sorties to the gunnery range at Salins d'Hyères for AA gunnery training and port visits along the Mediterranean coast. In June, the annual visit of the squadron to the ports of French North Africa took place.

The normal peacetime round of training and port visits would be interrupted by the Suez Crisis. It was decided that *Jean Bart* be reactivated to serve in her designated role as a command and fire support ship. From 8 July, the ship was a hive of activity as the

Jean Bart in 1953 with her new AA battery of 100mm and 57mm guns. She now has a full outfit of surveillance and fire control radars, and is in her final paint scheme of light grey overall with black anchors and blast bags.

SHELLS IN USE[1]

Gun	Shell Model	Weight	Charge	MV	Range	Remarks
380mm	OPfK Mle 1936	890kg	C1	800m/s	36,500m	APC: orange dye
	OPfK Mle 1943[2]	885kg	C1	800m/s	36,500m	APC: orange dye
	OEA Mle 1945[3]	884kg	C1	800m/s	36,500m	HE
	OEA Mle 1949	879kg	C3	632m/s	24,800m	HE
152mm	OPfK Mle 1931	55.8kg	C1	861m/s	26,100m	SAP: orange dye
	OEA Mle 1943[2]	47kg	C1	914m/s	24,900m	HE[4]
	OEA Mle 1947	51kg	C1	894m/s	24,850m	HE[4]
100mm	OEA Mle 1945	13.32kg	BM7	855m/s	17,000m	HE[4]
57mm	OEA Mle 1950	2.96kg	BM4	850m/s	11,630m	HE

Notes:
[1] The list does not include exercise rounds
[2] The 380 OPfK Mle 1943 and the 152 OEA Mle 1943 were of US manufacture.
[3] The 380 OEA Mle 1945 was of British manufacture.
[4] The 152 OEA Mle 1943 and Mle 1947 and the 100 OEA Mle 1945 could be used against surface or aerial targets; AA shells were time-fuzed; the 100mm OEA Mle 45 shell had a German Zt Z S/30 mechanical time fuze; later versions had a very sensitive nose fuze.

AMMUNITION ABOARD JEAN BART, JANUARY 1957

Gun calibre	380		152			100		57	
Shell type	OPfK Mle 43	OEA Mle 45	OPfK Mle 37	OEA Mle 47	OEA Mle 54	OEA Mle 45	OEcl	OEA Mle 52	
No. of shells	328	406	750	2284		8906 D	600	28,525 D	
						3000 N		14,531 N	
No. of charges	3000		1800 C1; 380 C2 (D)			(fixed ammunition)			
			750 C1 (N)						

Notes:
OPfK = <u>O</u>bus de <u>P</u>erforation (APC/SAPC) with 'K' colorant; 380 colorant was orange, 152 yellow
OEA = <u>O</u>bus <u>E</u>xplosif en <u>A</u>cier (HE: contact or time-fuzed AA)
OEcl = <u>O</u>bus <u>E</u>clairant (starshell)
D = day rounds; N = night rounds

Source: Inventory from Devis de Campagne of CV Digard (31.05.55-27.01.57)

Below, left:
View of the 152mm turrets and after tower. Note the twin dish reflectors of the ACAE fire control radar on the face of the secondary directors above and below the funnel. (Jean Moulin collection)

Below:
Close-up of the forward tower of Jean Bart in 1953. In the centre of the picture is one of the four gyro-stabilised directors for the 100mm guns; note the twin dish reflectors of the ACAE fire control radar on its face. To the right is one of the five smaller directors for the 57mm Bofors guns with its DRBC 30B fire control radar. (ECPAD)

Right:
Jean Bart arrives in New York 13 July 1955. (*US National Archives*)

Below:
Jean Bart in Laninon Dock No. 8 at Brest in 1955; she would be moved out of the dock on 15 April. Moored in the roadstead is the recently completed cruiser *De Grasse*, which began her sea trials in April 1955.

COMMANDING OFFICERS AND FLAG OFFICERS (1943-70)

Commanding Officers

CV Ansaldi	15.03.43 – 18.04.47
CV Delattre	18.04.47 – 01.06.48
CV Robin	01.06.48 – 23.04.50
CV Cirier	23.04.50 – 06.12.51
CV Lefevre	06.12.51 – 29.06.53
CV Barnouin	29.06.53 – 31.05.55
CV Digard	31.05.55 – 27.01.57
CF Dupuis	09.11.56 – 27.01.57[1]
CV Salmon	28.01.57 – 18.11.57
CF Chevillotte	18.11.57 – 04.01.58[1]
CV Gisquet	04.01.58 – 18.11.59
CV Ghilini	18.11.59 – 20.12.61
CV de Muizon	20.12.61 – 01.02.64
CV Bouvet de la Maisonneuve	01.02.64 – 21.07.66
CV Walter	21.07.66 – 25.05.68
CV Guttinger	25.05.68 – 18.12.69
CV François	18.12.69 – 14.01.70

Note: [1] interim/provisional command respectively

Flag Officers

CA Brannellec	11.05.49 – 16.04.50
VA Lambert	26.06.50 – 03.07.50
CA Champion	01.07.55 – 26.07.55
CA Cirier	21.10.55 – 13.07.56
CA Galleret	25.01.57 –

Notes:
CF	*Capitaine de frégate*	(RN equivalent rank: commander)
CV	*Capitaine de vaisseau*	(RN equivalent rank: captain)
CA	*Contre-amiral*	(RN equivalent rank: rear-admiral)
VA	*Vice-amiral*	(RN equivalent rank: vice-admiral)

Below:
Jean Bart at anchor off Newport, United States, 8 July 1955. The visit was to commemorate the 175th Anniversary of the landing of Rochambeau's troops during the American War of Independence. (*US National Archives*)

RADARS 1946-56

Surface surveillance

DRBV 10	1948-50	Atop CT	Ex-GBVS; replaced by DRBV 11
DRBV 11	1951-6	Atop mainmast	Combined surface/air; unsuccessful
DRBV 30	1948-56	Atop mainmast	Successful; moved to foremast 1951

Air surveillance

DRBV 20	1949-56	Lower mainmast	Ex-GBVA; successful; moved to foremast 1951
SP	1951-6	Lower mainmast	From *Bois Belleau*; modest performance

Fire control

ABM	1948-50	Face main director	For 380mm; replaced by DRBC 10 1951
ACAE	1950-6	Face secondary director	For 152/100mm; unreliable
DRBC 10A	1951-6	Face main director	For 380mm; replaced ABM
DRBC 30B	1951-6	Face AA director	For 57mm; successful

Notes:
GBVS	*Grand Bâtiment Veille Surface*
GBVA	*Grand Bâtiment Veille Air*
ABM	*Artillerie But Marin*
ACAE	*Artillerie Contre Avion Eloigné*
DRBV	*Détection Radio-électrique Bâtiment (de surface) Veille*
DRBC	*Détection Radio-électrique Bâtiment (de surface) Contrôle*

ship's complement, soon to increase from 757 to 1280 and assisted by dockyard personnel, worked to get her ready. Turrets II (380mm) and VII (152mm), together with two groups of 100mm and three groups of 57mm guns were fully manned. The ship was worked up from late August until mid-October. On 7 September, gunnery practice took place in company with the cruiser *Georges Leygues* off the North African coast, and there were regular firings of the anti-aircraft guns.

OPERATION 'MOUSQUETAIRE'

On 24 October, *Jean Bart* left Toulon for Algiers, arriving two days later after conducting various exercises en route. From 29 to 31 October, the élite Commando Hubert and soldiers of the 1st Parachute Regiment, Foreign Legion embarked. *Jean Bart* then joined the *Force Navale d'Intervention*, activated specifically for this operation. In addition to *Jean Bart*, the force comprised the carriers *Arromanches* and *Lafayette*, the cruiser *Georges Leygues*, the new EE *Surcouf*, *Kersaint*, *Cassard* and *Bouvet*, plus the *Groupe d'action sous-marine* (GASM). Its mission was to support a landing in the Suez Canal Zone in conjunction with the British.

Jean Bart left Algiers on 1 November, arriving at Limassol (Cyprus) three days later, having made the passage at 25 knots. Here she transferred the troops embarked to the amphibious landing force. The following day she left to conduct a bombardment off Port Said. She fired only four rounds of 380mm in support of the landings before the operation was called off. *Jean Bart* left Port Said on 7 November, returning

to Toulon on 13 November via Limassol. On 1 December, she rejoined the GES.

THE LAST YEARS

The last training sortie by *Jean Bart* took place during 11-19 July 1957, when all of her guns were fired for the last time. On 1 August, she was placed in Reserve A.

Aerial view of *Jean Bart* in the Mediterranean in 1955. (*ECPAD*)

Jean Bart at Algiers on 1 November 1956, having embarked the élite Commando Hubert and soldiers of the 1st Parachute Regiment, Foreign Legion, in readiness for the Anglo-French Suez operation. (*ECPAD*)

By this time, the postwar naval construction programme of the Marine Nationale was in full swing. Despite the major injection of US funding that accompanied French membership of NATO, budgets remained tight, and *Jean Bart* was not only expensive to maintain but also would need further costly modifications if she were to remain an effective operational unit. Battleships also made heavy demands on personnel. The reconstructed AA cruiser *De Grasse*, which had recently entered service, had a complement of 950, and each of the new *escorteurs d'escadre*, of which twelve were now in service with a further five building, had a complement of 350.

The Marine Nationale had already invested considerable funding and manpower in the reconstruction of *Jean Bart*, and there was a natural reluctance to see this investment come to nothing. The end of 1957 therefore saw further reconstruction projects: the first envisaged the replacement of both the 100mm Mle 1945 and the 57mm Mle 1947 mountings by the latest 100mm Mle 1953 single mounting; the second by a combination of 100mm Mle 1953 mountings amidships and missiles on the quarterdeck (see table for details).

However, none of these projects came to anything, and from August 1957 *Jean Bart* became a floating barracks. On 1 January 1961, her reserve status was downgraded to Reserve B. *Jean Bart* spent the next nine years in this category, until stricken on 10 February 1970, when she was redesignated hull Q466. She was sold to a French firm of breakers on 21 May of the same year, and was subsequently towed away and broken up at Brégaillon.

THE LAST PROJECTS

Project 1: Modernisation of AA Guns (1957)
– replacement of twelve 100mm CAD Mle 1945 by twelve 100mm CAS Mle 1953[1] (some modifications to magazines and hoists)
– progressive replacement of ten 57mm ACAD Mle 1948 forward and amidships by ten 100mm CAS Mle 1953
– replacement of four 57mm ACAD Mle 1948 on quarterdeck either by four 100mm CAS Mle 1953 or missiles (see below)
– directors for 152mm guns to be linked to after 100mm directors for long-range AA fire

Note:
[1] The 100mm Mle 1953 mounting was to be evaluated during 1958.

Project 2: Guided Missile Cruiser (1958)
Solution A
– suppression of four 57mm ACAD on quarterdeck + associated director + FC station 1
– construction on quarterdeck of central missile hangar by extending the shelter deck to the towing capstan; missiles to be stowed horizontally at 45 degrees to the centreline; capacity 24-44 missiles
– installation of three horizontal launch ramps on either side of the hangar
(This solution was considered simple and practical, requiring few structural modifications. There was, however, some concern regarding possible concussion damage from the after 152mm guns.)

Solution B
– suppression of four 57mm ACAD on quarterdeck + associated director + FC station 1
– extension of the shelter deck as far as the towing capstan to form the roof of the missile hangar, and removal of the upper deck beneath the hangar structure to permit the missiles to be stowed vertically; capacity 75-150 missiles
– installation of six launch ramps with vertical reloading on the roof of the hangar
(This solution was attractive because of the much-increased missile capacity. There was also considered to be less risk of concussion damage to the missiles from the after 152mm guns than in Solution A.)

Solution C
– suppression of four 57mm ACAD on quarterdeck + associated director + FC station 1
– removal of upper deck and some crew accommodation for vertical stowage of missiles; capacity 75-90 missiles
– installation of six launch ramps flat on the quarterdeck but with vertical reloading
(This solution was attractive because it minimised topweight additions, albeit at the expense of crew accommodation. There was also considered to be less risk of concussion damage to the missiles from the after 152mm guns than in Solutions A and B.)

Solution D
– suppression of 380mm turret I and the two 57mm ACAD located on the forecastle
– extension of the shelter deck to the forward or after breakwater to provide missile stowage and accommodation for the missile crews; eighty-five missiles to be stowed in the former magazines and barbette + 125 missiles in the deckhouse
– three or four launch ramps
(There was concern regarding blast and concussion damage from turret II. The stowage of 125 missiles in the deckhouse was dependent on these concerns proving unfounded.)

Solution E
– suppression of both 380mm turrets to permit a taller and more capacious missile hangar capable of stowing missiles vertically above upper deck level; extending this hangar to the forward breakwater would give a capacity of 325 missiles (provided the hangar was unarmoured)
– six or eight launch ramps
(Neither of the solutions involving the complete or partial replacement of the main guns by guided missiles was seriously pursued because the NGS considered removal of the 380mm gun turrets premature.)

Project 3: Terrier Missile Conversion
– removal of centreline 152mm turret
– installation of a US Mk 10 twin-arm missile launcher
– stowage for three missiles only beneath the launcher
(This installation was proposed only for the training of personnel. It was envisaged that the missile launcher would be removed and the turret replaced following` trials.)

A rare view of the after group of 100mm turrets trained to starboard, dating from 1956. (*H Landais collection*)

Below:
The three major school ships which formed the GES, seen here in 1959. From left to right: *Jean Bart*, *Suffren* and *Montcalm*. In the foreground is a the former German torpedo-boat *Lorrain* (ex-*T 28*), attached to the anti-submarine training school at Toulon.

The guns of turret II, seen here in 1953. Note the unusual configuration of the blast bags, which are supported on hinged frames which move with the gun when it elevates. These were first fitted in *Richelieu* and the light cruisers during their reconstruction in the United States. (*Courtesy M Moulin*)

Below:
Jean Bart being broken up at Brégaillon in 1970. She was sold, together with the cruiser *Montcalm* (seen here in the background on the right) to the Société des Abeilles for 2,980m FF. The two ships provided work for 200 men over two years, and yielded 30,000 tonnes of scrap iron and 750 tonnes of nickel. (*Martinelli*)

CONCLUSION

DUNKERQUE **AND** *STRASBOURG*

The relatively short active service life of these two ships makes a full appreciation of their strengths and weaknesses a difficult task. Given the radical nature of their design when compared with the French battleships that preceded them, it would have been surprising if everything had worked as intended and if there were no flaws in the design which would need to be addressed. In the event, it took almost six years to complete *Dunkerque* and to bring her to full operational readiness. When war was declared on 3 September 1939, her sister *Strasbourg* was a brand new ship whose entry into service had been accelerated due to the deteriorating international situation.

Many of the defects of these ships which became apparent during their early war service would have been remedied had France not been driven out of the conflict in June 1940. As in British and US ships, more effective light AA weapons with centralised fire control would undoubtedly have been fitted in numbers. A variety of radars would have been fitted for surveillance, target designation and fire control, as they were in *Richelieu* and in the French cruisers and *contre-torpilleurs* that survived 1942 and subsequently rejoined the Allied cause. Modifications to the replenishment and loading systems of the main and secondary guns would undoubtedly have made them more robust and reliable, and less prone to breakdown.

Nevertheless, there were more fundamental weaknesses that became evident during the ships' limited war service during 1939-40, and others which became apparent only when *Dunkerque* sustained serious damage as a result of Operation 'Catapult' in July 1940. The following observations are based on the reports of the COs and flag officers under whom these ships served.

Seakeeping

Despite their outstanding manoeuvring qualities, *Dunkerque* and *Strasbourg* suffered from a combination of an exceptionally fine hull-form forward – a feature adopted to secure a high maximum speed – and inadequate freeboard. The bow was judged to have insufficient sheer and flare; in heavy weather speed had to be reduced, otherwise the forward quadruple 330mm turret was completely submerged and suffered ingress of water, and the lightly built bow section was vulnerable to structural damage. *Dunkerque* suffered particularly badly during winter 1939-40 when she operated in the North Atlantic, and *Strasbourg* experienced similar problems in the Bay of Biscay during November 1939 when returning from West Africa. The following is an extract of VAE Gensoul's report dating from that period:

> During the October/November sorties *Dunkerque* struggled in heavy seas. The bow section was devastated. Palliatives are required, and I use this word advisedly, as these ships will always lack the requisite two metres of freeboard (cf. the modifications made to

Scharnhorst-Gneisenau and *Prinz Eugen*).[1] In the course of the crossing from Halifax to Brest *Dunkerque* was exposed to heavy seas coming from the beam or the starboard quarter, and one cannot say that she came through this experience with flying colours. There was ingress of water into Turret IV (130 starboard after).[2] Severe vibration in the after part of the ship caused the starboard main servo-motor for the rudder to again break down. This meant that for a second time *Dunkerque* returned to port with only the port servo-motor operational. The same vibrations also resulted in substantial play in the lower collar of the rudder. These defects were reparable but would, like the bow section, be subject to constant repair.

Strasbourg at her moorings. The unusually fine hull-form forward was adopted to secure a high maximum speed, and the sheer and flare of the bow was judged insufficient to cope with the heavy seas experienced when operating in the North Atlantic.

There would also be regular failures in the electrical transmission for the tiller flat, which put the ship at risk in confined waters.

Value as a fighting unit

The propulsion machinery proved totally satisfactory. It was also economical and bestowed on the ship a good radius of action.

However, the main and secondary guns were fragile and complex, the remote power control (RPC) never worked properly, and the main guns suffered from

---

[1] Authors' note: These ships, together with the earlier heavy cruisers *Admiral Hipper* and *Blücher*, were given an 'Atlantik' bow with exaggerated flare and sheer after early problems experienced with their original straight stems. The initial design for *Bismarck* also featured a straight stem but as with *Prinz Eugen* this was modified before the ship's completion.

[2] Authors' note: Gensoul is in error here: this would have been turret V; turret IV was the port midships (twin) 130mm.

excessive dispersion (200-1100m). The problem was later assessed as being the close proximity of the paired guns, which resulted in blast interference when a half-turret salvo was fired.[3]

A fuller report on the qualities and defects of *Strasbourg* by Admiral de Laborde and dated 16 December 1941, makes a number of interesting observations:

The following defects are evident in the conception and realisation of *Strasbourg*:

From a seaworthiness point of view the construction of the bow is too light and its configuration is poor; the ship does not handle as well in a seaway as one would expect for a ship of her size; it is a hull-form best suited to a testing tank.

As for protection, the conception appears to be correct; however, the realisation is defective in that the tunnels for the cabling are not water- or gas-tight – a defect which, when aggravated by explosions in combat, would probably render the theoretical invulnerability of the citadel illusory. In future the aim should be to increase the autonomy of the various compartments of the ship either by decentralising the electrical switchboards or by at least a partial return to hydraulic systems.

In addition to the problem of water/gas-tightness, the dangers of fire when in action are now excessive due to the flammable nature of the cable insulation, and also to the quantity of flammable furnishings in the accommodation spaces which dominate the upperworks. These constitute a carefully prepared bonfire waiting for someone to strike the match. In future warships should be furnished as follows:

Flameproof installations capable of sustaining every aspect of life at sea during wartime made of steel and painted with flame-resistant paint, mouldings of asbestos board, chrome furniture with desk- and table-tops of thick glass;

Peacetime furnishings intended to make the spartan wartime furnishings more luxurious and comfortable, e.g., hangings, rugs, cushions, etc., to be disembarked in wartime.

In terms of armament, the concentration of the main armament forward is a serious error; the ship should be able to fight while being pursued if circumstances demand. The 130mm calibre of the secondary armament is not heavy enough to engage surface targets, but too heavy and unwieldy for effective AA fire.

Some further observations from the authors

Due to circumstances, *Dunkerque* and her sister *Strasbourg* were never given the opportunity to show what they could do in combat. Had they encountered any of the surface raiders that they were designed to hunt down and fight, the German *Panzerschiffe* of the *Deutschland* class, there can be little doubt as to the outcome.

How well they would have performed against the larger, more powerful *Scharnhorst* and *Gneisenau* is less easy to say. The German ships, built to match *Dunkerque* and *Strasbourg*, were heavier (32,000 tons against 26,500 tons standard) and had thicker

armour. However, their protection system was dated, leaving many of the major communications spaces and much of the electrical and telemotor cabling exposed above the level of the main armoured deck. They were also armed with the relatively lightweight 28cm main gun, firing a 330kg shell, against which the protection system of the French ships had been designed. The Germans of course fully intended to remedy this deficiency by replacing the triple 28cm turrets by the twin 38cm turrets planned for *Bismarck* and *Tirpitz*.[4] However, this measure was pre-empted by the outbreak of war, and the *Scharnhorst*s were left with a gun which had good penetration characteristics against belt armour but a relatively poor performance against armoured decks. *Dunkerque*'s inclined belt would have been vulnerable against the 28cm at shorter ranges, but it was unlikely that the German shell would have penetrated her thick 115-125mm armoured deck, which was backed up by a 40mm splinter deck. The citadel of *Strasbourg*, which had a thicker armoured belt than her sister (283mm against 225mm), should have proved invulnerable to the German 28cm at probable combat ranges.[5]

It should be noted that the German battleships, which had even less freeboard than their French counterparts, suffered just as badly in the heavy seas regularly experienced during the winter months in the North Atlantic. When operating off Norway during April 1940 *Scharnhorst* and *Gneisenau*, despite their specially modified 'Atlantik' bow, shipped huge quantities of water over their bows. During the action with HMS *Renown* both ships suffered ingress of water into 'A' turret, putting the training motors out of action in *Scharnhorst*, and the latter ship also had two of her open-mount 15cm secondary guns put out of action.

By May 1940, *Dunkerque* and *Strasbourg* had been redeployed to the Mediterranean in readiness for action against the Italian *Regia Marina*. The last-minute entry of Italy into the conflict frustrated French plans for a decisive fleet action in that particular arena. The Italians were content to await the anticipated collapse of the French Army rather than risk battle against the fully trained and battle-ready French Atlantic Fleet now based on Mers el-Kebir. The new Italian 35,000-ton battleships of the *Littorio* class were still working up, and reconstruction of the *Duilio* class had yet to be completed. The Italian battle line currently comprised only the two older reconstructed ships of the *Cavour* class. These were three-four knots slower than the *Dunkerque*s, their rebored 320mm guns fired a lighter shell (525kg against 560kg for the French 330mm), and their protection was still barely adequate; their 270mm side belt and 80/100mm

---

[3] In 1948, thyratron retarders were fitted to one of each of the paired guns in *Richelieu* (qv) and appear to have resolved the problem.

[4] As early as 1934, it was proposed to replace the 28cm triple turrets of *Scharnhorst* and *Gneisenau* with twin 35cm turrets at a later date.

[5] German figures suggested they were confident of penetrating the 225mm armour belt of *Dunkerque* up to 20,000 metres; however, the same figures show that *Strasbourg*'s 283mm belt could not be penetrated beyond 15,000 metres. Given that there was little improvement in German AP shells between the two world wars, even these figures may be considered optimistic.

decks would have been penetrated at most ranges by the French 330mm APC shell.

In short, *Dunkerque* and *Strasbourg* could have been expected to fight with a good chance of success against any of the capital ships in service with Germany and Italy until late 1940, and by that time the Italian *Littorio*s with their 381mm guns (shell weight: 885kg) would be matched by the similarly armed *Richelieu* and *Jean Bart*. The one European navy whose ships *Dunkerque* and *Strasbourg* could not expect to engage with any chance of success during 1939-40 was that of Britain, whose fifteen first-line capital ships were armed with guns of 15in or 16in calibre (shell weights were 870kg and 930kg respectively), and with the exception of the battlecruisers *Repulse* and *Renown* had armour belts 12-14in (305-356mm) thick. This should not have been a concern to the French, as the British were their allies. The arrival of Force H off Mers el-Kebir on the morning of 3 July 1940, with the French ships moored facing the mountainous shore, their all-forward guns unable to bear on the aggressor, overturned all previous assumptions about how (and what) these ships would fight. The escape of *Strasbourg*, almost completely unscathed, in the most adverse circumstances imaginable is all the more remarkable.

RICHELIEU AND JEAN BART

Although larger, heavier and significantly more powerful than *Dunkerque* and *Strasbourg*, these ships were broadly similar in conception and design and therefore shared many of the latter ships' strengths and weaknesses.

Seakeeping and manoeuvrability

Richelieu and *Jean Bart* appear to have been better sea boats than their smaller predecessors, able to sustain high speed even in heavy seas. Although the bow section remained comparatively fine, it had greater freeboard and a more exaggerated sheer. The increased length of the ships, together with their more compact superstructures, enabled the main turrets with their heavy armour to be moved farther aft, which made it easier for them to ride the swell. The bow section of these ships was also structurally much stronger, with the 40mm armoured deck forward of the citadel providing both strength and a degree of rigidity.

Despite their size they proved to be extremely manoeuvrable, with *Richelieu* in particular demonstrating this repeatedly during her passages through the Suez Canal, her entry into narrow graving docks at Gibraltar and Durban, her manoeuvres in confined and crowded anchorages such as Trincomalee, and during her replenishment of accompanying destroyers in the Indian Ocean.[6] Her performance in this respect was often favourably remarked upon by the British flag officers under whom she served.

Protection

Richelieu and *Jean Bart* were incontestably well armoured; their 330mm inclined belts, 150-170mm heavy armoured decks and their main turrets and barbettes (430mm and 405mm max. respectively) were more than a match for all contemporary construction. However, the comparatively lightly protected ends of the ships, together with the comparatively low percentage of the waterline that was armoured, meant that hits in these areas caused considerable ingress of water which then tended to seep into the armoured citadel via the shaft and cable tunnels. The extension of the water-excluding compound, *ébonite mousse*, to the large compartment immediately forward of the citadel, would undoubtedly have mitigated the effects of a torpedo hit on the unprotected bow section. However, *ébonite mousse*, although effective in excluding water, was to prove a mixed blessing. When impregnated with oil, which was highly likely in the event of underwater damage, it became particularly combustible, and fires resulting from the use of blowtorches in close proximity were common during ship repairs. Compartments filled with *ébonite mousse* – which was in the form of bricks – were difficult to maintain due to poor access, and as the ships aged this caused serious rust problems. Repairs were also complicated where these compartments were involved; it appears that in some of the damaged after compartments of *Richelieu* cork was used as a temporary measure.

Armament

The main armament of *Richelieu* was not fully combat-ready until after her modernisation in the United States in mid-1943. There can be little doubt that the extensive teething problems with the replenishment systems and with the defective 380mm APC shell would have been resolved more quickly had the ship been able to remain at Brest on her completion in June 1940. However, the provision of radar for fire control would have always been reliant on British goodwill and co-operation; in the event this would have to wait until the winter of 1943-4. The dispersion problem remained, and became fully apparent only when *Richelieu* was operating alongside British battleships during 1944. It was finally resolved in 1948 following extensive firing trials which would have been difficult to conduct under the pressures of war and active service.

The 152mm Mle 1930 employed for the secondary armament was an excellent weapon. However, the triple turret developed for dual-purpose firing was every bit as complex as the unsuccessful 130mm model fitted in the *Dunkerque*s. Although theoretically capable of 90-degrees elevation, loading was difficult at angles greater than 45 degrees and the gun was prone to jamming. The heavily armoured triple turret had a relatively slow training speed, and the elevating mechanism for the guns could not cope with fast-moving aerial targets. The upper director which was intended to provide AA fire control was never operational and was removed during modernisation in 1943. Effective AA barrage fire was possible only after *Richelieu* was fitted with the British Type 285 radar and its associated Auto Barrage Units (ABU) during the winter of 1944-5.

The limitations of the 152mm DP mountings were at least recognised while the ships were still building, and the midships turrets replaced by six 100mm CAD Mle 1931 mountings before the ships were completed. However, as a result of this, the secondary armament could realistically fire only on after bearings, which reinforced the move towards a 'double-ended' layout in *Gascogne*. Moreover, although the 100mm Mle 1930

---

[6] Commented on by her CO during this period, CV Merveilleux de Vignaux.

Richelieu on her speed trials
following her refit in the USA
in the summer of 1943.
(US National Archives)

was a reliable, robust HA gun comparable to the British 4in Mk XVI, other navies had by this time moved on and developed high-performance guns in fully enclosed mountings better suited to installation on board a battleship (e.g., the US Navy's 5in/38, the British twin 4.5in/45 BD/UD mountings, and the *Regia Marina*'s 90mm/50).

The protracted development and eventual cancellation of the 37mm ACAD Mle 1935 gun was an undoubted blow to the Marine Nationale, as the CAD Mle 1933 was not an effective weapon against modern high-performance aircraft due to its comparatively low rate of fire and lack of a properly integrated fire control system. The failure to replace the 13.2mm Hotchkiss MG with the more capable 25mm guns entering service with the Army in 1939 was equally costly, and highlighted the relatively low priority accorded by the Marine Nationale to air defence before the Second World War. During the refit of *Richelieu* in the United States in 1943, both the 37mm guns and the 13.2mm MG were stripped out and discarded in favour of the more effective director-controlled 40mm Bofors quad with multiple 20mm Oerlikon guns for close-in defence.

Propulsion

Both *Richelieu* and *Jean Bart* proved capable of sustained high speed throughout their service lives; the downside was the quantity of black smoke they emitted. Although the advanced Sural boilers otherwise functioned well, the forced-draught fans appear to have been inadequate, resulting in poor combustion and the sooting-up of boiler tubes, which had to be regularly replaced. Although the problem was mitigated postwar by planned maintenance in properly equipped bases it was never completely resolved.

FIN DE PARTIE

After the tumultuous years of 1940-5, the postwar history of France's two last surviving battleships was inevitably an anticlimax. Despite the effort and funding lavished on *Jean Bart*, her completion owed more to the heart than the head. For the French people, she became the symbol of a navy raised from the ashes, but from her considerable shadow a new Marine Nationale was emerging, a navy centred on carrier air power and anti-submarine warfare. After a brief revival in 1956 for the Suez campaign, the big guns were silenced.

SOURCES

Technical

Campbell, John, *Naval Weapons of World War Two*, Conway Maritime Press, 1985, reprinted Conway (London, 2002).

Dumas, Robert, *Les cuirassés Dunkerque, Strasbourg, Richelieu & Jean Bart*, Marines Editions 1992-93, republished as collection (Nantes, 2001).

Dumas, Robert and Guiglini, Jean, *Les cuirassés de 23 500 tonnes*, Lela Presse (Outreau, 2005).

Friedman, Norman, *Battleship: Design and Development 1905-1945*, Conway Maritime Press (London, 1978).

Friedman, Norman, *Naval Radar*, Conway Maritime Press (London, 1981).

Friedman, Norman, *US Naval Weapons*, Conway Maritime Press (London, 1983).

Friedman, Norman, *Naval Firepower: Battleship Guns and Gunnery in the Dreadnought Era*, Seaforth Publishing (London, 2008).

Sarnet, René and Le Vaillant, Eric, *Richelieu*, Marines Editions (Nantes, 1997).

Plans and other documentation from the Archives de l'Armement, Châtellerault, and from the Service Historique de la Marine (www.servicehistorique.sga.defense.gouv.fr).

Historical

Antier, Jean-Jacques, *Le Drame de Mers el-Kébir 1940*, Presses de la Cité (Paris, 1990).

Antier, Jean-Jacques, *La Flotte se Saborde: Toulon 1942*, Presses de la Cité (Paris, 1992).

Caroff, CV, *Les Débarquements Alliés en Afrique du Nord*, Service Historique de la Marine (Paris, 1960).

Cressman, Robert J, *USS Ranger 1934-46*, Potomac Books (Washington, 2003).

Lassaque, Jean, *Les C.T. de 2 880 tonnes du type Mogador (1936-1945)*, Marines Editions (Bourg-en-Bresse, 1996).

Lassaque, Jean, *Les C.T. de 2 800 tonnes du type Le Fantasque*, Marines Editions (Nantes, 1998).

Le Hir, Martial, *Mers el-Kébir & Catapult: les marins de l'oubli*, Marines Editions (Rennes, 2005).

Marder, Arthur, *From the Dardanelles to Oran: Studies of the Royal Navy in War and Peace, 1915-1940*, Oxford University Press (London, 1974).

Marder, Arthur, *Operation 'Menace': The Dakar Expedition and the Dudley North Affair*, Oxford University Press (London, 1976).

Moulin, Jean, *Les croiseurs de 7 600 tonnes*, Marines Editions (Bourg-en-Bresse, 1993).

Roskill, Stephen, *Churchill and the Admirals*, Collins 1977, reprinted Pen & Sword (Barnsley, 2004).

SOURCES OF PLANS BY JOHN JORDAN

Introduction

Normandie class: profile + plan: LANGUEDAPL1915APL10
Normandie class: master frame section: LANGUEDAPL1915APL8

Chapter 2

Inboard profile + plan 3rd FP: DUNKERQ1935C1-19 & C1-26
Hull Sections: DUNKERQ1935C1-21 & C1-22
Main gun arcs + AA as designed: DUNKERQ1935C2-01
Protection (longitudinal section/master frame/cross-sections/CT): DUNKERQ1935C1-39
Disposition of armour plates: DUNKERQ1935C1-40-2
Machinery layout: DUNKERQ1935C1-26

Chapter 4

Inboard profile: RICHELI1940C220b
Hull Sections: RICHELI1940PL223b
Main gun arcs + AA as designed: RICHELI1940PL223b

152mm mount Mle 1936: CAA
152mm OEcl: (see caption)
Protection (longitudinal section/master frame/cross-sections/CT): J BART1940C2-07
Machinery layout: J BART PL7900.9A/B & PLA.664/665
Catapults: RICHELI1940PL001

Chapter 6

C&G Projects: ST1017/1019/1020
G decks (1939): ST1448 & ST1358
Protection (longitudinal section)/152mm turret armour: ST1153 (Clem) & ST1184 (Gasc)
CT armour (*Clemenceau*): ST1271
G aviation arrangements: ST1435

Chapter 8

100mm Mle 1945 on CAD Mle 1946 mounting: CAA

INDEX